Winfield Scott and the Profession of Arms

Winfield Scott

and the

Profession of Arms

ALLAN PESKIN

The Kent State University Press

KENT *&* LONDON

© 2003 by The Kent State University Press, Kent, Ohio 44242

ALL RIGHTS RESERVED

Library of Congress Catalog Card Number 2003004414

ISBN 0-87338-774-0

Manufactured in the United States of America

07 06 05 04   5 4 3 2

Library of Congress Cataloging-in-Publication Data

Peskin, Allan.

Winfield Scott and the profession of arms / Allan Peskin.

p.   cm.

Includes bibliographical references (p.   ) and index.

ISBN 0-87338-774-0 (cloth : alk. paper)

1. Scott, Winfield, 1786–1866. 2. Generals—United States—Biography.
3. United States. Army—Biography. 4. United States—History, Military—19th century.
5. United States—History—War of 1812—Biography. 6. Mexican War, 1846–1848—
Biography. 7. United States—History—Civil War, 1861–1865—Biography.   I. Title.

E403.1.S4P47 2003

355.'0092—dc21

2003004414

British Library Cataloging-in-Publication data are available.

To Barbara,

whose persistence, patience, and love

have brought both this book and its author

to completion.

CONTENTS

PREFACE AND
ACKNOWLEDGMENTS

"It is comparatively easy to build a big book," warned Winfield Scott. "It is only necessary to pile line upon line, document on document, Pelion on Ossa—and bulk is obtained."[1] In writing his own memoirs, Scott did not heed this injunction, and perhaps some will say neither have I. In extenuation I can only plead that Scott was a big man and deserves a large book. Whether his life story deserves this particular book is another question, and not one for its author to decide.

With an active career that spanned more than half a century, Winfield Scott had a hand in the major military, political, and diplomatic events of his long lifetime. It was this versatility that initially attracted my interest. Having completed a biography of James A. Garfield, who played a similar role in post-1860 American life, I was looking for a project of equivalent magnitude. The usual practice among academic historians is to stake a claim to some small furrow of the past and keep plowing it deeper. I found myself unable to follow this path. Having said my piece on Reconstruction and the Gilded Age, I wanted to move on to something else. Envious of my Europeanist colleagues who take entire centuries as their province, I thought it might be fun to dip into the first half of the nineteenth century.

A study of Scott was appealing not only on that count but also for the practical reason that no scholarly biography had appeared since Charles Winslow Elliott's path-breaking 1937 work, *Winfield Scott: The Soldier and the Man*. As should have been expected, I ran up against what might be called Mitchell's Second Law. As promulgated by Memory F. Mitchell in her delightful essay, "Publishing in State Historical Journals," it reads, "No matter how obscure a subject, more than one person is studying it and writing about it." (The First Law states, "Human beings have four basic needs: food, clothing, shelter, and the desire to see themselves in print.")[2]

While I was plugging away at my customary leisurely pace, not one but *two* biographies of Scott appeared: the first by John S. D. Eisenhower in 1997 and the second by Timothy P. Johnson in 1998. This embarrassment of riches might seem to render the present work superfluous, but it could be argued that Scott was big enough to support numerous interpretations. The differences can be seen in the titles. To Eisenhower, Scott's significance was as the *Agent of Destiny,* "both for the consolidation of the nation as a single unity and for its expansion." Johnson saw the key to the general's career in more personal terms as *The Quest for Military Glory.* His Scott can be understood as a glory-hungry elitist and "as a social and political conservative who spent his life struggling against what he believed to be the degenerative force of democracy."[3] For reasons that should become clear to the reader, neither of these approaches seemed wholly satisfactory. As I immersed myself in Scott's life, it struck me that the key to its meaning could be found in his commitment to military professionalism. In this reading, Scott appears as a modernizer, not as Johnson's reactionary, and as an active force rather than Eisenhower's passive agent. His greatest activity was directed toward the creation of a professionalized, bureaucratized military organization as opposed to the ad-hoc peoples' army favored by Presidents Jefferson, Jackson, and Polk and by various frontier-schooled officers. For this reason, I was as interested in the peacetime military establishment as much as in its exploits during occasional wars.

This is not, however, a purely institutional study. Scott's outsized personality could not be contained by any such formal restrictions, and I found myself following him into various byways of private life. Part of the charm of biography lies in the capacity of a human life to be so various, contradictory, and unpredictable that it is full of surprises. Although I doubt whether Scott and I would have hit it off had we ever met, I was frequently surprised, and sometimes delighted, by the man I uncovered. I hope some of this carries over into the narrative that follows.

In thanking those who contributed to this project, the brevity of these acknowledgments does not reflect the extent of my gratitude. Cleveland State University generously assisted with travel and photocopying expenses, as well as with sabbatical leave for research and writing. My special thanks goes to the indefatigable Maggie Smith of interlibrary loan for patiently scouring the nation's libraries to satisfy my requests for arcane source material. Other librarians, especially at the National Archives, the Library of Congress, the New York Public Library, the Pennsylvania Historical Society, and the Clements Library, put up with my demands with good humor and efficiency.

Fellow scholars were generous with assistance, most notably Emily Apt Geer, William P. MacKinnon, and the late Frank Byrne, each of whom brought Scott items to my attention. John Hubbell prodded me to stay on task, as did my wife Barbara. Both she and our son, Larry, lent their keen eyes and exacting standards to the reading of proof when, I am sure, they would have preferred more interesting activities. Finally, the editorial staff at the Kent State University Press tolerated my foibles, humored my authorial vanity, and patiently changed "that" to "which," and vice-versa, at every opportunity.

CHAPTER ONE

HOTSPUR

In 1808, when Winfield Scott first entered the U. S. Army, it numbered less than six thousand soldiers, and its annual budget was less than three million dollars. It had no commanding general nor general staff, no strategic doctrine, and few serviceable manuals. Only a handful of its officers had been trained at the recently established military academy; the rest were either self-taught or relics of the Revolutionary War. Few had ever commanded a unit as large as a regiment.[1]

More than fifty years later, when Scott retired in the midst of a great civil war, the army he commanded was heading toward a million-man force with a budget of over a billion dollars. It had been transformed not only in magnitude but also in its very nature. When Scott had begun his career, an officer's calling was something like a trade, and not an entirely reputable one; by the time he resigned it had become a *profession*. More than any other individual, Scott, in his life and work, was responsible for the transformation.

Winfield Scott was born June 13, 1786, on a modest farm outside Petersburg, Virginia. His paternal line, as its name implies, came from Scotland. His grandfather, James Scott, had backed the wrong side in the "Bonnie Prince Charlie" uprising of 1745 and was forced to flee to America, settling in Virginia, where he practiced law. His son, William, farmed; served as a Virginia officer in the American Revolution; married a well-connected neighbor, Ann Mason; fathered four children; and died young. Winfield, who was barely six at the time of his father's death, scarcely mentions him in his *Memoirs;* most of his childhood memories were of his mother.[2]

Unlike most young widows of her day, Ann Scott never remarried. Very likely she received some help from her family in raising her children, particularly from her wealthy brother Winfield. Young Winfield was named after this rich uncle and was expected to inherit the estate, but as in so many of the novels of the period, his great expectations were dashed when Winfield Mason married late in life and fathered several children as his heirs.[3] The nephew would have to make his own way in the world.

His mother, by all accounts a strong-willed, quick-witted woman of independent spirit, was the great influence on his formative years. In later life, when he made the obligatory tribute that successful men are expected to pay to their mother's example, his words rang true. "And if," he said, "I have achieved . . . anything that my countrymen are likely to honor . . . , it is from the lessons of that admirable parent that I derived the inspiration." It was likely the memory of that formidable woman that accounted for Scott's gallantry, amounting almost to timidity, in his dealings with women. Even in the freewheeling masculine environment of the army, Scott was never known to succumb to temptation. Nor, he insisted, did he ever once stray from his marriage vows.[4]

Scott rebelled only once against his mother's authority. One Sunday, when he was seven, he refused to go to church. His mother cut off a switch from a poplar tree and prepared to apply it to her refractory son. Thinking quickly, the precocious lad cited the Gospel of St. Matthew to the effect that "Every tree that bringeth not forth good fruit [should] be cast into the fire." The delighted mother threw away the rod and spared the child.[5] Scott would grow up to become one of the great pettifoggers of his day, continually raising farfetched but ingenious arguments to justify his actions. Perhaps the memory of this childhood triumph fortified his belief that he could wriggle out of scrapes by legalistic appeals and that, if he were only clever enough, all transgressions would be forgiven.

His mother died when Winfield was seventeen, leaving him to finish his schooling on his own. That education had been haphazard. Virginia, like most Southern states, had no comprehensive, state-supported public school system. In the fashion of the English gentry, young Virginians of quality were either tutored at home or packed off to boarding schools, usually of indifferent merit. Scott was enrolled in two such schools in nearby Richmond. One, run by a respected Quaker pedagogue, James Hargrove, was more concerned with molding character than with imparting knowledge. The other was operated by James Ogilvie, an eccentric Scottish drug addict who soon gave up the classroom to tour the country, dressed in a toga, declaiming Ciceronian orations of his own devising.[6]

Even in these undemanding institutions, Scott did not stand out for scholastic prowess. As he later admitted, "the charms of idleness or pleasure often prevailed over the pride of acquisition." Nonetheless, he managed to pick up a smattering of Greek and Roman classics, Scottish metaphysics, rhetoric, logic, mathematics, political economy, and a good reading (though not speaking) facility in French, which would later provide invaluable access to French military manuals and texts.[7]

This education was, as he himself conceded, superficial: "Too much was attempted within a limited time, by republican short cuts to knowledge." Yet Scott somehow acquired a love of reading that persisted throughout his life (though an aide maliciously hinted that his reading was largely confined to title pages and prefaces rather than complete books). His literary tastes remained fixated on the authors he had studied early in life: Gibbon and Hume among historians; Adam Smith, Locke, and Hobbes among philosophers; the essayist Richard Addison; poets Milton, Dryden, and Shakespeare; Fielding and Goldsmith for fiction. Except for Sir Walter Scott, Washington Irving, and James Fenimore Cooper, he scarcely noticed the writers of his own day. But within that narrow compass Winfield Scott could hold his own in literary and philosophical discussions with the likes of Washington Irving or Harvard's learned Dr. Channing.[8] His old-fashioned education also equipped Scott with the elaborate courtesies and ponderous prose of an earlier day and helped create that impression of pedantic pomposity that sometimes made him a figure of fun.

In 1805 Scott enrolled at the College of William and Mary but soon discovered that his educational preparation had been inadequate for its demanding curriculum. He spent a year studying natural philosophy and law and then dropped out to read law in the office of Petersburg attorney David Robertson. This sort of apprenticeship, rather than a college law school, was the customary training for lawyers in the nineteenth century, and it was sufficient to prepare Scott for admittance to the Virginia bar in 1806. He went to work in Robertson's office, along with another aspiring attorney, Thomas Ruffin, whose brother Edmund, later such a rabid secessionist that he reputedly fired the first shot at Fort Sumter, remembered Scott as being, even then, remarkably pompous and vain.[9] For a while, Scott rode the judicial circuit with other young lawyers, doing clerical chores and picking up odds and ends of business.

A welcome diversion from this weary routine soon presented itself. The treason trial of former U.S. vice president Aaron Burr for some shadowy intrigue he had allegedly plotted opened in Richmond. All other legal business came to a standstill as local lawyers flocked to witness this clash of forensic titans. The trial was held in the chamber of the Virginia House of Delegates, which was so packed with spectators that Scott had to find a perch on the massive bronze lock of the rear door.

From that vantage point he carefully observed the great men: presiding judge John Marshall, jury foreman John Randolph, lawyers William Wirt and

Luther Martin, reporter Washington Irving (with whom he struck up a life-long friendship), and witness Andrew Jackson, whose reckless diatribes and unbridled show of temper astonished him. The most interesting witness was the obese and oily senior officer of the U. S. Army, Brig. Gen. James Wilkinson, whose testimony against Burr to cover up his own involvement in the mysterious plot earned Scott's lasting distrust. The defendant himself, "as immovable as one of Canova's living marbles," seemed oblivious to the spectacle around him, but he was actually taking everything in, including the tall young lawyer on the uncomfortable door lock. Years later, when the two were formally introduced, Burr would astonish Scott by recalling every detail of his appearance.[10]

It was not surprising that Scott should be so noticed. Over six feet, four inches tall, with oval face, wide eyes, aquiline nose, and dark hair brushed stiffly back from his forehead, he struck Burr as "the most magnificent youth in Virginia." He was then remarkably slim for his height, weighing less than 150 pounds. In old age, when his body had become bloated from too much hard living and French cooking, he would look back on his early self as wistfully as Falstaff recalling his days as a page for the Duke of Norfolk. "I am thin as a beanpole," he would sigh. Thin as a beanpole.[11]

Only a few weeks after Scott had settled in to observe the Burr trial, another sensational event diverted his attention. On June 22, 1807, the American frigate *Chesapeake* was attacked off the Virginia coast by the British warship *Leopard*. Over twenty of her crew were killed or wounded, and four others, claiming American citizenship but suspected of being British deserters, were hauled off to be tried in a British court. The great European war, then nearing its final act, now threatened to cross the ocean.

For well over a century, England and France had been locked in a vast conflict for European supremacy. The United States had attempted to steer a middle course between the contending giants, but as their conflict approached its final showdown, neutrality in a world in flames was increasingly difficult to maintain. Both sides regularly violated American rights, but the *Chesapeake-Leopard* affair was the most flagrant violation, and in its wake, war fever swept the United States.

President Thomas Jefferson deplored war as irrational and expensive. He preferred to employ what he called "peaceable coercion," or what a later age would term "economic sanctions." Later that year, he would impose a far-reaching embargo on all overseas trade, but as an immediate response to the *Chesapeake* provocation, he closed American ports to British warships. Volunteer troops were called up to patrol the coastline and to prevent British ships from obtaining provisions.

Young Winfield Scott, ca. 1820. Smithsonian National Portrait Gallery.

On an impulse, Scott bought a horse, borrowed a uniform, and joined one of these volunteer companies. He had no military experience nor, up to that time, any apparent soldierly inclinations. It seems to have been a spur-of-the-moment lark, but it soon took a serious turn.

One evening, while Scott was acting as lance corporal in charge of a small patrol, he heard the sound of muffled oars. Charging across the sand dunes and into the muddy creek, his squad captured a rowboat from the hated *Leopard* containing two midshipmen (boys, really) and six oarsmen on an illicit provisioning expedition.[12]

Scott was proud "as Hotspur" of this feat of arms, though, as he conceded, it was the more easily done since the British were unarmed and their boat was stuck in the mud. President Jefferson, however, was embarrassed by the incident, which he feared might lead to a war with Great Britain. He ordered Scott's prisoners to be returned with apologies. Instead of his expected commendation, the young Hotspur was slapped with what he called an "imbecile admonition" not to do it again. The *Chesapeake* excitement passed, the volunteer companies were dissolved, and Scott returned to the prosaic life of a lawyer. Still, he had tasted military excitement and found it good. "The young soldier had heard the bugle and the drum. It was the music that awoke ambition."[13]

It was not an ambition that seemed likely to be gratified. At the end of 1807, the entire U. S. Army consisted of fewer than 150 officers commanding less than three thousand men.[14] Americans were uncomfortable with the idea of a standing army, fearing it might be turned against their own liberties. In times of crisis, patriotic volunteers and militiamen were expected to flock to the colors to augment the tiny regular army. Such an army could patrol the borders, guard public property, and make an occasional show of force to awe restless Indians, but it presented few opportunities to satisfy Scott's dreams of glory. He returned the borrowed uniform and went back to his law books.

Virginia, however, was overstocked with bright young lawyers, so he decided to try his luck in South Carolina. Had he been successful there, who knows but that he might have wound up on the other side in the Civil War; however, he ran afoul of the one-year residency requirement for admission to the state's bar.[15] While he was marking time in Charleston, word came that, in view of the deteriorating relations with England, Congress was considering a bill to enlarge the regular army. He set sail at once for Washington and arranged to meet with President Jefferson.

On the European continent, the officer class was reserved for the nobility. In England, commissions were bought and sold. In the American meritocracy, military careers were theoretically open to talent, but it did not hurt to have some political pull. Scott wisely brought to the interview a Petersburg neighbor, the influential senator William Branch Giles, to vouch for his political bona fides. A few words convinced the president that the young petitioner was personally presentable, well connected, and politically sound—sufficient qualifications, apparently, to be an officer in the U. S. Army.[16]

A few months later, in May 1808, the eagerly awaited commission arrived. Rather than starting at the bottom as an ensign or even a lieutenant, Scott found, to his delight, that he was to be made a captain in command of a company of light artillery. Without a moment's hesitation, he accepted the offer, flamboyantly pledging *"my life, my liberty and sacred honor"* to be worthy of the trust the president "has thought proper to confide in my valor and patriotism."[17]

Now came the best part. He had himself fitted by a Richmond tailor, and when his uniform was ready he impatiently rushed home, locked the door for privacy, and maneuvered two tall mirrors into the corners of his largest room. For two happy hours he admired his dazzling new outfit: white britches; blue coat; high, stiff collar; and lofty "tar bucket" helmet topped with a feathery pompon. Had anyone spied upon him, he later said, "I should have proceeded at once to put him to death."[18] But it speaks to the essential innocence of Scott's famous vanity that he told the story on himself.

One can imagine him turning this way and that, critically adjusting the angle of his hat, fluffing up his gold epaulets, patting his red sash, and drawing his sword smartly from its scabbard, rapt in the contemplation of his new self.

Old Fuss and Feathers was born.

CHAPTER TWO

CAPTAIN

For all the dazzle of his glittering new uniform (which he himself had to purchase out of his forty-dollar monthly salary), young Captain Scott was not yet a full-fledged soldier. His company existed only on paper. In the casual manner of the old army, he had been assigned no subalterns, no troops, no arms or equipment, no drill manuals, and precious few instructions. Throughout the summer of 1808, Scott labored to remedy these deficiencies. He rented temporary quarters, scrounged up supplies, and conducted drill and instruction in whatever moments he could spare from his recruiting forays.[1]

Recruiting was Scott's most onerous task: "of so disagreeable a nature," he sniffed, "that I am sensible no gentleman would engage in it." Even with the hard times brought on by Jefferson's embargo, it was difficult to induce free-born Americans to submit to military hardships and discipline for seven dollars a month. Much of the army had to be drawn from the ranks of foreigners and what was disdainfully described as "the scum of the population" of the native residents.[2] Immigrants were scarce in Virginia, but "scum" were plentiful. To attract them, Scott scoured the vicinity of Richmond, delivering patriotic speeches and exuding false bonhomie, all the while guarding against bounty jumpers, deserters, and underage applicants. To keep his recruits content until their pay arrived, he was compelled to advance them small sums from his own pocket, with the informal understanding that the amount would later be deducted from their salaries. This makeshift arrangement would return to haunt him.

By fall the company had reached its full complement of seventy privates (including four musicians) and eight noncommissioned officers and was ready to march. It proceeded to Norfolk, there to await the arrival of other companies before embarking for its ultimate destination of New Orleans. Until the arrival of these two fresh units, Scott had been the senior officer at the depot. The new captains, however, had claims (though imperfectly documented) to the same seniority as his. Who should command the detachment while en route to New Orleans? Scott vigorously pressed his claim. General Wilkinson, passing through Norfolk on his way south, broke the impasse by quite sensibly ordering the contending officers to draw lots. Scott lost, though not gracefully.[3] Festering resentment of this injustice would embitter his relations with his commanding general, with consequences that would almost put an end to his military career before it was even fairly begun.

More significantly for the long run, this petty squabble would be prophetic of one of the great running themes of Scott's career. Disputes over relative rank would consume much of his energy over the next three decades, leading to a string of bitter quarrels with his fellow officers. "Desire for promotion is almost universal in democratic armies," observed that shrewd French tourist Alexis de Tocqueville; "it is eager, tenacious, and continual. All other desires serve to feed it, and it is only quenched with life itself." Scott's career could serve as a gloss on that text. "The right of promotion," he would insist, "will be regarded by every officer as the most important attached to his commission."[4] In pursuit of that right, he would sour relations with colleagues and superiors, including various presidents, detracting from his considerable achievements by making himself appear both selfish and foolish. In the callow captain of 1809 could be seen the haughty general of later years.

The journey to New Orleans proved a nightmare. The *Nancy* set sail on February 4, 1809, and promptly got lost, sailing all the way around Cuba. It nearly foundered in a storm and then ran aground at the mouth of the Mississippi River, where it waited three weeks for a new rudder. Not until April 1 did the weary warriors finally set foot on land again at New Orleans.[5]

It was hardly worth the effort, at least as far as Scott was concerned. New Orleans was a steamy, indolent, unhealthy city that seemed to belong, in spirit, more to the Mediterranean littoral than to the United States. American troops fell all too readily under the spell of its corrupt, easygoing ways. By mid-April, more than one-fourth of the two-thousand-man detachment was on sick call, struck down mainly by tropical and venereal diseases.[6]

Their commander, Maj. Gen. James Wilkinson, was right at home in this freewheeling atmosphere. He was reputedly up to his ears in corrupt contracts with local suppliers and had long enjoyed an overly cozy relationship with Spanish authorities, who slipped him a secret retainer in return for intelligence tidbits.[7] Even without full knowledge of Wilkinson's questionable activities, Scott had ample reason to distrust his commander, dating back to the

Burr trial and the perceived insult over rank on the voyage to New Orleans. He soon had more substantial grounds to question the general's competence as well as his integrity. News of the appalling sick list led Secretary of War William Eustis, himself a former military surgeon, to order Wilkinson to move his headquarters to a healthier site on higher ground upriver. Reluctant to leave his business (and romantic) connections in New Orleans, Wilkinson instead moved a few miles down the Mississippi to a soggy pasture known as Terre aux Boeufs. Aside from its convenient location, the campground's only asset seemed to be that its owner was an associate of Wilkinson who stood to make a handsome profit from the deal.

For the hapless soldiers, Terre aux Boeufs was a nightmare of mud, snakes, filth, and vermin. Their meat was rancid, their bread crawled with unwelcome visitors, and their drinking water was fouled with camp waste. Overworked and underfed, they were struck down by the hundreds by dysentery, malaria, and exhaustion. By the time they finally moved to a healthier campsite near Natchez, their numbers had been reduced by death and desertion from 2,036 to 1,184, making this the greatest peacetime disaster suffered by the American army.[8]

By then Scott was safely back in the comfort of his Virginia home, his brief military career seemingly at an end. Almost from the moment he had arrived at New Orleans, his ardor had begun to ooze away. The routine of garrison life was not what he had dreamed of when he first put on that dazzling uniform. Nor were his brother officers the sort of people with whom he cared to associate. He found the officers of the old army to be "coarse and ignorant men" who were generally "sunk into either sloth, ignorance, or habits of intemperate drinking." The new appointees were scarcely any better. Most owed their commissions to political connections (as did Scott himself) and consisted largely of "swaggerers, dependents, decayed gentlemen, and others—'fit for nothing else,' which always turned out *utterly unfit for any military purpose whatever.*"[9]

After only a few weeks of this sort of companionship, life as a Virginia lawyer seemed more attractive to Scott, and he asked the general to accept his resignation from the service. Wilkinson would later condemn Scott as "a vainglorious coxcomb" who was chief among that band of "idle, dissipated and unprincipled malcontents who . . . had shrunk from duty, at New Orleans, and abandoned the recruits they led to the country," but at the time, he was considerate enough to offer Scott a suggestion that saved his military career. Instead of resigning, he advised Scott to ask for a furlough. That way the government would pay for the return trip to Virginia, and Scott could keep his options open in case he should change his mind.[10]

The leave was approved in time for Scott to miss the worst horrors of the Terre aux Boeufs encampment. Nonetheless, even though he did not mention it in his memoirs, the episode must have made a profound impression upon him. He would ever after be a stickler for proper camp hygiene, and in his compilation of army regulations, he would pay particular attention to matters of sanitation and nutrition. More importantly, he would remain forever leery of military operations in the tropics. During the Mexican War, his great fear would be the "vómito," or yellow fever, and his strategic timetable would be dictated by efforts to escape the unhealthy coastal regions before the onset of the sickly season. Even later during the Civil War, his famed "Anaconda Plan" was designed, in part, to avoid the necessity of large-scale land operations in those Southern climes, which had already demonstrated their lethal potential.[11]

After his return to Virginia in July 1809, Scott blew hot and cold on his military future. At first he acted as if he intended to continue in the army, and in an interview with Secretary Eustis at Washington, he made the extraordinary suggestion that he be sent to Europe as a military observer. This displayed remarkable presumption on the part of a junior officer with so little experience, but it also revealed considerable insight. The Napoleonic Wars, with their vast armies, flexible tactics, and innovative weaponry, were transforming warfare, yet few of these developments were appreciated in the United States.

Scott wanted to learn it all: engineering; horse artillery, recently introduced into the American service but as yet imperfectly understood; "the manner in which large bodies of troops take up and pursue the line of march; on manoeuvering in advance and retreat in the face of an enemy; the mode of encamping—together with an internal view of their organization and police." All these "points of professional knowledge," he said, "constitute a *desiderata* which it is believed no diligence could supply within the United States."[12] With this revealing phrase, "professional knowledge," Scott first sounded the note that would resonate throughout his long career. Virtually alone among the self-taught officers of his day, he understood that war was not merely something to be fought that it was also an intellectual discipline to be studied with the same rigor and dedication as the law or medicine.

When Secretary Eustis understandably ignored his brazen request, Scott once again considered hanging up his sword and studying war no more. With unconscious effrontery, he laid down conditions for his retention in the service. He informed the secretary that he could not return to New Orleans due to "certain principles deemed sacred" (presumably his antagonism to General Wilkinson) but that he would be willing to serve under other generals, such as Wade Hampton. Otherwise he would "leave the service without a murmur, but not without regret."[13]

This threat was withdrawn almost immediately upon receipt of a piece of disquieting news. Scott learned that shortly after he had left the Terre aux

Boeufs camp, charges of embezzlement had been leveled against him. There was a kernel of truth to these accusations. Scott had reimbursed himself from out of his men's salaries for the monies he had advanced them in the early days of the company's formation. In the hands of the vindictive Wilkinson, this excusable irregularity was magnified into the serious charge of absconding with two months of the pay rightly due his soldiers.[14]

No Virginia gentleman of honor could resign under such a cloud. Scott now had to stay in the service to clear his name. His threat to resign was withdrawn on July 29, less than a week after it had been made, under the pretence that renewed danger of war with England made his retention in the army a patriotic duty.[15] It was a duty he was in no hurry to fulfill. Scott did not reach camp at Washington, in the Mississippi Territory near Natchez, until November, overstaying his leave by at least two months. Once there, he found himself in a camp seething with intrigue and discontent. Wilkinson had been superseded in command by Brig. Gen. Wade Hampton but remained in camp preparing his defense for the Terre aux Boeufs court of inquiry. Junior officers inevitably became partisans of one general or the other, which aggravated the endemic sniping and backbiting that characterized the peacetime army.

Those drawn to the military life tended to be daring, bellicose, active men, yet in the peacetime army, they found mostly boredom, idleness, and routine. Except during rare intervals of war, the only target for their aggressive instincts was each other. Throughout his long career, Scott would be especially notorious for the zeal with which he attacked brother officers. Later in life he would reveal that he understood this problem, but he failed to realize that it applied to himself. Writing in 1859, he said:

> In the army, there is always, in time of peace, much unoccupied energy, spirit and talent amongst our educated officers of the junior classes, which from the want of fit occasion of display, sometimes merely to escape from *ennui,* get up a little game of war against an unlucky commander, in which the interest consists in harassing him with petty complaints of injustice;— in endeavors to perplex and wear him out with subtle distinctions on points of duty and acts of captious but intangible opposition. In this perverse career, the most restless officer—a stickler for rights, with indifference to duties—is sure to take the lead. Supporters, however, from sympathy with mischief, readily fall in, and then, in the animation of the conflict—notwithstanding some prudent reserve at the beginning—"good order and military discipline" are soon brought to an end.[16]

In this shrewdly drawn portrait, did the aged warrior of 1859 recognize some trace of his younger self? Scott's later successes should not obscure the fact that, until the War of 1812, he did not stand out from the other officers of his generation. True, he was younger, smarter, and taller than most, but otherwise his behavior was similar. Proud to the point of arrogance, contentious, ambitious for rank, a gossip and a duelist (he received two challenges in one day while at New Orleans), he was not entirely out of place in the fractious atmosphere of the Washington cantonment.[17] Quite understandably he supported Hampton, recklessly indulging in pothouse bluster against his nemesis Wilkinson. At various times and places, Scott publicly denounced his hated superior as a scoundrel, a liar, and a traitor while threatening that if he went into battle, he would carry two pistols—one for the enemy and the other for Wilkinson. All this, of course, was instantly carried to Wilkinson's ear. The chief talebearer seems to have been Dr. William Upshaw, surgeon of the 5th Regiment, whose dislike of Scott dated back to an obscure quarrel in New Orleans that would have led to a duel had the doctor not been too ill to respond to the challenge.

A military court was convened on January 6, 1810, to deal with charges preferred by Upshaw. Scott was arraigned on two counts: withholding the pay due his men and making threatening and abusive remarks against a superior officer. The trial dragged on for most of the month and sometimes wandered far afield. The defendant, who acted as his own counsel, was acquitted of fraudulent intent in detaining his men's pay but judged guilty of unofficer-like conduct in the matter. The charge of mutiny, potentially the most serious accusation, was thrown out, but the court could hardly overlook the derogatory statements Scott had made about Wilkinson.

Under the Articles of War, that should have been sufficient grounds for dismissal from the service, but instead Scott was merely suspended "from all rank, pay and emolument for the space of twelve months." As a further expression of sympathy for the young officer (and a slap at the generally detested Wilkinson), the court recommended that all but three months of the sentence be suspended, a recommendation General Hampton did not see fit to approve.[18]

Before leaving camp, Scott had one last duty to perform. The long-deferred affair of honor with Dr. Upshaw, to which recent events had given added urgency, could be put off no longer. On February 3, 1810, the two hot-headed antagonists, accompanied by their seconds and a crowd of several hundred spectators, crossed over the Mississippi to the Louisiana side and sought satisfaction with pistols. Scott missed, but Upshaw's steady surgical hand was nearly fatal. His bullet grazed the top of Scott's skull, leaving him with a bloody, painful, and embarrassing memento of the price of honor.[19]

Scott had now been a soldier for almost two years and had seen active duty for only a few months. During that time, he had resigned and reconsidered, had been court-martialed and suspended, and had come under hostile fire only from a fellow officer. It was not an auspicious beginning. Now he faced a year in limbo while he pondered his future.

He moved into the Petersburg home of a slightly older friend, Benjamin Watkins Leigh, a respected lawyer and political figure of scholarly bent, whose well-stocked library was placed at Scott's disposal to help while away his enforced leisure. Prominent on the shelves was a collection of British military manuals. The precise volumes owned by Leigh are not known, but they probably included such standard works as William Armstrong's *Practical Considerations on the Errors Committed by Generals and Field Officers Commanding Armies and Detachments, from the Year 1745 to the Present Time* (1808) and Thomas Simes's *A Military Course for the Government and Conduct of a Battalion . . .* (1777). From them Scott learned the details of drill, maneuver, fortifications, and entrenchment. How to form a hollow square in the face of a cavalry attack, how to reform a line of battle so that it changes its front, how to conduct a siege, how to maneuver an entire regiment and even a battalion—all this was a revelation to Scott, whose practical experience had been limited to the company level.[20] Henceforth he would be known as a "scientific" soldier who would always be accompanied by a portable library of works on military history and theory from which he would draw inspiration and advice.

It is tempting to conclude, as some have done, that in Leigh's library Scott experienced an epiphany that transformed him from a dilettante into a serious student of military science. In fact, he remained ambivalent about his future career. To a friend, he confessed, "though not unmindful of the studies connected with my present profession . . . , my military ardor has suffered abatement."

What then? For a landless, well-bred Virginian with social aspirations and no tangible assets, there were few career choices available: the law, the military, or a brilliant marriage. Scott had no marriage prospects at hand, and his military fling had proven disappointing. That left the law. "Indeed," as he put it in his stilted fashion, "it is my design, as soon as circumstances will permit, to throw the feather out of my cap and resume it in my hand." Still, he left open the possibility that, "should war come at last, my enthusiasm will be rekindled; *and then, who knows but that I may yet write my history with a sword?*"[21]

As the likelihood of war with Britain increased, Scott badgered the secretary of war for reinstatement, employing the sort of legalistic pettifoggery of which he would become a master. He ingeniously argued that since his suspension had been for twelve "months," this implied lunar months, or forty-eight weeks rather than the solar year of fifty-two weeks. Although Scott cited Blackstone in support of this novel theory, Eustis was not moved. Nor was he persuaded by the claim that Scott was actually entitled to promotion to his regiment's vacant majorship (with back pay, no less) despite his suspension.[22]

Eustis could not help but be impressed by Scott's ardor, if not his logic, yet he kept the impatient captain waiting until October before assigning him to active duty under General Hampton. Scott accompanied the general, an immensely wealthy South Carolina planter with Revolutionary War experience, to the regiment's Southern headquarters.[23] Along the way, they passed through Indian territory, where Scott observed with interest the habits of those tribes he would force a quarter century later into exile along the Trail of Tears. At a stopover in South Carolina, Scott revealed that his commitment to the soldier's life was still uncertain. He asked Secretary Eustis to assign him to duty in Charleston since, as he admitted, he intended to resign his commission soon and hoped to establish residence to qualify for the South Carolina bar.[24] Eustis ignored the request, and Scott proceeded on to Baton Rouge as a member of Hampton's staff.

In Louisiana, Scott still toyed with the possibilities of a legal career. He began to study the Napoleonic Code used in that state and even had the gratifying experience of prosecuting a successful court-martial against a former crony of his old tormentor General Wilkinson. Conviction was a foregone conclusion, but Scott could not resist the temptation to indulge in the sort of spread-eagle oratory then fashionable. In his peroration, he declaimed: "Mercy, too far indulged towards a prisoner, is a wrong to the public. . . . [T]here is a time when humanity, even humanity! bathed in tears and sickened with pity, must yield herself up a sacrifice on the altar of public JUSTICE!"[25] From this, the only case on record that Scott ever argued, it would not seem that the legal profession was the loser when he decided to devote his talents exclusively to the military.

That decision was made for him by the rapid onrushing of events. By the spring of 1812, all signs indicated that war with England could not be avoided. Anxious to get to the likely seat of battle, Hampton and Scott hastily returned to Washington.

The month-long voyage would later serve as one of the stories with which Scott would regale his captive audience of young aides. After passing through furious storms and tedious calms, his ship entered Chesapeake Bay on June 20, just after Congress had declared war. The news was not yet generally known, and Scott's ship peacefully passed a British frigate off the coast. Two hours later, the British warship was informed that a state of war existed and that it would have been entitled to intercept the American vessel. "What a happy escape for me!" the future general later rejoiced. "Had the New Orleans ship been captured, I might, as a prisoner, have chafed and been forgotten, for months—perhaps years—in a British prison!"

Further perils awaited. The ship ran aground, and the impatient Scott decided to walk the sixteen miles to Baltimore. After four miles, he stumbled onto a militia meeting so consumed with patriotic enthusiasm that it insisted the bedraggled captain mount a table and declaim the declaration of war. In return, they offered him a ride to Baltimore, but the drunken driver twice overturned the gig, and Scott had to take the reins himself.

Arriving in Baltimore, still smoldering from fires set by anti-British rioters, Scott learned the astounding news that he had been promoted two full grades. He could hardly believe his good fortune: "a lieutenant-colonel in rank, at the age of twenty-six, with a hot war before me—seemed to leave nothing to be desired but the continued favor of Providence!"[26]

CHAPTER THREE

DEFEAT

The War of 1812 may have begun on the high seas, but to most Americans it was about land, particularly the enticing land to the north—Canada. Considering that the United States had barely explored, much less settled, the vast Louisiana Purchase acquired only a few years earlier, such land hunger might seem excessive. At the time, however, there seemed compelling reasons for coveting Canada. For one thing, it contained the sort of densely forested land in which the American frontiersman felt at home. The Louisiana Purchase, with its grasslands (and perhaps even deserts) presented environmental challenges with which he was not yet prepared to cope. For another, it was widely believed, with some justification, that the British were encouraging client Indian tribes to take to the warpath against the isolated American settlements in the West. Defeat of the British could end the menace of their savage allies and remove the chief remaining obstacle to westward expansion.

The conquest of Canada had been attempted once before, during the American Revolution, but the military situation of 1812 seemed more auspicious than that of 1775. England had its hands full in dealing with Napoleon, then at the peak of his power. With its resources stretched to the limit, there was little to spare for a remote, backwater conflict halfway round the world. Still, even a wounded lion can bite. The United States, however, was virtually toothless. Its deep-water navy was effective but tiny, and its regular army could only muster 6,744 men on the eve of conflict despite its recently authorized increase.[1]

Undeterred by the long odds against them, Americans blithely went to war, confident that patriotic volunteers and militiamen would make up in enthusiasm and numbers what they lacked in professional polish. This faith was at the heart of the Jeffersonian military system. In 1801, in his first inaugural address, Jefferson had assured his countrymen that they enjoyed "the strongest Government on earth" because it was "the only one where every man . . . would fly to the standard of the law, and would meet invasions of the public order as his own personal concern."[2] The next few years would put that faith to the test.

British defense of Canada rested in the hands of ten thousand British and Canadian regulars, plus whatever militia and Indian allies they could muster. Since this force was strung out along a thousand-mile border, American strategy seemed obvious: use its superiority in resources and manpower to launch simultaneous attacks on these thinly stretched British forces. Three likely invasion routes presented themselves: from Detroit, across the straits; from the Buffalo area across the Niagara River; and from Lake Champlain north to Montreal.

The advance to Montreal had to be called off when New England governors refused to call out their state militia for a war they opposed. The Niagara theater was so disorganized that the U.S. commander, Henry Dearborn, had to ask for a truce while he tried to put his affairs in order. This freed the enterprising British general Sir Isaac Brock to dash west to Detroit. There he was able to bluff the timorous American commander, Isaac Hull, into an ignominious surrender of his entire force.

While the American invasions of Canada were crumbling on all fronts, Lieutenant Colonel Scott was mired in Pennsylvania, trying to recruit troops for his regiment and finding few takers. By early September he grew impatient. Hearing rumors of impending action on the Niagara frontier, he begged for permission to hasten to the front with his two completed companies, led by Captains Nathan Towson and James Barber. Transported by boat to Albany, they then struck overland for the three-hundred-mile trek to Buffalo. On the march, the raw recruits began to toughen into soldiers. A young lieutenant of Towson's company marveled how "after marching twenty miles I can rise the following morning as cheerful and light for twenty more as if I had not marched a mile." Scott pushed his men hard but won their respect and affection. The same lieutenant assured the folks back home, "I am very pleased with the Col. (he does everything to make us happy and comfortable)."[3] On October 4, only a month after leaving Philadelphia, Scott's battalion arrived in Buffalo and reported for duty to Brig. Gen. Alexander Smyth, the senior American officer on the Niagara frontier.

The Niagara River runs thirty-six miles due north from Buffalo. Through it the waters of Lake Erie and the Upper Great Lakes pour into Lake Ontario on their way to the St. Lawrence. Halfway in its course, the river plunges down the famous falls, not yet the obligatory destination of tourists and newlyweds ("The second great disappointment of an American honeymoon," Oscar Wilde

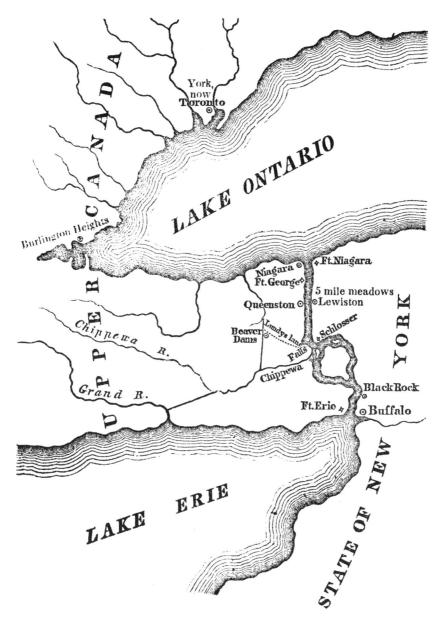

Niagara Frontier. Edward D. Mansfield, *The Life and Military Services of Lieut.-General Winfield Scott* (New York: N. C. Miller, 1862), xii.

would later quip). Because of these falls, all traffic between Lower and Upper Canada had to be portaged across the Niagara peninsula. To protect this vital passage, forts were erected on both sides of the river. At the southern, or Lake Erie, end, the British constructed Fort Erie across from the American forces at Buffalo and Black Rock. Farther north, near where the river empties into

Lake Ontario, the British troops in Fort George and their American counterparts at Fort Niagara glowered at each other across the narrow strait.

Scott would spend the next two years trying to wrest this little strip of land from the enemy's grasp. In pursuit of that goal, he would fight three pitched battles as well as numerous raids and sorties. Hundreds would be left dead on the field and hundreds more would be wounded, including Scott himself.

In later years, when he had trained himself to think in strategic terms rather than in the specifics of battlefield tactics, Scott would conclude that the whole effort had been misdirected. The proper course, he argued, should have been to mass American strength for an invasion of *Lower* Canada (Quebec), the farther east the better. With American control established on the St. Lawrence, all British positions upriver would wither on the vine.[4] This instinct to strike at the heart of the enemy, rather than fritter away at peripheral objectives, would serve Scott well during the Mexican War thirty-five years later. In 1812, however, such high strategic decisions were beyond the competence of an untested lieutenant colonel. Scott had come to Canada to fight. Within a few days he would get his chance.

His first assignment was to guard the shipyard at Black Rock, commanded by naval lieutenant Jesse Duncan Elliott. Throughout the War of 1812, the United States and Great Britain would be engaged in a unique sort of naval arms race. Trees lining the banks of Lake Erie would be fashioned on the spot into warships, and whichever side launched the most recent ship could control the Great Lakes until the other side launched *its* latest vessel.

Shortly after Scott's companies arrived at Black Rock, two new British warships were spotted at Fort Erie across the river: the *Caledonia* and the somewhat larger brig *Adams,* captured as part of Hull's surrender and now insultingly rechristened *Detroit.* Elliott asked Scott to detach fifty soldiers to help capture these British ships by a surprise attack. The colonel assembled his men and asked for volunteers. To his unconcealed delight, every man instantly stepped forward. Sixty were chosen and put under the command of his adjutant, Lt. Isaac Roach. Some officers were also eager to participate, but Scott decided no one on the expedition should outrank Roach. At this, Captain Towson went to his tent, wrote out his resignation from the service, and offered to volunteer as a citizen. Scott relented.[5]

At one o'clock on the morning of October 9, this handpicked detachment, along with three dozen sailors, rowed with muffled oars across the Niagara. Two hours later, they boarded the unsuspecting British vessels, and within ten minutes they had overwhelmed the skeleton crews aboard. The *Caledonia* was brought safely to the American shore, but the *Detroit* ran aground and had to be burned to keep it out of British hands. Even so, the night's work was profitable: two ships subtracted from the British fleet, one added to the American; thirty American prisoners from Hull's fiasco rescued; a quantity of small arms and British prisoners bagged—all at a cost of two American dead and thirteen wounded.[6]

To an America reeling under a string of humiliating defeats, this was the first bright spot in an otherwise dispiriting war, and Scott enjoyed some reflected glory from the incident. His precise role is unclear. Lieutenant Elliott's report neglected to mention his name, and Scott's own memoirs merely noted that he spent "a busy day."[7] Most likely, his participation was limited to providing artillery cover during the seesaw struggle for possession of the *Detroit*. Before the week was out, he would find opportunity to win much greater distinction.

It was an opportunity he almost missed, but then the whole story of this Niagara campaign of 1812 was one of missed opportunities. On their side of the river, the Americans had assembled between five and six thousand men. At Lewiston, the first navigable point below the dreaded Whirlpool, Maj. Gen. Stephen Van Rensselaer, an aged New York politician and philanthropist, commanded over 2,600 state militiamen. About 1,300 soldiers of the regular army were stationed farther north at Fort Niagara, and almost 1,700 more, including Scott's companies, were in the Buffalo area under the command of Brig. Gen. Alexander Smyth. On the other side, General Brock could scrape together only about 1,500 British and Canadian soldiers plus some 250 unreliable Indian allies.[8]

The American numerical advantage was dissipated by its generals. Smyth refused to obey, or even meet, Van Rensselaer, whom he scorned as a militia officer and, even worse, a Federalist. Instead, Smyth devoted his energies to drafting pompous pronouncements (for example, "Think on your country's honor torn! her rights trampled on! her sons enslaved! her infants perishing by the hatchet!").[9] For his part, Van Rensselaer had his hands full trying to control his restless New York militiamen, who demanded either immediate action or immediate release.

To appease his troops, Van Rensselaer planned a two-pronged invasion, with simultaneous attacks on Fort George and the Canadian village of Queenston, directly across the river from Lewiston. The Fort George attack had to be scrapped due to Smyth's foot dragging, but the Queenston expedition was pushed ahead because of the militiamen's impatience. On the stormy night of October 10, Van Rensselaer's troops assembled on the riverbank only to discover that a Lieutenant Sims, otherwise unknown to history, had loaded all the available oars onto the lead boat and rowed off with them into the darkness, never to be seen again.[10] The militiamen retired to their quarters with their clothes drenched and their ardor dampened. The attack had to be rescheduled for the morning of the thirteenth.

While all this was going on, Scott was less than ten miles away, unaware of any pending military activity. He learned about it purely by chance. Around sunset on October 12, as Scott's command was pitching their tents for the night, Capt. James Collier happened to pass by. Noticing the tall commanding officer, who was, he later said, "the finest specimen of a man I ever saw," he politely inquired if he knew what was planned for the next morning. "No sir," Scott replied, "I have not heard from head-quarters for several days. Is there any thing in the wind, sir?"[11]

As soon as he learned what was afoot, Scott ordered the tents struck and his troops to the march while he dashed ahead to Lewiston to offer his services to Van Rensselaer. The general was more irritated than grateful for this unexpected reinforcement. The arrangements for the expedition were already made, he complained, and he suggested that Scott's unwanted battalion stay away. Perhaps more to the point, command of the expedition had already been assigned to the general's kinsman, Lt. Col. Solomon Van Rensselaer; as a regular officer of the same rank, Scott would supersede him. Some other regular officers had offered to waive their rank for this occasion, but Scott adamantly refused such an uncharacteristic act of abnegation. Finally, a compromise was reached whereby Scott and his men were allowed to provide artillery support for the invasion, but Scott would have to stay on the American side of the river.

The tiny Canadian village of Queenston was situated some 250 yards across the Niagara from Lewiston, just below the rapids. The current at this point was swift but navigable enough to permit a regular ferry service in peacetime. Directly south of the village towered the three-hundred-foot-high Niagara Escarpment, over which twelve thousand years earlier had poured the falls of the Niagara before beginning its slow retreat to its present location. These heights dominated the position. From them one could see, as if laid out on a map, every detail of the road to Fort George and, on a clear day, all the way across Lake Ontario to the provincial capital of York (now Toronto).

The American embarkation began at four o'clock on the morning of the thirteenth. Scarcely a dozen boats were available, which meant that the invaders would have to be ferried across in driblets. About three hundred militiamen and an equal number of regulars, recently arrived from Fort Niagara, were scheduled for the first wave. Many did not make it across: the river was swollen by recent storms, the civilian boatmen were understandably timid, and the well-posted British artillery took a heavy toll on the defenseless boats. Of the five hundred regulars who were sent across that day, only about half arrived on the opposite shore; the rest were either killed, wounded, captured, or forced back. The militia fared somewhat better, but their commander, Lieutenant Colonel Van Rensselaer, was so severely wounded that he had to withdraw.[12]

Before retiring, Van Rensselaer ordered Capt. John E. Wool of the 13th Infantry, then at the beginning of a military career that would rival Scott's in longevity, to seize the high ground of the escarpment, where a British 18-pounder was wreaking havoc on the Americans below. These heights were considered unscalable, but Wool discovered a little-used path up the nearly perpendicular cliff that led him and his men slightly to the rear and above the unsuspecting British artillery squad.

Directing that squad was none other than General Brock himself, who had just arrived from Fort George ahead of his main detachment. Caught by surprise, he barely had time to spike his gun before scampering to the safety of Queenston. From there he organized a counterattack that he led personally. Unlike some of his rank, Brock was known for his tactical daring and reckless courage. On Queenston Heights, these traits proved fatal. As he was readying his charge, an American sniper stepped out of the brush and shot him dead.

Wool was also injured, though not fatally, by an embarrassing wound in the buttocks (which the official report diplomatically transposed to his thighs). He left the field, nursing both his wound and his resentment against Scott for not giving him sufficient credit for his role in the battle.[13] The wound would heal; the grudge would not. Over fifty years later Wool would still be complaining about Scott's attempts to hog all the glory for himself.[14]

By midmorning the Americans seemed on the verge of victory, while their foe was leaderless, demoralized, and for the moment, outnumbered. On the opposite shore, Scott chafed with frustration as he watched these stirring events unfold while he "was confined, by the orders of my chief, or rather by the want of suitable boats," to a passive role.[15] But with every American field-grade officer now rendered *hors de combat,* General Van Rensselaer relented and allowed Scott to cross the river and take charge of the invading force. As a result of a series of accidents, Scott now found himself commanding a battle that, had it not been for Lieutenant Sims and Captain Collier, he would have missed altogether.

Scott arrived during a lull in the fighting and went up the heights to reconnoiter. He ordered defensive works constructed, but since no entrenching tools had been sent across the river, the work was slow going. Then he turned his attention to repairing the spiked British cannon, though to no avail. In the meantime, the fighting was renewed. Indians infiltrated from the nearby forest and threw themselves repeatedly at the improvised American line. For all their fierce war whoops, they inflicted little damage but did manage to keep Scott distracted until the main British force arrived from Fort George.[16]

That column of eight hundred redcoats, now under Maj. Gen. Roger Sheaffe, could be clearly seen from the heights as it slowly snaked its way south. Unlike the impetuous Brock, Sheaffe took no chances. He cautiously bypassed the village of Queenston, looping around to the west to gain the heights by the back door. Scott skillfully re-formed his line, but without reinforcements, his position was hopeless. A hasty count revealed that he had less than three hundred troops at his command, which meant that out of the six thousand Americans under arms in the Niagara region, less than 5 percent could be deployed at the critical time and place.[17]

Realizing that "without succor, our situation had become desperate," Scott could only hunker down behind his lines and await the promised reinforcements. They were not forthcoming. On the American side of the river, the New York militiamen could clearly see Scott's perilous position and decided that they wanted no part of it. Belatedly discovering constitutional scruples, they concluded that their terms of enlistment required them only to defend their own state, not to invade another. Van Rensselaer sent a pathetic note to Scott: "I have passed through my camp. Not a regiment, not a company is willing to join you. Save yourself by a retreat, if you can. Boats shall be sent to receive you."[18]

It was at this point, according to folklore and ballad, that Scott jumped on a log and addressed his men. "The enemy's balls begin to thin our ranks," he supposedly said. "In a moment the shock must come, and there is no retreat. . . . Let us then die, arms in hand. . . . Those who follow will avenge our fall and their country's wrongs. Who dares to stand?" "ALL!" was the answering cry.[19] This inspiring fiction was belied by events. After a brief stand, Scott and his men took Van Rensselaer's sensible advice and clambered down the cliff. No boats awaited them. They had been abandoned and had no alternative but to surrender.

The captives were marched to the pretty little village of Newark (now Niagara-on-the-Lake) adjacent to Fort George. The number of prisoners—about nine hundred—astonished Scott, who had commanded only three hundred men in the action. About two hundred more had been captured early on when their boats had been swept downstream by the current. Most of the remaining four hundred or so were skulkers (mainly militiamen) who had been hiding during the fighting. With a hundred more killed and an equivalent number wounded, American losses were severe. British casualties were comparatively light. Excluding the Indians, who, as was their custom, carried away their dead and wounded, the English army suffered only fourteen deaths, but that total included the irreplaceable loss of Brock.[20]

What had begun as an American victory had somehow turned into another humiliating defeat. In the postmortems that followed, Scott was generally exempt from blame. Indeed, for his gallant stand, he emerged as something of a hero: the first that America had produced in the course of this ineptly conducted war.

Although he happily basked in the adulation, Scott privately conceded that he shared some of the blame. In retrospect, he realized that his activity on

Queenston Heights had been misdirected. The key to success lay elsewhere. In his after-battle report, he concluded: "Every officer who had a principal command . . . appears to have committed an error in not descending from the heights and occupying the village of Queenston, and the batteries before it. This, I neither heard suggested by others at the time, nor did it occur to my-self."[21] The heights were important as an observation post and an artillery platform, but the position should not have consumed Scott's entire attention. Nor should he have wasted his own efforts on the mundane task of unspiking the captured cannon when he had subordinates perfectly capable of performing that chore.

The battle, and perhaps the war, might have had a happier outcome if Scott had concentrated his troops down below to clear the British garrison out of Queenston. With the beachhead secured and enlarged, reinforcements from Lewiston would have crossed over more readily, perhaps even on the boats that must have been available in a fishing village like Queenston. Advance parties could then have been sent down the road to Fort George to impede Sheaffe's advance by tearing up bridges and constructing defensive works. Such an early success might even have induced General Smyth to throw his idle brigade into the fray.

Instead, Scott adopted a passive role. The books in Benjamin Leigh's library had taught him how to maneuver troops but not how to win battles. He had learned to be a soldier but not yet to be a commander.

This failure of command extended all the way up the line. Planning for the operation was virtually nonexistent. Neither Scott nor any other officer seems to have received any instructions on what to do once they crossed the river. No one seems to have been responsible for ensuring that such vital supplies as cannon, ammunition, and entrenching tools were sent over. There was a failure to coordinate with other commanders in the area. Ample boats and skilled boatmen could have been had from Lieutenant Elliott at Black Rock. They were not called for. Smyth's battalion of regulars could have provided a steadying influence on Van Rensselaer's untrained militia. They were unused.[22]

There was ample blame to go around, yet it was the militia that became the scapegoat for the defeat at Queenston. The spectacle of New York militiamen passively watching an American defeat while staying safely on their side of the river was seized upon as a refutation of Jefferson's military policy. Never mind that by this time the battle had already been lost and that, in any event, there were no boats to transport them even if they had been willing to cross. The difference between regular troops and militiamen was not as clear-cut as popular judgment would have it. Some militiamen fought bravely on Queenston Heights, while some regulars were later found hiding in the cliffs.[23] The militia commander, Stephen Van Rensselaer, may have botched his invasion, but at least he tried, which is more than can be said for General Smyth of the regular army. And as for Scott himself, was his refusal to waive his rank for the sake of the common cause all that different from the insubordination of the recalcitrant militia?

Scott certainly thought so. To the end of his life, he blamed the Queenston debacle solely on those "vermin, who . . . no sooner found themselves in sight of the enemy than they discovered that the militia of the United States could not be constitutionally marched into a foreign country!"[24] From that experience dated his determination to create a disciplined, dedicated army of career soldiers bound together by dependable professional pride, rather than by evanescent patriotic enthusiasm. Scott had found his life work.

CHAPTER FOUR

ROCKET

For the United States, the defeat at Queenston Heights was just another in a humiliating string of failures, but for Scott it was something of a triumph. Unlike other commanders in this dispiriting war, the young lieutenant colonel had displayed both skill and bravery. The battle may have been lost, but Scott's reputation was made. From this point on, his ascent through the ranks, like those Congreve rockets employed by the British, would be precipitous and dazzling.

It almost sputtered out before it was launched. Taken as a prisoner to Newark, Scott was lodged in a local inn. He had barely arrived when two Indians accosted him in a narrow hallway, tomahawks in their hands and murder on their minds. As Scott told the story, in the third person he affected for his memoirs: "God and his own stout heart must save the American from instant butchery. With one mighty spring he seized the hilt of a sword. . . . [T]hen springing back he faced the enemy and occupied the narrow space between the staircase and the opposite wall. . . . In this strong position he could not be attacked by two assailants at once, and was sure to fell the foremost, though he might be assassinated by the second." At this delicate moment, a British officer fortunately happened to pass the hallway. He ordered the Indians to the guardhouse and escorted the prisoner to dinner.[1]

Aside from this near-fatal encounter, Scott's interlude as a captive was not particularly unpleasant. As an officer, he was treated more as a guest than a prisoner. This was an age when the phrase "an officer and a gentleman" was not yet an empty formula. The European officer class was drawn exclusively from the ranks of the aristocracy. As members of an international fraternity, they had more in common with each other (even if, for the moment, enemies)

Scott attacked by Indians. Mansfield, *The Life and Military Services of Lieut.-General Winfield Scott,* 48.

than they had with the soldiers they commanded. This courtesy was extended to Americans, so Scott was free to come and go on his honor and even shared dinner with his captors. Reciprocating in kind, Scott arranged for the American artillery at Fort Niagara to join the salute during the funeral of Brock at Fort George. General Sheaffe was deeply moved by this chivalrous gesture.[2]

The same chivalry did not extend to enlisted men, as Scott soon discovered. He and the other captive American regulars were to be paroled, that is, sent home after giving their word ("parole") that they would not fight until properly exchanged for British prisoners of equivalent rank. (As a gesture of contempt, the captive militiamen had already been sent home without these formalities.) While Scott was busy in his cabin of the prison ship moored at Quebec, he heard a commotion on the main deck. Darting up the ship's ladder, he found the American prisoners lined up and being interrogated by their captors. In a replay of the *Chesapeake* outrage, the English were searching for suspected British subjects. Already, they had sequestered twenty-three whose accents seemed to betray British birth and who now faced being hanged as traitors.

Scott sprang into action. His commanding voice cut through the din as he ordered his men to refuse to answer any further questions. The British commissioners tried to bully him, but unfazed, Scott warned that his government would not hesitate to retaliate in kind if any prisoners were harmed. No further Americans were disturbed, but the unlucky twenty-three were hauled off to an uncertain fate.[3]

A month later, after "a thousand hardships," Scott was back in the United States.[4] After making arrangements at Boston for the care of his 255 fellow prisoners, Scott hastened to Washington, arriving just in time to attend a White House soiree.[5] The dashing young bachelor-hero found himself the social star of the evening, forced to tell and retell the story of the outrage at Quebec. President James Madison was so indignant that he asked Scott to prepare an official report on the incident. When passed along to Congress, this resulted in a law empowering the United States to retaliate. Twenty-three British prisoners of war were set aside as hostages. The British then raised the ante by taking another forty-six American soldiers hostage, which number was then matched by the Americans. There the escalation ceased, but the point had been made. No one on either side would be executed.[6]

Capitalizing on his newfound celebrity, Scott improved his time at the capital by lobbying for himself and his friends. These men consisted largely of young officers who supported Gen. Wade Hampton in his feud against Gen. James Wilkinson. Not exactly a cabal, this was more in the nature of a generational resentment against being commanded by generals "crippled with gout and palsied with age."[7] Almost fifty years later, during another war, the young George B. McClellan would grumble in almost identical terms about Scott himself.

In March 1813 Scott moved another step up the ladder. Promoted to full colonel, he was given a joint appointment as adjutant general and commander of his old regiment, the 2d Artillery, which was then being augmented by fresh recruits from Pennsylvania. For the second time in less than a year, he made the grueling march to the Niagara frontier, suffering the usual delays and hazards along the route.[8] On May 13, he arrived at Fort Niagara and reported for duty to Maj. Gen. Henry Dearborn.

Dearborn had once done honorable service as an officer in the Revolution, though more recently as secretary of war, he had been considered something of an irresolute old fussbudget. Now sixty-two years old, he was ailing and crabby. Scott was willing to forgive Dearborn's rude, unpolished manners in light of his unquestioned patriotism and courage, but he could hardly overlook the general's deplorable "want of method." He reluctantly concluded that "nature never designed him for *a great General.*" Putting aside his private reservations, Scott plunged into his work as Dearborn's chief of staff, a position virtually unknown in the American army and which Scott helped define. Drawing upon the latest French texts, he reorganized the department along Napoleonic lines and soon had it humming with unaccustomed efficiency, infusing into headquarters the energy and method that Dearborn so conspicuously lacked.[9] Within three weeks, the army was ready to take the offensive.

The military situation was much like the one that had confronted Van Rensselaer the previous spring. On their side of the river, the Americans had once again assembled a force that considerably outnumbered the more sea-soned British and Canadian troops commanded by Brig. Gen. John Vincent. This time, however, Scott was able to profit from Van Rensselaer's mistakes in at least four ways.[10]

First, he maintained the element of surprise. Instead of assembling his forces in full view of the enemy and landing them within range of their artillery, Scott gathered 4,700 men on the shore of Lake Ontario, some three miles east of Fort Niagara, where they could not be readily observed. To distract the enemy and mask his real intentions, he kept up an artillery barrage on Fort George throughout May 26, giving the impression that a direct assault on that point was imminent. In the predawn darkness of May 27, his force boarded ships that carried them to a point on the Canadian shore a bit to the west of Fort George, which they could then attack from an unexpected direction.

Second, unlike Van Rensselaer, Scott coordinated his efforts with the navy, which, for the time being, was enjoying supremacy on Lake Ontario. His friend, the promising young officer Oliver Hazard Perry, assembled a flotilla of six-teen transports, each of which towed a string of rowboats, all packed to the gunwales with soldiers. As a bonus, fire from the warships silenced the enemy's shore batteries and provided cover for the landing.

Third, in contrast to the hit-or-miss attack on Queenston, Scott made careful advance preparations. Field artillery, sufficient ammunition, and other essen-tial supplies were carefully loaded beforehand. The landing site was recon-noitered and marked to minimize the inevitable confusion of battle, and each assault wave was instructed on how to proceed once ashore.

Finally, instead of trusting to luck, Scott had a strategic plan. His immedi-ate goal was Fort George, but his objective was to bag Vincent's army. To that end, Col. James Burn, with two troops of dragoons, was to cross the river a few miles upstream and block the enemy's anticipated retreat. Caught be-tween two American forces, the British would either have to surrender or fight on unfavorable terms.

It almost worked. At six o'clock on a foggy morning, the first boats came ashore on a narrow, sandy beach, with Scott in the lead. The British were waiting atop a steep bank about ten feet high and tried to throw the Ameri-cans back with bayonets. In dodging one thrust, Scott tumbled down the embankment. From his observation post aboard the flagship *Madison,* Gen-eral Dearborn thought him killed "and honored the supposed loss of the chief of his staff with a tear," but he was relieved to see Scott scamper back up the bank, unharmed.[11]

As successive waves of Americans embarked, the British gave way. Scott "borrowed" a horse from a wounded British officer and led the pursuit to the gates of the now nearly abandoned Fort George.[12] At that point, a tremendous explosion threw him from his horse, breaking a collarbone—the departing enemy was blowing up the powder magazines and spiking their guns. Too keyed up to attend to his injury, Scott entered the fort and had his men stamp out the fuses, while he hauled down the British flag as a souvenir.[13]

Scott then resumed his chase of Vincent's fleeing army, but his carefully laid trap failed to spring. By the time Colonel Burn crossed the river, the British had already gone. Scott stopped briefly to integrate Burn's dragoons into his own command, and while he was halted, Brig. Gen. John P. Boyd rode up with orders to cease the pursuit. Scott protested that if given another hour he could crush or disperse Vincent's army, but to no avail; the British were allowed to slip away unmolested. The next day, when Scott was ordered to track them down, he found that "the bird had flown."[14] Vincent had fled cross-country to Burlington Heights, at the western end of Lake Ontario, with his army intact.

Dearborn hailed the expedition as a victory, but Scott was "disappointed and dispirited" at the result. Secretary of War John Armstrong, equally disappointed, reminded the general: "Battles are not gained when an inferior and broken army is not destroyed. Nothing is done while anything that might have been done is omitted."[15]

By the time Dearborn nerved himself to take the offensive, Vincent was ready for him. Early in June, an American force of two thousand men, led by Brigadiers General John Chandler and William Winder, marched on Burlington Heights. They camped at Stony Creek but neglected to post pickets, allowing Vincent to fall upon them in the darkness with only seven hundred men. In the confusion, both Chandler and Winder wandered into the enemy lines and were captured. The leaderless Americans fled back to the safety of Fort George.

This fresh humiliation left Dearborn in such a state of nervous prostration that he begged the War Department for permission "to return to some place where my mind may be more at ease."[16] Command devolved upon General Boyd, whom Scott regarded as "the most destitute of capacity of any man of his rank and experience in the world." Although he conceded that his new commander could be "courteous, amiable and respectable as a subordinate," as a chief he proved "vacillating and imbecile beyond all endurance."[17]

Secretary of War Armstrong evidently agreed, for he kept Boyd on a short leash, forbidding further offensive operations. "Thus," Scott lamented, "the army of the Niagara . . . stood fixed in a state of ignominy for some two months." Cooped up in a narrow strip of the Niagara peninsula between Forts George and Erie while its enemy was free to move at will, the American army rusticated. Among its idle officers, intrigues festered and tempers flared. Scott was not immune: he even came near to fighting another duel. Bored and frustrated with his routine as chief of staff, he moaned, "Office duties will kill me." He repeatedly tried to resign, but Boyd insisted that he could not command the army without Scott's help. Finally, the general bowed to Scott's repeated pleas to be relieved from "the sedentary habits" of staff work and allowed him to return to his regiment.[18]

The 2d Artillery, Scott realized, had become "infected with the general dullness which pervades our army."[19] It needed the stimulus of action, but no major operations were possible so long as Boyd commanded the army and the British controlled the lake. Scott had to settle for minor skirmishes.

Minor though they were, these actions posed a major peril to Scott personally. A high-level dispute over the prisoner-exchange agreement supposedly concluded earlier in the year now cast doubts on the legitimacy of Scott's parole. A stiffly worded note from British colonel John Harvey disingenuously inquired whether Colonel Scott was the same person taken captive at Queenston. If so, Harvey warned, "it is impossible that he can be recognized in any other capacity than a British prisoner of war, he having given his parole of honour (of what value is not proved), not to serve again until regularly exchanged." This meant that if Scott should again fall into British hands, he would not be invited to share their dinner, as before, but would be summarily shot. In his response, the usually hot-blooded Scott overlooked the slur cast upon his honor and calmly placed his trust in the assurances given by his superiors that his exchange had been proper. "Should any misunderstanding exist as to the correctness of the exchange," he concluded, "it may afford questions for the two governments, but certainly not for the individual implicated, who is bound to obey his orders, regardless of consequences."[20]

Fatalistically, Scott took his chances, leading a series of raids, foraging expeditions, and reconnaissance probes. The most ambitious of these sorties took place in late July, when control of Lake Erie had seesawed back to the American fleet under Commodore Isaac Chauncey. This raised the possibility of swooping by sea upon Vincent's supply depot at Burlington Bay while his forces were still scattered. Scott loaded over two hundred soldiers aboard the *General Pike,* but "light and contrary winds" so slowed their progress that Vincent had ample time to recall his forces and prepare a formidable defense by the time Scott and Chauncey arrived.[21]

The Americans pulled anchor and sailed instead to York, where, it was reported, ample British supplies were stored. They found the little provincial capital virtually stripped of defenders and almost destitute of the rumored booty, except for some four hundred barrels of flour, which they confiscated, and a handful of American prisoners, whom they liberated. The public buildings were then put to the torch, perpetuating that cycle of incendiary vandalism that would culminate in the British burning of Washington the following year. Spared from the flames was the personal property of British officers, including a portrait of Colonel Harvey's wife, which the chivalrous Scott, overlooking the recent aspersions cast upon his honor, returned to its rightful owner.[22] Harvey would be grateful for this gesture, and a warm respect would be kindled between the two antagonists that would, in later years, facilitate diplomatic relations between their governments.

These raids were uniformly successful but, from Scott's point of view, unsatisfying. He had become a soldier to win glory, not to steal flour. He dreamed of waging warfare in the grand manner, not in this petty fashion. "It was his ambition," Scott confessed, "to conduct sieges and command in open fields, serried lines and columns."[23]

In this revealing admission, Scott would inadvertently supply the key to both the successes and failures of his military career. As a "scientific" soldier, he had initially acquired his professional knowledge from books, and in the absence of an American military tradition, those books were necessarily European. Consequently, his inspiration was found in the lives of the great European captains, from Wallenstein to Wellington. To match their achievements, however, required a war in the European mold. When such a war occurred, as in 1812 or 1846, Scott could rise to the challenge brilliantly, but these opportunities would be rare. In the long intervals between conventional wars, the American army's mission would be less heroic: fighting small-unit engagements with Indian foes who would not play by the European rules of war. In that sort of irregular warfare, Scott's professional skill would be less useful, and his success would be less conspicuous.

Throughout the summer of 1813, Scott marked time, impatiently awaiting the long-rumored arrival of General Hampton to assume command. Instead, the War Department had an unpleasant surprise in store: Scott's old nemesis, General Wilkinson, had been ordered north. He arrived at Fort George in early September, and Scott promptly paid a courtesy call on the "unprincipled imbecile." Oily as ever, Wilkinson assured Scott that he bore no grudge for their past differences and would treat him with all the courtesy his present rank deserved.[24] Yet when the general issued his orders for the long-awaited offensive into Lower Canada, he pointedly left Scott behind.

Wilkinson's plan was to advance down the St. Lawrence River with about four thousand men and capture Montreal, supposed to be only lightly garrisoned. Hampton's force would simultaneously proceed north from Lake Champlain, and the two armies would winter at Montreal and prepare for a campaign in the spring. The glaring flaws in this plan were apparent even to its authors, Wilkinson and Armstrong. For one thing, the season was late. For another, the British naval base at Kingston would be left free to operate on Wilkinson's rear to cut his line of supply and potential line of retreat. Finally, Wilkinson and Hampton were not on speaking terms. These obstacles might have been overcome through speed and audacity, but the sickly Wilkinson was capable of neither.

Scott, who might have supplied some of the energy and boldness that his commander so conspicuously lacked, was ordered to remain at Fort George in command of its diminished garrison. That post was still in disrepair from the battering it had received the previous May and vulnerable to an attack from Vincent, encamped only five miles away. Scott and his men labored around the clock to repair the walls and install artillery while Vincent obligingly stayed his hand.[25]

Shortly after the works were completed, Vincent burned his stores and beat a hasty retreat to Burlington Heights, driven there not by any fear of Scott but by a sudden change in the military situation. William Henry Harrison's victory over the British and their Indian allies at the Battle of the Thames compelled the scattered British troops to go on the defensive. Assuming (incorrectly) that this signaled an imminent British withdrawal from the Niagara region, Scott decided to abandon his post at Fort George and join Wilkinson's advance. "My situation," he wrote the general, "has become truly insupportable, without the possibility of an attack at this post, and without the possibility of reaching you in time to share in the glory of impending operations below."[26]

Assigning a small detachment of militiamen to guard the fort, Scott marched his eight hundred regulars to the mouth of the Genesee River, where Wilkinson had promised that transport ships would be waiting. As he should have anticipated given his previous experience with Wilkinson, the ships were not there. He pressed on through constant rain to near Utica, where he encountered Secretary of War Armstrong, who gave Scott permission to push on ahead of his men. Leaving his regiment behind (which meant, of course, that it was available neither to protect Fort George nor to participate in Wilkinson's advance), Scott and an aide dashed fifty miles through mud and sleet, reaching the main army just as it was preparing to run the enemy's shore batteries at night. "The scene was most sublime," he later recalled. "The roar of cannon was unremitting, and darkness rendered visible by the whizzing and bursting of shells and Congreve rockets."[27]

The next day, November 7, he was assigned to command the vanguard battalion of about eight hundred men, charged with clearing the way for the advance of the main body of the army. On November 11, he encountered a British force under Lt. Col. James B. Dennis, about equal to his own, that was well positioned to guard a bridge across Hoople's Creek.[28] Rather than risk a frontal assault, Scott posted a field battery across Dennis's front to mask his own movements and "to amuse the enemy." While Dennis was thus amused,

Scott led the bulk of his force across a ford about a mile above the enemy's position, hoping to trap them in a vise. This was Scott's first use of the turning maneuver that would become his trademark during the Mexican War, where it would be used with good effect at Cerro Gordo and Contreras. At Hoople's Creek it almost worked. Dennis managed to extricate himself just before the trap snapped shut, but at the cost of a hasty retreat in which a number of his men were taken prisoner.[29]

On the same day that Scott was winning fresh laurels at Hoople's Creek, fifteen miles to his rear, at a place called Chrysler's Farm, the rest of Wilkinson's army was suffering another defeat. Two thousand Americans, most of them regulars, were routed by less than nine hundred British. The next day Wilkinson turned his back on Canada and headed home. Scott was disgusted at the outcome of this campaign—"begun in boastings, and ended in deep humiliations." He thought Wilkinson deserved to be shot. "Shall not fatuity, incapacity, ignorance, imbecility," he sputtered, "—call it as you may—in a commander—of whatever rank—be equally punished with cowardice, or giving aid and comfort to the enemy?"[30]

Scott's fighting spirit clouded his judgment. He was convinced that Montreal was virtually defenseless and could easily have been taken had Wilkinson not lost his nerve. The general, however, knew some things Scott did not. For one thing, the British garrison actually stationed in the city may have numbered a mere six hundred, but there were an additional fifteen thousand in the vicinity available to assist them if needed.[31] Furthermore, he had just learned that Hampton had decided not to join him as promised but had, instead, settled into winter quarters at French Mills, New York. Wilkinson's army soon joined him, and together they spent a difficult winter, full of hardships.

Scott was spared the rigors of French Mills. By direct orders from the president, the colonel was summoned to Washington to report on the recent train of northern disasters. It must have been a heady experience for a young officer to have the president and the secretary of war hanging on his words, but Scott, already known to his friends as "the vainest man in the army," probably took it in stride.[32]

In the midst of Scott's high-level conferences, a delegation from upstate New York arrived at the capital. The Niagara frontier was in flames, and they demanded help. The specific savior they had in mind was Winfield Scott, the only officer who had emerged from the Niagara campaign with reputation enhanced. The colonel was accordingly dispatched to New York.[33]

During his absence, the Niagara frontier had collapsed. Fort George was abandoned without a fight and Fort Niagara captured by stealth. Defenseless villages, including Buffalo, were burned by the British in retaliation for alleged American atrocities. To a degree, Scott was responsible for this situation. By withdrawing his regiment from Fort George the previous October, he had left the frontier exposed. Now he was called upon to repair the damage.

His first stop was Albany. There he conferred with Governor Daniel Tompkins and struck up a friendship with a promising young legislator, Martin Van Buren. Scott presciently forecast that his new friend would someday become president, and Van Buren returned the compliment by naming his newborn son (who died in infancy) Winfield Scott Van Buren.[34]

As Scott began to prepare for a winter campaign to retake the Niagara peninsula, he found himself in a "truly embarrassing" situation. His orders were from the secretary of war, but he was operating within the military district commanded by Wilkinson. The general had no intention of allowing this "fawning hypocrite" of a colonel to operate independently within his jurisdiction. To thwart this "outrage on military subordination and the feelings of a gentleman," Wilkinson threw up obstacles at every turn, refusing to allow his troops to be detached for Scott's campaign and even siphoning off for his own use units earmarked for Scott. An accomplished intriguer, he tried to undercut Scott's standing with Governor Tompkins by hinting that the haughty young colonel was too proud to work well with militia. (There was some truth to this charge. Scott angrily predicted, "We shall be disgraced if we admit a militia force either into our camp or order of battle," and he threatened to resign from the army rather than serve under a militia general.)[35]

Scott fought back, appealing directly to Secretary Armstrong for support. In this he was doing what later as commanding general he would not tolerate from a subordinate—communicating directly with the secretary of war over the head of his superior officer. Despite his efforts, he seemed to be checkmated by the wily old general. "My prospects are most gloomy," Scott sighed.[36]

Then with dazzling suddenness, his situation was transformed. In a longoverdue housecleaning, the War Department swept out from their high commands the aged generals of defeat. Gone, or on their way out, were both Wilkinson and Hampton. Gone too were Dearborn, Lewis, and Boyd. A new set of young, vigorous, and aggressive general officers filled their places. Three new major generals, including Jacob Brown in the North and Andrew Jackson in the South, would now take command, aided by four newly minted brigadiers: Alexander Macomb, Eleazar Ripley, Edmund P. Gaines—and Winfield Scott.

Only three years earlier, Scott had been a disgraced captain serving out his term of suspension from office. Three years before that, he had been a law student, drawing up wills and deeds. In 1812 the average age of an American general had been sixty; by 1814 that had been reduced to thirty-six, and Winfield Scott, at twenty-seven years and nine months of age, was the youngest of them all. That "favor of Providence" he had invoked at the war's commencement had indeed smiled upon him.

CHAPTER FIVE

VICTORY

Early in April 1814, Brig. Gen. Winfield Scott arrived at Buffalo to assume his first command. His superior officer was newly promoted Maj. Gen. Jacob Brown, a one-time Quaker from upstate New York who was unschooled in military science but possessed of a fighting spirit and an unflappable disposition.[1] Brown was soon called to Sackett's Harbor, at the eastern end of Lake Ontario, which put Scott in full command of the "Left Division" of Military District No. 9, along the Niagara frontier.

The Left Division initially numbered about 1,600 regulars, but from April to June, fresh detachments of recruits and militiamen dribbled in, raising the total to about 3,500.[2] Scott had been given no specific orders of what to do with this force in Brown's absence other than to act as he thought best. With this vague mandate, he had a free hand to carry out his ideas on how an army should be run. Scott cleared a campsite at Flint Hill, a little west of the burned-out ruins of Buffalo, and there he opened a "camp of instruction," subjecting the men under his command to the rigors of what later generations would call basic training.

Contrary to myth (propagated largely by Scott himself), this was not the only training camp in the American army, but it was the most thorough. No detail, Scott boasted, was overlooked: "the service of outposts, night patrols, guards, and sentinels organized; a system of sanitary police, including kitchens, etc., laid down; rules of civility, etiquette, courtesy—the indispensable outworks of subordination—prescribed and enforced, and the tactical instruction of each arm commenced."[3] For almost two months, the men were drilled up to ten hours a day, seven days a week.

They needed it. Although the enlistees of the War of 1812 were less likely to be immigrants and were drawn from somewhere higher on the social scale than the recruits of the old army, they were still unpromising material. "Our standing army," complained Secretary of War John Armstrong, "is but a bad and ill-organized militia; and our militia not better than a mob."[4] Unlike the British "lifers," whom the Duke of Wellington famously described as "the scum of the earth, enlisted for drink," American soldiers were amateurs who signed up largely for the cash bounty. As such, they were prone to an unmilitary sense of independence, often leading to disobedience and even desertion.

To curb these insubordinate tendencies, many officers relied on iron discipline and brutal punishments. "The situation of Virginia slaves is enviable compared to that of American soldiers," declared one disgusted officer. "They are beaten and even whip'd with cowhides without trial, fed on bad provisions, compelled almost incessantly to labor without extra pay, and every third or fourth night lose their rest [in sentry duty]. It is not to be wondered at that they desert in such numbers. It is impossible men thus treated should be faithful soldiers." Although flogging was far less severe than in the British army, where up to five hundred lashes could be imposed, recalcitrant American soldiers could be subjected to a variety of punishments and humiliations, ranging from branding and mutilation to ducking, bucking, bread and water, ball and chain, solitary confinement, and deprivation of whiskey rations.[5]

Scott, however, preferred to instill discipline through professional pride rather than fear. Although some punishments were inevitable, brutality was discouraged. One officer who struck a soldier was suspended from duty for six months.[6] By May, Scott could proudly boast, *"I have not had occasion for a provost guard!"* When it came to a serious offense, however, Scott could be implacable. In June, he ordered four deserters to be shot. (A fifth was spared because of his youth, but not before facing a firing squad with blank cartridges. When the supposedly fatal volley was fired, he fainted from sheer terror.)[7]

Determined not to repeat the horrors of Terre aux Boeufs, Scott took pains to ensure the health and well being of his men. Ample supplies of wholesome bread were always on hand, and inspectors made sure that the kitchens were clean and that the latrines were kept far from the drinking water. The men were even ordered to bathe three times weekly under the paternal supervision of an officer who made sure that they did a thorough job. The results astounded old soldiers: only two deaths from disease were reported, and "even the demon diarrhoea appeared to have been exorcised by the mystical power of strict discipline and rigid police!"[8]

Scott was less successful in clothing his men than in feeding them. Many of his soldiers, he complained, were "almost in a state of perfect nakedness," and ten to fifteen out of every company went ragged and barefoot. He blamed

Wilkinson for diverting to his own troops supplies earmarked for Scott's army, but the roots of the problem ran deeper. Preindustrial America could not readily meet the massive demands for uniforms that wartime mobilization created. Even though four thousand tailors and seamstresses were busily stitching away in Philadelphia alone, shortages persisted. Regulation blue cloth was especially hard to come by, and the cheaper gray uniforms used by militias often had to be substituted. A shipment of these gray uniforms finally reached Flint Hill in June, just as Scott was preparing to break camp and go on the offensive.[9]

Until then, barefoot or shod, in sun or rain, heat or cold, the men of the Left Division were put through their paces. In the morning after breakfast, corporals drilled their squads for an hour. From 11:00 A.M. to noon, captains took over, drilling entire companies. After lunch, the whole brigade was assembled for large-scale evolutions and maneuvers. Scott personally presided over these arduous exercises, profanely urging the men to ever greater exertions. "General Scott drills and damns, drills and damns, and drills again," one of his captains reported.[10] The object of all this effort was to turn a thousand or so individuals into automatons, as was required by the imperatives of Napoleonic-era warfare. The basic weapon of that style of warfare, as it had been for over a century, was the muzzle-loaded flintlock musket. Its strengths and weaknesses determined the battlefield tactics of the day.

The deficiencies seemed obvious. The musket's range was limited, and its accuracy was poor. Unlike the rifle, which Americans were accustomed to using in hunting game and fighting Indians, the barrel of the musket was smooth bored, lacking the rifling, or incised spiral grooves, that could impart a stabilizing spin to its projectiles. Musket balls plopped out of their barrel rather than spinning straight and true to their target. This gave them an effective range of only forty or fifty yards compared to the hundreds of yards within a rifleman's range. Contending armies, as at Bunker Hill, had to get close enough to see the whites of the enemies' eyes. Furthermore, these muskets were so inaccurate that the British manual of arms dispensed with the command "Aim." The undersized musket ball bounced around so erratically in its journey down the barrel that it hit its target only by chance.[11]

These drawbacks were more than offset by the musket's dependability and speed of operation. A rifle might do to pluck off an unsuspecting deer, but the thirty seconds or more required to load and fire its tight-fitting bullet was simply too long for battlefield conditions. Besides, after the first volley, armies were so clouded with black smoke that it was impossible to see any specific target at which to take aim. In the hands of a well-trained soldier, a musket could be fired up to six times a minute. If a thousand men fired into that smoke at precisely the same time, the resulting wall of lead could compensate for the deficient marksmanship of the individual soldier.[12]

Such speed and precision required extensive training. The twenty separate motions required to fire a musket had to be so deeply ingrained that they could be performed automatically, even in moments of panic. Entire companies, and even regiments, had to load and fire with the coordination of a corps de ballet. They had to keep their ranks dressed, even while crossing broken terrain, and they had to have enough confidence in their ability (and sufficient fear of their own officers) that they could stand firm in the face of the murderous fire directed against them.[13]

The United States was such an unmilitary nation that its army lacked standardized drill manuals and training procedures. Its store of military knowledge was so meager that John Armstrong found it necessary to prepare a small guidebook to instruct *generals*.[14] The rank and file had no such handbook, or rather, what was worse, suffered from a multiplicity of inadequate and contradictory manuals. Some units still relied upon Baron Steuben's Revolutionary-era *Blue Book;* others, the various manuals prepared by William Duane, a newspaper editor with military pretensions.[15]

Scott liked none of them. He considered Steuben's "meagre Book" obsolete and Duane's "miserable handbook" an "abortion." He much preferred the French system: "the most perfect of the didactic kind that has yet fallen under my notice." This preference made sense. Although the British formation of "the thin red line" was theoretically superior to the French practice of maneuvering by columns, it required more professional skill than the American army could muster. Postrevolutionary French armies, composed of levies of citizen-soldiers, provided a better model for the amateur American forces. The problem was that there were no French manuals available for the use of Scott's army other than the ones he carried in his own personal library. Patching together pieces from the existing handbooks with procedures derived from his own sources, he devised a system of drill that he taught to his officers who then conveyed it to the troops. The system worked, but as Scott complained, if he "had been furnished with a text book, the saving of time and labor would be immense." He resolved that some day he himself would remedy the deficiency.[16]

After two months of this regimen, the troops of the Left Division looked forward to combat as a welcome respite from the rigors of drill. Scott thought they were ready. They "are already broken into habits of subordination; are becoming expert in their tactical exercises and," he predicted, "will ... if I have not grossly deceived myself, possess the firmness and cohesion of veterans." "I have a handsome little army," he boasted. "If, of such materials, I do not make the best army now in the service by the 1st of June, I will agree to be dismissed from the service."[17] These bold words would soon be put to the test.

As with so much else in this muddled war, the offensive of 1814 arose out of confusion, misdirection, and cross-purposes. Initially, the objective was supposed to be Kingston, the major British navy yard on Lake Ontario. Its capture was advocated by many military strategists, Scott included, who realized that it was the key to control of the Great Lakes and, consequently, all of Upper Canada. In late February, Secretary of War Armstrong authorized General Brown to prepare an attack on Kingston, but as a *ruse de guerre,* he enclosed a second letter, intended to fall into British hands, that ordered an expedition against Fort Niagara.

Armstrong was too clever by half, or at least too clever for Brown, a straightforward soul unaccustomed to deceit. Interpreting the second letter as a legitimate alternative, Brown assembled his forces for a Niagara campaign. By the time the bewildered general was set straight, it was too late to attack Kingston, so Armstrong gave the Niagara project his blessing, urging Brown to "go on and prosper. Good consequences are sometimes the result of mistakes."[18] Actually, as the secretary realized, there was little to be gained from yet another Niagara campaign so long as Commodore Chauncey was unable to obtain naval supremacy on Lake Ontario. The Left Division, however, was now thoroughly trained and ready for action; it would be a shame to let it stand idle. As Napoleon once said, one can do anything with bayonets except sit on them.

Armstrong authorized Brown to conduct a limited operation "to give immediate occupation to your troops, and to prevent their blood from stagnating." He suggested that they capture the lightly garrisoned British outpost at Fort Erie and then push north to Chippewa. After that, Brown should "be governed by circumstances in either stopping there or going further"—an injunction that betrayed by its vagueness how little store the secretary placed in the project. Scott had somehow gotten the idea that he was to command the invasion and could scarcely conceal his disappointment when, at the end of June, Brown returned to take charge.[19] Nonetheless, Scott's role would be substantial. Brown divided the army into two battalions. The larger, led by Scott, was to cross about a mile north of Fort Erie; the other, commanded by Brig. Gen. Eleazar Ripley, would simultaneously land about the same distance on the other side of the fort.

The campaign was scheduled to begin July 3, but both generals urged delay. Scott, with an eye toward public relations, thought that a battle fought on the "Glorious Fourth" would make a bigger splash. Ripley, betraying the first signs of that tendency toward hesitation that would blight his military career, argued that his force was inadequate and threatened to resign. Brown overruled them both.[20]

The crossing began shortly after midnight on July 3. For the third time in as many years, Winfield Scott was rowed across the Niagara River to invade Canada. This trip was almost fatal. As he approached the shore on the lead boat, he had what he called "a most critical adventure." Determined to be the first ashore, he shouted, "Follow me!" jumped into the surf, and promptly sank beneath the unexpectedly deep waters. Dragged down by the weight of the uniform of which he was so proud, he nearly drowned but, fortunately, was plucked by comrades from the depths, spluttering, soaked, and embarrassed.[21]

That was the greatest danger Scott faced the entire day.[22] The rest of the invasion was carried off with surprising ease. Fort Erie was quickly secured without even waiting for the arrival of Ripley, who was late in crossing. The British garrison of only two hundred men realized the hopelessness of their situation and surrendered after token resistance. At a cost of only four American dead (and one Englishman), Brown had gained a toehold on the Niagara peninsula. Maintaining it would prove more costly.[23]

When the British commander, Maj. Gen. Phineas Riall, got wind of the American invasion, he gathered his scattered forces, but by the time his advance guard reached Chippewa, word came that Fort Erie had already fallen. There he stopped to await the reinforcements from York that were expected the next day. Had Brown heeded the pleas for delay from Scott and Ripley, he would have faced substantial opposition, and his landing might have met the same fate as Van Rensselaer's had two years earlier.[24]

July 4 was hot and muggy. Wasting no time on a holiday celebration, Brown sent Scott's brigade down the road to Chippewa. For twelve hours they fought a running battle with British skirmishers, who skillfully delayed the Americans' advance by ripping up the planks on the many bridges they had to cross. By sunset, Scott reached the Chippewa River, which at that point was about 150 feet wide and too deep to wade. Behind it was massed the main British army in a strong defensive position. Scott withdrew about a mile to Street's Creek to wait for the rest of Brown's army to catch up with him.[25]

The next morning both armies were encamped along the Portage Road behind their respective streams—with the Niagara River on their east flank; a dense woods to their west; and a mile of open plain, covered with tall grass, in between. They remained in this position for much of the day, probing at each other's defenses.

Convinced that there was no serious action in store, Scott allowed himself to relax from his previous day's exertions. Invited to breakfast by Mrs. Street, wife of the wealthiest local landowner, he recklessly accepted. As he and two aides were beginning to sip their coffee, one officer happened to glance out the window and spotted a number of Indians and British soldiers closing in on the house. "General," he shouted, "we are betrayed!" Dashing out the door and dodging bullets, they made it across the bridge to safety, with the long-legged general, as befit military protocol, in the lead. Scott realized that this indiscretion could have ended his career in disgrace. He was so filled with "shame and mortification" that he could scarcely concentrate on his duties. Even in the heat of battle later that day, his thoughts kept drifting back to his earlier embarrassment. Such was his chivalrous idealization of womankind that he could scarcely believe "a lady of cultivation and refinement capable of such an act." Over half a century later he was still brooding over the incident.[26]

This was not the only example of Scott's carelessness on that momentous day. By noon, he decided that his brigade could afford the luxury of a belated holiday celebration. He ordered a special dinner prepared and afterward, "to keep his men in breath," intended to hold a dress parade on the plain that separated the two armies.[27] Considering that his exercise would take place in full view of an enemy of uncertain numbers, this whim might have seemed the height of folly, but Scott was convinced that only a skeleton British force lay behind the Chippewa.

Brown was more cautious. Disturbed by the Indians who had been infiltrating through the woods on his left flank, he ordered militia general Peter Porter into the woods to clear them of enemy skirmishers. Meanwhile, Riall had not been idle. Having been reinforced, he was even then preparing an attack. At about 4:30 he sent his artillery and three regiments of infantry across the Chippewa into the plain and another infantry brigade through the woods to flank the American camp. It was this force that Porter stumbled upon while he was chasing Indians. Quickly turning tail, his militiamen fled through the woods to the safety of camp, spreading the alarm as they ran.[28]

Scott was unaware of all this activity. High brush screened the British from his view, and he had unaccountably neglected to send out scouts. Oblivious to the impending peril, he was preparing to cross the bridge for his parade when Brown galloped by and shouted, "You will have a battle!" Convinced that there could not be more than three hundred British in his front, Scott initially shrugged off the warning, but the brisk cannonades from the enemy's well-placed artillery soon undeceived him.[29]

Scott was in a perilous position. He had to shepherd his brigade across a narrow bridge under heavy fire, while they were vulnerable as a line of ducks. Fortunately, most of the British shells went high, passing over their heads and then bouncing across the water like children's skipping stones. The men crossed the bridge safely and in good order and, once on the open plain, coolly deployed into line of battle. General Riall was astounded. From the Americans' gray uniforms, he had assumed he was dealing only with the despised militia, but the cool competence they displayed under fire made him realize that he was facing something else. "Why, these are regulars!" he was supposed to have exclaimed in surprise.[30]

Now the tedious weeks of training at Flint Hill demonstrated their value, as discipline overcame fear and ingrained habits triumphed over confusion. Previously arcane military maneuvers, such as attack en echelon, deployment

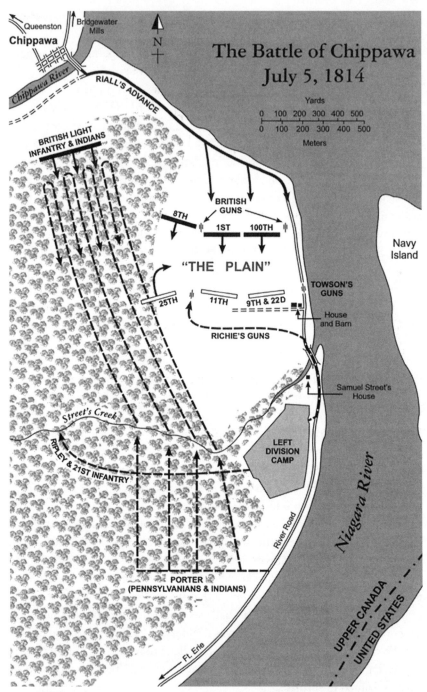

The Battle of Chippewa. John D. Morris, *Sword of the Border: Major General Jacob Jennings Brown, 1775–1828* (Kent, Ohio: Kent State Univ. Press, 2000), 101.

from line to column, enfilading fire, and the oblique approach now made practical, even lifesaving, sense.

They formed their line of battle three ranks deep and marched with precision through the waist-high grass, as snatches of music from the military bands sounded incongruously between the bursts of artillery fire.[31] Canister and grapeshot from those guns thinned Scott's line somewhat, but counterfire from Capt. Nathan Towson's battery silenced it with a lucky shot that blew up the enemy's ammunition wagon. Throughout all this carnage and confusion, Scott's troops maintained their poise as if they were on the parade ground. "Now the musketry of the enemy began to rattle," recalled Capt. James Hall,

> pouring bullets thick as hail upon our ranks. Still, not a trigger was drawn, not a voice was heard on our side, save the quick, peremptory tones of command. General Scott rode along the line, cheering and restraining his troops—then passing from flank to flank to see that all was as he wished. ... The British rushed forward with bayonets charged; but they were struck with amazement when they beheld those whom their commander had tauntingly called *militia,* standing motionless as statues; their muskets erect, their arms folded across their breasts, gazing calmly at the hostile ranks advancing furiously with levelled bayonets![32]

As the two advancing lines approached within musket range, Scott noticed that the British line extended beyond his own. To prevent his line from being enveloped, he extended the gaps between his own regiments, pushed the flanks forward, and held back the center so that he formed a shallow V. As the British advanced into it, they were caught in the crossfire from Scott's musketry and raked by the artillery posted on their flanks. Mowed down like wheat beneath the sickle, the British line hesitated. Scott then ordered a bayonet charge and incredibly, for the first time in this war, it was the British line that "mouldred away like a rope of sand," as the redcoats broke and ran.[33] The Battle of Chippewa was over. From start to finish it had not lasted ninety minutes.

The retreat was covered by the British reserves, who held off the American advance long enough for the army to cross the river into the village of Chippewa, destroying the bridge behind them. Scott pursued to the river's edge, but the British batteries on the northern bank were too strongly entrenched to be stormed.

The battle ended with the Americans in command of a field strewn with dead and wounded; the majority of these wore red uniforms. Total British casualties numbered 515, with 148 dead and 320 wounded, including many officers picked off by unsporting American marksmen. The Americans lost 60 killed, 248 wounded, and 19 missing. Twenty-five percent of the men engaged on both sides were casualties, and 90 percent of the American dead and wounded were from Scott's brigade, indicating that it had borne the overwhelming brunt of the day's action.[34]

When the fighting was finished, Ripley's brigade finally appeared on the battlefield. Brown had earlier sent it through the woods on the left, hoping it would emerge behind the British line and trap it. Ripley, however, took a wrong turn, and by the time he found his way, it was too late. Brown had taken a large and unnecessary risk in dividing his forces in the face of a potentially superior foe, but Scott's success redeemed the blunder. But that was not the only mistake made that day: the failure to reconnoiter the enemy was another. "We were all young soldiers," explained an American officer in retrospect, "and the wonder should be, not that we blundered, but that we did not blunder more, and that our talented and veteran enemy should have out blundered us."[35]

British mistakes stemmed from overconfidence. Years of easy victories had made them careless and led Riall into taking needless risks. One of his colonels bluntly concluded that his commander's actions were "ill-advised and the movements ill-executed." Riall's excuse was that he was outnumbered by about six thousand to fifteen hundred, but in truth, the forces on the field were almost equally matched—about fourteen hundred on the British side to over thirteen hundred under Scott.[36]

From a strategic point of view, the Battle of Chippewa was inconclusive. Riall's army had been bloodied, but it was still intact. From the standpoint of morale, however, the results were decisive. The British aura of invincibility had been shattered, and their dispirited Indian allies returned for a time to their villages. American valor won new respect, even from their foes. "The important fact is, that we now have an enemy who fights as bravely as ourselves," an English journal observed, and it drew a discouraging lesson from that fact. "They have now proved to us what they are made of, and they are the same sort of men as those who captured whole armies under Burgoyne and Cornwallis; that they are neither to be frightened nor silenced; and that if we should beat them at last, we cannot expect to do it without expending three or four hundred millions of money. . . . These are the natural consequences of battles such as that of Chippewa."[37]

In the United States, the news was received with rejoicing. "Everywhere bonfires blazed; bells rang out peals of joy; the big guns responded, and the pulse of Americans," according to Scott, "recovered a healthy beat." Enlistments rose and defeatist voices fell silent. Such was the influence of the victory that, according to military folklore, the cadets at West Point ever after wore the gray uniforms of Chippewa in commemoration. (Unfortunately for that charming legend, modern research has established that the U.S. Military

Academy adopted gray uniforms solely for the practical reasons that they were cheap and functional.)[38]

Brown generously gave his subordinate full credit for the victory. "Brig.-gen. Scott," he wrote, "is entitled to the highest praise our country can bestow—to him more than any other man am I indebted for the victory of the 5th of July. His brigade covered itself with glory."[39] Scott himself could not have put it better.

CHAPTER SIX

HERO

Despite all the pealing of bells and quickening of the nation's patriotic pulse, the victory at Chippewa did not significantly improve the situation of General Brown's little army. Still cooped up within the Niagara peninsula, cut off from naval support, their ranks thinned by the Chippewa bloodbath, all while the enemy was receiving fresh reinforcements, the Americans spent three weeks in aimless maneuvering, unable to capitalize on their famous victory. During this lull, nerves jangled and tempers flared. Even the hero for whom the victory bells tolled was uncommonly edgy. When Winfield Scott read Brown's initial report on the battle, he was disappointed to see that his officers received what he considered insufficient praise—so disappointed, in fact, that he huffily threatened to resign his commission. Brown tactfully soothed his young eagle's ruffled feathers, and Scott, mollified, withdrew his resignation.[1]

The British could not be dealt with so easily. For two days after the battle, both sides buried their dead and tended their wounded, while the Americans searched for a crossing upstream to turn General Riall's position at Chippewa. Declining to be outflanked, Riall pulled back all the way to Burlington Heights, leaving a garrison at Fort George to inhibit Brown's pursuit.

The American commander was undecided whether to bypass Fort George or to attack it. After a council of war, he determined to deal with the fort before moving farther. Scott's role in that decision is unclear. Thomas Jesup, then a major, later recalled that most of the officers favored an immediate advance on Riall's position but that Brown allowed his judgment to be swayed "by the zeal and importunities of General Scott, who stood almost alone in favor of attacking Fort George." Defeat Riall first, while we still have numerical superiority, Jesup argued, and then take the fort "at our leisure." In retro-spect Scott agreed. "Perhaps it had been better," he conceded, "after masking these works, to have moved at once upon Riall," especially since Brown lacked the heavy artillery needed to breach the fort's walls, which, ironically, had been strengthened by Scott's exertions of the previous summer.[2]

As it turned out, these apprehensions were justified. The Americans demonstrated before Fort George for a day and then withdrew to Queenston, giving up the strategic initiative. While reconnoitering the fort, Scott had a narrow escape, which he managed with a coolness that confirmed the admiration of his men. As the regimental drummer boy told the story:

> Genl. Scott was sitting on his horse, a few rods in front of the line, about noon, the soldiers lazily reclining upon their arms, some preparing and some eating their dinner, when a shell was fired from the fort. In a moment we all saw it, and heard it buzzing through the air, and were all upon the lookout to ascertain where it was going to fall. Genl. Scott threw up his sword, in such a manner as to take sight across it at the bomb, and found it would fall upon him and his charger, unless he made his escape instantly. He wheeled his spirited animal to the left, and buried his spurs in his sides. The whole army was gazing upon the scene with intense anxiety, for the safety of their beloved commander, and with the highest admiration of his decision of character in such an emergency, when the shell *actually dropped upon the very spot,* he had a moment before occupied and without damage.[3]

The camp at Queenston seemed to present a formidable aspect, with thirteen different regiments, detachments, and corps arrayed in a vast semicircle. A junior officer was stirred by the imposing spectacle: "The various guards mounting; the drills and parades, the regimental beats and bugle-calls, converging from so many different points at once; retreat-beating and parade, at sundown; and above all, the fine old spirit-stirring reveille of Baron Steuben, at the earliest dawn of day. These beats commenced, generally, with the regiment on the extreme right; then the next; the next; and so on; till the whole circumference was one grand chorus of the most thrilling martial music."[4]

Appearances were deceptive. General Brown and his senior commanders realized how precarious the army's position really was. Three campaigns in as many years had swept the Niagara peninsula bare of the resources needed to sustain armies, and as the war grew uglier, with villages burned and patrols bushwhacked, cooperation, or even neutrality, from the embittered civilian population could no longer be expected. In the meantime, the British were being resupplied by lake schooners and reinforced with enough fresh troops under Sir Gordon Drummond to give them numerical supremacy.[5]

Unless the American fleet could provide similar assistance, Brown's land-locked army would be in a desperate situation. Brown urgently renewed his pleas to Commodore Chauncey at Sackett's Harbor. "Meet me on the lake-shore north of Fort George with your fleet, and we will be able, I have no doubt, to settle a plan of operations that will break the power of the enemy in upper Canada. . . . For God's sake," he begged, "let me see you." Chauncey, cautious and sickly, had no intention of risking his precious fleet on such mundane tasks as transporting troops and supplies. The navy, he insisted, had been given a "higher destiny—we are intended to seek and fight the enemy's fleet," and he regarded Brown's request as "a *sinister attempt* to render us [the navy] subordinate to, or an appendage of, the army."[6] Brown's army would have to fend for itself.

Hoping to lure the British into battle before the odds tilted too strongly against him, Brown fell back to Chippewa in simulated panic. Riall, burned once before, did not rise to the bait but pursued cautiously, waiting for Drummond's promised reinforcements from York. They began to arrive on the morning of July 25.

It was a beautiful day, warm and lazy, and the American army was, as Scott put it, "unbuttoned and relaxed" as the soldiers caught up on their laundry and lolled around the camp. About noon, word was received that British ships had been sighted off the mouth of the Niagara, but their numbers and intentions were as yet unknown. A bit later a message arrived from a militia officer at Lewiston that the British were landing in force and proceeding down the American side of the river.[7] Without bothering to check further, Brown instantly concluded that the British objective must be the American supply depot at Schlosser, between Lewiston and Buffalo. He further concluded that the best way to drive the British back to their side of the river was to threaten Queenston and Fort George, which, if the reports were true, must have been depleted to provide the troops for the Schlosser attack.

The reasoning was sound, but unfortunately, the premise was false. There was no British advance toward Schlosser, only a brief minor sortie near Lewiston that panicky militia officers had magnified into a major threat. In fact, Drummond's reinforcements, consisting largely of seasoned veterans of the European wars, were even then disembarking on the Canadian side and making their way to a preselected position near Niagara Falls where they would join up with Riall's forces.

It was late in the afternoon before Scott's brigade of twelve hundred men was put on the march. Scott had been chafing for action, but Brown, who suspected that his ambitious subordinate's chief concern was to "cover himself with additional glory," gave orders that Scott was merely "to report if the enemy appeared—then to call for assistance if necessary." This was confirmed by one of Scott's officers, who understood that the objective was "to make a reconnaissance and create a diversion should circumstances require; and if we meet the enemy, we shall probably feel his pulse."[8]

When his fighting spirit was aroused, Scott heard what he wanted to hear, and his understanding was that Brown had given orders "to find the enemy and beat him." He also saw what he wanted to see and brushed aside reports that a large body of the enemy had been spotted near Niagara Falls. Not even the increasingly frequent sightings of British scouts could shake his conviction that he faced "only a small body, detached from an inferior army that had committed the folly of sending at least half of its numbers to the opposite side of the river." When he reached Willson's Tavern at Table Rock near the falls, a touch of reality began to intrude. At his approach, British officers poured out of the tavern, jumped onto their waiting mounts, and sped away, though not before one, in a nice touch, smartly saluted the oncoming enemy, who courteously returned the gesture. Mrs. Willson greeted the Americans at the door "with well-affected concern," and exclaimed, "Oh Sirs, if you had only come a little sooner you would have caught them all." General Riall was nearby, she said, with eight hundred regulars and three hundred militiamen ready to give battle.[9] Her information was correct, so far as she knew, but even as she spoke, Drummond was bringing up additional troops that doubled Riall's forces.

Though skeptical, Scott sent a messenger back to camp urging Brown to make haste and, without waiting for a response, recklessly plunged ahead. About a mile past the falls, the Portage Road crossed a lane that passed by William Lundy's farm. The advance of Scott's column approached this junction about seven o'clock. Lengthening shadows signaled the approach of sunset, and rays from that setting sun mingled with the mist from the nearby falls to arc a rainbow over the American army just as it marched into the arms of the British.[10] Scott had no time to ponder the meaning of that ambiguous omen. Spread out before him was a British army at least as large as the one he had faced at Chippewa. This time, however, they were in a well-chosen defensive position, with their line in a slightly concave arc anchored by dense woods on either side. A steep hill lay in the middle of that line, and on it was posted an artillery battery well situated to command the lane and the surrounding clearings.

Scott was stunned, torn between surprise and anger over the faulty intelligence that had so misled him. Even after the lapse of fifty years, he fumed in his memoirs, "he cannot suppress his indignation at the blundering, stupid report made by the militia colonel."[11] Scott should have directed some of that anger at himself. This was the second time in three weeks that he had precipitated a battle by stumbling upon a British army. By this time, he should have appreciated the necessity of advance scouts, or at least a minimum of caution. Recriminations would have to wait. For now, Scott had to make a split-second decision: stand, advance, or retreat. Perhaps he should have pulled back to a defensive position and awaited reinforcements. The British were not likely to abandon their high ground to launch an attack on an enemy of unknown strength at sunset, particularly after Riall's experience at Chippewa.

Scott rejected this alternative for a number of reasons, none of which seem wholly convincing: he feared that a pullback might degenerate into a rout; that it might throw the oncoming reserves into panic; that it might dim the "extravagant opinion [that] generally prevailed throughout the army in respect to the prowess—nay, invincibility of Scott's brigade." There was some merit to these arguments, but they have the air of after-the-fact rationalizations. Up to this point in his career, Scott's strong suit as a commander had been audacity, not prudence. All his instincts led him to prefer the offensive, and these instincts had served him well at Chippewa. At Lundy's Lane, he reasoned that a bold attack would convince Riall that he faced the entire American army and persuade him to pull back. It almost worked. The British commander was so unnerved that he ordered a withdrawal, but it was countermanded by the timely arrival of Drummond.[12]

His bluff called, Scott could only stand his ground and wait for help. His position was an unfortunate one. At four to five hundred yards from the British line, he was too far away for effective musketry but close enough to be within the range of enemy artillery. Scott's men now served as human target practice for those guns while they depleted their own ammunition in largely futile musket fire. Unable to go forward, unwilling to go back, Scott was frozen in place while his ranks were thinned by canister and grape. "Dread seemed to forbid his advance, and Shame to restrain his flight," observed a British officer of literary bent.[13]

The sole bright spot in this stage of the battle came from Jesup's regiment. Slipping undetected through the woods on the British left, Jesup rolled up their flank and, for a time, found himself behind enemy lines, where he was able to bag a large catch of unsuspecting English in the confusion of dusk. So many fell into Jesup's hands that they encumbered his movements. When he saw his men pull out their knives, he feared they were taking a direct way to rid themselves of that encumbrance and, horrified, ordered them to stop. The men patiently explained that they were merely cutting the British suspenders, since, "if compelled to hold up their breeches with their hands they could not run to make escape." Even so, there were too many to guard. Rather than put them to death, Jesup looked the other way as they returned to their lines, some, no doubt, hopping to safety with trousers flapping round their ankles.[14]

The prize catch did not get off so lightly. General Riall himself, badly wounded in the arm, was being escorted to what was thought safety. "Make room there men, for General Riall," ordered his aide. The quick-witted, aptly

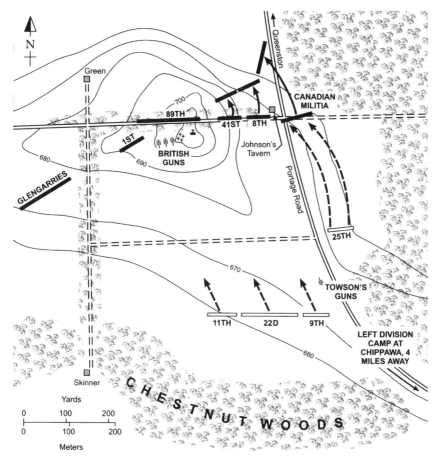

The Battle of Lundy's Lane, ca. 7:30 P.M. Morris, *Sword of the Border*, 116.

named Capt. Daniel Ketchum of Jesup's regiment replied, "Aye, Aye, Sir"; let them pass; and then grabbed them. "But I am General Riall!" the British commander sputtered. "There is not doubt on that point," the captain smoothly replied, "and I, Sir, am Captain Ketchum, of the United States Army." "Ketchum!" Riall muttered. "Well! you *have* caught us! sure enough!"[15]

Back at their camp at Chippewa, the rest of the American army was folding their laundry and preparing for the final parade of the day when they heard the sound of distant gunfire. Instantly divining its source, General Brown put his men on the march without waiting for Scott's messengers. By the time they reached the battlefield, Scott's brigade had been reduced by an appalling 40 percent.[16] Brown pulled it out of the line of battle and held it as a reserve. Consequently, Scott was relatively inactive during the next, and most successful, stage of the battle, which was fought largely by Eleazar Ripley's Second Brigade.

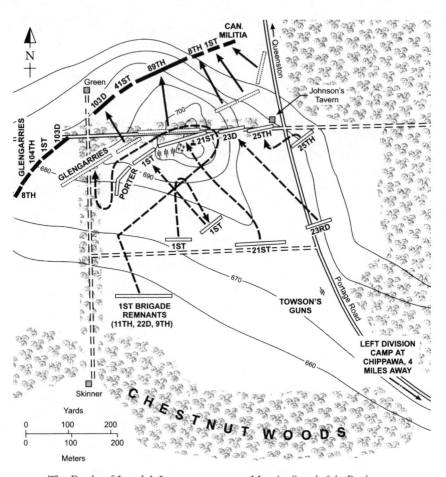

The Battle of Lundy's Lane, ca. 9:00 P.M. Morris, *Sword of the Border*, 121.

Assisted by fresh troops and by the near-total darkness that now obscured the battlefield, Ripley was able to attempt what Scott could not—an assault on the British artillery. This was the key position in the British line, but distracted by his own wounds, Drummond had carelessly left it virtually undefended. Guided personally by Scott, Col. James Miller stealthily maneuvered his 21st Regiment through the darkness to within pointblank range of the unsuspecting enemy gunners. A withering musket volley, a bayonet charge, and the artillery that had decimated Scott's brigade was now in American hands. The battle had turned.

Three British counterattacks were launched and beaten back. Each time the Americans waited fearfully as the whispered commands drew nearer, and each time they allowed the British to fire first and then took aim at the flash reflected off the enemy's brass buttons. This was too much punishment for even the famed thin red line. The Americans were left in possession of the hilltop battery and, soon, of the entire field.

In the meantime, what was left of the First Brigade was sufficiently re-freshed to return to action. Forming them into a column, in the French man-ner, Scott "resolved to try an experiment" of piercing the British line and then wheeling to the left so as to envelop a portion of it. Unfortunately, his path took him between the British and American lines, exposing his men in the darkness to fire from both friend and foe. Caught in the crossfire, which one officer said "cut us up most dreadfully," the column disintegrated. Scott's horse was shot out from under him, but he led another attack on foot, with much the same deadly result as before.[17]

By now the First Brigade, which had begun the battle with between eight and nine hundred men, was reduced to less than one hundred. Nonetheless, Scott was rallying them for yet another charge when a bullet ploughed through his left shoulder, shattering the bone and rendering him insensible. Aides tenderly propped him against a tree until he recovered consciousness. "Un-able," Scott recalled, "to hold up his head from the loss of blood and an-guish," he was carried off the field and sent back to Chippewa on a jolting ambulance. For Winfield Scott, the Battle of Lundy's Lane was over.[18]

At the same time, in another part of the field, Brown was wounded too. As he was carried off, he turned command of what was left of his army over to Ripley with orders to return to Chippewa. From the quiet that now descended over the field, it appeared that the British had already pulled back, leaving the Americans in possession. Exhausted and almost maddened by thirst (while in sight of the greatest fresh-water cataract on the continent), the Americans retired in good order to their camp. The captured British artillery, which had cost so much blood, was left behind on its hilltop due to confusion and a lack of horses and proper gun carriages. Brown was furious at this oversight. He needed those cannon to support his claims to victory. He sent Ripley back to secure them, but by the time he returned, the British had recovered the guns. As Brown had feared, Drummond cited this as proof of a British victory.[19]

On the American side, Lundy's Lane was hailed as a triumph comparable to Bunker Hill and Saratoga. By the standard of the casualty lists (what Scott would later scornfully call "the butcher's bill"), the Americans came out somewhat ahead. According to initial reports, the British lost 878 men against 860 American casu-alties, though, considered as a percentage of the troops involved, the Americans suffered more than their foes.[20] In a strategic sense, the British came out ahead, for the Americans retreated all the way to Fort Erie, conceding the Niagara pen-insula to Drummond. From the point of view of morale, however, the Ameri-can cause gained a welcome boost, for the army had demonstrated once again that it could stand up against the best that England could bring to the field.

Perhaps the final judgment on the controversy was expressed by a British colonel, Hercules Scott. "We boast of a 'Great Victory,'" he wrote his brother, "but in my opinion it was nearly equal on both sides."[21] Or, as the Dodo said to Alice after the Caucus race, "*Everybody* has won, and *all* must have prizes." Among Scott's prizes were promotion to major general (by brevet—a distinction that would later cause intense controversy), a gold medal awarded by a grateful Congress, and commemorative swords from both New York and Virginia. Counties were named in his honor, as were innumerable children.

Only a few dissenting voices were raised against this near-universal adulation. One complained that Scott had shown himself "utterly regardless of human life and willing to make any sacrifice for his own personal renown." Rather than being promoted for the battle, Scott should have been drummed out of the service, he argued. A hostile critic like Wilkinson could easily tear apart Scott's conduct at Chippewa and Lundy's Lane point by point, from his selection of a camp site at Street's Creek to the "rashness and folly" of his attacks at Lundy's Lane.[22] Yet most Americans could readily see that Wilkinson, for all his pretensions to military "art," consistently failed, while Scott, despite his flaws, succeeded. Scott's veneer of military knowledge may have been thinner than he liked to think, but it covered a fighting heart.

After Lundy's Lane, the wounded hero was transported back to the United States in a triumphant progress. When military hospitals proved inadequate, he was borne south on a litter. At the edge of every town, prominent local citizens vied for the honor of carrying the general to the next. He passed through Princeton, New Jersey, as the college was holding its commencement exercise. Learning of Scott's presence, faculty and trustees dragged him from his bed, "almost by main strength," to the platform at Nassau Hall, where he was "assailed with all the powers of oratory" and awarded an impromptu honorary degree.[23] Finally, in late September, escorted by a military parade, he arrived at Philadelphia to be placed under the care of the eminent Dr. Physick (a real person and not, as the name might suggest, a grotesque out of an E. T. A. Hoffman fantasy).

While Scott's bones knit and his body healed, the war proceeded without him. On the Niagara front, Brown's army was cooped up for a time in Fort Erie, but even though it succeeded in beating off attacks by Drummond, it eventually pulled back to Buffalo, giving up the ill-starred invasion of Upper Canada. Even worse, the British brazenly attacked the American capital itself, brushing aside Washington's feeble defenders and wantonly burning its public buildings. On a brighter note, a British invasion of upstate New York was turned back by Brig. Gen. Alexander Macomb at Plattsburg and naval captain Thomas Macdonough on Lake Champlain.

Scott was unable to participate in these stirring events. While he slowly recovered the use of his left arm, he was assigned command of the Tenth Military District, headquartered in Washington and embracing Philadelphia and Baltimore. Militarily this was a backwater, but politically it had the advantage of proximity to the seats of power. Scott utilized this opportunity to cultivate relations with the new secretary of war, James Monroe, bombarding him with projects to reorganize the militia, increase the regular army, reform the procurement system, upgrade the Corps of Engineers, and, in many ways, reshape the military establishment to his ideal. Monroe also turned to him for advice as to which officers should be promoted and which discarded.[24]

Barely twenty-eight years old, Scott was now a power behind the scenes. He allowed himself to dream of superseding Andrew Jackson (then rumored to be ill) as commander of the southern army or else to be put in command of the next invasion of Canada. "It has been the first object of my ambition," he unblushingly confessed to the secretary, "to attain a rank that would give me . . . the chief control of those operations." That rank might even be lieutenant general, left unfilled since the retirement of George Washington.[25]

These lofty hopes were dashed by the unexpected news that a peace treaty had been signed. The war was over. There would be no invasion of Canada for Scott or anyone else to command. Monroe tried to console him. "The peace has robbed you, and many others of glory," he said, "but you will feel an indemnity for it, in the advantage derived from it by your country." Uncomforted, Scott admitted that his "breast was violently agitated by opposite currents of feeling"—joy for the country and disappointment at his own thwarted ambition.[26]

At the same time, another piece of glorious news proved equally unsettling. On January 8, 1815, a British army was annihilated by Andrew Jackson near New Orleans. The British, all seasoned veterans of the European wars, lost over two thousand men; the Americans, a rag-tag assemblage of backwoods volunteers, Gulf pirates, and New Orleans free blacks, had only seventy casualties. If an untrained Indian fighter could defeat highly trained professionals with troops like these, then some might question Scott's cherished project of creating a professional army along European lines. Scott himself feared that "Jackson and the Western militia seem likely to throw all other generals and the regular troops into the background."[27]

The coming of peace posed an even greater threat to the regular army. It was bound to be reduced in both size and esteem, but Scott was determined that it would not sink back into its slothful prewar ways. His challenge now was to use his newfound prestige and influence, not merely to preserve the army, but to transform it.

CHAPTER SEVEN

PROFESSIONAL

Scott often used the term "profession" to describe the military career he had chosen to follow, but it is hard to tell what exactly he meant by it. Such imprecision was not Scott's alone. Even a dictionary definition (*Webster's Collegiate* 5th ed.)—"The occupation, if not commercial, mechanical, agricultural or the like, to which one devotes oneself; a calling: as, the *profession* of arms"—is not very helpful. Perhaps professionalism is one of those concepts best explained by pointing to its characteristics rather than by defining its essence.

By that standard, a profession can be described as a self-regulating group of people who have mastered a practical, specific body of knowledge. They have a lifelong commitment to their craft. From it they derive their livelihood, and to it they give their deepest loyalty, rather than to their nominal employer. Its operations are regular rather than capricious, bureaucratic rather than personal. Its outward manifestations are found in journals, schools, and accreditation. Internally, it is characterized by esprit de corps and by contempt for the untrained laity. Its members are meritocratic in regard to each other, aristocratic in regard to the outside world. They are neither dilettantes nor amateurs. Theirs is a calling, not an occupation.

Later in the century, with the formation of national bar associations, academies of medicine, and even scholarly organizations such as the American Historical Association, professionalization would become commonplace in the United States. With all due respect to other claimants, however, it can be argued that in America the military is the oldest profession and that Scott (however imperfectly he may have understood his role) was its prophet. The "rascally regulars," as he called professional soldiers with affection, were his family; preserving their integrity and increasing their effectiveness was his lifework. In this, he prefigures the twentieth-century technocrat who places loyalty to his profession above all else.[1]

This put Scott somewhat out of touch with the spirit of his own age. Politically and socially, pre–Civil War America was becoming a mass society, characterized by the decline of deference and by an ever-increasing sense of equality and individualism. As an advocate of professionalism, with its hierarchic body of initiates, Scott was misinterpreted as a figure out of an aristocratic past, rather than as the precursor of a technocratic future. Consequently, he often had to settle for half-measures and partial victories. This was particularly true in the immediate aftermath of the War of 1812, when he fought a rear-guard battle to preserve the regular army in the face of a near-universal demand for retrenchment.

Before news of the peace treaty reached Washington, Scott had been drafting ambitious plans for army expansion. He envisioned a regular army of 65,000 men commanded by six lieutenant generals, thirteen major generals, and thirty-six brigadiers. If necessary, these troops would be raised by conscription.[2] With the arrival of peace, Scott's grand scheme had to be shelved. He prepared a scaled-down plan for an army of 20,000, but a penny-pinching Congress would authorize no more than 10,000 soldiers, a figure that half a dozen years later would be further pared to less than 6,000.

A board consisting of the two major generals, Andrew Jackson and Jacob Brown, and four brigadiers (Scott, Edmund Gaines, Alexander Macomb, and Eleazar Ripley) was appointed for the "painful duty" of recommending reductions in the officer corps. In the absence of his seniors, Scott usually presided. The first order of business was easily dispatched. The board recommended that six generals be retained for the peace establishment. By no coincidence, the six generals selected were the six members of the board that did the choosing. This was not as self-serving as it may have appeared, for each had already been confidentially assured by Secretary of War Alexander J. Dallas that they would be retained in their rank. The hard part was weeding out the surplus lower-ranking officers. Over 2,270 officers were currently on the rolls, but less than 500 of them could be retained. Such ruthless winnowing, admitted Dallas, was bound to work hardship on "honorable men, whose misfortune it is, by age, by infirmities, or by wounds, to be disabled from rendering further service to their country; but," he concluded, "the task must be performed."[3]

It also presented an opportunity to improve the caliber of those officers. The fact could not be disguised, Scott admitted, that "the army, as it stands, is but indifferently officered." Scarcely ten field-grade officers, he estimated, were capable of commanding a brigade. According to Ethan Allen Hitchcock (later of Scott's staff), those drawn to the army by the War of 1812 were not much better, on the average, than the timeservers and bunglers of the prewar establishment. Selected largely through political connections, they were, he claimed, "nearly all them alike, ignorant of the profession of arms, there were great confusions, discords and quarrelling, and there was not enough stability of character among the officers of what might be called 'the old army' to act as a wholesome restraint." Duels were common, drunkenness near universal, and "most of the officers dissipated in the worst sense of that word: profane, indecent and licentious." It is not surprising, therefore, that "approved moral character" was ranked first, along with "military merit," among the criteria enumerated by the secretary of war to guide the board's deliberations. After that, the generals were asked to consider seniority, capability of making a living in civilian society, "the pecuniary situation of the parties," and as a last resort, all else being equal, as Wilkinson had once suggested to Scott years before, the board was advised to draw lots.[4]

The six board members labored diligently, preparing list after list that the president and secretary of war personally scrutinized. Yet despite all their efforts, Hitchcock complained, "the leaven of evil had spread so far and wide that the character of the Peace Establishment did not materially differ from that of the War Establishment out of which it had proceeded."[5] Ultimately, improvement of the officer corps would be brought about, not by personal decisions and individual choice, however well intentioned, but through the impersonal, bureaucratic accreditation standards of that instrument of professionalization, the U.S. Military Academy at West Point.

Reduction of the swollen ranks of enlisted men could proceed in two ways. The easier was to eliminate entire regiments so as to bring the aggregate numbers down to what Congress was willing to support. Such a course would mean, in effect, a return to the prewar Jeffersonian military policy of a bare-boned regular army as the first line of defense, augmented in time of crisis by volunteer citizen-soldiers. This approach appealed to those who stood by the old republican virtues of economy in government and a distrust of standing armies as a threat to the people's liberty. Tension between the charms of liberty and the demands of power had been, and would long remain, one of the central themes of the American experiment. Those who advocated a wholesale reduction in the postwar army plumped for liberty over power. "One of the best features in our Government," declared one, "is its unfitness for war."[6]

To Scott and other military professionals, such an attitude betrayed an almost perverse blindness to the lessons of 1812. They feared that an indiscriminate demobilization would deprive the Republic of their hard-earned skills during the next military crisis. If the army had to be reduced at all, they advocated maintaining what George Washington had once called a "skeleton" organization: that is, the retention of the current regimental structure and officer cadre but with a diminished number of enlisted men in each company. In time of danger, additional flesh could readily be put on these organizational bones.[7]

Washington's 1783 proposal had been largely ignored, but in 1815, Secretary of War James Monroe (with Scott very likely whispering in his ear) advocated much the same plan. It too was ignored by Congress, but two years later, with Monroe president and fresh reductions being threatened, Scott proposed to the new secretary of war, John C. Calhoun, a similar plan that would reduce each infantry company to only fifty-five men while retaining the full complement of officers. The War Department's chief clerk, Christopher Van Deventer, palmed off Scott's plan as his own, and in that guise it became the genesis of what Calhoun would call "the expansible army."[8]

The matter rested until the depression year of 1821, when Congress determined to reduce the army to only six thousand men as a measure of economy. Although it balked at a wholesale endorsement of the expansible army concept, Congress did give the generals much of what they wanted in that the reductions bore more heavily on the enlisted ranks than on the officers. In 1814, the army had one officer for every sixteen enlisted men; in the shrunken army of 1823, the ratio was on the order of one to eight.[9]

The officer class thus had performed one of the prime duties of a profession—the protection of its own. It had also ensured that its professional skills would not be unduly dispersed or diluted but would be available when once again needed. In the long run, however, the expansible army would prove inadequate to preserve its professional monopoly. Both the Mexican War and the Civil War, despite Scott's misgivings, would be fought largely by volunteer citizen-soldiers, rather than by the professionals of the regular army.

Demobilization was not Scott's only concern in the aftermath of the War of 1812. Kept busy on boards, committees, and courts-martial and always free with advice to the president, secretary of war, assorted congressmen, senators, and anyone else who would listen, he had a hand in virtually every aspect of military policy. One project was particularly close to his heart. Ever since his experiences with the training camp at Flint Hill, Scott had been determined to bring some order out of the confusion caused by inadequate and contradictory training manuals. Some officers still clung to Baron Steuben's antiquated method, others swore by one of Duane's manuals, and yet others by Smyth's, while some, like Scott, made up their own system. When these different units fought side by side, the result could be chaotic.[10]

In December 1814, Congress appointed a board of officers, headed by Scott, to prepare an official manual of infantry tactics and drill based on the French system. In less than two months of effort, "laborious and tedious in the extreme," the board produced a three-hundred-page handbook prescribing the school of the squad, the company, the battalion, and the evolution of the line.[11] With various alterations and fresh editions (some of which Scott disowned), it would serve as the basic handbook for the next four decades. The first edition could be completed so rapidly because it was closely patterned after its French models, with only minor adjustments to meet American conditions. This led some critics to dismiss it as a mere translation and others, more harshly, to accuse the board of outright plagiarism. These detractors missed the point. What the army needed was not originality but uniformity. In this, it was anticipating yet another significant development of American society—the rise of big business.

The army was both a promoter and a precursor of the new industrial age. As the nation's largest customer, it promoted the techniques of mass production, most notably with the famous contract with Eli Whitney for ten thousand muskets, which some have credited as stimulating such manufacturing innovations as standardized, interchangeable parts and the assembly line. Scott would not display much interest in these revolutionary developments: his education had been essentially literary and legal, not technological. But his work did contribute to a related aspect of the new age of industry—the managerial revolution.

The army was not only America's first national profession but also its first big business, a distinction usually ascribed to the railroad. The similarities were striking. Both employed large numbers of men strung out over distances too vast to allow for personal supervision. Both were dangerous occupations in which the penalty for confusion or misunderstanding could be fatal. Each, therefore, required consistent, systematic modes of operation, rather than the idiosyncratic rules of thumb acceptable in lesser enterprises. In the new age of giant organizations, standardized procedures would be as important as standardized parts. It was no coincidence that early American railroads recruited army officers as their executives or that the operating manual for the Baltimore and Ohio was directly modeled on the army regulations drawn up by Scott.[12] His *Tactics* were a precursor of the bureaucratized regulations that would be essential to the emerging corporate era.

Scott did not fully comprehend the significance of this innovation, but he did appreciate, intuitively, the need for managerial reform, as can be seen in another proposal he made at this time. Throughout the war, the army had relied on private, civilian contractors to provide it with supplies. The result was that troops often went hungry and ragged, while the contractors grew rich. Late in 1814, Scott was ordered to preside over a board to investigate these abuses. He sharply condemned "the petty villainies which contractors are daily tempted to commit to the prejudice of the troops" and recommended that army officers, rather than civilians, be made responsible for the procurement and distribution of supplies.[13] In this recommendation, Scott and his fellow officers were anticipating those modern management principles that stress efficiency over economy, accountability over irresponsibility, clear lines of command rather than divided authority, and regularity instead of improvisation. The industrial giants of the Gilded Age, the Carnegies and Rockefellers, would understand the importance of maintaining control of each step of their operations. So did Scott.

President Madison was so taken with Scott's advice that he asked him to become secretary of war. Demonstrating that prudence did place some limitations on his ambition, Scott wisely declined, "from feelings of delicacy towards his seniors."[14] If he had accepted, he would either have had to resign from the army or else retain his commission. If he resigned, his military career would be over when he was just thirty. If he did not, he would find himself in the impossible position of issuing commands to his superior officers, Jackson and Brown. Scott sidestepped the dilemma and instead permitted himself two peacetime indulgences: first he took a vacation, and then he took a wife.

Strictly speaking, Scott's European tour was official business rather than a pleasure jaunt. This was the trip he had dreamed of ever since 1809, and he planned to make the most of it. Initially, he had hoped to spend as much as three years abroad, but the War Department would only consent to a two-years' leave, which as it turned out, would prove more than ample.[15]

Scott's official position was that of military observer attached to the French army. For years, it had been his hope to witness war conducted according to the European model he had so assiduously studied in books. Chippewa and Lundy's Lane had been but pale reflections of that model, and he eagerly looked forward to seeing the real thing. "Our late war," he admitted, "afforded no such spectacle and . . . without enjoying that advantage, no man can pretend to be a *general*. He may lead a single column very well, but will never be able to combine the movements of many columns on a given object until he has seen it accomplished in the face of an enemy." The administration also expected him to do a little discreet snooping to sound out the intentions of the European powers toward the United States but, aware of his French sympathies, enjoined upon him strict neutrality.[16]

Scott set sail on July 9, 1815. He was now such a celebrity that his passage was considered worthy of notice by *Niles' Register,* then the closest thing to a national American journal. The editor was confident Scott would acquit himself well. "His person, his manners, his brave achievements will furnish him a *passport,* wherever he goes. He is a favorable specimen of the American character."[17] But by the time he arrived in Europe, the war was over, Napoleon was again in exile, and any opportunity to observe warfare in the European style would have to wait another forty years.

In the meantime, there was always Paris. Scott made the usual tourist rounds, including the Louvre; polished his French; purchased military books for his library; and developed a taste for haute cuisine, which would become a lifelong passion. He cultivated friendships with Russian and German officers, caught glimpses of heads of state—Czar Alexander, "as affable and courteous as a candidate for office"; Francis of Austria, "grave to sadness"; and the King of Prussia, "glum, incapable of any lively emotion"—and, to tweak the British, hosted a dinner to commemorate the Battle of New Orleans. The sentimental highpoint of his stay was a visit to the ailing Marquis de Lafayette, then in rustic retirement at La Grange, surrounded by grandchildren and memorabilia of the American Revolution.[18]

Official business was not entirely neglected. As he had been instructed, Scott kept his eyes and ears open, even at receptions and balls, and relayed to Washington any gossip or information regarding the great powers' intentions. Of greatest concern in this regard was Spain: Did it intend to retake its recently lost Latin American colonies? Would it go to war to keep Florida out of the hands of the United States?

The future conqueror of Mexico was in 1815 a stout champion of Latin American independence. He advised Monroe to extend recognition to the South American republics, assuring him that England would not support Spanish claims to that continent and that the Spanish navy was inadequate to defend those claims by itself. If it should come to war, Scott was confident that the American navy could sweep Spain's from the seas and that the army could easily overrun Florida. A few regiments, he calculated, should be sufficient to do that job, and he offered to lead them himself, though, he added characteristically, "if the force employed should *principally be militia,* I should very willingly yield my pretensions." By 1816 that war seemed so imminent that the administration called him home. Scott was not sorry to cut short his European stay. For one thing, he was embarrassingly low on funds, and for another, he was growing "not a little *home-sick.*" As for so many Americans abroad, a taste of the Old World only confirmed his patriotism, and he declared himself "very well content to remain at home, for the remainder of my life."[19]

Home at last by late spring of 1816, Scott reported for duty to General Brown, commander of the Northern District, who assigned him to Department Three, headquartered in New York City. The post was far enough removed from any likely scene of military action that Scott had ample time to pursue his romantic interests. Shortly before he had left for Europe, his suit had been rebuffed by a haughty Philadelphia lady, but now gossips began to link his name with that of a Miss Maria Mayo of Richmond, Virginia.[20]

The Mayo family of Richmond confounds the easy stereotype of the Southern gentry as a landed aristocracy with a precapitalist mindset. Demonstrating a work ethic as intense as any Yankee's, the first American Mayo, Major William, was a civil engineer who laid out the city of Richmond. His grandson, Col. John Mayo, was a bridge builder and entrepreneur who married

Miss Maria D. Mayo, the "reigning belle" of Richmond.
Charles Winslow Elliott, *Winfield Scott, the Soldier and
the Man* (New York: Macmillan, 1937), 215.

Abigail De Hart, daughter of a New Jersey delegate to the Continental Congress. Maria, their eldest daughter, was born in 1789, making her only three years younger than Scott and, at twenty-seven in 1816, perilously older than was deemed proper for an unmarried lady of her time and station. Her prolonged single state was not due to a lack of opportunities: according to local tradition, she had spurned over one hundred suitors. Accomplished on both piano and harp, fluent in French, and capable of dashing off genuinely clever light verse, she was hailed by the doyens of Richmond society as "the reigning belle of the day." From her portrait, she appears to have been pert rather than conventionally beautiful, with an upturned nose; deep, warm eyes; and the hint of what must have been a deliciously wicked smile. "No young lady in the South," it was claimed, "has been so much admired as she."[21]

General Scott was one of those admirers, but for how long was a matter of dispute. According to gossip, he had been pursuing her heart for a decade, first as a penniless lawyer, then as a young officer, but only won her hand as a famous general. A close friend, however, insisted, "Mrs. Scott told me with her own lips that she never made his acquaintance until he was a General."[22] If that were true, then the couple had probably been thrown together at the White House, where Maria, a protégé of Dolley Madison, was a frequent guest.

However long the courtship may have been brewing, its conclusion was unexpectedly rapid. As late as November 5, 1816, Scott confided to a friend with (perhaps feigned) indifference that, though he respected Miss Mayo, "I deeply regret not being in love and not having a prospect of marriage." Only one week later, he reported to General Brown, "My charming country-woman, Miss Maria Mayo, has just consented to unite her fate to mine," and he breathlessly begged permission for a furlough from military duty. "There is nothing wanting but your consent to make me the happiest of men."[23]

An early wedding date was set, but sudden illness in the bride's family caused delay. This postponement gave Scott time to persuade his prospective in-laws to drop their condition that he resign from the army before they would give the union their blessing. The pending nuptials provoked considerable excitement among members of the Richmond social set, who anticipated "the grandest party that ever was heard of," but the actual ceremony was a simple one. It was held at "Belleville," one of Colonel Mayo's many mansions, on March 11, 1817, before a small company of family and friends, including Maj. Gen. William Henry Harrison. The groom, resplendent in the new uniform he had brought back from Europe, quite stole the show from the bride, at least according to one catty guest, who purred: "The bridal simplicity of Maria's dress was extremely becoming to herself. You know she is not remarkable for her taste."[24]

The newlyweds embarked on a wedding trip to Niagara, not to see the falls, but to tour the fields on which the husband had won his fame.[25] They then set up housekeeping in Elizabeth Town (now Elizabeth), New Jersey, in another of the Mayo family mansions. This was close enough to the general's headquarters in New York City to allow for some family life, though duty would often call him away to the more distant reaches of his command.

In this "present season of Peace and leisure," these routine departmental duties could not satisfy Scott's restless energy and ambition. To fill his time, he turned to a project he had long considered—the compilation of a definitive body of regulations for the army. In June 1817, he broached the subject to General Brown, and the following year he laid a formal proposal before Secretary of War Calhoun.[26]

Although separate manuals existed for specialized topics, such as infantry tactics, there was no handbook that contained within one convenient set of covers all the regulations and procedures used by the army. What Scott proposed to Calhoun was to replace the current hodge-podge of conflicting regulations, inconsistent procedures, oral traditions, and improvisation with a comprehensive, detailed, systematic, and uniform code of operations. He was aware of the magnitude of the project and, with unaccustomed (and unconvincing) humility, claimed, "far from arrogating to myself any peculiar fitness for the employment, I have constantly wished . . . that some other officer, better qualified, might present the army with such a work," but in the absence of such a paragon, he concluded, "I offer myself as a volunteer."[27]

Scott labored on the *General Regulations for the Army* (or *Scott's Institutes,* as he preferred to call it) for two years, devoting five to six hours a day to that "*cursed* book which has given me so much trouble." By late December 1820, it was finally completed and by the following July approved, with some modifications, by the administration.[28]

The result justified the effort. Into the book Scott crammed everything he had learned in the past decade, from baking bread ("The crust ought not to be detached from the crumb. On opening it . . . one ought to smell a sweet and balsamic odor") to winning battles ("one ought always seek to take the *lead,* that is, to reduce the enemy to the defensive").[29] He specified how to pack a knapsack; the size and type of paper on which to record court-martial proceedings; how often hands, face, and clothing should be washed; and, of course, a detailed description of proper uniforms. Demonstrating what put the fuss in Old Fuss and Feathers, he included a lengthy section on spot removal (for rust, use anvil dust "well sifted through an old stocking and moistened with sweet oil"; for brass buttons, literally apply spit and polish).

The work was saved from being a catchall by three qualities that Scott brought to it. First, it was logically constructed. Unlike the French and English manuals he had studied, *Scott's Institutes,* so its author claimed, demonstrated "a due logical connection and dependance between the parts."[30]

It began with the essential feature of military organization, that is, discipline, which Scott defined as "a gradual and universal subordination or authority, which, without loss of force, shall be even, mild, and paternal, and which, founded in justice and firmness, shall maintain all subordination in the strictest observance of duty. It requires that enlisted soldiers shall be treated with particular kindness and humanity, that punishments, sometimes unavoidable, shall be strictly conformable to martial law; and that all in commission shall conduct, direct and protect inferiors, of every rank, with the care due to men from whose patriotism, valor, and obedience they are to expect a part of their own reputation and glory."[31] From this base of mutual obligation and respect, he then derived the duties of the various ranks to promote esprit de corps and mutual well being, which, in turn, led to the heart of the work, a detailed description of the procedures to be followed in order to achieve both harmony and efficiency.

Second, the organization was not only logical, it was also comprehensive. In its pages, officers could find instructions for each task they might be called upon to perform, from the twenty-five steps necessary to conduct a proper inspection to the amount of forage they should feed their horses (fourteen pounds of hay and twelve quarts of oats daily).[32] The book, therefore, served as a pocket-sized ready reference manual, indispensable in resolving disputes as well as in providing advice.

Finally, the *Institutes* imposed uniformity. One might smile at Scott's minute description of the thirteen (no more and no less) record books required for each company, but to an officer transferred to a new post, such uniformity meant that he could assume his new duties with a confidence born of familiarity. It meant that the army could operate as a vast machine in which its personnel were as interchangeable as Eli Whitney's standardized parts.

Scott's Institutes has been called "the first comprehensive management manual published in the United States."[33] With it, the author was creating a system of accountability, responsibility, division of labor, and chain of command, all bound together by a paper trail of standardized printed forms and account books. Scott literally wrote the book on army procedures. It was his major contribution to the professionalization of the American profession of arms.

CHAPTER EIGHT

MIDLIFE CRISIS

As he entered the 1820s, Scott would seem to have every cause for satisfaction. The acknowledged master of a profession he loved, second only to Andrew Jackson as a national hero, and married to a rich and accomplished woman, he had traveled far from the penniless, unknown captain of ten years before. Why then was he not happy? Instead of contentment, he displayed contentiousness, instead of fulfillment, frustration.

Halfway through his biblically allotted span, Scott seemed to be undergoing what a later era would diagnose as a "midlife crisis." His mind, he complained, had lost "its wonted vigour and independence," and he yearned "for the opportunity of once more respiring the air of freedom."[1]

His angst stemmed from the usual causes: money, family, and career. Marriage into the wealthy Mayo family had not brought Scott his anticipated financial security. Quite the contrary, his father-in-law, who died in 1818, made provisions in his will that effectively cut off his daughters' husbands from any direct control of the estate. Scott was allowed to maintain the Elizabeth Town mansion as his home, but the title remained firmly in the hands of his mother-in-law, who kept him on a tight monetary leash. To his friends, Scott confessed his "mortification" at "being dependant on the caprice of [her] sordid avarice," but he had no choice but to try to make do on his army salary.[2]

That salary may have seemed lavish to most of his countrymen, but to Scott it was barely adequate. In the two-year span from October 1, 1821, to September 30, 1823, he received $11,756, including expenses and brevet pay. This was $1,100 more than General Gaines was paid during the same period and only $24 less than Jacob Brown, the commanding general of the army, yet

Scott was continually asking for more in the way of double rations, brevet salary, and extra compensation for compiling the army regulations. Congress, however, was in a cheeseparing mood, and the military establishment was the favorite target of its perennial economy drives. Yesterday's heroes, Scott complained, now found themselves "represented as mendicants at the Treasury, and otherwise rendered odious in the eyes of their fellow citizens."[3]

Scott's obsession with money, which would become one of his less attractive traits in later life, dates from these years, when he was trying to support a growing family and a wife with expensive tastes on an officer's salary. Raised in luxury and not a little spoiled, Maria Scott's demands were one cause of the tension that occasionally strained their married life. Two such strong personalities were bound to clash from time to time. As a friend perceptively noted: "General Scott was a born commander while *Madame la Géneral* from her earliest life had the world at her feet. Such a combination naturally resulted in an occasional discordant note, which was usually sounded in public." Maria's sharp wit was sometimes directed at her ponderous husband, as in her definition of "ennui": "a tallow candle, a game of whist, and General Scott."[4]

All this, plus her long absences at various European watering spots, gave rise to rumors that all was not well with the Scott's family life. Gossips clucked over their frequent separations and hinted darkly that the cause lay in the husband's sexual inadequacy. "Nobody but his wife," Mary Chesnut claimed to have heard, "could ever know how little he was." Closer friends, however, testified to the mutual respect and affection that warmed the Scott household. "Their private life," insisted one, "was serene, and they were invariably loyal to each other's interests."[5]

The steady stream of children that issued from the union should have put to rest the imputation that it was lacking in passion. The first to appear was Maria Mayo Scott in 1818, followed the next year by John May. Additional children arrived at regular two-year intervals: Virginia in 1821, Edward Winfield in 1823, and Cornelia in 1825. Then, after a European sojourn to restore her understandably weakened health, Mrs. Scott returned home and gave birth to Adeline Camilla in 1831 and Marcella in 1834, for a grand total of seven children—five girls and two boys. Only the girls survived beyond infancy. Little John died of the croup in 1820 at only seventeen months of age while his family was visiting former president Madison's Montpelier home and was laid to rest in the president's family plot. The grief-stricken parents inscribed their sorrow on the little headstone: "My soul melteth away for very heaviness. Comfort Thou me, oh Lord!" Seven years later, four-year-old Edward, "a child of the finest figure and promise," succumbed to the same dread disease. "Mrs. Scott and myself are broken hearted," the bereaved father lamented. "It would seem utterly impossible for us to recover any thing like cheerfulness of mind."[6]

Family woes and money worries intensified the discontent Scott felt over the course his life was taking. Even his military career had lost some of its savor. Scott's dazzling string of wartime promotions had spoiled him for the plodding pace of peacetime advancement. And instead of the adulation he had come to expect, he now found "every sort of contempt and contumely" directed at those so recently hailed as saviors of their country. "I am grown sick of my position in the army," he confessed to President Monroe. So sick, in fact, that he seriously considered turning in his uniform, "whilst I am yet young, and before the mind sinks into dejection, or the habits become fixed in professional rigidity."[7] But what then? Neither his training nor his inclinations had equipped Scott to engage in private pursuits. That left public service, either in politics or in the diplomatic corps, as the only alternative.

Swallowing his pride, he asked President Monroe to appoint him to some foreign post, preferably in France, though he would settle for Portugal or Mexico. With unconvincing humility, he acknowledged, "I cannot boast of any particular fitness" for diplomacy, other than "some knowledge of history, geography, municipal and public law, classical literature, french, a little spanish . . . to which I will add—a *capacity* to acquire whatever mere zeal and labour dare attempt." Apparently, these qualifications were not enough, for although the president briefly toyed with the idea of sending Scott to one of the newly independent Latin American nations, nothing came of it.[8]

Nor did anything come of Scott's various forays into the political arena. Although he insisted that he burned with an "ardent desire . . . to lead a life of *political activity and usefulness,*" no suitable office presented itself. He considered resigning his army commission to run for the Virginia legislature, but the salary was too meager to support his family. The U.S. Congress was another tempting possibility, but his home district was likely to be represented by William S. Archer, an old friend from college days whom he could not, in good conscience, oppose. Raising his sights to the governorship, he asked his Virginia friends to take discreet soundings on the gubernatorial situation. They reported back the discouraging news that, with several strong candidates already in the field, Scott's prospects were poor, which seemed to shut the last door to a political career.[9]

If he could not win political laurels on his own, perhaps Scott could rise by hitching his wagon to someone else's star. The presidential sweepstakes of 1824 presented intriguing possibilities for a would-be kingmaker. America was about to undergo one of its periodic changing of the guards. Monroe, the last president to wear knee britches, was also the last of that string of Revolutionary War veterans who had dominated politics since the establishment of the Republic. Standing in the wings to replace him was a new generation brought into prominence, as was Scott himself, by the War of 1812.

Conspicuous among these hopefuls was Secretary of War John C. Calhoun. Only four years older than Scott, Calhoun had risen rapidly by virtue of intellect, industry, and ambition. Building on his reputation as the most effective leader the War Department had yet seen, he now felt ready to make a bid for the presidency.[10]

Calhoun's cause was aided by a coterie of army officers before whom he dangled hints of preferment. Scott was the most active of this group. The tradition that the military should abstain from politics had not yet been established, so he felt no compunctions against plunging into a political race. His strategy was to build newspaper support for Calhoun while attacking the "false pretensions" of Secretary of Treasury William Crawford, then seen as Calhoun's chief rival. To this end, Scott helped establish a Calhoun organ in New York City, the *Patriot,* edited by his wartime aide, Charles K. Gardner (who would later introduce the postage stamp to America). Scott helped finance the venture with six hundred dollars of his own money, secured subscriptions, and solicited articles from his friends, including James Fenimore Cooper. Taking up the pen, Scott published some anti-Crawford pieces in the *Richmond Enquirer* under the pseudonyms "Pendleton" and "Roanoke."[11]

Scott persuaded himself that a Calhoun victory was virtually assured, but the candidate himself knew better. Convinced of the hopelessness of his cause, Calhoun dropped out of the race, settling for the vice presidency and leaving his allies in the lurch. Crawford was disabled by a paralyzing stroke, and the election of 1824 was fought out among three contenders Scott had not even considered: Henry Clay, John Quincy Adams, and Andrew Jackson. None received a majority of the electoral vote, but the House of Representatives chose Adams, much to Jackson's chagrin.

In this, his first foray into national politics, Scott displayed the same trusting naiveté and tone-deaf ear to public opinion that would mark his own later political ventures, including his 1852 campaign for the presidency. Wrapped within a military cocoon, he was cut off from many of the concerns of the civilian world. In the early 1820s, he attempted to break free from this "military incumbrance," but all his efforts were frustrated. Embittered for a time by his inability to change the direction of his life, he was, he moaned, "Stung to madness at the vexations I have experienced in this service."[12]

The most conspicuous evidence of this frustration was seen in a series of highly public quarrels Scott conducted with fellow officers and prominent politicians. He was well aware that such indecorous squabbling could "have the effect of deeply injuring the army in the estimation of the nation," and he had vowed in 1816 to follow the path of "dignified forbearance."[13] It was not a vow he could keep. Within a year he was crossing swords with none less than Andrew Jackson.

It began innocently enough at a dinner party in June 1817. During a lull in the conversation, Governor DeWitt Clinton of New York asked Scott what he thought of a recent controversial order issued by General Jackson. An officer in Jackson's Southern Division had been reassigned by the War Department without prior notice having been given to Jackson. Old Hickory was quite properly offended by this breach of the chain of command, but he overreacted by issuing a general order prohibiting his men from obeying any directive from the War Department that did not pass through him. Scott replied that such an order could, in some circumstances, be considered as an incitement to mutiny.[14]

A meddlesome eavesdropper slipped a distorted version of these remarks to the press, and an anonymous troublemaker passed it along to Jackson, with the warning that Scott was spearheading an administration plot to discredit him. Instead of pitching this communication into the trash basket where it belonged, Jackson asked Scott for an explanation. Scott replied that his remarks had been made at a private gathering with no sinister intent. Had he left it at that, so Jackson later told President Monroe, it would have been the end of the matter, but Scott never knew when to stop. In a condescending, schoolmasterish tone, he undertook to instruct the Hero of New Orleans as if he were addressing a not-overly-bright cadet. "Take any three officers. Let A be the common superior, B the intermediate commander, and C the common junior," and so on in that vein for page after pedantic page.[15]

Scott actually expected Jackson to be as impressed by this lecture as his mother had been by his boyhood scriptural exegesis. "I should expect your approbation," he naively concluded, "as, in my humble judgement, refutation is impossible." Instead, the hot-tempered older general exploded in fury at this "tinsel rhetoric" dished out by a "hectoring bully." "Pray Sir," Jackson inquired, "in what School of Philosophy you were taught; that to a letter . . . clothed in language decorous and unexceptionable, an answer should be given couched in pompous insolence and bullying expression." No one dared patronize Andrew Jackson: "I think too highly of myself to suppose that I stand at all in need of your admonitions; and too lightly of you, to appreciate them as useful."[16]

This could be interpreted as an invitation to a duel, but Scott had too much respect for Jackson's public services (and for his marksmanship) to rise to the bait. He evaded the implied challenge with a mocking, supercilious response that must have infuriated the humorless Jackson, who chose to regard it as a cowardly capitulation by a "vain, pompous nullity." With that, the correspondence ceased. "It seemed cruel to disturb so much happiness," Scott loftily claimed, so he "left his enemy in his glory."[17]

Such equanimity was clearly an afterthought. At the time, Scott was so frustrated that he lashed out at another target, DeWitt Clinton, calling him a liar and an intriguer and blaming him for instigating the controversy. Clinton responded in kind, to which Scott, forgetting the religious scruples he had expressed to Jackson, made the retort discourteous and challenged the governor to meet him on the field of honor. Clinton contemptuously brushed aside this invitation in a twelve-page, insult-laden response.[18]

Scott emerged badly from both of these affairs. John Quincy Adams, a friend, though not an uncritical one, feared that "Scott's vanity was leading him to his ruin."[19] The haughty general had made two powerful enemies for no reason more compelling than gratifying his pride. He had allowed himself to appear foolish before the public, clouding his heroic wartime reputation. And he had displayed the first signs of that compulsive urge to justify himself at tedious length that would so blight his later years.

The Clinton imbroglio would die down, but the one with Jackson would linger a few years more. Scott helped keep it alive by an act of insubordination more blatant than the one for which he had condemned Jackson. Upset that Jackson had allowed some friends to see a sanitized version of their correspondence, he demanded the right to publish the letters entirely, even though such publication was forbidden by the regulations he himself had written. He badgered Secretary Calhoun and President Monroe for permission, and when that was denied, he went ahead and published them anyway.[20]

The correspondence consumed almost the entire edition of *Niles' Register* for April 10, 1819, testifying to the widespread public interest in the matter. Yet rather than the vindication he had anticipated, Scott found mostly embarrassment. "The whole pamphlet is weak and inconsiderate," declared John Quincy Adams, who was dismayed by Scott's "verbal subterfuges" and "casuistical sophistry." Scott, Adams said with his usual perception, "exhibits an unnatural mixture of the soldier and the attorney." President Monroe displayed remarkable forbearance. Rather than disciplining his temperamental warriors, he tried to play the peacemaker, proposing that they "forget the past, and be friends."[21] Jackson, however, was in no hurry to allow Scott to wriggle off the hook on which he had impaled himself. He bided his time until reconciliation could confer maximum political benefit.

Jackson's opportunity came in December 1823, when he arrived in Washington to take the Senate seat to which he had recently been elected. This threw him and Scott into proximity for the first time. Scott had reason for apprehension: he had heard repeated reports that Jackson had threatened to cut off Scott's ears if ever they should chance to meet. Never one to back off from a fight, Scott threw himself in Jackson's path at every opportunity, but the old general ignored his presence. Scott was finally reduced to sending Jackson a note. "One portion of the American community has long attributed to you the most distinguished magnanimity," he wrote, "and the other portion, the greatest desperation." He left it to Jackson to decide which view was correct. Jackson chose magnanimity: "Whenever you shall feel disposed to meet me on friendly terms, that disposition will not be met by any other than a corresponding feeling on my part."[22]

A public reconciliation was conducted at a crowded reception thrown by Adams in Jackson's honor. The two heroes parted on friendly terms, but when Scott returned home, he discovered that his pocket had been picked of six hundred dollars. It was an omen. Jackson had not really changed his opinion of Scott; he was using him to burnish his own image. Burying the hatchet with Scott, Jackson gloated, undercut those "enemies who denounced me as a man of revengeful Temper and of great rashness. I am told the opinion of those . . . prepared to see me with a Tomahawk in one hand, and a scalping knife in the other has greatly changed."[23]

Jackson was too good a hater to surrender a grudge. Over the next dozen or so years, he would continue to treat Scott with suspicion and ill-disguised contempt. For his part, Scott remained ambivalent in his relations with Jackson. He admired his vigor but deplored his violence. He opposed his politics yet revered his patriotic services. He would suffer numerous embarrassments at Jackson's hand, including a vindictive court-martial stemming from the Seminole War; yet in 1845, when he learned of Jackson's death, he could pay a touching and sincere tribute to his old antagonist. "A great man has fallen among us. ANDREW JACKSON, after filling the world with his fame, and crowning his country with glory, departed this life." If his flaws were great, so too were his virtues. Everything about Jackson, Scott concluded, was larger than life: "Nothing little can ever find a place in his soul."[24]

Scott would not be so generous to lesser foes. For Edmund Pendleton Gaines, his rival general, Scott had nothing but contempt, unleavened by any trace of admiration. The two conducted a running feud for nearly three decades, ending only with Gaines's death in 1849. The rivalry began in 1821. The army reduction act of that year not only slashed the army's authorized size from ten to six thousand men but also eliminated half the generals. Of the four brigadiers, Ripley resigned to pursue law and politics, and Macomb, theoretically the senior, was reduced in grade to colonel in charge of the engineers, though retaining his brevet rank and pay. This left Gaines and Scott, who agreed to alternate the command of the Eastern and Western Departments. With Jackson about to take up the territorial governorship of Florida, Jacob Brown would be the sole remaining major general, with his headquarters at Washington.

As an unanticipated consequence of this reorganization, the army now had, for the first time since George Washington, a single commanding general. The position's precise functions were undefined, which created an opportunity for someone with energy and determination to place his stamp upon both the office and the army. Brown, however, was distracted by private affairs and was, in any event, too feeble from a debilitating stroke to give the office his full attention.[25] His tenure was likely to be brief, and when it should end, Scott wanted to be his replacement. This would be the culmination of his military ambition, and all that seemed to stand between Scott and his heart's desire was Edmund P. Gaines.

Nine years older than Scott, Gaines had entered the army in 1797. His ascent through the ranks was similar to Scott's, but his conception of the army was very different. A gruff, frontier-schooled Indian fighter in the Andrew Jackson mold, though lacking his fellow Tennessean's iron will, Gaines had no use for those effete officers "who have acquired distinction only in the mazes of French books . . . better adapted to the Quackery of Charlatans, than the common sense science of war." Foremost among those charlatans, of course, was Scott, who Gaines mocked as "the vain-glorious Giant votary of science." He was equally scornful of the entire professional military establishment. West Point–trained officers, he conceded, might have "more knowledge of *the science of war as it was in the last century,*" but patriotic volunteers possessed more "*common sense practical knowledge.*" He scoffed at Frenchified theories and nitpicking regulations. "The brave people of the West," he insisted, "need no other preparation than what their own *strong arms, good Rifles and sound hearts* will at the moment furnish."[26]

This was an echo of that same old Jeffersonian heresy that Scott had dedicated his life to stamping out. It was unthinkable that he would tamely allow its spokesman to take command of his army. The problem was that Gaines's name stood above his on the army register, making him Brown's heir presumptive. Scott bent every effort to correct that unfortunate technicality. He pled his case before the War Department in letter after letter, but Secretary of War Calhoun evaded making a final decision. With his sights set on the presidency, Calhoun was unwilling to antagonize either of his politically well-connected generals.

Despite his later reputation for stubborn integrity, Calhoun here played a skillful double game. At a meeting in May 1821, he managed to give Gaines the impression that he favored his case.[27] A bit later, he sent Scott a private letter assuring him that he was the president's choice to succeed Brown.[28] Scott set great store on this promise, unaware that Calhoun had secretly made a similar pledge to Gaines. Later, when Scott discovered the extent of the secretary's duplicity, he was disillusioned that someone whose presidential aspirations he had promoted was motivated by nothing more than "*heartlessness and the finesse of a deep politician.*"[29] It would not be the last time that the trusting general would allow himself to be misled by false friends who knew how to play to his vanity and ambition.

Early on in the controversy with Gaines, Scott had uncharacteristically pledged to "submit in silence" to whatever settlement was reached, but as

Monroe's second term drew to a close with Brown still an invalid and no decision in sight on his eventual successor, he broke his vow.[30] Seeking to force a decision while a presumably friendly administration was still in place, he requested that a board of officers be convened to rule on the question of seniority between himself and Gaines.

Scott supported this request in a lengthy communication, which Gaines would deride as a "book." As usual when he took pen in hand, Scott overdid it. He piled argument upon argument, diluting his strong points with some that were irrelevant, such as the practice of the British army, and others that were just plain silly, such as the claim that Gaines had once allowed Scott to take the seat of honor at a public dinner. Somewhat more plausible was the contention that Gaines had forfeited his seniority by briefly resigning from the army just before the War of 1812.[31]

Scott's strongest argument dealt with the vexing and unsettled status of brevet rank. This was a critical element of Scott's case. Both men had been promoted to colonel and then to brigadier general on the same date. Scott's only claim to priority lay in his brevet rank as major general, which had been conferred on him some three weeks earlier than it had on Gaines.

Brevet rank was a species of quasi-rank conferred for honorary or temporary purposes. Since the United States did not regularly award medals for extraordinary service, a brevet promotion seemed the only way to reward military distinction. It could also be assigned to officers performing duties above their grade level and, as such, was considered temporary in nature. Did it confer upon its bearer precedence over an officer who held lineal rank? No one knew. Or rather, no agreement seemed possible since the question was so tangled in self-interest that no officer could reach a dispassionate conclusion. According to one contemporary authority: "The annals of the army show more disputes to have arisen in consequence of this brevet rank than all other matters in dispute. It seems to have had the property of transmuting the calmest and best-tempered men into hectoring and quarrelsome Bobadils."[32]

This certainly was the case with Scott and Gaines. For more than a half dozen years, they engaged in a steadily escalating war of words as each demonstrated, at mind-numbing length, his irrefutable claims to precedence over his rival. Both happily consumed quires of paper, engrossed in a controversy that seemed to take on a life of its own. One of Scott's productions when published required eighty-five closely printed pages, to which Gaines responded with equal verbosity.[33]

Inevitably, the quarrel crossed the line into personal abuse. Scott accused his opponent of indulging in "puerility, egotism and vulgarity" and of committing such a gross fraud upon the public that it deserved a court-martial. Gaines retaliated by ladling sarcasm on Scott's "extreme fondness for casting his dazzling and eccentric light on the paths of those whose misfortune it is, in his judgment, to be groping in the dark."[34] For once at a loss for words, Scott responded by challenging his tormentor to a duel, in clear violation of the regulations Scott himself had written.[35] Gaines declined, citing those regulations, leading Scott to indulge in some unseemly gloating over his rival's cowardice.[36]

Scott's hundreds of pages of argument could be boiled down to three words: "rank is rank," whether conferred by brevet or otherwise. To him, that proposition was "so exceedingly plain and easy that it was impossible any impartial and intelligent mind should hesitate concerning it."[37] This was wishful thinking. In the real world, informed military opinion overwhelmingly rejected Scott's claims.

The high-level board of officers to which Scott had referred the issue ruled unanimously that Gaines was entitled to seniority over his rival, notwithstanding his attempted resignation in 1812. That same commission found itself unable to resolve the broader issue of brevet rank that Scott had thought so plain and easy. The chairman, General Brown, though a personal friend of Scott, concluded that Gaines had the stronger case. So did James Barbour, secretary of war under John Quincy Adams.[38]

Earlier, as governor of Virginia, Barbour had been a sponsor of Scott's career, but he had now become alienated by his former protégé's persistent insubordination. The last straw was Scott's demand that he be allowed to go public with the materials generated by his quarrel with Gaines. Permission was denied, but, as in the earlier controversy with Jackson, Scott published anyway. The tone of the resulting pamphlet, according to President Adams, was "not only full of coarse invective upon Gaines, but offensive in several passages to the Secretary of War himself." At Barbour's request, a special cabinet meeting was called to deal with the transgressions of these squabbling warriors. The cabinet's first instinct was to order both of them arrested and tried by court-martial, but after lengthy debate, it was decided that, for the present, letters of reprimand would be sufficient. President Adams asked what should be done if, as was possible, these letters should be met with insulting responses, especially from Scott. Cashier them! the exasperated cabinet ministers replied.[39]

The uneasy truce imposed upon the combatants was shattered by the death of General Brown on February 24, 1828. The old hero was scarcely cold in his grave before the scramble to replace him began. Gaines, who was then commanding the Eastern Department, was able to argue his case in person before the president; Scott, stationed at Cincinnati, initially had to rely on his friends to speak for him.[40] President Adams was noncommittal, not even revealing his inclinations to his cabinet when it met on April 14 to resolve the matter.

That meeting consumed an entire afternoon. The conflicting claims, by now so familiar, were thrashed over at length. Secretary of State Henry Clay was Scott's strongest advocate; no one spoke for Gaines. After three hours of debate, most of the other cabinet members were unenthusiastically coming round to Scott, except for Secretary of the Treasury Richard Rush, who had been silent all afternoon. When President Adams asked for his opinion, Rush argued that Scott and Gaines had both disqualified themselves by their behavior. Rather than reward either of them, he suggested a novel way to cut the Gordian knot—award the vacant major generalship to Alexander Macomb. At that, the president, according to Rush's recollection, "straightened himself up in his seat, and in his peculiar manner said 'and I think so too.'"[41]

This bombshell broke up the meeting and nearly broke up the cabinet as well. Clay was so angered that he threatened to resign and bring the administration down with him. Rush calmed Clay's wrath, and the next day, when Macomb's surprise nomination was submitted to the Senate, Clay raised no objections. The appointment was speedily confirmed.

Adams had been quietly leaning toward Macomb for some time. Gaines and Scott, he thought, "have both made themselves obnoxious by continual acts of insubordination and contempt of the civil authority. Their controversy for rank and precedency has been carried on by both not only with rancor but with indecency."[42] In their ceaseless attacks upon each other over a seven-year span, each had succeeded in his aim of destroying the other, but each brought himself down as well. As with the Kilkenny cats of the nursery rhyme:

> There once were two cats of Kilkenny.
> Each thought there was one cat too many;
> So they fought and they fit,
> And they scratched and they bit,
> Till, excepting their nails
> And the tips of their tails
> Instead of two cats, there weren't any.

Scott was thunderstruck when he heard the news. He considered himself the senior officer of the army; how could he obey his junior? "If I were to do so," he explained, "I should not only be considered as a degraded man . . . but what is worse, I should be lost forever in my own esteem." When Macomb presumed to give him an order, Scott not only refused to obey but also actually demanded that Macomb be arrested and tried for "this act of contempt and insubordination . . . towards me, his senior and therefore commanding officer."[43]

Three more cabinet meetings had to be convened to deal with this one refractory officer. President Adams displayed remarkable indulgence. Despite Scott's deliberate provocations, he was reluctant to dismiss him from the army, as strict discipline might require, bearing in mind the gallant services the general had rendered to the country. Furthermore, Adams noted that though Scott scorned Macomb's "illegal" orders, he seemed to be carrying them out anyway. That was so. Scott carefully maintained the pretence that Macomb was merely suggesting things Scott had already intended to do.[44]

Scott continued his defiance for over a year, continually bombarding authorities with a barrage of justifications, explanations, and expostulations. War Department clerks were kept busy transcribing his appeals. In June, there was a twenty-two-page screed that the president dismissed as "a long argumentative letter . . . full of his rights and his wrongs"; in November, a fifty-page printed pamphlet with 302 numbered paragraphs; and in January, a "hasty" summary of only 119 numbered paragraphs. It was a lonely battle. Scott found no support for his stand. The War Department, the cabinet, Congress, and once-friendly newspapers such as *Niles' Register* all condemned his course.[45] And with his wife and family off in Europe, there was not even support from the home front.

Finally, even President Adams's patience ran out. Although he and Scott genuinely liked each other, enough was enough.[46] The contentious general's affairs, the president complained, "absorb all the faculties of my soul, and leave me scarcely time to perform the remnant of my official duties." He decided to dismiss Scott from the army, should he be reelected to the presidency, but as he wryly noted, the voters dismissed him instead.[47] Adams merely suspended Scott from active duty, leaving it to the incoming Jackson administration to determine his fate.

Given the stormy nature of their prior relationship, Scott had little reason to expect leniency at the hands of Andrew Jackson. He prepared himself for the worst. "My good friend," he told a sympathizer, "my military career is over." To the War Department, he informally announced his "fixed intention" to resign from the service by March 1829.[48]

The proud general had painted himself into a corner. On the one hand, he had committed himself so publicly to a defense of his rights that he could not back down. "'Tis not my intention to yield any point or principle which I have heretofore contended for," he insisted. On the other hand, he had no prospects in civilian life, "but I must work, tho' I know not well how, *where,* or at *what.*" He would not again solicit a position in the federal government, "if it should be necessary to save me from starvation," and public office in Virginia was ruled out by his refusal to take the required antidueling oath. "Such are my prospects, which I think [all] will admit, are bad enough," he concluded, in something close to despair.[49]

A way out of this dilemma was unexpectedly offered by the Jackson administration. The new president lifted Scott's suspension, and Secretary of War John Eaton granted him an extended furlough to join his family in Europe.

Apparently recovered from her ailments, Maria had made something of a social splash in France, winning the title "la Princess sauvage" for her appearance as an Indian at a fancy-dress ball. She had also renewed her husband's acquaintance with Lafayette. When Scott called at LaGrange and recited his woes, the venerable patriot gave the headstrong American some sage advice: "I beseech you general, consider it maturely. Be assured that your great services and your high rank have put it out of your power to follow, in this matter, the bent of your inclinations. Who so proper, in fact, to set the example of obedience—that great virtue of the soldier—as he who has purchased fame and station with his blood?"[50]

Lafayette provided the cover behind which Scott could beat a graceful retreat. Coming from such a revered source, it was almost as if the voice of Washington himself was telling Scott to submit. And submit he did. With newfound humility, he informed the War Department that he was prepared "to sacrifice my own convictions and feelings to . . . the repeated decision of the *civil* authority of my country." He withdrew his resignation and, like a good soldier, reported himself for duty.[51]

For over a decade, Scott's pride had been at war with his professionalism. The struggle had led him to the brink of abandoning a military career that promised much for himself and for his country. Now, with the onset of a new decade, Scott rededicated himself to his profession. His Bible taught him that he who ruleth his spirit is greater than one who conquereth a city. Scott would do both.

CHAPTER NINE

TROUBLESHOOTER

Even as Winfield Scott was reconciling himself to the army, the army was trying to justify itself to the nation. The decade of the 1830s, sometimes called the Age of Jackson and characterized by the so-called Rise of the Common Man, was not sympathetic to those who claimed special status by virtue of professional expertise. President Jackson, speaking for many of his countrymen, insisted that "The duties of all public officers are ... so plain and simple that men of intelligence may readily qualify themselves for their performance."[1]

That included the military. From his own experience, Jackson had concluded that standing armies were "dangerous to free government in time of peace." He pledged not to enlarge the regular army but rather to rely upon the militia as "the bulwark of our defense ... which in the present state of our intelligence and population must render us invincible."[2]

As memories of the War of 1812 began to fade, the army found itself under attack for its supposedly undemocratic ways. The Military Academy at West Point was particularly offensive to outraged Jacksonians who charged, "There is not on the face of the earth, a more aristocratic, anti-republican and monopolizing establishment." A movement to abolish the academy gained strength in Congress, much to the delight of an unwilling cadet, Ulysses S. Grant, and to the dismay of Scott, who proposed an elaborate (and unworkable) scheme to save the school by opening it up to navy midshipmen.[3]

As it turned out, neither Grant's hopes nor Scott's fears would be realized. The academy survived these attacks, but they sent a signal that the professional army would have to prove its worth to a skeptical nation. For Scott, that meant demonstrating that, even in the absence of a foreign foe, he and his army could make themselves useful to the Republic. In pursuit of that mission he would crisscross the country for a decade, dealing with crisis after crisis, with scarcely a pause for rest. He would become a roving troubleshooter, ranging from the tropical swamps of Florida to the frozen wastes of Maine, and from the Aroostook Valley to the Mississippi frontier, wherever the latest emergency called him.

The first of this series of special assignments came in June 1832. The Sac and Fox Indians in Illinois and the Wisconsin Territory were on the warpath, led by a sixty-five-year-old chieftain named Blackhawk.[4] Strictly speaking, this would seem to be none of Scott's concern, since the action took place within the jurisdiction of the Western Department, then under command of General Gaines, who was, unlike Scott, an experienced Indian fighter. The implacable President Jackson, however, had begun to suspect that his one-time friend Gaines had grown overly sympathetic to the Indians, and so ordered the presumably more reliable Scott to take command.

After years of desk-bound inactivity, Scott wasted no time in scooping up whatever forces were available in the East and hastening them to the scene of action via steamboats, then a novelty on the Upper Great Lakes. With what Macomb praised as "a rapidity which is believed to be unprecedented in military movements," he transported some artillery companies the eighteen hundred miles from Fort Monroe in Virginia to Chicago in only eighteen days. Eight hundred regulars and six companies of mounted rangers were accompanied by the entire West Point class of 1832, including the son of Secretary of War Lewis Cass, which had unanimously volunteered for the expedition.[5]

At Buffalo, Scott chartered four steamers. Officers and men boarded the *Sheldon, Thompson,* and *Henry Clay;* provisions and equipment were loaded onto two other ships—a division that would later prove unfortunate. While en route, Scott used the time by drilling his West Pointers on the fine points of the *General Regulations.* His only concern seemed to be that he might, through impatience, get to the scene of action before all proper preparations had been made. Then, just as the fleet approached Detroit, an ominous event occurred. A soldier on the *Henry Clay* was stricken with cholera. His first symptoms appeared at 5:00 P.M. on July 4. By two o'clock the next morning, he was dead.[6]

Cholera morbus—the Asiatic cholera—is caused by the bacillus Vibrio cholera, which lodges on the intestinal lining and interferes with the digestive process. The first symptoms are abdominal pains and muscle cramps, followed by severe diarrhea and vomiting. The victim can lose up to four gallons of fluid a day. In about half the cases, death from dehydration follows quickly. The disease is spread through water contaminated with infected fecal matter and can readily be prevented by boiling the water before drinking. None of this was understood at the time. The disease, then sweeping the world in a massive pandemic, was regarded as an "unaccountable phenomena in the laws of existence by which God visits the sins of men with the sweeping devastation of pestilence."[7]

Scott suspected a more mundane cause. Noting that many of the victims were habitual drunkards, he fingered Demon Rum as the culprit. A pioneer temperance advocate, Scott had published the lengthy "Scheme for Restricting the Use of Ardent Spirits in the United States" as early as 1821. Now, convinced that drunkenness caused the dreaded plague, he stepped up his campaign, ordering that all intoxicated soldiers be forced to dig a suitable grave for themselves "to spare good and temperate men the labor of digging graves for their worthless companions."[8] Since the disease was spread by water rather than whiskey, Scott's measures probably proved counterproductive.

The surgeon on board the *Henry Clay* evidently was unconvinced by Scott's theory, for as soon as the epidemic broke out, he got drunk and stayed that way, leaving Scott to care for the victims. Disregarding his own safety, the general personally nursed the sick and attended to their needs, consoled the dying, and cheered the healthy, winning the devotion of his men and the admiration of a junior officer who hailed his commander "not only as the hero of battles, but as the hero of humanity."[9]

By the time the fleet reached Detroit, the *Henry Clay* had become "a moving pesthouse." City officials refused to allow it to land, so it sailed a bit farther to Fort Gratiot. As soon as she docked, the men, disregarding their officers, dashed ashore and tried to flee from the pestilence that, in all too many cases, they already carried within themselves. Their corpses were later found strewed along the road to Detroit, half-eaten by hogs and wolves.[10]

Scott transferred his headquarters, along with the officers and the cadets, to the as-yet-uninfected *Sheldon Thompson*. A few days later, with the end of the voyage almost in sight, cholera struck again. The first victim was wrapped in a blanket and buried at sea by a veteran sergeant named Davis. Within a few hours, Davis himself was dead, along with a dozen others.[11]

Landing at Chicago, then a settlement of less than fifty people, Scott hastened to send the precious cadets back East to safety and moved the rest of his command to Fort Dearborn, where he isolated the sick from the well and took stock of his situation. "What a calamity has come upon the expedition!" he moaned. Of the 208 recruits commanded by Col. David E. Twiggs, 30 were dead and 155 had fled into the forest. Other detachments suffered similar losses. In all, of the 850 soldiers who left Buffalo two weeks earlier, scarcely 200 could now be found fit for duty.[12]

In the face of such a catastrophe, which rivaled the Terre aux Boeufs disaster, Scott's campaign against Blackhawk, begun with such confidence, seemed on the verge of collapse. He was, he complained to the War Department, "so baffled and crippled by the hand of Providence, as to be left almost without the possibility of doing good." To add to his woes, the supply ships carrying much needed tents, medicine, and ammunition were stranded somewhere between Detroit and Chicago.[13]

Despairing of bringing his remaining troops up to combat readiness, Scott departed Chicago for the front on July 29, accompanied only by his three aides. By the time they arrived, the Blackhawk War was over. On August 2, Brig. Gen. Henry Atkinson cornered the fleeing Indian band at the mouth of the Bad Axe River and decisively defeated them without any help from Scott. (Another tardy warrior who missed the fighting was a young Illinois militia captain, Abraham Lincoln.)

Scott then took charge of the peace negotiations with the remaining Indians. His glittering uniform and his aura of *gravitas* enabled him to strike the pompous, dignified tone deemed proper in dealing with a savage warrior race. Addressing them as "My children," with frequent references to "the Great Spirit" and "the Great Father at Washington" in the obligatory pidgin English Indians were accustomed to hearing from whites, Scott made the desired impression, particularly since he held all the high cards.[14]

By terms of the treaty he negotiated (or rather imposed), the Indians were to be relocated across the Mississippi River in return for token payments. Scott supervised all the arrangements while overseeing the demobilization of the volunteer army and managing the affairs of the encampment at Rock Island. A fresh outbreak of cholera incapacitated most of his staff (though not fatally), leaving much of the administrative burden on Scott. "I have written more and have laboured harder in other ways than in any other two months of my life," he complained.[15]

At this difficult time, General Macomb tactlessly reopened an old wound. He rebuked Scott for bypassing the commanding general's office by corresponding directly with the secretary of war. A few years earlier, such a reproach would have been met either with stony silence or by a furious outburst. Now, Scott demonstrated his newfound self-control with a soft answer. "For Heaven's sake," he apologized, "don't complain of neglect. None was intended."[16] The midlife crisis of the 1820s was definitely over.

His mission accomplished, Scott prepared to return home. He carried with him an enhanced reputation. Governor John Reynolds of Illinois hailed Scott as "a very efficient Commissioner," adding, "mercy for the unfortunate Indians is conspicuous in all his actions." From Secretary of War Cass came a generous commendation for "the fortunate consummation of your arduous duties . . . during a series of difficulties requiring higher moral courage than the operation of an active campaign." President Jackson went a step further. "The campaign," he said, "has evinced the efficient organization of the army and its capacity for prompt and active service."[17] This, coming from the nation's chief advocate of the militia, demonstrated that both Scott and his army had succeeded in their goal of justifying themselves, even to skeptics.

After an arduous overland journey, an exhausted Scott rejoined his family, then staying at West Point, on November 4. He had little time to enjoy the reunion. Three days later, he received a confidential order from the War Department summoning him immediately to Washington for some unstated purpose. He reported directly to President Jackson at the White House. The Union, the general was told, was in danger of coming apart. Scott was to go to South Carolina to help hold it together. Even as they spoke, a specially elected convention was assembling in the state capital of Columbia to defy (or "nullify") the laws of the United States.

The ostensible grievance was the Tariff of 1832, regarded by many Southerners as a discriminatory tax that protected the industries of the Northeast at the expense of the cotton-exporting states of the South. Many were convinced (on flimsy statistical grounds) that such a measure cost them forty bales of cotton out of every hundred they produced. When Congress and the administration failed to provide relief, they determined to resist, egged on by Vice President Calhoun, who maintained that individual states had the constitutional power to nullify laws they considered destructive of their rights. However, the underlying grievances ran deeper than abstract constitutional arguments.

Whether based on the declining price of cotton, resentment over competition from the fertile lands of the Southwest, or an unspoken but pervasive fear for the future of the institution of slavery, their resentment was genuine and widespread. In the election of 1832, the nullifiers swept to control of the South Carolina state legislature. They promptly called for a special convention that, on November 24, declared the federal tariff act to be "null, void and no law" insofar as South Carolina was concerned.

President Jackson was not interested in root causes or in finely spun constitutional arguments. His response to Calhoun's subtleties was simple and direct: "Our Federal Union, it must be preserved." He was not, however, averse to some sort of compromise, but until it could be reached, he wanted to make sure that events in South Carolina did not spin out of control. Scott's mission was to prevent that from happening.

The general proceeded at once to Charleston under the thinly disguised cover of conducting his regular tour of inspection. When that pretence was challenged, Scott tried to bluff his way through. "On what evil days have we fallen, my good friend, when so common place an event gives rise to conjecture or speculation!" he replied sadly. Actually, he was carrying secret instructions from the War Department (though not so secret as to keep them from being leaked to the newspapers within a few months). His first charge was to strengthen the forts and arsenals in and around Charleston against the possibility "that in the first effervescence of feeling, some rash attempt may be made" to seize the weapons stored there.[18]

This was not an idle fantasy. In Charleston, rebellion was in the air. Armed mobs roamed the streets, and the recent elections had been marred by brawls and riots. Carolina hotheads proudly affixed palmetto cockades to their hats as a badge of defiance and cheered the most extravagant rhetoric of disunion. "Let the tariff be got rid of by *Resistance*," urged one. "If war should result the government could not put the State down."[19] Unionists, contemptuously dubbed "Submissionists," were unnerved and unorganized.

In such an explosive atmosphere, Scott had to tread warily. He discreetly surveyed the forts, strengthened their defenses, quietly slipped in reinforcements, and transferred officers of doubtful loyalty to distant posts. To avert incidents, he kept his men under tight discipline, reminding them that, although the nullifiers "have, no doubt, become exceedingly wrong-headed," they were still fellow citizens and had to be treated with respect and forbearance. Soldiers walking the streets were ordered to give way to all civilians, no matter how rude, and not to be provoked by insults, mud throwing, or even brickbats. To ingratiate his troops further with the citizens, he treated Charlestonians to a spectacular display of fireworks on Washington's Birthday, and when a real fire threatened to destroy the warehouse district, he sent soldiers to help put it out (for which service they received no thanks from sullen city officials).[20]

Drawing on the friendships he had made during his prewar stay in South Carolina, Scott also engaged in quiet diplomacy with leading citizens. To unionists, such as James L. Petigru and Joel Poinsett (developer of the red-leafed Christmas plant that bears his name), he offered assurances of the administration's resolve. To nullifiers, he extended the olive branch. Unlike the cynic in the later secession crisis who bluntly reminded South Carolinians that their state was too small for a nation and too large for an insane asylum, Scott breathed sympathy and conciliation. He guaranteed that the government had no aggressive intentions against their state and was, even then, working toward a reduction of the obnoxious tariff. What was needed, he repeatedly insisted, was a period of calm "to give time for wisdom and moderation to exert themselves." "My ruling wish," he repeatedly maintained, "is, that neither party take a rash step that might put all the healing powers at defiance."[21]

Whether through Scott's agency or simply by the operation of common sense, his wish was fulfilled. No violence erupted to derail the settlement of the crisis. When Congress reconvened, a bill providing for a reduction of the tariff in stages was proposed and passed so quickly that, as Senator Thomas Hart Benton marveled, members were putting on their coats for dinner when the bill was introduced, and it was approved before those coats had got on their backs, "and the dinner which was waiting had but little time to cool before the astonished members, their work done, were at the table to eat it."[22]

With that concession, the nullification crisis came to an end, though not the dream of disunion that many South Carolinians continued to cherish. To Scott, it was a nightmare. "I cannot follow out the long, dark shades of the picture that presents itself to my fears," he confessed with apprehension. Allow one state to withdraw, even peacefully, he predicted, and then "the whole fabric of the Union will tumble in," leaving two, or perhaps even three, separate nations "out of its broken fragments. . . . I turn with horror from the picture." If that day should come, he insisted, "My humble support will be given to the Union," but he qualified that pledge by adding (in a passage that he prudently excised from his later memoirs) that it would be given only if his native state of Virginia should remain within that Union. "If *she* withdraw, I hope no longer to be on the scene."[23] But thirty years later, he *was* still on the scene and would be compelled to confront the choice he now found so unpalatable.

With another mission successfully behind him, Scott returned to Washington in March 1833 to receive the acclaim he thought his due. His old Albany friend Martin Van Buren, now vice president of the United States, effusively thanked him for his services, but from President Jackson came only "a few terms of measured praise," reawakening the suspicion that Old Hickory still nursed his ancient grudge despite conciliatory professions.[24] Winning Jackson's approval was important to Scott, but for now he would have to be content with near-universal applause from press and public as he returned to New York to rejoin his family and resume his duties as commander of the Eastern Department.

For the next few years these official duties would largely be routine. His family life, however, would be darkened by another tragedy, "one from which we can hardly yet perceive the possibility of recovery," he lamented. Maria Mayo Scott, his firstborn child, died in late 1833 at the age of fifteen. Grief from this "severe dispensation" was not mitigated by the birth of the Scotts' last child, Marcella, in January 1834, which seems to have plunged the mother into a prolonged postpartum depression. Her condition was aggravated by worries over her sickly daughter Virginia, who was afflicted with "inflammatory rheumatism" virtually every winter.[25] In 1838, Maria took the children again to Paris. They would not return until 1843.

Gossiping tongues were again set wagging over this fresh separation. "The devil take such women!" exclaimed Scott's New York friend Philip Hone. "They break their part of a solemn contract, and would have no right to complain if their husbands were to seek in other arms, the comfort and consolation which they deny them." A longtime aide to Scott, however, insisted,

"The animadversions upon their frequent separation were always much exaggerated," and he testified to the pride and affection the couple always displayed toward one another. The general himself was never heard to complain of his unusual domestic arrangements and, rather than seeking the solace in some other arms that Hone suggested he was entitled to find, insisted that he had always managed to subdue "the mutinous appetites" of the flesh. Raising his hand toward Heaven, Scott swore: "I have never violated my marriage vow, nor did I ever give a human being cause to imagine that I desired to violate it. I pledge my soul, my honor and my life that all I say now is strictly true."[26]

To combat his personal "grief and seclusion," Scott busied himself with public affairs. In particular, he immersed himself in the activities of the newly formed Whig party. Dismissed too readily by subsequent historians as a conservative, elitist faction, the Whigs were actually a nationalist, modernizing party unafraid of utilizing the power of the federal government to promote both economic prosperity and social reform. Strongest in New England and those areas settled by Yankees, it also attracted followers as diverse as the young Abraham Lincoln and (for a time) John C. Calhoun.[27]

One thread binding together these otherwise dissimilar types was opposition to the policies of Andrew Jackson, especially his crusade against the Second Bank of the United States. Scott hardly needed additional inducement to join an anti-Jackson party. Although in awe of Jackson's military feats and intimidated by his forceful personality, he scorned the president's policies as products of "passions, predilections or prejudice."[28]

The president, in turn, barely bothered to hide his irritation over Scott's politics. At a White House dinner in January 1836, he turned to the lady seated between them and informed her, "in a tone of labored pleasantry, that is, with ill-disguised bitterness," that Scott opposed all his policies. Scott demurred, citing his support of the nullification proclamation and the special message on the French indemnity question. "That's candid!" the president snorted. "He thinks well of two—*but two!* of my measures."[29]

Yet only four days later, on January 20, Jackson called on Scott to deal with still another crisis, this time in Florida.

CHAPTER TEN

FAILURE

On December 28, 1835, Maj. Francis L. Dade was leading a column of over one hundred regulars on a leisurely march from Fort Brooke on Tampa Bay to Fort King in north-central Florida. It was a chilly, peaceful morning, and the unsuspecting officer had sent out neither scouts nor flankers. As his men neared Wahoo Swamp, a band of Seminoles hidden in the pine woods opened fire. Before the day was out, Dade and his entire command would be dead, except for a handful of wounded who staggered back to camp to report the massacre. That same day, in a concerted attack, Osceola, the Seminole chief, ambushed Indian Agent Wiley Thompson as he was enjoying an after-dinner stroll outside Fort King and distributed pieces of his scalp among his braves as trophies. The Second Seminole War had begun.[1]

The First Seminole War (1817–18) had been conducted by Andrew Jackson when he was yet a general and while Florida was still under Spanish rule. Disregarding diplomatic technicalities, Old Hickory had stormed through Florida, defeating the Seminoles, hanging their British supporters, and so weakening the nominal Spanish authority that it soon surrendered Florida to the United States.

The Seminoles, however, remained as an irritant to American settlement, particularly in view of their association with "maroons," those escaped slaves who had found a degree of freedom in the Florida wilderness and whose presence was regarded by the Americans as a possible incitement to slave uprisings. A solution to the problem seemed to have been reached in 1832 with the Treaty of Payne's Landing, which called for the removal of the Indians to the West. The Seminoles, however, resisted this forced relocation, and by 1835, as Major Dade so tragically discovered, they decided to take up arms again.

Scott happened to be in Washington on January 20, 1836, when news of the Dade disaster arrived. He was briefed on the situation by Secretary of War Lewis Cass late that afternoon and volunteered to leave for the front that very night.[2] Cass was impressed by his eagerness but asked the impetuous general to wait at least another day in order to receive instructions.

By these instructions, Scott was authorized to take command of the campaign against the Seminoles and given complete charge of military operations. In making peace, however, his discretion was severely limited. No terms or conditions were to be allowed the Indians other than their unconditional acquiescence to relocation in the West. Furthermore, no peace terms would even be considered until "every living slave in their possession belonging to a white man is given up." Almost as an afterthought, Scott brought up a potential embarrassment. The line dividing Scott's Eastern Department from the Western Department, commanded by his archrival Gen. Edmund P. Gaines, ran through the likely theater of war. Scott was ordered to ignore that "imaginary" distinction, but whether Gaines would meekly agree to be superseded remained to be seen.[3]

Scott immediately hastened south, gathering militia troops along the way, arranging for supplies, and plotting his strategy. This was the first time he had ever been in command of a military campaign; all his prior experience had been as a subordinate. Furthermore, that experience was more than twenty years in the past and had been conducted under conditions very different from those he now faced. He had never fought Indians, nor had he ever set foot in Florida.

Nothing in his experience had prepared Scott for the inhospitality of central Florida's environment. Part of it consisted of barren sandy wastes with low shrubs unsuitable for animal forage, unlike the grassy prairies of the northern part of the territory. Slightly farther south, one could find only marshes and swamps, with unpronounceable names and impenetrable paths, swarming with alligators, rattlesnakes, and, most deadly of all, mosquitoes. The most characteristic feature of this landscape were the "hammocks," densely packed groves of exotic trees "where a goat could not penetrate," though an Indian could easily slip through and be lost to sight within ten feet. "Fancy a surface chequered at convenient distances, for the Indians, with hammocks, cyprus swamps, savannahs and scrubs," said Scott. "Every hammock and scrub is more difficult, being pre-occupied with Indians, to storm and to carry than any field work it was my fortune to take in Canada."[4]

Such terrain offered little opportunity to gratify Scott's long-held ambition "to conduct sieges and command in open fields, serried lines and columns."[5] Called upon to wage what was, in effect, America's first jungle war, Scott was reluctant, nonetheless, to abandon the hard-won professional skills he had acquired through his study of European models, however inappropriate they might be. Rather than adapt to the unusual conditions he now confronted, the general chose to impose his view of warfare upon them. He devised an intricate plan designed to end the war at one blow. Convinced that most of the Seminoles were concentrated around the Cove of the Withlacooche, he divided his army into three columns, each of which would converge upon the enemy from different directions, surrounding them and preventing their escape into the wilderness.

Gaines openly scoffed at such "visionary plans . . . according to the Napoleon tactics!! (excellent for operations against troops of civilized nations—but fruitless for wilderness swamp, against savages)." Even the War Department was skeptical, but Secretary Cass, true to the American military tradition of allowing the commander on the spot full leeway, was reluctant to interfere.[6] Actually, Scott's strategy was not without merit. It held out the enticing possibility, if all went well, of bringing the conflict to a speedy conclusion. Even if not completely successful, the projected attack could channel the escaping Indians away from their swampy strongholds in the south and into the more open country of the north.

All, however, did not go well. In fact, almost nothing went as planned. As Scott surveyed the war zone, he realized that he needed more soldiers, especially mounted troops, than he had initially called for. Horses, however, were in short supply, as was the grain to feed them. Most of the promised provisions, including rations for both man and beast, were on the aptly named supply ship *Arctic,* still ice-bound in the Chesapeake Bay. A shortage of rifles left Scott in a "state of disappointment and vexation," as did the government's refusal to provide state militiamen with much needed knapsacks. Even if sufficient supplies had been available, Scott lacked the means to transport them to the front—a situation for which he enumerated no less than seven different excuses. To make matters worse, the "zeal and patriotism" of the Georgia militiamen "evaporated" under the Florida sun, and—shades of Queenston Heights—they refused to be mustered into the service. "It will be seen that human agents are as little to be relied upon as the winds and waves," the frustrated general complained. "All have fought powerfully against me."[7]

The crowning blow to Scott's rapidly unraveling plan came from an unexpected quarter—Edmund P. Gaines. That general was in New Orleans when he learned of the Seminole uprising. Without waiting for orders, he enrolled a regiment of Louisiana volunteers and headed for Tampa Bay. While he was en route, Cass's order placing Scott in command of the operation caught up with him, but Gaines decided to ignore it. Gathering up whatever supplies were available at Tampa, he marched inland, with no particular plan other than to seek out Indians and, if possible, defeat them. He found them, or rather, the Indians found him, not far from the scene of Dade's massacre, whose victims Gaines had recently buried.[8]

Gaines escaped Dade's fate by constructing log breastworks, which he grandly named Fort Izard, in honor of a lieutenant who had been killed early in the fighting. His men hunkered behind these works from February 28 to March 5, waiting for a relief expedition from Brig. Gen. Duncan Clinch, who was thought to be nearby. Gaines himself was wounded in the jaw while defending against one of the many Indian attacks, but the tough old soldier, whose personal courage not even Scott ever questioned, calmly spat out his teeth, made a joke, and kept on fighting. His position, however, was no laughing matter. Trapped inside his fort, unable even to make a sortie (which he claimed was a deliberate strategy to prevent the Indians from scattering), he and his command were reduced to eating their own horses.[9]

On March 5, the Indians asked for a parley. While it was going on, Clinch arrived, and the Indians dispersed. According to Gaines, the Indians were about to surrender, but that seems unlikely since, if they had wanted to cease fighting, they had merely to slip away. It was more probable that they proposed the talks to feel out Gaines's position. Gaines, however, chose to believe that "the enemy was beaten and sued for peace." As a parting dig at his rival, he signed this proclamation as "Commanding General" and referred to Scott only as "the diplomatic agent of the War Department."[10]

Declaring that the war was now over, Gaines returned to Louisiana. On his way back, his path finally crossed that of Scott at Fort Drane. It was not a cordial reunion. Compelled to spend a day together, they were observed "sitting at the same table, and showing as much courtesy to each other . . . as two men can, who take no notice of each other." Scott felt that he had good reason to act so cool. He blamed Gaines's unwanted intrusion for derailing his own carefully laid strategy. "All my plans are thwarted," he angrily complained. He charged that the hungry Louisianans had gobbled up the rations and supplies Scott had stockpiled for his pending offensive. Furthermore, Gaines's premature attack threatened to scatter the Seminoles into their swampy strongholds before Scott's trap could be sprung.[11]

Scott had, in fact, been so vexed by Gaines's unwelcome appearance that his first reaction had been to let the impetuous general stew in his own juice. Learning of Gaines's predicament at Fort Izard, he ordered Clinch to make no move to rescue him or even send supplies to the starving troops. "Let him, therefore, in time extricate himself from the embarrassment he has placed himself in," Scott coldly commanded. A few days later, he relented.[12] Clinch, in the meantime, had wisely disobeyed the order, but the damage had been done, and an opportunity had been lost.

Having become so enamored of his plan, Scott lost sight of its purpose—to chastise the Seminoles. Gaines's appearance with a thousand fresh, eager troops may have been unexpected, but war is full of surprises. A resourceful commander would have incorporated this fresh development into his strategy and improvised a new plan to take advantage of changed circumstances. Scott, who wrote the book on American warfare, was still very much a bookish soldier. He was not so rigid, however, that he could not learn from mistakes. Ten years later, in Mexico, Scott would throw away the book and demonstrate a flexibility and ingenuity that was absent from his Florida campaign. The lessons Scott learned from his failure in the 1830s would help pave the way for his 1840s triumph.

Meanwhile, in Florida, there was still a war to be lost. With Gaines out of the way, Scott could resume his long-delayed plan. His three columns were set in motion to converge upon the supposed Indian hideaway, according to a rigorous predetermined timetable. They soon discovered that, as a later general ruefully observed, "we have, perhaps, as little knowledge of the interior of Florida as of the interior of China." The only passable road was the one on which poor Dade had been bushwhacked, while the others were mere wilderness trails so rugged that it took one column two days to traverse seven miles. The only way these scattered columns could communicate with each other was to fire off artillery at predetermined times. This, plus the music from the camp bands that Scott ordered to sustain morale, was as audible to the Indians as to the Americans, which tended to diminish the element of surprise.[13]

Scott's column arrived at its rendezvous point roughly on schedule; the others straggled in late. The Indians, as might have been expected, were gone. With four hundred of his soldiers on sick call and the term of enlistment of his volunteers about to expire, there was little more the frustrated general could do but send out search parties in a futile attempt to discover the hiding places of the Seminole women and children. All in all, Scott estimated, scarcely sixty Seminole braves had been killed during the war, leaving another twelve hundred to be dealt with.[14]

Far from being over, as Gaines had so grandly claimed, Scott was convinced that "the war, on our part is, in fact, scarcely begun." He recommended that a new army of 2,400 foot soldiers and 600 mounted men be assembled to resume the struggle once the sickly summer season had passed. As for himself, he had had his fill of this dispiriting war. "I have no particular desire to conduct the operations of the new forces," he informed the War Department. "That is a duty which I shall neither solicit nor decline."[15]

In the very next sentence, however, he let slip an undiplomatic remark that ensured he would not be welcomed for any further activity in Florida. We need *"3,000 good troops (not volunteers),"* he said. Scott's recent experience had given no cause to abate his longstanding animus against volunteer soldiers. Undisciplined, insubordinate, and unreliable, they were willing enough to kill Indians (even friendly ones) but often balked when ordered to perform such inglorious tasks as road construction or camp police. "Associated with such officers and men, no man's honour is safe," Scott declared in disgust.[16]

When word of this slur upon Florida's citizen-soldiers leaked out, effigies of the tactless general were set ablaze across the state. Scott tried to apologize, but he only made matters worse by an ill-tempered general order issued on May 17. With portions of Florida in a panic because of reported Indian outrages, the general attempted to stiffen their collective backbone. Scoffing at those timid souls who saw "nothing but an Indian behind every bush" and then "fled without knowledge whether they ran from squaws or warriors," he urged manly self-defense. He ended the insulting communiqué on a note of self-pity for "the general who has the misfortune to command a handful of brave troops in the midst of such a population."[17]

The order succeeded in arousing the Floridians' fighting spirit, but it was directed against Scott rather than the Indians. Demands for his removal swept the state. Joseph M. White, the territorial delegate to Congress, informed President Jackson, "The feelings of the people are outraged by representations calculated to degrade and expose them to ridicule throughout the United States." He demanded that Jackson immediately replace the obnoxious general.[18] The president, already impatient with Scott's excuses and delays, needed little persuasion. He immediately ordered the general's recall, but the matter was, for the time being, moot. Secretary of War Cass had already ordered Scott out of Florida, though not in disgrace. His services had been suddenly required in Georgia to deal with yet another Indian uprising. Scott had been given a second chance.

He was eager to make the most of it. "Thank God!" he rejoiced upon his arrival in Georgia, "here an enemy may be reached." That enemy was the Creek Indians, a formidable tribe in southern Georgia and Alabama. Emboldened by the example of the Seminoles, Creek warriors rampaged throughout the frontier, burning villages and setting off a panic-stricken flight by white settlers. Alabama governor Clement C. Clay pleaded with Scott for immediate assistance. "The people on our frontier are in a wretched condition, their lives and property being at the mercy of the savages."[19]

Scott, however, was still in the cautious mode he had adopted in Florida. "I must avoid all premature and false movements," he insisted. This meant a series of exasperating delays while he awaited the arrival of sufficient troops, twenty days' worth of rations, an artillery train, ammunition, and four steamboats. To the impatient authorities, he explained, "if we fight the Indians, with inferior numbers, we should, nevertheless, in all probability, beat them; but with a great loss of valuable lives on our part; whereas, if we wait for the arrival of all, or nearly all of our forces . . . and till we have ample means of subsistence . . . , the war may be successfully terminated on our part with but a small loss of lives." This consideration, he admitted, "has great weight with me." Despite all obstacles, the general was bursting with confidence. "I like difficulties, and I hope to know how to conquer them."[20]

As in Florida, he had a plan. The strategic objective was to prevent the Creeks from joining with the Florida Seminoles. One wing of Scott's army, composed largely of Alabama militia and friendly Indians, would maneuver to the south and west of the main Creek concentration, driving them up the Chattahoochee, away from Florida, and into Scott's waiting arms.[21]

This column was to be commanded by Maj. Gen. Thomas Jesup, Scott's old comrade in arms from the War of 1812. Jesup was now serving as the army's quartermaster general, but the distinction between line and staff officers was not as rigid as it would later become, and it was not thought odd that he should be ordered to leave his desk and take to the field. Scott carefully explained his plan to Jesup and was confident that, unlike his unhappy Florida experience with Gaines, he had a fellow officer upon whose cooperation he could rely.

That confidence turned out to be misplaced. Rather than waiting until his commander's preparations were perfected, Jesup embarked on what Scott called a "private adventure" of his own. Prodded by his impatient Alabama militiamen and their flighty Indian allies (and perhaps by the urge to make the most of his reprieve from inglorious desk work), Jesup launched an unauthorized attack on the Creek camp. He succeeded in capturing Chief Neho Mico and hundreds of his warriors, though as Scott had feared, several hundred more managed to escape in the direction of Florida. The frontier, Jesup proudly reported, was now nearly tranquilized.[22]

Scott received this good news with bad grace. "I will not believe that you have declared your independence of my authority," he angrily told Jesup, and he ordered an immediate halt to the unwanted offensive. It seemed to be the story of Gaines all over again: a rival general keeping Scott in the dark while off pursuing personal glory at the expense of the carefully laid plan. Scott could understand such behavior from Gaines, but not from Jesup. "All of this is infinitely strange," he chided his old friend, "and was the last thing in the world that I expected from *you*."[23]

The Indian war now gave way to a war of words between the two generals. Both men were ill and very likely more irritable than usual. Scott had been bedridden with a debilitating fever, which he attributed to the premature shedding of his winter underwear. Jesup was suffering from an excruciating attack of "gravel," that is, the passing of kidney stones. When he received Scott's initial rebuke, he shot back with an insubordinate "apology" obviously designed to score points when reprinted in the public press: "I regret that my operations have met your disapprobation, but they were commenced and have been continued for the purpose of staying the tomahawk and scalping knife. . . . I acted in accordance with what I believed to be the spirit of your instructions; but even were my conduct in direct opposition to your instructions . . . , the altered circumstances of the country is, I should think, a full justification. I consider it so, for I have none of that courage that would enable me to remain inactive when women and children are daily falling beneath the blows of the savage." A few days later, still smarting, Jesup complained to Scott: "You have treated me with a degree of harshness which is cruel in the extreme."[24]

Scott angrily rejected Jesup's charges and countered with some of his own. "Who gave you authority to roam at pleasure, thro' the Creek nation?" he asked. And why commence an offensive "without giving me the slightest intimation . . . and of course without waiting for my approbation and cooperation"? Scott was particularly incensed by Jesup's transparent attempts to court cheap popularity by inserting "two or three topics which would furnish a good basis for a popular appeal . . . as if it were for future use against me."[25]

Yet even as he wrote, Scott's anger began to subside. A phrase in Jesup's letter, referring to their longstanding friendship caught his eye. This was the sort of appeal that could not help but stir the sentimental side of Scott's nature, and he softened his wrath. "General, in haste, I have not intended to say anything to injure you," he apologized. "I have cherished for you, for more than twenty-two years, a warm and sincere affection, which I would not part with on any consideration. . . . Throwing, for a moment, seniority aside, I ask it of your ancient connection with me to be more careful. . . . It will give me sincere delight to put down this war with you and give you all the fame which I know you are so capable of winning."[26]

This letter was written on June 19. Either it was delayed in transit or else it failed to move Jesup, for on June 20, that general took a step that irrevocably shattered the "ancient" friendship and even threatened to derail Scott's military career. He wrote a letter to his Washington friend and neighbor, Francis P. Blair.

No casual correspondent, Blair was a highly influential Jacksonian. As editor of the official administration organ, the *Washington Globe,* and as a prominent member of that informal group of advisors dubbed the "Kitchen Cabinet," he had direct access to Jackson's ear. Just in case, however, Blair's sense of discretion might prove too delicate to convey a private communication to its actually intended recipient, Jesup added this instruction: "Let the President see this letter."

Dear Sir [Jesup wrote]: We have the Florida scenes enacted over again. This war ought to have been ended a week ago. I commenced operations on the Alabama side, and have succeeded in tranquilizing the whole frontier. . . . I was in full march, with a force sufficient to have terminated the war in five days, when my progress was arrested by an order from General Scott. He has censured me in the most unmeasured and unwarrantable manner; and I shall be compelled to have the whole subject of this campaign investigated. There was force sufficient . . . to have put an end to this war . . . but it was thought necessary to adopt a splendid campaign upon paper, and make everything bend to it. To have waited the developments of that plan would have left nothing to defend—bloodshed and conflagration would have pervaded entire counties of Alabama. If not arrested by General Scott, I shall apply to be relieved; for I disapprove entirely the course he has thought proper to pursue, and believe that his delay has been destructive of the best interests of the country.[27]

While this fateful letter was slowly wending its way north, Scott and Jesup enjoyed an unexpected reconciliation. Jesup seemed to accept Scott's pacific overtures and agreed to "cheerfully go on to the close of the campaign, and offer you every support in my power." Delighted that their breach had been so amicably repaired, Scott responded by return courier. "I already feel the return of all my ancient affection for you. As to my confidence in your high honour, intelligence and capacity for war, nothing has ever shaken that."[28]

Now that they had made up and were ready to "act together with best feelings toward each other and in perfect harmony," Scott asked the War Department to remove his angry letters from the official files, "so that, as we are now again friends, no trace may remain on record that we ever had the slightest misunderstanding with each other." Putting this newfound harmony to the test of action, the two generals worked in concert to mop up the remaining pockets of Creek resistance. By June 24, Scott could report that the war was substantially ended.[29]

The struggle between the generals, however, continued, at least on Jesup's part. What Scott thought had been a peace treaty was to Jesup merely a tactical maneuver. While his trusting commander's guard was down, Jesup renewed his offensive on another front. On June 25, he wrote another accusatory letter, this time directly to Secretary of War Cass, bypassing the customary chain of command. "*My* operations," he boasted, "have broken the power of the hostile chiefs." He repeated his complaints against Scott and again asked that they be laid before the president.[30]

The request was unnecessary; Jesup's earlier communiqué to Blair had already done its work. When Blair, as instructed, took his letter to the president, Jackson exploded in anger. The impulsive chief executive did not bother with an investigation or even wait to hear Scott's defense. He was already convinced of Scott's "want of capacity to fight Indians" and had concluded that the general should have "put this puny Indian war down in ten days." Snatching the letter from Blair's hand, Jackson scrawled on its back: "Referred to the Secretary of War, that he forthwith order General Scott to this place, in order that an inquiry be had into the unaccountable delay in prosecuting the Creek war, and the failure of the campaign in Florida. Let General Jesup assume the command."[31]

The unsuspecting Scott had no hint of these high-level developments. Not even an enigmatic order from Macomb that he turn over his command to Jesup and immediately report to Washington disturbed his tranquility. Bidding a hasty farewell to his troops, he headed north in all innocence. Not until he reached Norfolk, Virginia, was he made aware of the rumors that were swirling about his name.[32] Without even stopping to see his family, Scott dashed straight for the capital to seek an explanation.

The government, however, had closed shop for the summer. The president was at the Hermitage, the vice president was off attending to his own presidential campaign, the secretary of war was either in New York or Detroit, and General Macomb was taking the waters at Saratoga Springs. When Scott burst into the War Department, he found only the chief clerk, Cary A. Harris, as acting secretary. That functionary obligingly retrieved Jesup's damning letter from the department files, and armed with a copy of the incriminating document, Scott searched for someone in authority on whom to vent his rage. Finding none, he repaired to his home, as an amused newspaper reported, "like a good citizen, to report to his wife."[33] Scott would have to await the court of inquiry for an opportunity to tell his side of the story.

That court convened at Frederick, Maryland, on November 7, 1836, conveniently after the presidential election so that "whig slangwangers" could not exploit it as a campaign issue. Its jurisdiction had now been expanded to include Gaines's conduct in Florida. That general, whose wife was dying, wanted the court to relocate closer to his home base, and he also objected to its composition, claiming that Macomb and the other judges were biased against him. All of his complaints were overruled. Scott had no such objections; he was looking forward to the hearing as an opportunity for vindication. Although so ill he could scarcely hold up his head for fifteen minutes at a time, Scott managed to churn out over a hundred pages of a "summary" defense statement, in which he conceded not a single mistake. "If I can be convicted of having committed one serious blunder," he melodramatically declared, "let me be shot."[34]

Such a fatal outcome was unlikely. There was little chance that a court composed of professional soldiers would vote to condemn one of its own. After a lengthy (and, to civilian spectators, boring) trial, the judges reached their expected conclusion and exonerated both of their colleagues. (Gaines, however, was censured for intemperately comparing Scott to Benedict Arnold.)

President Jackson was so dissatisfied with this verdict that he remanded the case to the court for further consideration.[35] The judges prudently waited until Jackson was out of office and then resubmitted the verdict to his successor, Martin Van Buren, who approved it without comment.

Scott thought that Jackson was engaged in a personal vendetta against him, but the president insisted that he was only concerned that "the shameful proceedings in Florida . . . had tarnished the reputation of our army." If that were the question, then the recall of Scott did not provide the answer. Not long after Jesup took over command in Florida, he too was heard to complain that the war was unwinnable, and he even began to express some belated sympathy for Scott's plight.[36] Jesup was merely one in a line of hapless generals who found themselves bogged down in the Florida swamps. The war against the Seminoles would drag on until August 1842 at a cost of sixteen hundred American lives (mostly from disease) and $30 million.

The failure in Florida was not merely a blow to Scott's reputation; it was a setback for the cause of military professionalism. "It is the first time that a scientific combined military movement has been attempted against Indians," Jackson ruefully noted, "and I hope, from the results, it will be the last."[37] This complaint was shared by many of his countrymen, who feared that an army based on Napoleonic models was not only expensive and aristocratic but also irrelevant to American conditions.

But those conditions, as Scott realized, were transitory. He had his gaze set on a future in which the nation would require not Indian fighters, but an army that could confront European-style opponents in conventional warfare. That future would arrive for him in due course. In the meantime, he would continue as a roving troubleshooter, pursuing what his Harvard friend Dr. Channing hailed as "the purer and more lasting glory of a pacificator."[38]

CHAPTER ELEVEN

PACIFICATOR

After his failure at waging war in the tropics of the South, Scott would be given an opportunity to redeem himself by bringing peace to the frozen frontier of the North. For the next four years, he would patrol the Canadian border in an effort to prevent yet another war between his country and Great Britain.

Trouble had been brewing in Canada for some time. In 1837, it erupted in a short-lived rebellion. Some of the rebels, most notably William Lyon Mackenzie, fled for safety across the border to the United States. They set up a provisional government, headquartered in a Buffalo tavern, and began to recruit American supporters. Drawing on the deep reservoir of anti-British sentiment dating back to the Revolution and on the economic desperation brought about by the depression that began in 1837, they established a network of self-styled "Patriots," Americans who were pledged to liberate Canada from English rule and secure free land for themselves in the process.

Estimates of Patriot strength ranged from 500 to 200,000. Scott favored the higher estimate, though the lower figure was far more realistic. Initially, he sympathized with their cause. "God grant them success!" he prayed. "My heart is with the oppressed of both Canadas."[1]

He was aware, however, that the Patriots' activities carried the risk of provoking war with Great Britain. But Scott was not totally averse to that prospect. Only "a good hot foreign war," he argued, could heal such "cankers of a long peace and a calm world" as anti-Masonry, peace societies, nullification, Mormonism, abolitionism, and kindred "moral distempers" that afflicted American society in those turbulent times. If the occasion for a just war should present itself, he declared, then "every *American* patriot ought to fall upon his knees and return thanks to Providence for the blessing."[2]

This belligerence was tempered by Scott's awareness of American military weakness. With an army of only seven thousand men, over half of whom were still bogged down in the Florida swamps, the United States was in no position to challenge Great Britain, no matter how therapeutic such a conflict might be. Scott estimated that at least thirty thousand additional regulars would have to be recruited, an expansion unlikely to be approved in the best of times and doubly difficult in the midst of a severe depression. In any event, to be dragged into war "wrong end foremost" by the Patriots was not what Scott had in mind.[3]

Instead, the general was ordered to the northern frontier to inspect its defenses and recommend "the minimum force" necessary for its protection. Scott balked at making such a reconnaissance during the winter season, snidely offering "to provide myself with snow-shoes" if the War Department insisted. The authorities relented and allowed him to prepare his report from the comfort of his Elizabeth Town home (where he had relocated Eastern Division headquarters on the pretext that New York City rents were too steep).[4]

Now that his old antagonist, Andrew Jackson, had at last retired to his Tennessee plantation, Scott was once again a welcome guest at the White House. Its new occupant, Martin Van Buren, was an old friend from wartime Albany days. Even though political differences had strained that friendship, the two remained on cordial terms, their relationship strengthened by the intermediation of the president's son, Maj. Abraham Van Buren, who had served as Scott's aide de camp during the Seminole War.[5]

On the evening of January 4, 1838, Scott was invited to a presidential dinner party along with other prominent Whigs, such as Henry Clay, and a sprinkling of Democrats. The dinner hour came and went but not the president, who, it was reported, was tied up in an emergency cabinet meeting. All the guests, Scott recollected, "were equally hungry, ignorant and merry." As they occupied themselves at the presidential sideboard, they jokingly speculated on the reasons for their host's delay. Finally, a grimfaced Van Buren appeared. Pulling Scott aside, he whispered: "Blood has been shed; you must go with all speed to the Niagara frontier."[6]

There, the Patriots had transferred their headquarters to Navy Island, on the Canadian side of the Niagara River, directly across from Scott's 1814 battlefield at Chippewa. About 150 recruits had drifted in, led by a self-proclaimed "general," the redundantly named Rensselaer Van Rensselaer, a dissolute and recklessly ambitious son of Col. Solomon Van Rensselaer, under whom Scott had refused to serve at Queenston.

With a force of over 2,500 Canadian militiamen waiting for his tiny army across the narrow strait, the young Van Rensselaer actually posed more of a nuisance than a genuine threat to the British. For provisions, he had chartered the steamboat *Caroline,* whose operations so irritated the Canadian authorities that they resolved to make an example of her. On the night of December 29, 1837, six small boats, led by Andrew Drew, a half-pay British naval officer, rowed silently to the unsuspecting *Caroline,* then moored near Schlosser, well within American waters. After a brief struggle, the ship was secured, set afire, and sent drifting toward Niagara Falls. In the melee, a stray shot killed a bystander, a Buffalo stage driver named Amos Durfee (who may or may not have been black). When the news reached Governor William Marcy at Albany, the death toll had been inflated to twelve, and by the time word reached Washington, casualties had been magnified by rumor to forty innocent American citizens slaughtered in their sleep.[7] This was the report that led an alarmed President Van Buren to dispatch Scott to Buffalo.

Even the unvarnished facts were serious enough. American territory had been attacked by a foreign power. This could be considered an act of war, and indeed, war fever gripped the northern frontier. A Rochester paper demanded that the *Caroline* outrage be avenged "not by simpering diplomacy—BUT BY BLOOD."[8] The cry was echoed by the three thousand mourners who filed past Durfee's martyred remains on display at Buffalo's public square.

Scott's assignment was to cool these warlike passions, maintain the peace, and preserve the national honor. Yet he was given such meager tools to accomplish his mission that the *New York Herald* derided his as a "fool's errand." Unable to call upon regulars, all of whom were occupied elsewhere, Scott was forced to rely on New York militiamen, the memory of whose unreliability at Queenston still rankled. Furthermore, due to a deficiency in the American neutrality legislation, he was not authorized to prevent a Patriot invasion of Canada, only to intervene after such invasion was actually underway.[9]

His only available weapons, Scott complained, were "rhetoric and diplomacy," which he employed at every opportunity. Drawing on the prestige he had won by defending the region against the British a quarter century earlier, he addressed meeting after meeting, always in full military regalia while he preached his message of peace. "Fellow citizens," he would melodramatically conclude, "I stand before you without troops and without arms, save the blade at my side. I am therefore, within your power. Some of you have known me in other scenes, and all of you know that I am ready to do what my country and what duty demands. I tell you, then, except it be over my body, you shall *not* pass this line—you shall *not* embark."[10]

Scott was aware how hollow these bold words actually were. Without reliable troops or full legal authority, his position, as he informed the War Department, was "most awkward." Unable to use force, he tried to thwart the Patriots with behind-the-scenes diplomacy. On January 14, 1838, he was informed by the

British commander (with whom Scott had kept in close touch) that the rebels were planning to embark on the steamer *Barcelona,* presumably with the intent of launching their invasion of Canada. Scott stepped in and simply hired it and all other available transports out from under Van Rensselaer's nose. "General Scott's *money-bags* were too heavy for us," the Patriot "general" complained. Mackenzie urged that the rebels should seize Scott's vessels by force and proceed with the invasion, but after a "violent altercation," his rash scheme was overruled.[11]

Having thwarted the Patriots, Scott now had to demonstrate that he had not caved in to the British. The withdrawal of the *Barcelona* from Navy Island provided an opportunity for a dramatic, though risky, piece of diplomatic theater. Despite Scott's assurances that the steamer carried neither Patriots nor contraband, the British stationed a line of armed schooners to intercept her. Scott, in turn, posted a battery on the American shore, ready to retaliate if the *Barcelona* met the fate of the *Caroline.* With Governor Marcy by his side, and with the gleam from his own buttons and braids clearly visible from the opposite shore, Scott was, in effect, daring the British to start a war over his dead body. "The cannon on either shore were pointed," he recalled, "the matches lighted and thousands stood in suspense."[12] The British held their fire as the *Barcelona* safely ran the gauntlet. The matches were extinguished, the crisis passed, and Scott succeeded in conveying the impression that he had compelled the haughty English to back down.

It now remained to persuade the Patriots to disperse. Scott took Van Rensselaer aside and patiently explained that his enterprise, "in a military point of view, was rash and hopeless," that his transports were inadequate, his troops undisciplined, his position poorly chosen, and his prospects of success dim. Van Rensselaer attentively absorbed this lecture and returned to the United States, where he was promptly arrested and just as promptly released on bail.[13]

Scott had hoped that would be the end of the matter, but Van Rensselaer merely transferred his operations elsewhere. "The spirit of our boys is good," the Patriot leader assured Mackenzie. If no boats were available in Buffalo, they would "foot it," if necessary, to Detroit or anyplace on Lake Erie where they could obtain transport.[14] Everywhere they went, however, the rebels were frustrated by the vigilance of Scott's subordinates, Brig. Gen. Hugh Brady and Col. William Worth.

By the end of January, Scott could report that the entire border, from Lake Ontario to Lake Huron, had been tranquilized, and he headed back to Washington, bearing the commendation of the president for a job well done. On February 17, he reached New York City. When he checked into the Astor Hotel, he was handed a packet of mail, including an order from Secretary of War Poinsett directing him to return to the Canadian frontier to deal with a fresh outbreak of violence. Wasting no time, he left the Astor at precisely seven the next morning. With his black body servant, David, and his young aide, Lt. Erasmus Darwin Keyes, he went dashing through the snow in a four-horse covered sleigh. Nineteen hours later, at two in the morning, the trio pulled into West Point for their first stop.[15]

They would spend fifty-four nights sleeping while sitting up in sleigh or stagecoach. An unusually severe cold spell gripped the North, dropping the thermometer to ten or more degrees below zero. "My young blood was nearly congealed," Keyes vividly recalled, but the general "showed no signs of suffering or impatience," nor was he heard to complain. As they "trotted away in the direction of the North Pole," Keyes thought his commander "had the look of a tawny old lion slumbering quietly."[16]

One morning, around sunrise, Keyes awoke to find Scott regarding him with compassion. "My face was probably sorrowful to behold at that moment," he recalled, "for the general took out from his pocket a handful of parched corn and dropped five or six grains into my hand, one after another, keeping his eyes fixed on mine with an expression of affection like that of a mother watching her suffering child." The memory of this small act of kindness from a man the world regarded only as pompous and vain lingered fondly in Keyes's heart, even after the two had, many years later, angrily broken off relations.[17]

Dashing from Detroit to Vermont and back again, Scott "posted himself nowhere, but was by turns rapidly everywhere," putting out brush fires along an explosive eight-hundred-mile border. In the East, a mob of unruly Vermonters pelted British officers with snowballs. Along the Great Lakes, the Patriots planned a three-pronged invasion of Canada to coincide with Washington's Birthday. As might have been expected from their past performance, all three invasions fizzled out. Nonetheless, Scott and his tiny entourage were kept hopping as he served writs, tracked down Patriot fugitives, strengthened defenses, and at every opportunity, "by short and rapid addresses . . . succeeded in rallying all the friends of law and order who had been too long held in silent awe of the lawless band."[18]

All this peacemaking took its toll on Scott's health. By mid-March, he was so prostrated with exhaustion and severe pain from passing "sand" from his kidneys that he took to his bed. For the time being, the diplomatic crises seemed to be over. With the melting of Lake Erie's icepack under the spring sun, there was little chance that "the dispirited wrecks"[19] of the Patriot band could launch another attack until winter. His mission accomplished, Scott was ready to return home.

The government, however, had other plans. In April 1838, Scott was ordered south to supervise the forced removal of the Cherokee Indians to their new home beyond the Mississippi River, in what is now Oklahoma.[20]

Scott addressing the Cherokees. Mansfield, *The Life and Military Services of Lieut.-General Winfield Scott,* 310.

Of all the eastern tribes, the Cherokees were the most thoroughly acculturated, having adopted agriculture, representative government, a written language, Negro slavery, and other aspects of civilization. Even so, white settlers, especially in Georgia, coveted their lands and their newly discovered gold fields. Neither the Supreme Court nor longstanding treaty obligations were able to protect the Cherokees against the greed of the Georgians and the hostility of Andrew Jackson. A fraudulent treaty was cooked up that was agreed to by an unrepresentative sliver of the Cherokee Nation and that imposed removal upon the unwilling majority of the tribe.

Scott sympathized with the Cherokees' plight but, as a good soldier, was bound to do his duty, though he was determined to perform the distasteful task in a humane manner. "Every possible kindness," he ordered, must be shown by the troops. "And if, in the ranks, a despicable individual should be found capable of inflicting a wanton injury or insult on any Cherokee man, woman or child, it is hereby made the special duty of the nearest good officer or man . . . to seize and consign the guilty wretch to the severest penalty of the laws."[21]

He assured an assembly of Indian chieftains that his soldiers were "as kind hearted as brave, and the desire of every one of us is to execute our painful duty in mercy." Resistance, he warned, would not only be futile but could also provoke a war of extermination. "I am an old warrior, and have been present at many a scene of slaughter, but spare me," he begged, "the horror of witnessing the destruction of the Cherokees." The Indians, it was observed, received this plea "with a dead silence."[22]

They had good reason to be apprehensive. Scott may have been able to impose his "system of kindness" upon the regular troops, but the Georgia militiamen had longstanding scores to settle with their now helpless Cherokee rivals. With malicious glee, they rounded up the Indians, "with whooping and hallowing like cattle." Families were driven from their homes on a moment's notice, leaving behind livestock and treasured possessions to be seized by looters before the owners had even trudged out of sight. In the confusion, children were often separated from their parents, and the sick and elderly were herded to the detention camps in Tennessee at a merciless pace. "I fought through the civil war and have seen men shot to pieces and slaughtered by the thousands," a Georgia officer later testified, "but the Cherokee removal was the cruelest work I ever knew."[23]

Scott closed his eyes to these atrocities. Exercising his considerable capacity for self-deception, he persuaded himself that the Georgians had "distinguished themselves by their humanity and tenderness." He blamed the Cherokees for bringing their misery upon themselves by not heeding his warnings to prepare in advance for the evacuation.[24]

Once the seventeen thousand Indians had been herded into their temporary detention camps in Tennessee and were under Scott's direct supervision, their conditions improved. Three well-chosen campsites were laid out, the largest measuring over twelve by four miles. They had ample shade and firewood, plentiful springs and running water, and were well supplied with food and medicine. By Scott's orders, vaccination was introduced and liquor banned. Justifiably proud of his humanitarian exertions, the general boasted that "an almost universal cheerfulness" now prevailed among the Indians.[25] From his rosy description, one might think that the Cherokees were embarking on the Trail of Smiles. Living conditions in the camps, however, steadily deteriorated in the summer heat. At the same time, a severe drought left the navigable rivers too low for the Indians to be removed on schedule.

The private contractors who had hoped to conduct the evacuation grumbled at the delay, and they complained even more loudly when Scott decided to place the deportation arrangements in the hands of the Indians themselves. For some reason, this sensible decision infuriated Andrew Jackson. The ever suspicious former president fumed that it was part of a plot by Scott, "in league with Clay & Co. to bring disgrace on the administration," but actually, it saved the government substantial expense as well as eased the task of removal.[26]

The worst, however, was yet to come. Perhaps as many as four thousand Cherokees, one quarter of their nation, would perish during the eight-hundred-mile trek west, earning it the lasting name the Trail of Tears. Scott, however, was spared having to witness this tragic denouement: he was called away in October for yet another urgent mission.

With his part in the sad business of Cherokee removal almost completed, Scott had looked forward to a long-overdue rest, "for God knows, I have never been more overworked than in this service." Rest, however, would once again be denied him. Scott and his Indian charges had gotten no farther than Nashville when he was overtaken by dispatches from the War Department ordering him back to the Canadian border for the third time in less than a year.[27]

With the onset of frost, the Patriots had resumed their activity, hoping to draw the United States into a war with Great Britain. By now, familiarity had bred in Scott a contempt for these "miscreants." He no longer called down God's blessing on their cause but denounced those "mad and wicked people" at every opportunity, "in bar-rooms, whilst changing horses and warming myself, in village crowds and public meetings."[28] These exhortations, combined with the sobering spectacle of another botched Patriot invasion near Windsor, effectively dampened public ardor for further Canadian adventures. By February 1839, the border seemed sufficiently calm for Scott to consider a return to his routine duties, but a fresh crisis erupted that posed an even more serious threat to the peace.

The boundary between Maine and Canada had never been precisely demarcated. Negotiators for the 1783 Treaty of Paris had relied on inaccurate maps and flawed assumptions, leaving seven and a half million acres of disputed territory claimed by both New Brunswick and Maine. The region was so remote and sparsely settled, however, that few concerns were raised over its clouded title until the late 1830s. Canadian unrest in those years convinced British authorities of the military necessity of a road linking Upper and Lower Canada, and surveyors were sent into the disputed territory. At about the same time, American loggers began to drift into the Aroostook Valley, lured by its rich stands of pine trees.

Inevitably, the two groups clashed. Officials of both sides were arrested for trespass, and troops were called up to protect each nation's rights and honor. The standoff was tense. Only a small spark was needed to set these pine forests ablaze with war. On the American side of the border, there were many who would welcome such a conflict. Maine militiamen sang as they marched north:

> Britannia shall not rule the Maine,
> Nor shall she rule the water;
> They've sung that song full long enough,
> Much longer than they oughter.[29]

More ominously, a Maine legislator thundered that he would "rather see our State deluged in blood, and every field bleached with the bones of our citizens, than that we should re-trace our footsteps and submit to British arrogance!" "How long are we thus to be trampled on," asked Maine's governor, John Fairfield, "our rights and claims derided; our power contemned and the State degraded?" He requested that the legislature authorize an additional ten thousand militiamen.[30]

While Maine politicians angrily beat the drums for war, knowledgeable officers of the regular army shuddered at the prospect. With a rumored 25,000 British troops massed on a border protected by only 1,000 U.S. regulars, and with American arsenals depleted by the pilferage of the Patriots, "disgrace awaits us," warned Colonel Worth, in something close to hysteria. "God knows what is to come," he told Scott, "but . . . I cannot resist the apprehension that we are fast verging towards a contest, to meet which everything around us denotes the absence of preparation. In the minds eye one can already see the national honor for a time stricken in the dust."[31]

Scott was so alarmed that he dashed back to Washington for instructions in such haste that, as he complained, he did not allow himself to assume "a recumbent position" for eighty hours. He found the capital abuzz with talk of war. Even the normally levelheaded John Quincy Adams, now a congressman, seemed to regard a war with Great Britain as not only inevitable but perhaps even desirable.[32] President Van Buren, however, knew that the nation could neither afford nor support such a war. He sought a diplomatic solution, but until one could be negotiated, he needed Scott's help in maintaining calm along the troubled border.

The general did not underestimate the difficulties before him. "Mr. President," he said, "if you want *war*, I need only look on in silence. The Maine people will make it for you fast and hot enough . . . but if peace be your wish, I can give no assurance of success." "Peace with honor," was Van Buren's reply, and to that end, Secretary of State John Forsyth reached an agreement with British envoy Henry S. Fox. It provided that Maine would promise to withdraw all its armed forces from the disputed territory; in return, Great Britain pledged only that it would not use force to expel them.[33]

Selling this lopsided bargain to bellicose New Englanders would not be an easy task, especially since Scott's instructions from the War Department explicitly prohibited the use of force.[34] Scott had to play to three different audiences, and with each, he adopted a different role.

His first task was to calm the excited populace, who mistakenly assumed that he had come to lead them against the British intruders. To them, he played the part of the old warrior, continually referring to his War of 1812 exploits and giving hearty greetings to former comrades in arms. He was careful never to utter the word "peace" in public but, instead, assured his audiences, "should war come, he should be glad to be found shoulder to shoulder—breast to breast—with such soldiers."[35]

This sort of bombast might do for the general public, but the Maine legislators would be harder to satisfy. When he arrived in Augusta, Scott discovered that only a handful of lawmakers were willing to support the Fox-Forsyth memorandum. Their reluctance was based on political considerations. Whigs and Democrats alike feared to support compromise, lest the other party accuse them of betraying the state. To appease them, Scott doffed his uniform and played the role of politician, appealing to Democrats as an emissary of President Van Buren and to Whigs as one of their own. At a series of bipartisan banquets, he brought both sides together in an atmosphere of conviviality, which helped melt away suspicions. "A feast is a great peacemaker," Scott concluded, "worth more than all the usual arts of diplomacy."[36] After a few weeks of this hospitality, most Maine politicians were induced to back off from their bellicose stance and embrace a policy of conciliation.

Now all that was needed was to persuade British authorities not to rock the boat. By a happy chance, the lieutenant governor of New Brunswick, Maj. Gen. Sir John Harvey, was the same officer whose personal effects Scott had captured at York in 1813 and so chivalrously returned. The two had maintained a correspondence over the years, most recently by exchanging condolences on the deaths of their sons. Now their paths crossed again on the road to peace. "How happy may we esteem ourselves," Scott told his one-time foe, "if a personal friendship commenced in the field and in opposite ranks, can become, in any degree, conducive to the preservation of peace."[37]

Building on that friendship, Scott was able to serve as a trusted intermediary between Governors Fairfield and Harvey, assuring them that Maine would withdraw its troops voluntarily and that England would not take advantage of that concession. No one in authority had really wanted war, but neither side trusted the other. The Democrats feared that the Whigs would exploit any concessions as weakness; the British feared the rashness of the Americans; and the Americans doubted the good faith of the British. By winning the confidence of all parties, Scott was able to avoid a violent collision and buy time for the diplomats to do their work. Three years later, the Webster-Ashburton Treaty would provide for a comprehensive settlement of all outstanding differences between the two nations, including a compromise adjustment of the Maine–New Brunswick boundary.

Scott was immensely proud of his peacemaking efforts, but he looked beyond the settlement of the immediate crisis to a new era in Anglo-American relations. Donning the mantle of prophecy, he peered into the future to foresee not merely peace between the two nations but the creation of a special relationship that would, in the next century, unite them in the common defense of freedom throughout the world. As he told Harvey:

> I see no reason to apprehend another cause of serious misunderstanding between the two portions of the great Anglo-Saxon race for centuries to come. The ties of common blood, language, civil liberty, laws, customs, manners, interests must, in a reasonable period—that is, as soon as we can forget past wars, and they are almost forgotten—work out a strong compact of reciprocal feelings (far more binding than written engagements) which the other nations of the world would be wholly unable to dissolve or to resist. Such compact, altho' the two portions of the race are, and probably ever will remain, under separate governments and of different forms, is necessary to both—in war, as in peace; for who shall say what hostile combinations, in the next 100, 70 or even 30 years may not take place among the other nations to require the united strength of England and America for the safety of their common principles and interests?[38]

Scott's prophecy was almost exactly on target. World Wars I and II, which saw the United States and Great Britain fighting side by side, would come almost exactly on the years he had predicted and for the reasons he had foreseen.

CHAPTER TWELVE

POLITICIAN

The Great Pacificator returned to Washington in March 1839 amid universal plaudits. "Again through the pacific and civil services of this distinguished man," hailed an enthusiastic New York newspaper, "great and near danger of war has been averted from these United States." Secretary of War Joel Poinsett officially commended his accomplishments, and President Martin Van Buren hosted a White House dinner at which Scott was the guest of honor. (Sir John Harvey, in contrast, was recalled from his post for not standing up firmly enough to the Americans.) Scott's New York Whig friend Philip Hone rejoiced that the general "is now 'the observed of all observers'" and, looking forward to the next year's presidential election, wondered "who knows what he may be hereafter?"[1]

Scott had often asked himself the same question, but in public, he was careful to disavow any political ambitions. Aware that Americans of his day regarded the presidency as the one office that was supposed to seek the man, he repeatedly insisted that he was no politician, "that I was absolutely indifferent whether I ever reached the office of President . . . and that there were already presidential candidates enough before the public without the addition of my name." Scott's pose "is a hard one for him to play," reported an amused political observer, "but he does it with more discretion than some would have expected of him, and only overacts sometimes." To allay any suspicions the Van Buren administration might have as to his loyalty, Scott assured the secretary of war that he had never "committed the indecency of blending party feelings with public duty," never attended a political meeting and had scarcely ever voted, never supported any political candidate (except for Calhoun), nor ever failed to show proper respect for a president (except for Jackson).[2]

Despite these protestations, a Scott-for-president boomlet emerged, emanating largely from those counties in upstate New York where the memory of his military and diplomatic triumphs burned most brightly. In Rochester, a public meeting called for his nomination, and in Buffalo, Congressman Millard Fillmore hitched his wagon to Scott's star. "He has gained infinitely upon the affections and confidence of the thinking portion of the community," Fillmore reported to Thurlow Weed. If New York Whigs could unite behind Scott, Fillmore promised, "we will make the welkin ring with his name." Otherwise, he warned, the party was doomed to "drift on the *Clay Banks* where she will founder forever."[3]

To another New York Whig, a Scott candidacy presented an opportunity to outdo the Jacksonian Democrats at their own game by running a certified military hero of their own. Envisioning the sort of hoopla that would characterize the forthcoming Log Cabin campaign, he predicted that "Scott's name will bring out the hurra boys. . . . The General's lips must be hermetically sealed, and our shouts and hurras must be long and loud."[4]

Other Whig presidential aspirants looked on the Scott movement with alarm. The aged Indian fighter William Henry Harrison was "mortified" at the prospect that the party might prefer an upstart over him. "Can those who urge Genl. Scott," he asked, "recollect that I was at the head of an Army . . . whilst he was yet a subaltern?" Nor could party leader and perpetual presidential candidate Henry Clay have been reassured by Scott's promise of support when, in the next breath, Scott volunteered to lead "the forlorn hope" if Clay's campaign should falter.[5]

To New York Whigs, such a prospect seemed likely. Fearing that the Kentuckian had outworn his welcome with the voters, they hoped to avoid (as Fillmore put it) becoming *"stuck in the Clay"* by promoting a more available candidate, such as Scott. The movement was engineered by the formidable political team of Governor William Seward and Albany editor Thurlow Weed. Scott trustingly placed his fortunes in their hands, but others, aware of the Albany duo's reputation for deviousness and duplicity, suspected that he was only being used as a stalking horse to be discarded for Harrison at the proper moment.[6] This cynical interpretation was adopted by many subsequent historians, but those who have most closely scrutinized the matter have concluded that New York Whig support for Scott was genuine, though it may have been more expedient than sincere.[7]

It was with some relief that Scott turned from these tangled political maneuverings to the more familiar maneuvers of a military kind. Since the War of 1812, the U. S. Army had not only shrunk but also been dispersed. With many companies on detached service and others manning tiny, isolated frontier garrisons, few soldiers, or even officers, had experience in regimental, much less battalion, exercises and drill. Secretary of War Poinsett hoped to remedy this deficiency by bringing these scattered army units together for a summertime school of instruction, similar to Scott's 1814 training camp at Flint Hill.

Although reluctant to strip the troubled northern frontier of troops, Scott ordered his aide, Lt. Joseph Johnston, to search for a suitable campsite. His instructions revealed that Scott had not forgotten the lessons of Terre aux Boeufs. Johnston was to look for "dry ground and freedom from malaria and musquitoes; good water; partial shade, if practicable, for the tents," as well as access to transportation and sufficient open ground for at least three regiments to practice the evolution of the line and the school of the battalion.[8]

A location for the grand encampment was found at the Trenton Race Course, conveniently close to Scott's New Jersey home, but the general himself missed most of it. He was off on another troubleshooting mission, this time to Wisconsin, to persuade the Winnebago Indians to relocate west of the Mississippi. The Winnebagos, however, stubbornly resisted being uprooted, and as a Wisconsin paper wryly observed, "The 'Great Pacificator' has been less successful than usual this time."[9]

Scott returned east to supervise the encampment's final review. To a sympathizer (who was also prominent in promoting his presidential prospects), the general presented an imposing spectacle "in full uniform, and mounted on a steed which, though not less than sixteen hands high, seems diminutive beneath its lofty rider." A more critical spectator was less impressed. Indulging in the frontier style of exaggerated humor so popular in the Age of Jackson, he pretended to be awestruck at the sight of "the Pacificator of the East! of the West, of the North, and of the South . . . the hero of Florida, the subduer of Black Hawk, the remover of the Indians, the curber of the Canadian patriots— dressed in the full *costume d'armee* of a major general! . . . cocked hat, loop, cockade, tassels, yellow swans' feathers, drooping black silk stockings, shirt, brimstone colored vest, silk undershirt, osnaburgh suspenders, blue-and-brimstone coat, epaulets, buttons, trowsers, boots, gloves, sky-blue sash, sword knot, belt, plate, spurs, stockings, garters, drawers and pocket handkerchief!"[10]

Both the adulation and the mockery were signs that the political season was at hand and that Scott was regarded as a serious contender by friend and foe alike. Although he continued to insist that he supported Clay and was "personally wholly uninterested" in the nomination, an aide noted that Scott followed the political scene "with the eagerness of a falcon."[11]

The Whig National Convention assembled in Harrisburg, Pennsylvania, on December 4, 1839.[12] Unlike the raucous, mammoth political gatherings of later years that would attract tens of thousands of delegates, spectators, and reporters, this modest, quiet meeting fit easily into a local Lutheran church. It was the first such convention of the Whig party, and the ground rules had not yet been firmly established. The manner of selecting delegates was haphazard: some were chosen by state convention, others seem to have been self-appointed; four states sent no delegates at all, while Pennsylvania chose two contending sets.

An early straw vote showed Clay in the lead with 103 votes, mainly from slaveholding states that were unlikely to go Whig in the general election. Harrison pressed him hard with 91, and Scott trailed the field with 57, all from New York, New Jersey, and Vermont.[13] At this point, the Harrison forces, masterminded by Pennsylvania's wily Thaddeus Stevens, staged a procedural coup. They pushed through a set of rules providing that further balloting would be held behind closed doors under the unit rule. This was designed to nullify the scattered minority support for Clay found in various Northern states.

By the third day, Scott had edged up to 68 votes with the addition of Connecticut and Michigan, while Clay had slipped to 95. Virginia, whose delegation was led by Scott's old friend Benjamin Watkins Leigh, now had a chance to break the deadlock by a timely switch from Clay to its second choice, Scott. Leigh, a political naif, felt honor bound to stand by Clay a bit longer, and so the moment was lost. The New Yorkers, seeing no further movement to Scott, switched to Harrison, beginning that general stampede that resulted in the nomination of a presidential candidate whom Scott dismissed as being "insignificant and weak in person and mind." To compound the damage, Leigh was also responsible for the selection of a renegade Democrat, John Tyler, as running mate, a man Scott regarded as "utterly unfit" for high public office.[14]

While the convention was deliberating in Harrisburg, Clay and Scott were in New York, awaiting news of the result. Scott passed the time by playing endless games of whist, Clay by drinking heavily. When he learned of the convention's disappointing result, Clay flew into a monumental fit of rage and self-pity. According to the bearers of the bad tidings, "Such an exhibition we never witnessed before, and we pray never again to witness such an ebullition of passion, such a storm of desperation and curses." Pacing the floor and stamping his feet, Clay screamed: "My friends are not worth the powder and shot it would take to kill them! . . . I am the most unfortunate man in the history of parties; always run by my friends when sure to be defeated, and now betrayed for a nomination when I, or any one, would be sure of an election."[15]

He staggered over to Scott's card table, denouncing him fiercely and pummeling him on the back. Scott put down his cards and calmly said: "Senator Clay, I beg you not to lay your hand so heavily on that shoulder. It is the shoulder wounded at Lundy's Lane." Still raging, Clay was led away by Senators George Evans of Maine and John J. Crittenden of Kentucky. When Crittenden returned, Scott formally requested, "please do me the honor and favor" of delivering a note to Clay in the morning. Knowing that this was the language of a challenge, Crittenden exclaimed: "Scott, I am horror stricken. The code of honor says 'a blow can only be wiped out by blood'" "I care nothing for the code," Scott replied, "but I must have an apology from Mr. Clay." The next day, sober and contrite, Clay made the required apology.[16] The affair passed without further damage, and the nation was spared the services of two whose contributions would prove so valuable in the coming years.

Scott watched the rest of the political campaign of 1840 from the sidelines. While the country was going wild with log cabin fever in the most exciting presidential canvass yet seen, he went about his routine business. Yet despite the carefully feigned indifference with which he concealed his disappointment, he had been badly bitten by the presidential bug and would persistently seek the office for as long as the Whig party existed.

Had Scott been the nominee in 1840, he would probably have been elected, as any Whig would likely have been, given the voters' unhappiness with the economic hard times, which they blamed on Van Buren and the Democrats. Whether he would have been a successful president is impossible to know, but at least he would have served out his full term (unlike Harrison), and his party and country would have been spared the turmoil of Tyler's unhappy tenure. But, had Scott left the army for the White House, he would not have been available for the Mexican War, where his military leadership would turn out to be indispensable.[17]

On March 4, 1841, Scott attended his rival's inauguration. The capital was so crowded with Whig well-wishers and office seekers that the general had to share a room with a butcher, whose snores kept him awake much of the night. During the inaugural address, the longest on record and filled with interminable classical allusions, Scott found himself drifting off into slumber. By evening, he was sufficiently refreshed to attend the inaugural ball, resplendent in full-dress uniform with bright yellow plumes.[18]

Four weeks later, Scott had the melancholy duty of presiding over the military honors at President Harrison's funeral. Now the hasty choice of John Tyler as vice president came back to haunt the Whigs, as they saw the White House slip from their grasp and into the hands of a doctrinaire states rights Democrat, for whom Scott had little respect.

Less than three months later, there was yet another high-level state funeral. Alexander Macomb, commanding general of the U. S. Army, died on June 25, 1841. Wasting no time with mourning, Scott instantly asserted his claim to succeed him. "I take it for granted," he peremptorily told the new secretary of war, John Bell, "that my name will be sent, in a day or two, to the Senate to fill the vacancy." Scott added that he had "not the time, or the feeling just now, to give the curious history of the injustice done me by President

Adams," but he did just that, rehearsing at length his ancient grievances against Macomb, apparently unable to resist getting in the last word, even against a dead man.[19]

Secretary Bell had somehow gotten the idea that Scott was too interested in pursuing the presidency to be bothered with the responsibilities of commanding general.[20] But Scott quickly set him straight. Neither Bell nor President Tyler had the stomach to refight the battle that had caused John Quincy Adams so much anguish. They docilely submitted Scott's name to the Senate, where it was speedily confirmed.

On July 5, 1841, Major General (no longer by brevet) Winfield Scott, fifty-five years old and thirty-three years a soldier, at last assumed the command of that army to which he had devoted his life.

CHAPTER THIRTEEN

COMMANDER

The office of commanding general, which Scott assumed in July 1841, was an anomaly. Its authority was undefined by statute, and its functions had been shaped more by accidents of personality and circumstance than by conscious design. Its creation had been something of an afterthought, and its utility was often questioned by a skeptical Congress.[1]

It came about as a byproduct of the Army Reduction Act of 1821. With only one major general retained on the army register, that officer became, willy-nilly, the general in chief, under the operation of what then-senator William Henry Harrison called "the principle to which all yield assent, that superior knowledge is always found united with superior rank."[2] The commanding general, Harrison explained, should be to the army what a captain is to a ship or a colonel to a regiment: responsible for "everything relating to its instruction, subordination, equipment, supplies, and health." This imposed upon that officer a daunting list of duties. "He is," enumerated Harrison:

> the medium of communication between the government and the army. . . . To him are made the returns and reports of the Generals commanding Departments. . . . He receives and decides upon the confidential reports of the Inspectors General. . . . He has the general superintendence of the administration of justice. . . . The recruiting service, in all its details, is under his immediate superintendence; so is the school of practice for the artillery. It is his duty to make himself intimately acquainted with the characteristic features of the country, particularly upon the frontiers; its military positions and the best means of defending them, and of operating against an invading army.[3]

Scott conducted all this business in two overcrowded rooms at the War Department with the help of only one underpaid civilian clerk, though he could also draw on the services of military aides and secretaries. Much of the burden of paperwork was thrown on the shoulders of the general himself, but Scott's diligent work habits were up to the challenge. According to an admiring aide, "he would allow himself neither rest nor pleasure night or day, in sickness or in health," until his desk was cleared.[4]

Broad though his powers may have seemed, the commanding general's authority was far from absolute. It was limited, to a degree, by his undefined relationship to the staff bureaus, on the one hand, and to the secretary of war, on the other.

The seven staff departments—Quartermaster, Subsistence, Medical, Ordnance, Pay, Engineers, and Topographical Engineers—predated the commanding general's office. They had never been placed under his authority but continued to report directly to the secretary of war. The politician who usually occupied that post, however, seldom had either the inclination or the specialized knowledge to exercise effective supervision over the bureau chiefs. "The consequence is that they are without any control," complained Maj. Gen. Alexander Macomb, "and in a word act so independent that one would suppose they did not belong to the same service."[5]

Bureau chiefs ran their departments as little fiefdoms, transferring officers and granting furloughs without bothering to notify the commanding general. Scott insisted that "if the Command of the Army is given to me in reality and not simply in name," such independence would have to be curbed, but neither he, nor Macomb, nor various secretaries of war were able to rein in the bureaus. In 1852, Scott would offer a plan to rotate officers of the line into the staff departments and vice versa. As with all such proposals to reduce the independence of the bureaus, it was rejected by Congress after intense lobbying by the bureau chiefs. Ironically, Scott, the champion of professional autonomy, found himself thwarted by the staff departments' claim to an even more highly specialized professional expertise. Not until 1903 would the staff and line finally be integrated into a general staff capable of planning and coordinating military operations with unity, harmony, and efficiency, far too late, of course, to be of help to Scott.[6]

The relationship of the secretary of war to the commanding general was another potential source of difficulty. In theory, the secretary was the direct representative of the president and, as such, the embodiment of the principle of civilian control over military affairs. In practice, the secretary was usually too overworked and overextended to exert much control over the military bureaucracy. Although his duties also included supervision of Indian affairs, he was not even provided with an assistant secretary. It was easier for him to follow the path of least resistance and just let things drift. Furthermore, most secretaries came and went too rapidly to secure a firm grip on their department. From 1821 to 1861, there were only three commanding generals; in the year 1841 alone, there were four secretaries of war.

Scott argued the dubious proposition that the secretary had no statutory or constitutional authority to issue orders other than through the commanding general.[7] A determined secretary with the backing of his president, however, could always impose his will on the army. John C. Calhoun had been such a secretary, but the commanding general during his tenure, Jacob Brown, had been too sickly and too often absent from Washington to offer much opposition. His successor, Alexander Macomb, was made of sterner stuff, but he also enjoyed the advantage of dealing with secretaries who were either weak or distracted. If, however, a strong-willed general should be paired with an ambitious secretary of war, then sparks would fly, as Scott would later discover to his sorrow.

Until then, Scott would have free rein to shape the army to his own vision. That vision was surprisingly narrow, considering how long and how anxiously he had yearned for the position. As commanding general, Scott would make few far-reaching changes in the army's structure, contenting himself for the next twenty years with supervising its day-to-day operations and making minor reforms. There was really little need for him to do more, for the army was already so much his own creation. In addition to the monumental *Military Institutes* of 1821, Scott had also written the standard handbook of infantry tactics (a three-volume edition of which had appeared as recently as 1835) and had a hand in the compilation of similar manuals for the artillery and cavalry.[8]

His first major change had the color of an administrative reform, but it could also be interpreted as an act of spite against an old foe. Since 1815, the army had been administratively divided into two large geographic districts, each headed by a major general who, in turn, commanded a number of regional brigadiers. However tidy this arrangement might have seemed on an organizational chart, in practice, it meant that correspondence and orders between the War Department and the regional departments followed a path that was "zig-zag, uncertain and constantly in arrears."[9] Communications with Florida, for example, had to be routed through Troy, New York, the headquarters of General Wool, Scott's successor as commander of the Eastern Department.

By General Orders No. 40, issued on July 12, 1842, Scott abolished the Eastern and Western Divisions, leaving nine smaller departments, each directly responsible to the commanding general's office. Secretary of War John Spencer defended this arrangement in the name of efficiency, but friends of General Gaines thought they smelled a rat.[10] Under Scott's plan of organization, Gaines's position as commander of the Western Division would be abolished, and the general himself degraded in both rank and salary.

Although Scott had urged the elimination of the "absurd and frequently impractical" system of geographic divisions as early as 1817, well before the feud with Gaines had become so bitter, the friends of the Tennessee general were outraged at what they regarded as this latest expression of a vendetta against their hero. At a protest meeting in Memphis, they charged that Scott was motivated only by "selfish ambition, and the feelings of personal jealousy" toward a rival. Gaines himself angrily accused Scott of acting as "*a secret enemy,* seeking to traduce the character of his long known senior and superior officer by the most atrocious machinations." In retaliation for Scott's "prostitution of his position to the basest means for injuring his brother in arms," Gaines's friends in Congress attempted (unsuccessfully) to eliminate the office of commanding general and reduce Scott's pay.[11]

Scott struck back at that "superannuated old martinet," whose slovenly administration, unprofessional attitude, and "inveterate habit of insubordination" had so bedeviled him over the years. Gaines, he now concluded, was no longer in his right mind. His increasingly erratic behavior lent some credibility to this diagnosis. Gaines had, for example, recently hit upon a scheme for national defense that was so supersecret it could not be entrusted to the mails. Disregarding an explicit command from the secretary of war, he dashed to Washington to explain it in person. He had also somehow acquired the delusion that Scott, in his vanity, affixed two additional stars to his uniform and demanded two extra guns in salute. Under normal circumstances, Scott explained, he would have hauled the old general before a court-martial, but "honour and humanity forbid that I should prefer charges against an officer whom I solemnly believe to be mentally deranged."[12]

Despite his protestations of sympathy, Scott could not help but derive a measure of satisfaction from Gaines's humiliation. Far more satisfying, however, were the efforts he was able to make on behalf of the army's often abused and neglected enlisted men.

The U. S. Army was still a place where brutal and ingenious punishments were common, where officers treated their men with contempt and required them to perform menial and degrading tasks. Pay was low (seven dollars a month for privates), and the desertion rate was high (as much as 15–20 percent of the army's authorized strength annually). A social chasm separated the mostly American-born, well-educated officer class from the men under their command, over half of whom were foreigners and many of the rest Americans "who have led dissipated lives and incapacitated themselves for any respectable business."[13]

Faced with these tough customers, many officers, especially young subalterns insecure in their new authority, tended to resort to force. For alleged acts of insubordination, soldiers were beaten with swords, confined in damp cells, branded, tied to trees, and in extreme cases, shot to death on the spot.

The most common punishment was flogging. Although curtailed briefly during the War of 1812, whippings were resumed in 1832, with fifty lashes being the legal limit, though more were often applied. General Gaines spoke for many officers when he hailed the whipping post as a "salutary" means of enforcing discipline, but Scott regarded the practice as "perfectly intolerable." As early as 1821, he had vowed to suppress it, "or forfeit my commission."[14] As commanding general, he would conduct a twenty-year crusade against arbitrary and excessive punishments, culminating in 1861 with the abolition of flogging in the army, over ten years after it had been banned by the navy.

Scott was not opposed to all harsh penalties. On the contrary, he recognized that an army could be "a most dangerous machine . . . unless held in the strictest of discipline." But he also insisted that it not be "a *slavish machine*," that officers and men be bound together under the rule of law. To clarify his position, he issued a comprehensive general order in 1842. It has been learned, he said, that "blows, kicks, cuffs and lashes" have been inflicted upon soldiers by their officers. Although discipline must be maintained in the face of "insolence, disobedience and mutiny," the remedy for such offenses was already prescribed by the articles of war and must be administered with due process of law. Instead of waiting for the judgment of a court, however, too many "hasty and conceited" officers, "losing all self-control and dignity of command—assume that their individual importance is more outraged than the majesty of law, and act . . . as legislators, judges, and executioners. Such gross usurpation," he insisted, "is not to be tolerated in any well-governed army." He laid down guidelines for the minimum use of force necessary to secure order, even rejecting the use of "harsh and abusive" language toward an inferior in rank. Officers unable to follow these guidelines, he declared, should be dismissed from the service. "There is in the army of the United States, neither room, nor associates, for the idle, the ignorant, the vicious, the disobedient."[15]

This seemed clear enough, but the abuses Scott complained of continued. When word of them reached his ear, he would order a military court to try the offenders, but the officers who constituted those courts generally closed ranks to protect their own. In one notorious instance, a court not only refused to condemn Lt. Don Carlos Buell for striking a soldier with a sword but actually commended him for it. When Scott ordered the court to reconvene to explain its verdict, the officers refused and successfully lobbied authorities in Washington to sustain their disobedience.[16]

In other cases, Scott was more successful in erecting what he called "a fence of laws around the rights of inferiors . . . against caprice and violence on the part of authority." He regularly reduced or overturned the overly harsh sentences meted out to enlisted men, insisting that they were entitled to have all doubts resolved in their favor. He was not so indulgent to officers, whom he held to a higher standard. When the flamboyant playboy "Prince John" Magruder improperly employed enlisted men as waiters at one of his lavish parties, Scott slapped him down. Another officer, who loaded all his wagons with personal effects while the enlisted men had to trudge on foot through desert heat, was reprimanded for his indifference to the rights and comfort of those under his command. Such selfishness, Scott reminded that colonel, "is not the way to attach men to the service and make them proud of belonging to it."[17]

Scott seemed to have regarded his chief duty as commanding general to act as a tribune for the common soldier. No detail was too trivial to escape his paternal eye. Were the privies at Fort Columbus inadequate and disgusting? Scott ordered them repaired without delay. Did privates have to sleep two to a bed? The commanding general put a stop to that "unclean practice." Were sick soldiers at seacoast forts housed in dark and damp casements? Scott had them moved to healthier quarters.[18]

His concern for the well-being of his "rascally regulars" extended even beyond their term of service. With no provisions for retirement pay, old soldiers were either cast adrift to fend for themselves or forced to stay at their posts for years beyond their capacity to perform their duties effectively. This was particularly harmful to the officer corps, which was clogged with superannuated veterans whose presence blocked the promotion of younger men. In each of his annual reports to the secretary of war, Scott tirelessly pressed for the establishment of an old soldiers' home, not only for officers but also to allow "the worn out and decayed" of the rank and file to end their lives in comfort and dignity.[19]

Over the years, Scott acquired an unenviable reputation for vanity, selfishness, and ambition. The soldiers under his care must have seen him in a better, and perhaps even truer, light.

CHAPTER FOURTEEN

MIDDLE AGE

Now in his fifties, firmly settled into middle age, Scott seemed at the pinnacle of his career. To the world at large he presented an imposing figure. Towering above lesser mortals at six feet, four and a quarter inches (he always insisted upon that final fraction), "erect as an Indian chief," with his martial bearing, according to an aide, "enhanced by the remembrance of past exploits, by constant adulation, by self-content and many feasts," he appeared the very model of a major general. One impressionable young cadet, Ulysses S. Grant, was awestruck by his first glimpse of the legendary hero. "With his commanding figure, his quite colossal size and showy uniform," Grant thought him "the finest specimen of manhood my eyes had ever beheld, and the most to be envied."[1]

Not everyone was so bedazzled. A visitor to West Point, who had the privilege of dining at the general's table, noticed only "his pomposity and conceit" and found his stilted manners and speech ludicrous. Some bold young officers, resentful of Scott's interventions on behalf of enlisted men, openly scoffed at his "frequent, though fortunately unsuccessful attempts to thrust himself into public notice" and covertly mocked his mannerisms.[2]

As his military exploits receded into an ever-more distant past, Scott seemed to many a living relic of another age, out of touch with his own times. He would often delight in gathering young officers and cadets around him to recount his now-familiar war stories. It was predictable, recalled one, that "at a certain point in his narrative, he would throw his hand up to his shoulder and, assuming a look of pain, exclaim, 'Oh, Niagara! Niagara!'" to dramatize his wounds. Occasionally, bored junior officers would goad him into retelling these stories, just for the pleasure of exchanging knowing smirks behind his back. Scott sometimes suspected that he was being made the butt of jokes. After one such session, he turned to an aide and said, "Young gentleman! I hope . . . that you do not think me too great a fool to know that I sometimes say silly things." But he continued to say them because, as that aide concluded, the old general's nature was so open and trusting that he could not believe professed friends could prove false.[3]

Some of the young officers he took under his wing repaid his generosity with ridicule. Henry Heth (later a Confederate general) left a memorable account of an evening when he and his friend Winfield Scott Hancock (later a general on the Union side) were summoned to dine with the commanding general. Food was a serious business with Scott, bringing forth his most dogmatic pronouncements. Terrapin was "the best food vouchsafed by Providence to man!" Canvasback duck ran it a close second, in his estimation. Veal, however, was deemed unfit for any gentleman's table, while fried meat, he warned, was sure death "to any Christian man."[4] That evening, Heth recalled, the subject was potatoes.

> The General said, "Gentlemen, I wish to call your attention to the potatoes I will give you; they are the finest potatoes in the United States." General Scott had the happy faculty of believing that anything he had on his table was the best in the world. . . .
>
> As soon as Hancock got his potatoes on his plate, he commenced to mash them; the General turned around and said, "My God, my young friend . . . you cant tell the taste of a potato when mashed." Hancock replied, "I like my potatoes mashed," and continued to mash them. I saw how the General manipulated his potato and tried to imitate him; he was pleased to notice me and said, "Oh, I see you know how to eat a potato." "Yes General," I answered, "I cannot tell the taste of a potato when mashed." . . . Hancock caught my eye and looked as though he would like to annihilate me.

After dinner, the table was cleared for a round of whist, an old-fashioned game that neither young officer knew well. Nonetheless, the cards fell in their favor and Scott, a notoriously poor loser, began to berate his servant until his luck turned. "A girl was never happier with a new dress . . . than the General was now." He insisted that his young friends stay for a *petite supe*. When they finally made their escape, they found to their dismay that it was too late for a planned rendezvous with their lady friends.[5] Every hero, it has been said, becomes a bore at last. Scott's time had come.

According to another adage, no man is a hero to his valet. Scott's relations with his many aides put that saying to the test. Thrown into daily and intimate contact, these officers saw Scott with all his crotchets and foibles exposed. To some, he seemed at first cold and irritable, but after a while, he would unbend and dispense fatherly advice, not only on professional matters but also, á la Lord Chesterfield, on how to behave as a man of the world. His temper was short and his tongue could be sharp, but when the tempest passed, the general was not too proud to apologize, even to juniors. "His magnanimity," an aide explained, "will always cause him to make promptly the *Amende honorable* when he has been vexed by a person's not agreeing with him, and he will esteem them all the more for it."[6]

Seemingly petty infractions, such as to the fine points of English usage, could throw Scott into a rage. He fought a stubborn rear-guard action against the modern, Americanized system of spelling and grammar advocated by Noah Webster. Once, when enrolling a daughter at a boarding school, he spotted the despised dictionary on the headmistress's desk and instantly withdrew the child, rather than expose her to its corrupting influence. Even in the heat of battle, during the siege of Vera Cruz while the shells were flying, he could dress down an officer for minor errors in transcribing a dispatch: "My dear Colonel! . . . that interlineation should be *there* and not *here,* dont you see? The sense requires it! . . . You make me write nonsense! You will kill me! . . . I'll not survive it. What? Send this nonsense to the government? And here again . . . there should be a period and not a semicolon. The capital letter shows it. How *could* you make it a semicolon? Correct that on your life."[7]

Junior officers were expected to emulate their commander's sartorial perfection. Scott imposed an ironclad rule that jackets must always be worn at headquarters. One hot night in Mexico, when all were presumed asleep, a thirsty officer tiptoed through quarters in his shirtsleeves for a drink of water. He had barely lifted the cup to his lips when he heard the tinkle of a bell summoning the sentinel. "Take this man to the guardhouse," ordered the general.[8]

Of all Scott's foibles, the one most commented upon was his vanity. "He was vain beyond any man I have ever known," declared James Buchanan, and Horace Greeley bluntly called Scott "an immeasurably conceited, aristocratic, arbitrary ass." Virtually everyone who served with Scott could tell some story to illustrate that famous vanity. Yet those who knew him best came to regard it as a harmless, almost endearing trait, devoid of either selfishness or malice. "The jineral thinks well of himself and is fond of a compliment," conceded one old soldier, "but he is willing to give a compliment now and then in exchange, He is not like some men . . . who want all the compliments to themselves and never give any." The last word on the subject probably belongs to another aide, who concluded that the charges against his chief were exaggerated. "I entered his military family with some apprehension of tyrannous control and a demand for profound respect for something not worthy of it," he said. "To say that I saw no weakness, no evidence of vanity or self-conceit, would be to say that he was not human, or that I was more stupid than I am willing to admit. But I did see a man, not free from defects of temper, but trying to be just—a man absolutely intolerant of wrong when the wrong was clearly to be seen—as free from personal vanity as any man of the world I have ever met, but so singularly frank and confiding to those whom he trusted that the absence of that reticence of suspicion—which we so generally see—gave occasion to charges of vanity and conceit."[9]

His amusements were simple. Whist and chess were his favorite games; food, with its rituals of preparation and consumption, his chief hobby. He enjoyed wine and an occasional mint julep, and before the Mexican War, he indulged heavily in tobacco in all its forms. Despite his rural Southern up-bringing, he took no pleasure in outdoor sports, such as hunting and fishing, though he did enjoy puttering in his garden, nor did he relish formal enter-tainments—balls, parties, plays, or operas. His favorite diversion was conge-nial companionship within a circle of friends usually composed of politicians rather than fellow soldiers. With them he could unbend and enjoy food, games, and good conversation.[10]

Such activities were better suited to an old bachelor than to a family man, but the Scott family was so often scattered that its head usually had to fend for himself. Even when Maria was not in Europe, as she was from 1838 to 1843, she found reasons to avoid Washington, which she despised as "an ill-contrived, ill-arranged, rambling, scrambling village." "You see nothing but dust," she complained, "hear nothing but political discussions and . . . , the weather is sultry enough to make a dog mad."[11] She much preferred West Point, where she and the general often summered with their four daughters. She treated the cadets as surrogate sons, on whom she lavished delicacies, advice, and maternal affection. To them she dedicated a song that concluded:

> And here's a health to you also, ye bright chosen ones
> Columbia's honored, though juvenile sons.
> Be ye brotherly, diligent, upright of heart
> That when from your famed *"Alma Mater"* ye part
> As rays from a centre diverge, ye may spread
> Virtue's light o'er the devious paths ye may tread.
> Health to you and proud names such as valor begets
> And in every hearts *core* live the "Corps of Cadets."[12]

Perhaps she was compensating for the disappointments her own children brought her. Adeline Camilla was acknowledged as the most beautiful, a child whose angelic countenance resembled the cherubs in Renaissance paintings.

As an adolescent, she was considered an "impulsive and ill-regulated" girl, whose otherwise empty head was "filled with beaux and parties." At the age of twenty, she married Goold Hoyt, a wealthy, self-absorbed New Yorker with "the look and manner of a Spaniel puppy." Her mother was heard to blame this misalliance on "the tyrannous caprices and petty inflictions whereby the General made his household wretched," and she seldom spoke of her son-in-law with anything but contempt.[13]

The youngest daughter, Marcella, was described as "an undeniably lovely lady . . . but as cold and impenetrable and unexcitable as a fish." While still a schoolgirl, she caught the eye of Charles Carroll McTavish, a much older member of Maryland's most distinguished Catholic family and a sometimes soldier of fortune in the army of the Tsar of Russia. He pursued her doggedly, and they were married at a home ceremony presided over by New York's archbishop, John Hughes.[14] Maria was equally unhappy with this match, not only because of the age difference but also because of the Catholic connection. She blamed the Roman church for the great tragedy of her family life, the loss of her eldest daughter, Virginia.

Virginia Scott was a bright, haughty young lady who, with her gift for languages and music, most resembled her mother. During her long residence in Europe, she fell in love with a French count, but her parents made her break off the romance. Virginia sought consolation in the Catholic faith and, on her return to the United States, slipped away to a Georgetown convent. There, in a gesture of worldly renunciation worthy of a nineteenth-century melodrama, she took the veil. Resisting her parents' tearful pleas, she remained immured in her cell while she wasted away with the tuberculosis that would kill her within a year.[15]

Her mother never forgave herself or the Catholic Church for the sad fate of her "poor, poor Virginia," and her father, so friends noted, could seldom bring himself to speak of her. Both, however, found a ray of solace from an unexpected quarter. Cornelia, grown into "a haystack of a woman, with the face and bearing of a chambermaid," married her father's aide de camp, the fortuitously named Henry Lee Scott.[16] This meant that their son could bear the name Winfield Scott and so continue the family line, which his doting grandfather had thought lay buried with his own sons.

Despite Scott's loneliness, family troubles, and frequent illnesses, Erasmus Keyes concluded that the general was essentially "a happy man."[17] He was also an intensely ambitious man. The general's close brush with success in obtaining the Whig presidential nomination in 1840 had left him more eager than ever for that glittering prize.

As Scott surveyed the political field, each of his Whig rivals was found wanting. Incumbent president John Tyler, having thrown off the Whig mask and revealed himself as a Democrat at heart, had disqualified himself for the party's nomination. How could Scott support a candidate he despised as an unreliable, vindictive schemer? "I'll cut my throat first!" he declared.[18] Party leaders fared no better: Daniel Webster was too corrupt and Henry Clay too debauched to deserve the presidency. By process of elimination, this left Scott, so he calculated, as the logical choice to be the next Whig standard bearer.

Thaddeus Stevens of Pennsylvania had reached the same conclusion, though by a different route, and, as early as 1841, had launched a Scott-for-president boomlet in his native state. In October, he revealed his plans to his chosen candidate and asked Scott to prepare a biographical sketch for campaign purposes. This should be written anonymously, he suggested, and he further urged (unnecessarily) that Scott avoid false modesty in recounting his heroic deeds.[19]

Nothing came of this autobiography, but the proposal did stimulate Scott into clarifying his views on the leading political issues of the day. As expounded in a series of letters to would-be supporters, these views were largely conventional, middle-of-the-road Whig doctrine. He described himself as neither a Federalist nor a fanatical "Jacobin" but as an admirer of Thomas Jefferson and an opponent of the policies and practices of Andrew Jackson. Unlike the highhanded Jackson, Scott would, in his administration, respect the Supreme Court and restrict the use of the presidential veto. Above all, he would put an end to that abuse, inaugurated by Jackson, of turning the federal bureaucracy into an engine of political patronage. He pledged to put an end to that corrupt and disgusting practice and to make all his appointments solely on merit, without regard for political considerations.[20]

These principles, he insisted, were immutable, "for I shall not modify or suppress a conviction to be made President for life, with remainder to my posterity." But when some Whigs recoiled from the prospect of being denied their rightful rewards of office in a Scott administration, the candidate hastily backpedaled. He still believed government appointments should be based on merit, he explained, but since Whigs were by nature far more meritorious than Democratic riff-raff, they would naturally be entitled to the bulk of the offices at his disposal.[21]

On other matters, Scott was more forthright. He would support a high tariff to protect American industry "against the half-starved labor of foreign countries." Although not a member of any secret society, he would not, unlike the anti-Masons, outlaw such groups. He would, however, support measures to restrict, if not prohibit, the consumption of intoxicating spirits—"the bane and the curse of this land."[22]

Despite his Southern background, Scott hoped to see the elimination of an even greater curse that blighted the Republic—slavery. He was convinced that it was "a high moral obligation of masters and slaveholding States to employ all means, not incompatible with the safety of both colors, to meliorate slavery even to extermination."[23] How that goal could be reached—whether by compensation, education, or, perhaps, colonization—was less important than that it be done peacefully and gradually, without violence or fanaticism.

Scott was attempting to stake out the middle ground in an increasingly polarized situation. More and more Southerners were adopting John Calhoun's intransigent formulation that slavery was a positive good that should be extended. In the North, abolitionists were anathemizing slavery as a moral sin that had to be extirpated. Scott's ameliorative position harkened back to the Virginia of his boyhood, when such leaders as Jefferson and Monroe still proclaimed a faith in moral progress and human rationality. Although not a slaveowner, he could sympathize with their plight, even while condemning their peculiar institution as being "mutually prejudicial" to the interests of blacks and whites alike.[24]

This was classic Whig doctrine, not all that different from the position held by Henry Clay, but it failed to recognize that passions on this subject now ran so high that reliance upon the inexorable workings of Christian benevolence required greater forbearance than most Americans were able to muster. Scott also failed even to consider the issue that would dominate the upcoming political campaign of 1844—territorial expansion. With the United States poised to annex Oregon and Texas even at the risk of war with Great Britain and Mexico, most aspiring politicians felt compelled to explain their stand on these momentous questions, yet Scott was silent.

Despite this glaring omission, Scott spread his political views before the public in a thirteen-page pamphlet issued in October 1841 in response to Thaddeus Stevens's urging. Scott was delighted with the reception given to this statement of principles. Even Democratic journals, he reported, treated it as gingerly "as a puppy terrier would mumble a hedge-hog," while the response it evoked from Whigs performed the unlikely feat of making him "humble with their encomiums." Less infatuated observers, such as Daniel Webster's son, dismissed Scott's circular as a flash in the pan. Andrew Jackson and Henry Clay, who seldom saw eye to eye, agreed that, despite Scott's efforts, his cause had gained little support.[25]

By mid-1842, even Thaddeus Stevens had to concede that the Clay juggernaut was unstoppable. Scott grumbled that his Kentucky rival's name had always proved "fatal to the triumph of Whig Principles . . . and yet he claims to lead the Whigs up to the slaughter every fourth year to the end of his life," but after a brief sulk, he acquiesced. Consoling himself that his only flaw was a deficiency of "that vulgar quantity—called *availability*," he lent his unenthusiastic support to Clay, rather than face another four years of Democratic misrule, which, he groaned, "would render my present position miserable."[26]

Scott's forebodings proved prophetic. Clay lost a heartbreakingly close election to a hitherto obscure Democratic dark horse, James Knox Polk, whose "little strength," Scott soon discovered, "lay in the most odious elements of the human character—*cunning and hypocrisy.*" Dejected at the prospect of spending four more years battling a hostile administration, Scott faced the future with misgivings. "The last sixteen years," he said, "have been the *Middle Ages* of darkness and disgrace," and he expected worse to come.[27] The analogy was more apt than he knew. His own middle ages were about to be followed by an unexpected renaissance that would carry his career to dazzling new heights.

CHAPTER FIFTEEN

WAR

During the presidential campaign of 1844, the Whigs had made much of their opponent's alleged obscurity. Who, they asked mockingly, *is* James Knox Polk? They soon found out.

He was a Tennessee protégé of Andrew Jackson, whose political resume included a term as governor and a five-year stint as Speaker of the U.S. House of Representatives. Scots-Irish by descent, Presbyterian by conviction, Polk belied the stereotype of the Southerner as dashing cavalier. Instead, he was perhaps the last Puritan in American public life, as dour and implacable as any of Nathaniel Hawthorne's duty-tormented New Englanders.

From his faith, he had imbibed the self-righteousness of the elect coupled with an awareness of the innate depravity of the rest of mankind. One can search the pages of his massive diary in vain to find a consistently generous evaluation of a single human being, aside from his wife and a small circle of Tennessee cronies. All others, even his own cabinet appointees, were continually plotting against him.

Unable to delegate authority, Polk chained himself to his desk, rarely enjoying the indulgence of a vacation during his four-year term, after which he promptly died of exhaustion brought about by overwork. No aspect of government was too insignificant for Polk's direct supervision. That, of course, included the army. Although devoid of military experience, he did not hesitate to impose his authority on the most minute details of army management.

Like his fellow Tennesseans, Generals Jackson and Gaines, he distrusted the pretensions of military professionals. Standing armies, he warned, were "contrary to the genius of our free institutions" and "dangerous to public liberty." As had Jefferson and Jackson before him, Polk preferred to rely on the patriotism and gallantry of citizen-soldiers, "who will be ever ready, as . . . in times past, to rush with alacrity, at the call of their country, to her defense." Unlike these brave and selfless volunteers, the officers of the regular army, he grumbled, had degenerated into pampered timeservers—"so in the habit of enjoying their ease, sitting in parlours and on carpeted floors, that most of them have no energy and are content to jog on in a regular routine."[1]

Even worse, most of these officers were Whigs whose chief goal, Polk suspected, was to embarrass his administration. At the head and fount of this political-military conspiracy Polk placed the ambitious figure of his commanding general, Winfield Scott. This suspicion was not entirely a product of the president's imagination: Scott still yearned for the presidency. Indeed, with the recent defeat of Henry Clay, Scott seemed, by default, the most likely Whig candidate for 1848. "His prospects of the Presidency look bright to him," observed a political friend, and "*that* makes him happy. Like the consumption, this ambition . . . may be called a *flattering disease*."[2]

Convinced that his party now represented only a minority of the voters, Scott was persuaded that it had to reach out beyond its ranks to tap that popular "military mania" that had once swept General Jackson and the Democrats into power. "Perhaps *the hair of the dog may be good for the bite*," he argued. "As such humble remedy, I may be worth something to the Whigs considering our diminished numbers."[3]

To augment the diminished ranks of Whiggery, Scott proposed to ally his party with a new movement beginning to make a political stir—the crusade against foreigners. The influx of impoverished Irish and German immigrants, mainly Catholic in faith and Democratic in political allegiance, caused a number of old-line settlers to fear for traditional American values. Calling themselves Native Americans (or later, Know Nothings),[4] they began to organize politically in the 1840s. Scott not only sympathized with their views, but he even drafted manifestoes and newspaper articles (under the pseudonym "Americus") to advocate withdrawing voting rights from the foreign born.[5]

Scott's flirtation with bigotry was a temporary one, influenced, no doubt, by his daughter Virginia's tragic involvement with Catholicism. It would come back to haunt him in his 1852 run for the presidency, but in the 1840s his embrace of Know Nothingism promised political dividends. The *New York Herald* predicted that it would carry Scott to the White House, if only he could "keep a shut mouth for four years," a task that, it conceded, might prove "a pretty hard job" for the voluble general to perform.[6]

President Polk could not help but be alarmed by these political rumblings, which seemed to confirm his worst fears. Polk had placed himself in an awkward dilemma. He distrusted his generals, Scott most of all, on political grounds, yet he needed their assistance to implement his policies. His election had been secured on a platform of territorial expansion, which threatened collision, and perhaps even war, with England over Oregon and with Mexico over Texas and the Southwest. If it should come to war, he would have to find some way to win without at the same time enhancing the political prospects of his generals. According to the powerful Democratic senator Thomas Hart Benton, Polk "wanted a small war, just large enough to require a treaty of peace, and not large enough to make military reputations, dangerous for the presidency."[7]

War with England would be averted by a compromise that split the disputed Oregon Territory along the forty-ninth parallel. The Mexicans would prove more obstinate. The sticking point was Texas.

Americans had been drifting into the province of Texas for decades, initially at the encouragement of the Spanish and Mexican authorities. Like the proverbial camel with its nose in the tent, they soon crowded out the earlier inhabitants and, in 1836, staged a successful revolt against the lightly governed, corrupt Mexican administration and declared their independence. They had expected to be welcomed into the United States, but many Americans feared that the admission of a new slave state might unduly strain the sectional balance. Furthermore, the Mexican government had made it clear that the annexation of Texas by the Colossus of the North would be considered an act of war. So Texas remained in limbo as an independent republic until the waning hours of the Tyler administration, when it was admitted into the Union by joint resolution of a lame-duck Congress.

The incoming Polk administration was thus handed a not-unwelcome present, but, as with Pandora's box, the troubles came only after it was unwrapped. The parsimonious president had hoped to secure the new state (and perhaps California and New Mexico in the bargain) without the expense of war, but it soon became clear that Mexico was not bluffing.

Militarily, the North American colossus was more like a pygmy. The U. S. Army could count on only 5,300 effective troops, the lowest figure since 1808. Its fourteen undermanned regiments were scattered along thousands of miles of frontier, and only a handful of elderly veterans had ever seen a formal battle. Most of its energy over the past thirty years had been spent chasing Indians and building public-works projects. Because of the lack of a retirement policy, the upper ranks of the officer corps were clogged with the elderly and the incapacitated. Of the twelve field-grade officers in the artillery, for example, only four were fit for duty. Scarcely any high-ranking officers knew how to maneuver a regiment, much less a brigade, without the prompting of a West Point–trained subordinate.[8] These graduates of the U.S. Military Academy, unlike most of their commanders, were skilled professionals, but because of the slow workings of promotion by seniority, most of them were still subalterns in the mid-1840s.

Scott took what steps he could to remedy these deficiencies. He urged that the skeleton ranks of existing companies be filled up to their authorized strength of one hundred privates. This measure alone would increase the army's strength to about 16,000 men. Beyond that, he suggested that the government be authorized to raise up to 50,000 volunteers for the emergency. To meet the immediate crisis, he ordered Brig. Gen. Zachary Taylor and his "Army of Occupation" to proceed to Texas.[9]

Fresh from a triumph over the Seminoles, Taylor was a gruff career soldier in the Jacksonian mold. With his open contempt for the fine points of military science and his casual indifference to army protocol, "Old Rough and Ready" seemed the very opposite of the polished professional soldier, Scott, with whom he would later feud. To U. S. Grant, who served as a junior officer under both men, the contrasts were striking. Disdaining uniforms, Taylor dressed like a farmer and was often mistaken for one. He roamed freely through his camp, unaccompanied by staff, and enjoyed striking up informal chats with enlisted men. In battle, he would sit sidesaddle on Old Whitey and improvise orders to meet the unfolding situation.

Scott, for his part, "always wore all the uniform prescribed or allowed by law," and when he and his staff conducted their daily tour of inspection, "word would be sent to all division and brigade commanders in advance . . . so that all the army might be under arms to salute their chief as he passed." Scott's orders were precise and always planned for contingencies. Both generals, Grant concluded, were great soldiers, "true, patriotic and upright in all their dealings. Both were pleasant to serve under—Taylor was pleasant to serve with."[10]

Beneath these superficial distinctions in appearance and personality, there could be discerned a fundamental conceptual conflict on the proper role of an army in a democracy. To Taylor, the army was *of* the Republic, sharing its values and behaviors; to Scott, the army was *for* the Republic, a separate institution that guarded republican values even though it did not embody them.

Although Taylor was not his kind of soldier, Scott was able to overlook their differences in light of his stocky, rumpled, plain-speaking rival's selfless spirit and courageous heart. To compensate for Taylor's glaring gaps in military knowledge and formal education, Scott assigned to his staff Capt. William Bliss—such a strict martinet that his family had nicknamed him "Perfect" Bliss. This combination of head and heart, Scott noted with satisfaction, worked "like a charm."[11]

Although Taylor soon came to despise Scott, the commanding general did not respond in kind. In his *Memoirs,* Scott sketched an indulgent, almost affectionate portrait:

With a good store of common sense, General Taylor's mind had not been enlarged and refreshed by reading, or much converse with the world. Rigidity of ideas was the consequence. The frontiers and small military posts had been his home. Hence he was quite ignorant, for his rank, and quite bigoted in his ignorance. His simplicity was childlike, and with innumerable prejudices—amusing and incorrigible. . . . Any allusion to literature much beyond good old Dilworth's Spelling Book, on the part of one wearing a sword, was evidence . . . of utter unfitness for heavy marchings and combats. In short, few men have ever had a more comfortable, labor-saving contempt for learning of every kind. Yet this old soldier and neophyte statesman, had the true basis of a great character:—pure, uncorrupted morals, combined with indomitable courage. Kind-hearted, sincere, and hospitable in a plain way, he had no vice but prejudice, many friends, and left behind him not an enemy in the world—not even in the autobiographer, whom in the blindness of his great weakness . . . he had seriously wronged.[12]

On April 24, 1846, Taylor dispatched a party of dragoons under Capt. Seth Thornton to patrol the left bank of the Rio Grande. The next day, Mexican forces ambushed them. Several were killed and the rest taken prisoner. "The cup of forbearance," the president told Congress, has been exhausted; Mexico had "shed American blood upon the American soil," and national honor had to be upheld.[13] Polk now had his war.

It was not universally hailed. Some Americans, particularly reformers and New Englanders, looked upon it as a barefaced land grab. This, after all, was the war that inspired Henry David Thoreau to formulate the principles found in *Civil Disobedience* and James Russell Lowell to write his sardonic *Biglow Papers*. Some leading political figures, including Henry Clay and Daniel Webster (each of whom would lose a son in the conflict), also lacked enthusiasm for a war with a neighboring republic, and even some soldiers, such as young lieutenant Ulysses S. Grant, doubted the justice of the cause for which they fought.[14] Scott did too.

Even under the best of circumstances, Scott considered war "a great calamity." He conceded that sometimes it could not be avoided but insisted that statesmen had "the highest moral obligation" to ensure "that the cause of war is not only just but sufficient; to be sure that we do not covet our neighbor's lands; 'nor anything that is his.'" In his memoirs Scott listed the War of 1812 and the Civil War as examples of just wars, but he pointedly excluded the war with Mexico.[15]

In hindsight, a war between the powerful, wealthy United States and its impoverished, distracted southern neighbor might seem a blatant case of imperialist aggression. At the time, however, the conflict was not as one sided as it might appear in retrospect. At the commencement of hostilities, Mexico had perhaps 32,000 men under arms, far more than the United States could muster. True, the Mexicans' equipment was inferior, but their soldiery, consisting largely of peasants accustomed to obeying orders and enduring hardships, were, historically, the stuff of which great armies had been made. Their officers were actually more experienced in warfare than their American counterparts, having been tested in a long series of civil wars and foreign threats; some even utilized Scott's own books of tactics as their training manuals.[16] Finally, the Mexicans enjoyed the considerable advantages that came from fighting on home ground: short supply lines, a friendly populace, and familiarity with the terrain. One thing they lacked was an outstanding commander who could coordinate their efforts and infuse their cause with steadfast purpose and strategic vision.

Ironically, it was President Polk who helped the Mexicans take a giant step toward remedying this deficiency. Hoping to gain the war's objectives on the cheap, he permitted Mexican strongman Antonio López de Santa Anna, the self-styled "Napoleon of the West," to return from exile in Havana with the cooperation of the U.S. Navy. Currently at a low point in a turbulent political-military career that had seen him, at one time or another, on every side of Mexico's civil strife, Santa Anna had convinced the Polk administration that, for a price, he would deliver Mexico's northern territories to the United States if he were returned to power.

In light of Santa Anna's record of betraying every cause and party he had once supported, Polk's reliance on his promises revealed a touching faith in human nature that he seldom displayed in dealing with his own countrymen. Polk, who trusted no one, apparently trusted this master of deceit and was, for his pains, betrayed the instant Santa Anna touched foot on Mexican soil.

The peg-legged general (one leg had been shot off by French invaders and buried with appropriate military honors) breathed defiance against the Yankees and set about to mobilize his nation's defenses. Although no Napoleon on the battlefield, Santa Anna, unique among Mexican commanders, possessed determination and resilience. Time after time, he would rebound from defeat and raise fresh armies to continue the struggle. Polk had unwittingly supplied the Mexicans with their general; he would have much more difficulty finding a commander to lead his own forces.

To Polk's dismay, none of the top-ranking officers in his army seemed fit for command. Wool was too partisan, Gaines too erratic, and Scott was too "scientific and visionary in his views."[17] Even worse, all were "Whigs and violent partisans, and not having the success of my administration at heart seem disposed to throw every obstacle in the way of my prosecuting the Mexican war sucessfully."[18]

For want of anyone better, the president settled on Scott, but he was not happy with the choice. Aside from the political objections (never absent from

Polk's calculations), there was also a genuine reluctance to place the nation's fortunes in the hands of a sixty-year-old general whose last successful military campaign had been conducted more than thirty years earlier. The president was inclined to agree with Democratic senator John Fairfield's cruel appraisal that Scott "has seen his day and is now too much of an old granny." Nonetheless, on May 13, Polk summoned the aged general to the White House to inform him of his decision. "Though I did not consider him in all respects suited to such an important command," Polk confided to his diary, "his position entitled him to it if he desired it."[19]

Unaware of these high-level misgivings, Scott jumped at Polk's offer. "Wherever the heaviest knocks are to be given or received by the army, there I claim to be," he eagerly told the president. His only condition was that if, while he was in Mexico, war with his old foe Great Britain threatened, he would be assigned to meet it—"I should die if not recalled to meet the British," he insisted.[20]

Handed the greatest challenge of his professional career, Scott at once set to work. There was much to be done. Twenty thousand volunteers had been authorized, as well as an expanded roster of regulars. All of them had to be recruited, enlisted, officered, supplied, fed, and transported. Scott delegated much of the groundwork to the chiefs of the various staff departments, treating them as a little cabinet, but most of the burden of planning and coordinating fell upon his own shoulders. He spent between eleven and eighteen hours a day at his desk, issuing the thousand and one orders necessary to put such a vast assemblage into motion—"to distribute, to apportion, to settle rendezvous and routes, to regulate the supplies of arms, ammunitions, accoutrements, subsistence, medicines, means of transportation, camp equipage, and to raise the troops, have them properly organized, put in motion at the right time, and put upon the right points, etc."[21] This was not the work of a day, or even a month. Scott estimated that these troops could not arrive in Mexico until September and would require his constant attention while on the march.

This was not what Polk had in mind. Unversed in military matters, the president had somehow assumed that Scott would instantly pack his bags and dash off to Mexico, even without the formality of written orders. Instead, Polk grumbled, Scott "was constantly talking and not acting." The ever wary president suspected that Scott was engaged in a Whiggish plot to embarrass the administration for political gain. "I have myself," he smugly insisted, "been wholly uninfluenced by any references to the political opinions of the officers of the army in the conduct of the War."[22]

Polk's actions, however, belied such noble sentiments. According to Scott's informants, a delegation of high-level Democrats had descended upon the White House as soon as his appointment was made public and warned the president of its dire political consequences. Polk promised to undo the damage and, on May 19, introduced a bill into the Senate to provide for the appointment of additional generals drawn from civilian life. Despite his protestations of nonpartisanship, all of the newly minted generals were active Democrats.[23] Although not a student of Clausewitz, Polk believed, in a literal sense, that war was a continuation of politics by other means.

When Scott got wind of this military bill, he instantly *"smelt the rat."* The plot, he feared, was to use these newly sprouted "mushroom generals" (as the regulars contemptuously called them) to supersede the existing military command and then, at war's end, "disband every general who would not place Democracy [that is, the Democratic Party] above God's country."[24] This, he feared, was not merely aimed at him personally but also at the professional integrity of the army he had helped create, and he would not abide it. The stage was set for a stormy scene with Secretary of War William L. Marcy.

When Marcy had been governor of New York, he and Scott had stood side by side during the *Barcelona* incident to face down the British. Later, when Marcy took control of the War Department, Scott had advised him to keep politics out of army affairs, but this was advice that Marcy, the man who had coined the cynical phrase "To the victor belongs the spoils," was unable to follow. At Polk's instigation, he consistently favored reliable Democrats when making military appointments and promotions. Despite their political differences, Scott still retained some of his old affection, if not respect, for the secretary. Marcy, he conceded, "is not a bad man," but he was sadly "deficient in *candor* and *nerve*."[25]

On the evening of March 20, Marcy stopped by Scott's office and attempted to reproach the general for his alleged foot-dragging. Scott exploded: "No created man shall lecture me with impunity," he declared.[26] Behind Marcy, Scott discerned the cunning hand of President Polk, who, Scott now suspected, intended to discredit him with both the army and the public by pushing for precipitate action.

As was his habit in times of stress, Scott sought relief with his pen, dashing off yet another in his long series of indiscreet letters, which he now boldly "flung . . . into the teeth of the poor Secretary."[27] In eight tightly packed pages, he attempted to give the administration a much needed lesson in logistics. He explained that the required number of troops could not be raised until at least mid-June and that transporting the indispensable cavalry regiments the twelve hundred miles to Mexico would require another two months at best. Even if these matters could be expedited, the onset of the rainy season would make the terrain of northern Mexico unfit for military activity until mid-September.

Until then, Scott insisted, his place was at the capital, where he could supervise these highly complex operations. Yet, while engaged in "these multitudinous and indispensable occupations," he complained, "I have learned from you that much impatience is already felt, perhaps in high quarters, that I have not already put myself in route for the Rio Grande." To do so, however, without being accompanied by large reinforcements, would, he insisted, work an injustice upon the junior general whom he would then supersede. Scott refused to make himself "the unholy instrument of wounding the honorable pride of the gallant and judicious Taylor."[28]

Had Scott stopped at this point, he would have given the president no just cause for complaint, but once his blood was up, Scott never knew when to stop. "I am too old a soldier," he unwisely added, "and have had too much *special* experience, not to feel the infinite importance of securing myself against danger (ill will or pre-condemnation) in my rear, before advancing upon the public enemy. . . . My explicit meaning is—that I do not desire to place myself in the most perilous of all positions—*a fire upon my rear from Washington, and the fire, in front, from the Mexicans.*"[29]

This was a red flag waved in front of an already enraged president, but it also provided Polk with an opportunity. He had made up his mind to dismiss Scott even before Marcy showed him this offensive letter. Earlier that same day, some troublemaker had shown Polk a private letter in which Scott declined to endorse an officer for promotion on the grounds that he lacked influence with this administration. "Not an eastern man, not a graduate of the Military Academy and certainly not a whig would obtain a place under such proscriptive circumstances," Scott had claimed, and he refused to "dishonor" himself by making a futile recommendation. According to Scott's estimate, he had written some four hundred letters expressing similar sentiments. He should have realized that at least one would find its way into Polk's hands, and he should have foreseen what the president's reaction would be. Polk was predictably outraged at this further proof "that Gen'l Scott was not only hostile but recklessly vindictive in his feelings towards my administration" and was persuaded more than ever that his appointment had been a mistake.[30]

He could not, however, dismiss the general on the basis of a private letter that he had no business reading. The letter to Marcy, with its disrespectful "fire in the rear" accusation, provided Polk with the cover he required. Brushing aside Scott's logistical arguments as mere "pretext," he insisted that the general's blatant display of partisanship required that he be dismissed. A letter of reprimand was drafted, with cabinet approval, and Secretary of War Marcy was deputized to deliver the bad news.[31]

When Marcy called at Scott's office, he found that the general had stepped out for a bite of supper, so he had the letter forwarded to the restaurant. There, Scott read, with mounting dismay, of the president's displeasure at "the most offensive imputations" Scott had leveled against him. On what basis could such charges be made, Marcy asked with feigned indignation. "Had not the President in a frank and friendly spirit just entrusted you with a command on which the glory and interest of the country depended?" How could Scott indulge in such "illiberal imputations against the man who had just bestowed upon you the highest mark of his confidence?" Then came the bombshell. "Entertaining, as it is most evident you do . . . that such are the motives and designs of the Executive towards you . . . , the President would be wanting in his duty to the country if he were to persist in his determination of imposing upon you the command of the Army in the war against Mexico." Scott, therefore, was to remain in Washington while others would lead the military operations at the front.[32]

His appetite spoiled, Scott abandoned dinner and hastened back to his desk to dash off a response. It began badly, explaining that he had been absent from his office only "to take a hasty plate of soup." It grew worse, as Scott unconvincingly tried to wriggle out of his accusations of a fire in the rear from high quarters. This was purely hypothetical, he insisted, and besides, "high quarters" did not mean the president, or else he would have said "highest quarters." It ended with an obsequious attempt to flatter Polk for his "excellent sense, military comprehension, patriotism and courtesies."[33]

Polk was not moved. He accepted the flattery as his due but found nothing in the letter to lead him to change his mind about Scott. "He now sees his error, no doubt," the president coldly concluded, "but it is too late to recal[l] what has been done."[34]

Scott had made himself a laughingstock. His unfortunately phrased letters tickled the public funny bone and were "unmercifully ridiculed." Cartoonists delighted in portraying the general with fire erupting from his rear, and the "hasty plate of soup" earned him the nickname "Marshall Tureen," in mocking reference to the famous French soldier, Marshal Turenne. "General Scott has committed political suicide," concluded a friend.[35] Whigs everywhere jumped off his presidential bandwagon and hopped aboard that of Zachary Taylor, fresh from his twin victories at Palo Alto and Resaca de la Palma.

Scott bided his time. Drawing upon reserves of patience and humility, which his younger self would not have been able to muster, he soldiered on at his desk while awaiting a fresh turn of fortune's wheel. Scott later boasted that he regarded "this period of obloquy on the part of enemies and desertion of friends, as by far the most heroic of his life." By September, he was ready to test the administrative waters. He renewed his plea to be sent to Mexico, only to be rebuffed by Secretary of War Marcy with a "vulgar and *cold-blooded*" rejection.[36]

Unfazed, Scott drew up an elaborate proposal for a fresh Mexican strategy and submitted it to the War Department in October. Taylor's operations in northern Mexico, he argued, were too remote from Mexico's vital heart to force the enemy to the peace table. Scott suggested a fresh line of attack, following the path of Cortez, with the capture of the port of Vera Cruz, followed by a march to Mexico City.

Two obstacles had to be overcome. First, Vera Cruz was defended by a formidable fortress, San Juan de Ulúa, often referred to as the Gibraltar of the West. Scott rejected a direct attack on this castle as too costly in time and lives. He advocated, instead, a landing near Vera Cruz and the investment of the city, whose surrender would lead to the fall of the fortress. For this, he proposed a force of ten thousand men transported on specially designed landing craft. The second problem was the unhealthy climate of Vera Cruz, where the yellow fever, or *el vómito,* could be expected to rage every spring. Speed would be required in order to finish the campaign before the onset of this sickly season. Scott's timetable called for the invasion to commence by the beginning of 1847, which would allow three months to ensure the fall of the city. Once secured, the port of Vera Cruz could serve as the base for an advance through the healthier uplands toward the City of Mexico. Its capture, or perhaps even the threat of its capture, would, Scott predicted, force the enemy to sue for peace and bring the war to a speedy end. An additional ten thousand soldiers would be required for this part of the campaign. Scott suggested that they could be drawn from the "surplus" troops already under Taylor's command.[37]

Polk's first instinct was to reject this plan as another of Scott's attempts to embarrass the administration. On second thought, he realized that the elevation of Scott might serve to counter the alarming popularity of General Taylor, who Polk now regarded as an ungrateful, bigoted partisan whose weak mind had been "made giddy with the idea of the Presidency."[38]

With Taylor out of favor, Scott seemed the only choice to lead the Vera Cruz expedition. After long debate, neither president nor cabinet could come up with a better solution, and Polk reluctantly acquiesced. He still lacked confidence in his commanding general, insisting that "nothing but stern necessity and a sense of public duty" could induce him to make such an unpalatable decision. "The truth is, neither Taylor nor Scott are fit for the command of the army," but Scott, he now concluded, was the lesser evil.[39]

Scott was summoned to the White House on November 19 and offered the coveted assignment. Polk managed to conceal his misgivings, smoothly proposing "that by-gones should be by-gones." Scott was so pathetically grateful that his eyes welled with tears, and he left the interview, according to an amused president, "the most delighted man I have seen for a long time."[40]

And why not? This would be the culmination of Scott's military career. From the training camp at Flint Hill, to the compilation of his *Military Institutes* and tactical manuals, through the decades-long struggle with the likes of Jackson and Gaines, Scott's goal had been to lead a professional, European-style army capable of waging conventional warfare—"to conduct sieges and command in open fields, serried lines and columns."[41] Until now, his lifetime store of professional expertise had gone largely unused, and the army he had forged had been frittered away in fruitless chases after painted savages. Against the Mexicans, he could, for the first and perhaps the only time, wage the sort of war toward which his whole career had been pointed. It was an opportunity he had almost thrown away, and little wonder his eyes misted over at being offered this second chance.

Completely won over by Polk's repeated expressions of confidence and respect, Scott pledged his entire loyalty and support. "Not to have been deceived by such protestations," he later insisted, "would have been, in my judgment, unmanly suspicion and a crime." To demonstrate his appreciation, he willingly agreed to accept any of Polk's political generals (that is, spies) on his staff and wrote letters to leading Whigs, urging them to support the president's policies. He promised to put aside politics for the duration of the war. "On setting out on my present mission," he assured Secretary Marcy, "I laid down *whiggism,* without taking up *democracy,* but without reference to party or politics, I have felt very like a Polk-man. At least the President has all my personal respect, sympathy and esteem."[42]

Polk, who seldom laughed, must have allowed himself a sardonic smile at these sentiments. Even as the trusting general was wending his way to Mexico, the president was desperately searching to find some way to avoid "entrust[ing] the chief command of the army to a Gen'l in whom I have no confidence." Senator Thomas Hart Benton, the influential chairman of the Military Affairs Committee, suggested an ingenious solution to Polk's dilemma. Why not revive the rank of lieutenant general, dormant since Washington's day, and confer it upon someone with the energy, talent, and reliability to conduct the war successfully? In case Polk misunderstood his drift, Benton volunteered to fill the position himself.[43]

Although he had once served as General Jackson's aide de camp, Benton had never fought in a battle, though he had engaged in a number of spectacular barroom brawls, most notably with Jackson himself. Endowed with a legendary ego that surpassed even Scott's, he saw no liability in his lack of military experience and, oddly enough, neither did Polk. A bill to revive the grade of lieutenant general was pushed through the House with strong administration support, but it narrowly failed in the Senate.

When Scott got wind of this "vile intrigue," he was stunned by Polk's betrayal. "A grosser abuse of human confidence is nowhere recorded," he declared.[44] He did not know the half of it. Marcy was actually playing a double, or perhaps a triple, game. The secretary later claimed that he was responsible for assigning Scott to take command of the army in Mexico. The president initially objected: "It would never do; it would end in making him President!" The cunning cabinet minister replied, "Let him go to Mexico and get affairs in train, and before the war is ended we can easily take the wind out of his sails—he is sure to give us the opportunity"—as in fact he did.

Polk raised the further objection that Scott's appointment would anger Benton, whose support in the Senate was essential. Marcy knew how to handle that problem as well. He introduced the lieutenant-general bill, but, so he claimed, "I took care that it should never get through Congress!" Thus, Benton was retained as an administration supporter, "awaiting what never came," while Scott went off to win Polk's war and earn Polk's ingratitude.[45]

This was the first volley of Scott's dreaded fire in the rear and was delivered, so Scott exclaimed, "with a vengeance!!"[46] Resolutely, he refused to allow these distractions to sway him from his duty and vowed to remain:

> True as the dial to the sun,
> Although it be not *shined* upon.[47]

His confidence unshaken by the political wars through which he had passed, Scott approached his challenging new military venture with customary self-assurance. "Providence may defeat me," he recklessly boasted, "but I do not believe the Mexicans can."[48]

CHAPTER SIXTEEN

INVASION

As Scott headed south to take command of the American armies in the field, the war with Mexico had already been dragging on for over half a year, and no end was yet in sight. True, the United States had managed to pluck the remote, lightly defended provinces of New Mexico and California from Mexico's feeble grasp, and Maj. Gen. Zachary Taylor's Army of Occupation had scored some spectacular battlefield victories, most recently in bitter house-to-house fighting at Monterrey, but the enemy showed no signs of moving toward the peace table. Quite the contrary, even to consider such negotiations had been officially declared an act of high treason.

What then? Taylor, egged on by some "wiseacres at Washington," seemed to be advocating an advance from Monterrey toward the enemy's capital. Scott, who realized that hundreds of miles of wasteland lay between Taylor's position and his objective, preferred a more direct approach. "To compel a people, singularly obstinate, to *sue for peace,* it is absolutely necessary," he insisted, "to strike, effectively, at the vitals of the nation."[1] This meant opening a fresh front at Vera Cruz, from which point he could march on good roads, through relatively hospitable terrain, straight to Mexico City.

What role, if any, would Taylor and his army play in this campaign? Conventional military wisdom called for forces to concentrate rather than allow themselves to be divided with a hostile army in between, able to operate on interior lines against each segment separately. Contrary to those detractors who derided Scott as a by-the-book soldier in thrall to European doctrines (the "Giant votary of science," sneered Gaines), Scott decided on an unconventional strategy. If he were a European general, he told Secretary of War William Marcy, he would have stripped Taylor of all his troops and added them to his own. But out of respect for Taylor's gallant record (and for his growing political popularity), Scott would leave him enough force to stand passively on a defensive line in the north, while his own main army took the offensive.[2]

Persuading Taylor to submit gracefully to this decision would require a major diplomatic effort. Scott thought that he had already made ample gestures to soothe the prickly general's feelings, though he suspected that Taylor "may never know *half* that I have done for him." These services included lobbying friendly congressman to secure "the gallant and distinguished" Taylor a promotion to major general and to have a gold medal struck in his honor. Behind the scenes, Scott had maneuvered to protect Taylor from President Polk's efforts to replace him with a Democratic commander.[3]

None of this was sufficient to placate Taylor. The general, according to a member of his staff, was "a man of strong and blind prejudices, like many a strong-minded but uneducated man," and currently the strongest of those prejudices was directed against his commander. Taylor had somehow become convinced that Scott was his enemy and that President Polk (of all people) was his true defender. He suspected that he was the victim of an improbable plot concocted by Scott and Marcy "to have me at once killed off" politically so as to pave the way for a Scott presidency. Although Taylor ritually disclaimed any political ambitions of his own, he could not forgive Scott for "the dirty work" in which he was engaged: "it appears that General Scott not only knew the effect of a well-directed fire in the rear but understands the proper mode of directing it with effect on others." Taylor's brother was even angrier. He wildly charged that Scott was playing "the part of an executioner, by having General Taylor and his command destroyed" in order to discredit a political rival.[4]

Unaware of the depths of the hostility he faced in Taylor's camp, Scott tried to mollify his subordinate with honeyed words and "courteous soothings." "I am not coming, my dear General, to supersede you in the immediate command on the line of operations rendered illustrious by you and your gallant army," he assured the testy old warrior before delivering the bad news. "But, my dear General, I shall be obliged to take from you most of the gallant officers and men . . . whom you have so long and nobly commanded. . . . This will be infinitely painful to you, and for that reason, distressing to me. But I rely upon your patriotism to submit to the temporary sacrifices with cheerfulness."[5]

Unwilling to entrust his plans to dispatches, which could be intercepted, Scott counted on a face-to-face meeting with Taylor at Camargo to explain the details. Taylor, however, decided that his presence was needed elsewhere and decamped for the front, leaving his jilted commander "in the dark" as to his intentions. Scott was reduced to dealing with his absent subordinate by correspondence. As he had feared, his letters fell into the hands of the Mexicans, revealing to Santa Anna not only the plans for the Vera Cruz expedition but also the fact that, for a time, Taylor's depleted army would be perilously vulnerable to attack.[6]

Scott departed from the absent Taylor's headquarters on January 3, 1847, taking the cream of the Army of Occupation and leaving a sullen and resentful General Taylor "in the dumps." "I had expected more fortitude and cheerfulness on his part," Scott confessed, but he decided to allow Taylor "time to cool off" and swallow his disappointment. Taylor, however, continued to sulk in his tent like some latter-day Achilles. Wrapped in self-pity, he brooded over the "outrageous" treatment accorded him and complained that he and his army were being sacrificed to further Scott's ambition.[7]

Scott had his own troubles. Despite Polk's assurance of support, he was beginning to suspect that, "instead of a friend in the President, I had, in him, an enemy more to be dreaded than Santa Anna and all his hosts." Even before Scott learned of the intrigue to replace him with Benton, there were signs hinting at the president's hostility. Scott's choice for chief of his staff was rejected by the War Department, and the president refused the general's request to convene a court-martial to try those officers who had allowed Scott's letter to Taylor to go astray. "This neglect alone," he realized in retrospect, "ought early to have admonished me that I had no hope of support, at Washington."[8]

More-serious omens were the failures of the government to make good on its pledges of men and supplies. Scarcely half of the promised ships, soldiers, and heavy ordnance reached Scott in time for the Vera Cruz landing. Confident that the valor of his troops could overcome these deficiencies in material, the general pledged to carry out his mission "with even half the number I should *wish* to give any one of my juniors for the same service."[9] But he could not afford to wait any longer. The onset of the yellow fever season, expected in early spring, imposed a remorseless timetable on his operations. Scott would have to make do with what he had.

There was much to be done. To begin with, a massive flotilla had to be assembled. Applying a lesson he learned from the interservice rivalry that had hampered operations on the Great Lakes during the War of 1812, Scott took special pains to consult with Commodore David Conner and to instruct his own officers to cooperate with their sea-going counterparts.[10] In the jealous world of the military, such selfless teamwork was rare and would bear fruit not only in the combined operations in Mexico but also later with Scott's "Anaconda" strategy during the Civil War.

With the technical advice of naval lieutenant George M. Totten, Scott helped design a novel type of landing craft. Flat-bottomed to minimize draught and double-ended for easy entry and exit, these "surf boats" came in three sizes that nested cozily within each other so as to take up less deck space. Each could carry, on average, about forty men. One hundred and forty-one were built (with substantial cost overruns), but because of bureaucratic confusion, only sixty-five reached Scott's army in time to be of use.[11]

Delayed by a shortage of transports, each of which had to be chartered from private owners, and by contrary winds and violent storms, Scott's army assembled slowly, pushing his timetable further and further behind schedule. A rendezvous was set for the island of Lobos, 120 miles from Vera Cruz. A coral spit of less than two hundred acres, Lobos was uninhabited, except for crabs, lizards, ants, and unusually large rats. To the soldiers who had spent miserable weeks in cramped quarters below deck, beset by storms, seasickness, and the ever present stench of vomit, Lobos seemed like a tropical paradise, with its blossoming citrus trees "filling the air with delicious fragrance."[12]

Over the next few weeks, elements of Scott's army dribbled onto Lobos, received some much needed training, and were organized into three brigades (later divisions)—two of regulars and the third composed of volunteer regiments from Pennsylvania, Tennessee, and South Carolina along with scattered companies from other states.

The senior officer and commander of the first brigade of regulars was Maj. Gen. William Jenkins Worth. Now in his early fifties, Worth had begun his military career as Scott's aide, fighting side by side with his commander at Chippewa and Lundy's Lane, where both were severely wounded. Scott had solicitously promoted the career of his protégé over the years, and Worth, in gratitude, named a son in honor of his patron. Recently, however, Worth had begun to resent a lifetime spent in Scott's shadow and yearned for the recognition to which he believed his gallantry in Florida and at Monterrey entitled him. Consumed by both illness and ambition, he exhibited some disturbing signs of erratic behavior: jumping at shadows, engaging in petulant squabbles over rank and precedence, and taking unnecessary risks in pursuit of glory and advancement.

Worth even allowed himself to dream of the presidency.[13] This ambition might seem extravagant, but the examples of Jackson and Harrison had inspired many officers with the same hope. It was said that in Napoleon's army, every private carried a marshal's baton in his knapsack; in the American army, almost every general thought he had a presidential nomination in his saddlebag.

The commander of the second brigade of regulars, Brig. Gen. David E. Twiggs, was an exception, untroubled by thoughts of political glory. Indeed, his opponents, among whom Worth was the most bitter, would claim that Twiggs seldom thought at all. A hard-driving, hot-tempered bull of a man nicknamed "The Horse" and "The Bengal Tiger," he was not known for tactical subtlety or finesse but for his "faculty of getting more work out of men in any given time than any other officer in the army." Twiggs was also reputed to be the most creative curser in the army. Even the objects of his wrath would listen to his imaginative streams of profanity with rapt admiration.[14]

The first commander of the volunteer brigade was Maj. Gen. Robert Patterson, a Philadelphia merchant who had dabbled in military affairs since the War of 1812. Irish-born (and therefore immune to the presidential virus), Patterson was a cautious, colorless martinet whose ill health would force his return to the United States in May 1847. He would be succeeded by Gideon Pillow, a Tennessee political crony of President Polk (though not, as was often carelessly assumed, his former law partner). An accomplished intriguer who had helped secure the presidential nomination for Polk, Pillow doubled as the president's spy in Scott's camp, sending home gossipy reports designed to magnify his own importance and diminish that of his rivals.

Pillow's military credentials were less apparent than his political ones. His soldiers despised him as a vain, glory-hunting blowhard, and they relished telling and retelling the story of his blunder at Camargo, when he had ordered the dirt excavated from a ditch to be piled on the wrong side, so as to protect any would-be attackers.[15] Regular officers derided him as "a mass of vanity, conceit, ignorance, ambition and want of truth." Scott, who would suffer the most from Pillow's intrigues, regarded him as "an anomaly—without the least malignity in his nature—amiable, and possessed of some acuteness, but the only person I have ever known who was wholly indifferent in the choice between truth and falsehood, honesty and dishonesty."[16]

Most volunteer generals had political ambitions of their own, but unlike Pillow, some were able to put them aside for the duration of the war. Two in particular won the grudging respect of the professional soldiers: John A. Quitman and James Shields. Originally a Yankee college professor, Quitman had moved to Mississippi, taken up the practice of law, and turned himself into a Southern gentleman. His gracious manners won the hearts of his men, and his unassuming competence the respect of his peers. The Irish-born Shields, who had once come close to fighting a duel with Abraham Lincoln, was a professional politician who would hold the distinction of being elected U.S. senator from three different states: Illinois, Missouri, and Minnesota. Yet for all that, he was a good soldier, modest and brave.

These officers constituted the core of Scott's official family. It was not a happy family. Worth could scarcely disguise his contempt for Twiggs, while other officers openly resented Scott's apparent partiality toward Worth. Regulars despised volunteers as ignorant amateurs, and many of the volunteer officers threatened to go home rather than be relegated to a subordinate position in the coming battles. And all the while, behind the scenes, Pillow cunningly stirred the bubbling cauldron of discontent for his own purposes. No one who was not present, concluded a disgusted officer, "can form any adequate idea of the virulence that permeated rank and file alike."[17] Scott's challenge was to keep these warring egos working in harmony while directing all their energy and ambition against the Mexicans rather than against each other. His first test was at hand: the invasion of Mexico was about to begin.

On March 2, Scott's army boarded its transports, sails were unfurled, and the largest naval armada yet assembled by the United States was underway. With over one hundred vessels of all sizes, it seemed to an awed observer of metaphorical bent like "a great white cloud" or "a wall of canvass."[18] The fleet made anchorage on the leeward side of the coastal island of Antón Lizardo, only two miles south of Vera Cruz. There it lay while the commanders scouted their intended target.

It presented a formidable appearance. A walled city of some fifteen thousand inhabitants, Vera Cruz was protected from seaborne assault by a series of fortresses. The most impressive was the Castle of San Juan de Ulúa, built on a reef a thousand yards offshore, whose sixty-foot-high walls bristled with cannon. On the landward side, the city was ringed by a wall about fifteen feet high and some two-to-three feet thick.[19]

On March 7, Scott, his generals, and their staffs, boarded the steamer *Petrita* to inspect these defenses for themselves. As they passed by the castle, a puff of white smoke drifted from its ramparts, followed in short order by a shell across the *Petrita*'s bow. As the shells rained closer and closer, the little steamer beat a hasty retreat. Had it not, the entire leadership of the American army, Scott, Worth, Patterson, and Pillow, might have been lost beneath the waves, along with such notables of the next generation of military leaders as Robert E. Lee, Joseph Johnston, P. G. T. Beauregard, and George Meade.[20]

This near brush with disaster confirmed Scott in his intention to invest Vera Cruz from its weakly defended landward side rather than risk a frontal assault on its coastal fortifications. Scott, who knew all the military maxims, hardly needed to be reminded of Lord Nelson's advice that only a fool would attack stone forts with wooden ships.

Collado Beach, a sandy stretch of shore three miles south of Vera Cruz and beyond the range of its guns, was selected as the landing site. The fleet anchored off Point Antón Lizardo, a dozen miles farther south, where elaborate preparations for the landing were made. Each surfboat was carefully laid out on the shore, provisioned, and assigned a number so that the platoons could board their proper boats without confusion or delay. The precise order of embarkation was fixed, soldiers packed two days' rations in their haversacks, and by March 8, all seemed ready for the landing.[21]

A threatened storm set back the timetable one day, but the ninth dawned bright with cloudless skies and a smooth sea. At ten o'clock, the fleet, with surfboats in tow and decks packed with soldiers, set sail for the island of

Sacrificios, just offshore from Collado. Each vessel took its predetermined place, dropped anchor, and began transferring the troops into their boats. Despite the grim business that lay ahead, the disembarkment had the festive air of a holiday: bands played patriotic airs, pennants fluttered in the light breeze, and enthusiastic cheers greeted each appearance of the splendidly uniformed commanding general on the deck of his flagship, the *Massachusetts*.[22]

Despite his confident appearance, Scott was aware of the perils his army faced. He knew that his plans had been revealed to Santa Anna, and he feared that the entire Mexican army might be lurking behind the sand dunes ready to pounce upon the Yanquis as they landed on the beach. These fears seemed confirmed by the appearance of a squad of Mexican cavalry on the crest of a sand hill. A volley from a man-of-war's cannon drove them away, but who knew what else might be awaiting the invaders.

At about four o'clock in the afternoon, the first wave of surfboats was launched, forming a line nearly a mile from end to end. "It was a grand spectacle!" an eyewitness exclaimed. "On, on went the long range of boats, loaded to the gunwales with brave men, the rays of the slowly-departing sun resting upon their uniforms and bristling bayonets, and wrapping the far-inland and fantastic mountains of Mexico in robes of gold. On they went; the measured strokes of the countless oars mingling with the hoarse dull roar of the trampling surf upon the sandy beach, and the shrieks of the myriads of sea-birds soaring high in the air."[23]

The place of honor in this initial assault was given to Worth's First Brigade. The general himself was oppressed by a premonition that he would die in the attack, but despite his misgivings, he was determined to win glory. As the line of landing craft approached the shore, the general's cutter pulled ahead of the pack. Plunging into surf up to his armpits, Worth waded onto the beach, winning the coveted distinction of being the first American to invade Mexico by sea.[24]

He was followed in short order by the rest of the brigade. Quickly organizing themselves into companies, they fixed bayonets and charged up the sandy hill to meet whatever foe might be waiting. No one was there. Santa Anna had decided to deal with the weakened American forces under Taylor rather than face Scott's more formidable army. Marching his troops across 150 miles of northern Mexican desert, he had caught up with the outnumbered Americans at the pass of Buena Vista in late February and was soundly defeated. This left only the Vera Cruz garrison, under Gen. Juan Morales, to resist Scott's landing. For some reason, Morales chose to keep his troops safely behind the city walls and allowed the invasion to proceed unhindered.

The rest of the American army was rowed ashore in successive waves of surfboats, and by midnight, ten thousand soldiers were sleeping on their arms within a secure beachhead. Thanks to meticulous planning (and a little luck), the entire operation had been carried off more successfully than anyone could have predicted. Unlike a comparable amphibious assault conducted by the French against Algeria in 1830, in which forty lives had been lost to accidents, Scott's men suffered not a single casualty.[25]

Thirty-three years to the day since he first became a general, Scott was embarked on his last campaign.[26] It had begun well, but no one knew better than he just how many obstacles remained to be overcome along the road to victory.

CHAPTER SEVENTEEN

SIEGE

Once the American army was safely ashore, its next task was to draw a noose around the city of Vera Cruz. On a map, this looked easy enough: the city was already blockaded by the navy on its eastern, or Gulf Coast, side; all that remained was for the army to invest the western side by land.

The maps, however, gave no hint of the difficulties the soldiers faced. Vera Cruz was surrounded by sand dunes, some of which were two hundred or more feet high. The soldiers, who had not yet regained their land legs, had to trudge up and down these hills under a tropical sun, sinking over their boot-tops in the loose sand at every step. There was little water, and the principal vegetation was dense chaparral, which could shred a careless man's clothing and skin. From time to time, the wind whipped up fierce sand storms, coating men, supplies, and food with a layer of grit.[1]

The enemy could have made the Americans' lives even more miserable had they mounted a stiff defense, but, except for some desultory cavalry sallies, General Morales contented himself with lobbing occasional shells from the shelter of his walls. He chose to husband the nearly five thousand men under his command (mostly ill-trained militiamen) in the hope that either a relief column or the approaching sickly season would drive away the invaders.

By March 11, the city was surrounded, and within another week, a five-mile semicircle of American trenches and outposts effectively sealed it off from the outside world. Scott now faced a difficult choice. Should he storm the city or besiege it? To carry the city by storm would, he estimated, cost two or three thousand American casualties, not to mention the inevitable slaughter

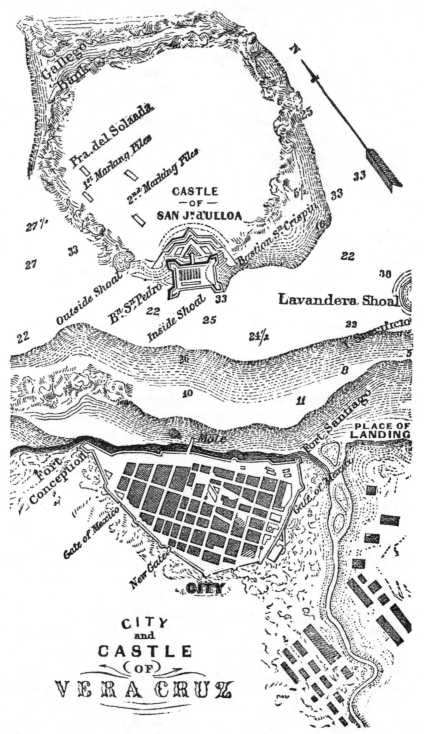

Vera Cruz. Mansfield, *The Life and Military Services of Lieut.-General Winfield Scott*, 368.

of civilians caught in the confusion of a night attack.[2] A siege, however, was slow, painstaking work, and it was uncertain whether the Mexicans and the mosquitoes would allow Scott sufficient time to complete it.

His impetuous generals, Robert Patterson and William Worth, were eager for the glory that could be won by leading a full-scale assault, but Scott was compelled by his responsibilities to be more cautious. He was inclined to pursue "the slow, scientific process" of siege warfare, but before committing himself, he laid the question before his "little cabinet."[3]

This was the name he gave to that circle of West Point–trained junior officers who formed what later generations would call a general staff. More than just aides, they were specialists, each with professional expertise that Scott could draw upon. The chief engineer was Col. Joseph Totten, one of the Military Academy's earliest graduates and an expert on fortifications. Col. Ethan Allen Hitchcock, a scholarly mystic who was an authority on military law and procedures, served as inspector general. Robert E. Lee of the Corps of Engineers was Scott's protégé, prized particularly for his uncanny eye for terrain. To an admiring messmate, Lee seemed to be "one of the most extraordinary men in the service. In the very prime of manhood, of remarkable presence and address, perhaps the most manly and striking officer in the service, of great grace of manner and great personal beauty. . . . His power of enduring fatigue is extraordinary, and his strength of judgment and perfect balance are conspicuous. For counsel, General Scott relies more upon him than any other." Rounding out the group was Lt. Henry L. Scott, the general's son-in-law, who served as his military secretary.[4]

The general told this group that he was inclined to take the city by the slower, but less bloody, method of siege. He was willing, however, to be persuaded otherwise. They weighed the alternatives carefully. "A death-bed discussion could hardly have been more solemn," Scott recalled, but in the end, all supported their commander's recommendation.[5]

"All sieges are much alike," Scott observed, and that of Vera Cruz was no exception.[6] After hundreds of years of experience, the techniques of investing a fortified position had become as ritualized and formal as a minuet. Once the attacking army was in place, it was expected that its commander would issue a request to surrender in order to avoid unnecessary bloodshed. His opposite number would politely refuse, insisting that he could hold out to the last extremity. The attacker would then dig a set of trenches to shelter his artillery and commence the bombardment. As the guns did their work, he would move the trenches ever closer. No fort could resist this approach, but the defenders were expected to delay the inevitable by sorties and counterfire. If they held out for a sufficient time (forty days was the traditional period), they would be allowed to surrender with the honors of war, retaining their sidearms and regimental colors, and released on their "parole." Otherwise, they faced not only disgrace but also possible massacre.

The only escape from this ever-tightening noose lay in rescue by a relief column from the outside. If, however, Morales was counting on support from Santa Anna, he was doomed to disappointment. After his defeat at Buena Vista, the Napoleon of the West had dragged his battered forces home and declared victory. Instead of hastening to the relief of Vera Cruz, he made for the capital, where an insurrection was then raging.

"What madness had seized the Mexicans," asked a frustrated patriot, "to provoke a civil war while a foreign army was lording over our cities and proudly occupying the national territory?" Its origins were suitably complex, as befit Mexican politics, but essentially the civil strife was a rupture along the old fault lines of class and religion. On one side were the "puros," who wanted to create an immediate and sweeping anticlerical democracy and to finance the war by appropriating church property. They were countered by the "polkas" (so-called because of the favorite music of their military bands), who wanted to retain the traditional privileges of church and society. Into this fray stepped Santa Anna. Adroitly playing faction against faction and promising something to everyone, he rose from disgrace to become, once again, Mexico's strong man.[7]

These intrigues detained the generalissimo in Mexico City, while at Vera Cruz, Scott prepared his siege. As a first step, he sent Captain Lee to scout out suitable locations for artillery batteries. Returning from one such expedition with Lt. P. G. T. Beauregard, he was challenged by an American sentry. "Who comes there?" "Friends," said Lee. "Officers," corrected Beauregard. At that, the trigger-happy volunteer fired, singeing Lee's coat but sparing Scott's favorite officer.[8]

Denied the heavy siege train he had requested of the War Department, Scott had to make do mainly with mortars. Since many of the expected horses and mules had perished on the sea voyage, these cannon had to be manhandled across miles of sandy beach, at night and in silence to escape detection. By March 22, they were finally in place, and as protocol required, Scott summoned the Mexican commander to surrender.[9]

The request was carried by Capt. Joseph Johnston of the Topographical Engineers. To spectators, the parley seemed like a scene from one of Sir Walter Scott's popular chivalric romances. With a medieval backdrop of crenellated walls and fluttering banners, with flag-bearing trumpeters preceding the gallant heralds, "all this was like the realization of a dream," said one entranced eyewitness. Morales, or course, responded with a defiant rejection couched in elaborate courtesies, inviting Scott to "commence his operations of war in the manner which he may consider most advantageous."[10]

The American general needed no further encouragement. Turning to an aide, he commanded: "Ride to the batteries as fast as possible, and tell them to commence firing! If they don't open within five minutes, I shall feel disgraced."[11] The bombardment began at four in the afternoon and continued through the night. Sailors in the fleet offshore crammed the decks and clambered up the rigging to admire the show, as if it were a harmless fireworks display.

> Suddenly, a vivid lightning-like flash would gleam for an instant upon the lines, and then as the roar of the great mortar came borne to our ears, the ponderous shell would be seen to dart upward like a meteor, and after describing a semicircle in the air, descend with a loud crash upon the house-tops, or into the resounding streets of the fated city. Then, after a brief but awful moment of suspense, a lurid glare, illuminating for an instant the white domes and grim fortresses of Vera Cruz, falling into ruins with the shock, and the echoing crash that came borne to our ears, told us that the shell had exploded and executed its terrible mission.[12]

For all the spectacular pyrotechnics of the American bombardment, its practical military effect was disappointing. With their high trajectory, mortars were able to rain shells indiscriminately into the city but were not well suited to battering down its walls or silencing its forts. Scott, however, had an ace in the hole and was ready to play it. Even though the War Department had denied him the heavy artillery he needed, the navy had an ample stock of big guns mounted on the ships patrolling nearby. All that was needed to pound Vera Cruz into submission was to transfer these monsters ashore.

The operation was begun with the cooperation of Commodore Conner and continued with his replacement, Matthew C. Perry, who added a stipulation that naval personnel had to man the guns, even when ashore. A site, dubbed the Naval Battery, that was close to the city walls but hidden from its view by a thick growth of chaparral was chosen by Lee. Six big guns, each weighing over three tons, were dismantled, loaded into surfboats, and then dragged by hundreds of hands through almost three miles of deep sand to their emplacements. The officers in charge, imagining themselves still on the quarterdeck, gave all their orders in naval jargon, much to the amusement of the soldiers. "More men on the starboard," they would shout, and the tars would cheerfully respond, "Aye, Aye, Sir."[13]

At ten o'clock on the morning of March 24, the masked battery exploded into activity, pounding the city's walls and forts with 32-pound shot and 8-inch explosive shells. The astonished Mexicans brought all their artillery to bear upon this new menace but were unable to silence it. By nightfall, a thirty-six-foot breach had been blasted through the city's walls, and its fortresses had been "drilled like a colander." Preparations to storm the battered walls were well underway. Scaling ladders were already constructed, and three columns—one of regulars, another of volunteers, and a third consisting of sailors and marines—awaited only a moonless night to commence the attack, which Scott feared could cost up to two thousand American casualties.[14]

Before the attack could be mounted, signals of weakening resolve from the besieged city indicated that it might not be necessary. The first such sign came on March 25 in the form of an appeal by the European consuls residing in the city for a partial truce to enable women, children, and neutrals to be evacuated. Scott rejected their plea with a reminder that he had given ample warnings of his intentions, which the neutrals had chosen to ignore. Now it was too late for any truce proposal to be entertained unless it came from the Mexican authorities and was "accompanied by a distinct proposition of surrender." Otherwise, he threatened, "the siege will go on with increased means and rigour." There was an element of bluff in this threat. Scott was running out of both time and ammunition.[15] But the Mexicans were in even more desperate straits. They accepted Scott's terms, and the next day, officers from both sides met under a flag of truce in no man's land just outside the city's walls.

The conference took place during a sandstorm so intense that soldiers could scarcely see two paces ahead.[16] The American negotiators—Worth, Totten, and Pillow—were also fumbling in the dark. Unversed in the subtle ways of diplomacy, they misread the Mexicans' intentions. Worth returned to headquarters that evening and bluntly reported that the negotiations were a failure. The Mexicans were only stalling for time, he told Scott, and he recommended an immediate assault upon their works.

When pressed, Worth admitted that the Mexicans had offered some propositions, which he had rejected out of hand. He handed Scott the paper but warned, "You will find it only a ruse to gain time." Angry at the possibility that he might lose his chance to lead an attack, Worth stomped out in disgust. "I wash my hands of it," he growled. After Worth had retired, Scott called his staff together. "Now let us hear the English of what these Mexican generals have to say." What the defenders had proposed turned out to be a surrender in all but the name. They agreed to evacuate the city but asked for some face-saving concessions, such as the retention of arms, a twenty-one-gun salute to their flag, and protection of the property and religious freedom of the inhabitants of Vera Cruz.[17]

Scott quickly drafted a set of counterproposals designed to salve Latin pride without sacrificing substance. Religion and property would be duly respected, the Mexican flag would be accorded the honors of war, officers could retain their horses and sidearms, but all other weapons and materials of war must be surrendered and the soldiers regarded as prisoners of war under parole. Most significantly, the Castle of San Juan de Ulúa, as yet scarcely damaged, was to be included along with the surrender of the city.[18] Contrary to Worth's dire predictions, the Mexicans accepted all of Scott's terms. After a siege of less than three weeks, Vera Cruz, the gateway to Mexico, along with its supposedly impregnable fortress, were in American hands.

The cost was surprisingly low. Anticipating what would later be called the American way of war, Scott chose to expend massive amounts of firepower rather than human lives. Up to 4,300 rounds of artillery had rained down upon the beleaguered city, but only ten American soldiers (including two officers) and nine sailors lost their lives, mostly from stray Mexican shells. Mexican casualties were harder to determine, but a British naval officer estimated about one hundred civilian deaths and eighty soldiers killed or wounded. This impressive achievement was lost on Scott's countrymen. As he had anticipated, a victory gained without a "long butcher's bill" of casualties won far less applause at home than the bloodier battles that made Taylor a popular hero.[19]

The formal surrender ceremonies took place on the morning of March 29 on the plains outside the city gate. The victorious army formed itself in parallel lines a mile long and a quarter mile apart, and their defeated foes marched between in submission, stacked their arms, hauled down their colors, and dispersed. Amid martial music and resounding cannon, the Stars and Stripes was raised over the city. The siege of Vera Cruz was over.[20]

With Scott at their head, the American soldiers entered the city and inspected their prize. From afar, the City of the True Cross, with its lacy spires and oriental domes, had seemed like something out of a fairy tale. Seen up close, it presented a less enchanted appearance, with filthy streets and dilapidated buildings. In addition, it was pockmarked with shell craters and littered with the bloated corpses of dead animals.[21]

Scott now had to restore order to the city he had recently tried to destroy. Worth was appointed military governor, and in short order saloons were closed, courts opened, streets cleared of rubble, and the blockade lifted—with American authorities assuming collection of customs' duties—and life returned to something approaching normal.[22]

A novel situation confronted Scott. There were hardly any precedents in the American experience for the military occupation of a foreign country. Common sense, however, suggested that it would not be wise for an army of only ten thousand to antagonize the entire Mexican population. Scott's occupation policy, therefore, was designed to combine firmness with fairness. It rested upon three legs. The first was martial law. In Taylor's Army of Occupation, unruly soldiers had literally gotten away with murder for want of any legal structure under which they could be punished. Scott imposed martial law upon American soldiers and, to show he meant business, flogged a thief and hanged a rapist for offenses against Mexican civilians.[23]

The second leg of his occupation policy was the prompt and reasonable payment for Mexican goods. The ever parsimonious Polk administration had advised its generals to seize supplies from the Mexicans without payment. Scott replied that if the army were to support itself in that way, "we may ruin and exasperate the inhabitants and starve ourselves," and he rejected the administration's self-defeating, penny-pinching policies.[24]

The third leg of Scott's policy was respect for the Mexican religion. Sentries were posted to guard each of Vera Cruz's many churches, and Scott and his officers ostentatiously attended mass. A candle was thrust into the bewildered general's hand, and he was maneuvered into joining the religious procession. His officers found the spectacle amusing, but the Mexicans were impressed by the gesture.[25]

With fears for their safety, their property, and their religion allayed by Scott's mild occupation, the citizens of Vera Cruz accepted their fate without overt resistance. The American commander, though, had little opportunity to enjoy this success. On April 9, two deaths from el vómito were reported.[26] It was time to move inland.

CHAPTER EIGHTEEN

ADVANCE

The National Highway, Mexico's finest road, stretched 280 miles from Vera Cruz to Mexico City. It passed first through the tierra caliente, the hot country of the coastal plain, and then climbed two mountain ranges, each with narrow passes and defiles ideal for bushwhacking and ambuscades. It cut through the cities of Jalapa, Perote, and Puebla of the central plateau, leading at last to the Valley of Mexico. Nestled within that valley, surrounded by lakes and marshes and accessible only by narrow causeways, lay the great prize, the Mexican capital itself.

One month after the U. S. Army first set foot on Collado Beach, it was ready to take up its march along that highway. Scott organized his force into three divisions, with Twiggs leading the way, Patterson's volunteers following, and Worth's regulars bringing up the rear. Worth regarded this arrangement as a personal affront. Scott's old friend, now grown, according to Hitchcock, "as arrogant and domineering as pride can make a man," stalked into headquarters and demanded to know why he was being so disgraced. Scott patiently reminded Worth of past favors but insisted that other officers were entitled to their turn at the post of honor. Worth sullenly withdrew from Scott's presence, a friend no more.[1]

Aware of Twiggs's propensity toward rashness, Scott took pains to restrain his impetuous general. Twiggs was ordered to march upon Jalapa, but if he should meet any serious opposition along the way, he was specifically commanded to "halt in some favorable position" and wait for Patterson to arrive and take command. Such a contingency, however, seemed unlikely, since Scott

From Vera Cruz to Mexico City, along the National Highway.

was somehow convinced that the road to Jalapa was wide open. This intelligence failure perhaps accounted for Scott's careless handling of his troops. Instead of keeping them together, he launched each division down the highway on separate days, which meant that if any segment should be attacked, the others would be too far away to render timely assistance.[2]

Had Santa Anna been more aggressive, he could have pounced upon the Americans during the early stages of their march while they waded through deep sand under a blazing sun. Unaccustomed to these rigors, volunteers and fresh recruits imprudently drained their canteens, tossed excess baggage by the roadside, and shuffled along on blistered feet. By afternoon, they were stretched out for miles along the highway under whatever shade they could find. "Three hundred resolute men could with ease have destroyed the whole division," estimated one exhausted volunteer.[3]

Santa Anna's next opportunity was at the National Bridge, spanning the Rio Antigua fifty feet below. Although work to fortify this bottleneck had begun, most of the workers fled in panic after the fall of Vera Cruz, allowing

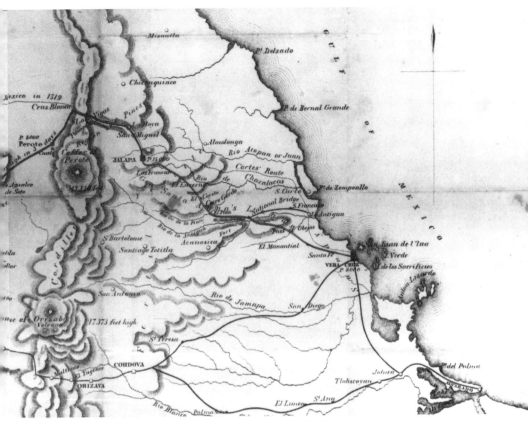

Courtesy Western Reserve Historical Society, Cleveland.

the invaders to cross without opposition. This lack of resistance confirmed Scott in his belief that Mexico was near collapse. Rather than facing Santa Anna's army along the highway, he half expected to find a delegation of "the intelligent, the wealthy and sober minded citizens" suing for peace. He rashly assured Secretary Marcy that the war would be over by summer, "if not earlier stopped by a treaty of peace."[4]

The Mexican dictator, however, had prepared a surprise for the overconfident Yankees. Near the village of Cerro Gordo, some dozen miles beyond the National Bridge, the highway passed through a rugged stretch of countryside. On its left was a sheer drop to the Rio del Plan, five hundred feet below; on its right, a series of steep hills behind which lay a jungle of dense forest and tangled chaparral. This was the point where Santa Anna, with his army of perhaps thirteen thousand, had chosen to make his stand.

The Mexican right was anchored on the ravine, and its left flank was protected by a wilderness so thick that, according to Santa Anna, not even a jackrabbit could penetrate its fastness. Its front was guarded by three hills from which batteries were capable of raking the highway. The rear was dominated by two conical peaks, also fortified: La Atalaya (The Watchtower) and El Telégrafo (sometimes called Cerro Gordo). The main body of the Mexican army was encamped along the highway about a half mile behind these hills.

The unsuspecting Twiggs almost blundered into this trap. Only a premature attack by Mexican lancers alerted him to the dangers ahead. After a cursory inspection, he decided to make a frontal attack upon the enemy's works, ignoring Scott's instructions to await reinforcements. The timely arrival of General Patterson's division on the evening of April 13 stayed Twiggs's hand. Patterson roused himself from his sickbed to assume command, cancelled the proposed attack, and sent word to Scott to hasten to the front with all available support. Scott arrived the next day, wearing an old straw hat and radiating confidence. Instantly, the confusion created by the earlier series of orders and counterorders, which one officer likened to "a game of battledore and shuttlecock," was dispelled, as the general's presence "calmed the rising storm, and brought order out of chaos."[5]

For three days, Scott carefully reconnoitered the enemy's position. It was not as impregnable as it first appeared. Indeed, a Mexican officer had earlier warned Santa Anna that, although the pass near Cerro Gordo was "advantageous for harassing the invading army on their march to Jalapa," it was "not the best point to dispute their passage, and much less to attempt a decisive victory." The weak point, as Scott discovered, was the supposedly impenetrable left flank. His engineers, first Beauregard and then the "indefatigable" Captain Lee, scouted a trail that, if improved, could outflank the Mexican defenders.[6]

By April 17, the trail had been widened, much of the underbrush cleared away, and artillery laboriously raised and lowered by hand up and down the steep ravines.[7] That morning, Twiggs's division was sent down the trail with orders to emerge somewhere near the National Highway behind the enemy's base camp; there they would prevent the Mexicans' escape after the victory confidently anticipated the next morning. Passing behind La Atalaya, the smaller of the two conical hills, his column was observed and fired upon, leading Twiggs to depart from the plan and storm up the hill.

After he had brushed aside the small Mexican garrison, Twiggs was asked for further orders. Carried away by the heat of battle, he roared, "Charge 'em to hell!" Taking him at his word, the Americans poured down the other side of La Atalaya toward El Telégrafo a half mile away. Unable to carry this better-fortified, eight-hundred-foot height, they were driven back to the refuge of La Atalaya.[8]

That evening, while Santa Anna was loudly trumpeting his "victory," Scott was maturing his plans for the next day's battle. He envisioned a two-pronged attack launched simultaneously on the enemy's front and rear. Twiggs, already part way there, would plant a portion of his division under Shields across the

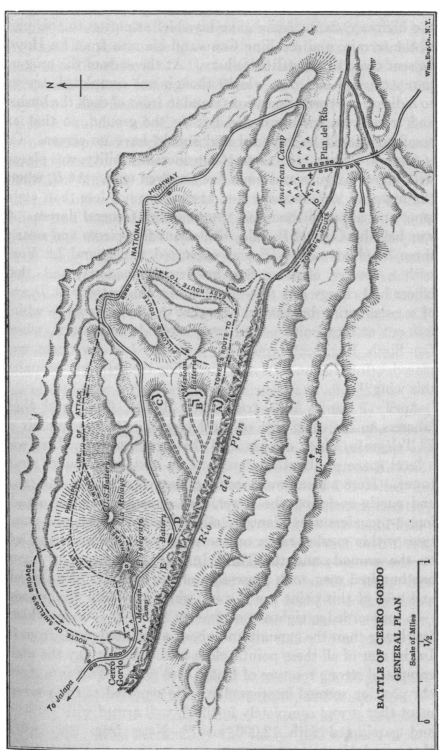

N

BATTLE OF CERRO GORDO
GENERAL PLAN
Scale of Miles
0   ½   1

Wm. Eng. Co., N.Y.

The Battle of Cerro Gordo. Justin Smith, *The War with Mexico* (New York: Macmillan, 1919).

National Highway to cut off the enemy's expected retreat, while the rest of his force would, if necessary, take the key position of El Telégrafo. At the same time, Pillow's volunteers would divert the Mexican front by attacking the three batteries emplaced there as soon as he heard the sound of Twiggs's guns.[9]

By dividing his force in the face of an enemy of superior numbers, Scott was deliberately violating a hallowed military maxim. Since his Florida fiasco, however, the old general had found a new flexibility. He had always known the rules, but now he understood when they should be broken. In this case, he had taken the Mexicans' measure and was confident they would stay behind their defensive works. His confidence was not shared by his generals, all of whom were squabbling on the eve of battle. Worth was sulking, both Patterson and Shields were angry at not having a greater share in the action, and Pillow was openly fearful that his "desperate undertaking" would fail. Unconvinced by Scott's assurances, the Tennessean finally muttered that he would go where ordered even if, as expected, "he left his bones there."[10]

In later years, a myth would grow to the effect that Scott's battle plan was so prescient that it could almost serve as a blueprint for what actually happened.[11] In fact, except for the victorious outcome, hardly anything went exactly as planned. The attack on El Telégrafo was launched prematurely by Col. William S. Harney, a bold and able, though chronically insubordinate, cavalry officer with a broad streak of sadism in his makeup. Harney led Twiggs's regulars straight into the cannon's mouth. They carried the redoubts at the base of the hill with bayonets and clubbed rifles, then pulled themselves up the slope by grabbing on to bushes and branches. They overwhelmed the defenders on the summit, slew General Vázquez, and sent his troops fleeing as the Mexicans' own guns were turned against them. General Scott, who was on the scene, shed tears of pure joy and declared that the charge up El Telégrafo was the most beautiful sight he had ever witnessed.[12]

It was all over so quickly that Shields did not have time to spring his trap tightly shut. Infected by the panic of their fleeing comrades, many Mexican soldiers in the rear abandoned their posts to dash pell-mell down the Jalapa road to safety. Santa Anna was among their number. Hopping onto a nearby mule, he made his exit from the field of glory in such haste that he left his carriage and his cork leg behind.[13]

Meanwhile, in another part of the field, Gideon Pillow and his volunteers were in trouble. Their instructions had been clear enough: Pillow was to march his brigade, consisting of two regiments each of Pennsylvania and Tennessee volunteers, along a previously scouted path to the three batteries that guarded the enemy's front. He would then attack one of the batteries, preferably that closest to the Rio del Plan, with the goal of piercing the Mexican line and then attacking the other batteries from the rear.[14]

Pillow decided to improvise instead. Rather than taking his column down the previously agreed-upon path, he impulsively chose another trail, over the protests of his engineers, and instead of concentrating on one enemy battery, he decided to attack two. Marching down the narrow, unscouted trail in single file, his troops became scattered and disorganized, with supporting regiments and attacking regiments scrambled together. Without waiting to sort things out, Pillow ordered a frontal attack on the middle battery, which exposed Col. William Haskell's 2d Tennessee Regiment to a murderous crossfire from all three batteries. A Pennsylvanian suspected that Pillow's intention was to win some glory for his home state, but this gallant and uncoordinated charge only resulted in sixteen Tennessee dead and forty wounded before it had to be abandoned.[15]

Pillow himself was wounded slightly in the arm by a stray chunk of canister and turned command over to Col. William Campbell of the 1st Tennessee Volunteers. A scene then ensued that would not have been out of place in an *opera buffa*. As a Pennsylvania volunteer observed:

> The Col. was in a most furious humor, perfectly rampant. He was mad and did not know exactly whom to blame or what to be mad about. Col. Roberts [of the 2d Pennsylvania Volunteers], who may be personally a brave man but who has not the slightest presence of mind, is running about perfectly bewildered. Campbell orders the Pa. Regt. to charge. As he does not designate either the 1st or 2nd neither obey him. So he damns the Pennsylvanians for a set of cowards. He next inquired who commanded our Regt. Being informed that it is Col. Roberts, he now orders Col. Roberts to advance with his Regt. Roberts, who is on the right, does not hear him and there is no movement. Campbell jumps about, damns the Pennsylvanians, damns Col. Roberts for a coward that he will expose him, etc. While Campbell is leaping about someone informs him that Roberts' Regt. is the supporting and not the charging Regt. and that Wyncoop commands the 1st Pa. This throws the honest Colonel into a new dilemma and while he is scratching his head the orders arrive to suspend operations that the works are covered by Twiggs and that the enemy have surrendered.[16]

Scott took Pillow's setback in stride, as if he had expected nothing better from that quarter.[17] He could afford to be forgiving. In less than three hours of hard fighting, the outnumbered American army had swept the enemy from its strong defensive position, killing or wounding over one thousand Mexicans and taking three thousand prisoners, including five generals. The rest, some six or seven thousand men, managed to escape with Santa Anna to fight another day, but in so depleted and demoralized a condition as to ensure that

that day would not be soon. American losses amounted to 63 killed and 368 wounded, including General Shields, at first feared killed by grapeshot that went clear through his chest, but who managed a near miraculous recovery.[18]

The spoils of war were so abundant that Scott found himself "quite embarrassed" with all the booty. Over four thousand Mexican muskets were smashed beyond further use, and forty captured cannon were spiked and dumped into the ravine.[19] Since guarding the prisoners would tie up too many of his own troops, Scott put them on their parole, served up a good meal, and sent them on their way.

The next day, April 19, the Americans again took up their march toward the enemy's capital. After passing the battlefield, reeking with the stench of dead horses and unburied Mexicans, they came to the city of Jalapa, famed for its cool breezes and hot peppers. With its gleaming white plaster buildings and its fragrant aroma of orange blossoms, the city at first seemed like "the Garden of Eden" to the weary Americans, though, on closer acquaintance, its overabundance of fleas and lice made it somewhat less of a paradise.[20]

The advance guard, under General Worth, pushed farther on. The dingy town of Perote surrendered to him without a shot on April 22. Its chief prize was a gloomy fortress-prison that had been abandoned by the Mexican army, except for one punctilious officer who gravely presented Worth with an itemized invoice of the castle's contents. The next stop was Puebla (more formally, Puebla de los Àngeles), Mexico's second city. Its residents had recently become disenchanted with the national cause due to Santa Anna's high-handed expropriation of civilian and church property and were receptive to Worth's offer to spare the city if it surrendered without resistance.[21]

While in command of this advanced outpost, Worth fell into a nervous funk, imagining that Santa Anna was hovering nearby with a vast force and that the Mexicans were engaged in some sinister plot to poison all the Americans. His orders and counterorders kept the army in a constant state of agitation until calmed by the arrival of Scott, after which, as Lieutenant Grant dryly observed, "nothing more was heard of Santa Anna and his myriads."[22]

At this point, about two-thirds of the way from Vera Cruz to Mexico City, Scott called a halt to his rapid advance, and, as he put it, "the career of conquest was arrested for a time."[23] Even though the enemy seemed defeated and the road to the capital unobstructed, the American general would mark time for four months after his victory at Cerro Gordo before again taking up his march along the National Highway.

CHAPTER NINETEEN

HALT

In the first flush of his victory at Cerro Gordo, Scott allowed himself to be carried away by euphoria. "Mexico has no longer an army," he confidently asserted, and he predicted that he could capture its capital without losing more than a hundred men.[1] Instead, it was the American army that was in danger of melting away, while the indefatigable Santa Anna was busy raising fresh troops.

Never large to begin with, Scott's army was depleted still further by the expiration of the volunteers' one-year term of enlistment. Much to the general's dismay, though not to his surprise, virtually all of the four thousand men affected chose to go home rather than reenlist. Along with them went General Patterson, too ill to perform his duties, and General Pillow, to exhibit the bullet that wounded him and to receive a major general's star from a grateful President Polk. After further subtracting the many sick and wounded, as well as those needed for garrison duty, Scott found himself with about four thousand effective troops to carry out a mission he had originally estimated would require twenty thousand. In something close to desperation, he begged Secretary of War William Marcy, "For God's sake give me a reinforcement of 12,000 regulars."[2]

This preference for regulars was consistent with Scott's longtime aversion to volunteers, a prejudice that his Mexican experience had done nothing to dispel. The contrast was clear to him. Within fifteen minutes after their evening halt, a regiment of regulars would have their tents pitched, arms secured, and kettles boiling, and the men would be "merry as crickets" under the benevolent eye of their officers. Volunteers, in contrast, would eat undercooked meat, lie down on wet ground, and expose their weapons to the elements. "In a short time the ranks are thinned, the baggage wagons and hospitals filled with the sick; and acres of ground with the graves of the dead!" So too in battle: the volunteers' lack of training and confidence in themselves and their officers, so Scott claimed, led to needlessly high casualty lists. "He who says otherwise is absolutely ignorant of the whole matter, or he lies," the general insisted.[3]

Junior officers echoed their commander's condemnation of volunteers by castigating them as "useless, useless, useless—expensive, wasteful—good for nothing." The precocious young lieutenant George B. McClellan, admittedly something of a snob, was shocked at their unmilitary behavior: "all hollow-ing, cursing, yelling like so many incarnate fiends—no attention or respect paid to the command of their officers, whom they would curse as quickly as they would look at them." To another West Pointer, volunteers were "expen-sive, unruly, and not to be relied upon in action. Their conduct towards the poor inhabitants has been horrible, and their coming is dreaded like death in every village in Mexico, while the regulars are met by the people almost as friends."[4]

In their eagerness to make a case for the superiority of the "rascally regu-lars," Scott and his officers overlooked some inconvenient facts. For one thing, the experience gap was not as unbridgeable as Scott assumed. The ranks of many regular regiments were diluted with half-trained raw recruits, while the volunteers proved capable of learning the military routine more quickly than might be expected. In March, for example, one Pennsylvania sergeant was amazed at the speed with which veteran soldiers struck camp; by July, he was proud that his own company was now equally efficient. For another thing, the disease rate did not bear out Scott's fears. Both volunteers and regulars suffered almost equally from sickness, each losing slightly less than a quarter of their numbers through death or discharge due to illness.[5]

True, as Scott maintained, many volunteer officers were lax and some-times stood helplessly by while their men committed atrocities "sufficient to make Heaven weep, and every American, of Christian morals *blush* for his country." But some of the regular officers, such as Colonel Harney, could be martinets whose excesses drove their men to desert and even to mutiny. Dur-ing the Mexican War, 9.2 percent of the regulars deserted the colors, and over 250 of them actually switched sides and fought for the Mexicans in the noto-rious San Patricio Battalion. In contrast, the desertion rate among volunteers was only 6.6 percent.[6]

Nor were volunteers noticeably less effective as warriors than their regular counterparts. Despite Scott's misgivings, the volunteer soldiers fought bravely and well. Even the enemy was astonished at their prowess. One Mexican ob-server could not understand "how those bands of vicious volunteers, with-out discipline, without subordination, and without experience in the management of arms, or knowledge of tactics, could have conquered our battalions, who were so well trained, instructed, obedient, patient, and, to say still more, so valiant."[7]

Admittedly, many volunteers were, as regular officers complained, unwashed, unruly freebooters whose unbridled rapacity and undisciplined behavior disgraced the flag under which they fought, but many others were drawn from the most respectable and industrious elements in American society. Out of the ninety-four members of a not-untypical Pennsylvania company, sixteen were lawyers and law students, two were teachers, and most of the rest were skilled craftsmen, such as printers, saddlers, blacksmiths, and tailors.[8] Not another army in the world at that time could boast a soldiery with comparable skills and education—certainly not Scott's beloved regulars, who were drawn largely from the ranks of immigrants and misfits.

In any event, with his invasion stalled and his undermanned, unpaid, ill-clad garrisons wasting away as they awaited reinforcements, Scott could hardly afford to be choosy: he would have to take whatever the administration sent. What it sent instead was an unwelcome visitor: Nicholas P. Trist, chief clerk of the State Department, who came armed only with the authority to negotiate a peace treaty. Scott had hoped to be given that authority himself, reminding Secretary Marcy "that he who is successful in combat, and backed by a powerful army, is more likely to be listened to, in negociations, than the ablest and most practiced diplomatist."[9]

To President Polk, however, it was bad enough that Scott might win this war; to allow him also to take credit for the peace would be intolerable. The cabinet considered a list of deserving Democrats for this honor but was unwilling to reward one at the expense of the others. This impasse was broken by Secretary of State James Buchanan, who had himself been anxious for the distinction. Buchanan proposed Trist, who not only was fluent in Spanish and versed in diplomacy but also sufficiently obscure so as to pose no political threat.[10] Trist, however, did not regard himself as an obscure functionary. His massive ego harbored grandiose ambitions. As the onetime private secretary to both Presidents Jackson and Jefferson (whose granddaughter he had married), he allowed himself to dream of following in their footsteps. Self-satisfied and contentious, this undiplomatic diplomat's temperament was enough like Scott's to ensure that the two would clash.

Their quarrel began even before they met. Instead of hastening to Scott's headquarters, Trist tarried at Vera Cruz, forwarding to the general a dispatch bag containing a sealed packet addressed to the Mexican foreign minister and a cover letter from Secretary Marcy. This mysterious packet gave the touchy general the impression that he was deliberately being left in the dark. Actually, it was a proposal for a peace treaty, and Trist was supposed to have given Scott a copy, but he neglected to do so. To compound the confusion, Marcy's letter was murky. It informed Scott that in the event of an unnamed "contingency," he was to suspend further military operations upon consultation with Trist.[11] The unnamed contingency actually referred to the signing of a peace treaty, but Scott jumped to the erroneous conclusion that Trist was empowered to usurp his military authority by negotiating an armistice with the enemy.

As always, when distressed, Scott took up his pen. To Marcy, he begged "to be spared the personal dishonor of being . . . required to obey the orders of the chief clerk of the State Department." This latest indignity, coming on the heels of "the many disappointments and mortifications" to which he had been subjected, led him to "beg to be recalled from this army"—a rhetorical flourish he would later have cause to regret. To Trist, he sent a chilly note, reminding him that an armistice was properly a military affair and, consequently, none of Trist's business. He bitterly complained "that the Secretary of War proposes to degrade me, by requiring *that I, the commander of this army, shall defer to you, the chief clerk of the department of state.*"[12]

Trist could have put Scott's misapprehensions to rest with a simple explanation, but he chose to respond with thirty pages of sarcasm and invective. The government's intent, he huffed, "is what any man of plain, unsophisticated common-sense would take for granted that it must be; and is not what your exuberant fancy and over-cultivated imagination would make. . . . The question is, whether the government of the United States is to be permitted by General Winfield Scott to discharge its international functions and duties in its own way." Furthermore, "greatly deficient in wisdom as the present (and indeed, any democratic) administration of the government must necessarily be, it has not . . . fallen into so egregious a blunder as to make [the negotiations with Mexico] . . . dependent upon the amiable affability and gracious condescensions of General Winfield Scott."[13]

Now in his element, Scott fired back: "My first impulse was to return the farrago of insolence, conceit and arrogance to the author; but, on reflection I have determined to preserve the letters as a choice specimen of diplomatic literature and manners. The Jacobin convention of France never sent, to one of its armies in the field, a more amiable and accomplished instrument. If you were but armed with an ambulatory guillotine, you would be the personification of Danton, Marat and St. Just—all in one."[14] And there matters stood for over a month, with the two highest-ranking representatives of the U.S. government refusing to take any further notice of one another, though thrown into close proximity at army headquarters in Puebla.

A box of guava marmalade brought them together. When the diplomat fell ill with a fever, Scott graciously offered the preserves as a get-well present. One thing led to another, and before long, he was able to report to Marcy "a happy change" in their relations. To his surprise, he found that Trist, in person, was "able, discreet, courteous and amiable," and once their differences had been patched up, they actually became good friends.[15]

The damage, however, had already been done. When word of the feud first reached Washington, the president was livid over the misconduct of "these two self important functionaries." The general, he told his cabinet, had been both insubordinate and unpatriotic in not delivering the peace proposals to the Mexicans as ordered. "The protraction of the war," he charged, "may properly be attributed to the folly and ridiculous vanity of Gen'l Scott," who deserved to be recalled from duty and tried before a court-martial. The cabinet agreed in condemning Scott's conduct but demurred at dragging a successful general home in disgrace in the middle of a war. The president reluctantly yielded to their views, "at least for the present."[16]

In the meantime, heedless of the fact that he lacked military experience, that he was thousands of miles from the scene of action, and that he relied on information that was weeks out of date, Polk regularly second-guessed Scott's decisions. He was continually looking over the general's distant shoulder: overruling his selection of staff officers, disapproving of his choice of roads, and even instructing him on the proper use of pack mules. Generous with advice, he was stingy with praise. Instead of the presidential commendation Scott expected for his victories at Vera Cruz and Cerro Gordo, he received only a carping complaint over his decision to parole Mexican prisoners.[17]

The president's wrath rose even higher when he heard reports of irregular transactions between Scott and the Mexicans. A British intermediary had suggested to Trist that the Mexican authorities might be more amenable to peacemaking if they first received a cash advance. Scott wrestled for a time with the morality of such a bribe, but he ultimately persuaded himself that "in this miserably governed country," one had to conform to the local customs.[18] A ten-thousand-dollar *doceur* was slipped to a Mexican official with the promise of a million more to come if the Mexican Congress could be persuaded to rescind its ban on peace negotiations.

The matter was properly one between Trist and the Mexicans, but Scott felt honor bound to lay it before his generals. He called a council of war at Puebla on July 16 and canvassed their opinion. Pillow spoke up first with a well-rehearsed set speech eloquently defending the plan—as well he might, considering that he had been in on it from its inception. His was the only strong supporting voice. Quitman warned that public opinion at home and abroad would condemn a treaty achieved by such "disreputable" means, and Shields believed that "peace made by such foul means would stain the Government of the United States with an infamy and disgrace that could not be blotted out in two centuries." Twiggs was for any means, fair or foul, that would end the war. Brig. Gen. George Cadwalader, only recently arrived, had no opinion, and Worth was no longer attending meetings called by Scott. Scott himself was ambivalent: although he spoke in favor of the plan, he harbored grave reservations.[19]

As it turned out, nothing came of the scheme. Exemplifying the classic definition of a dishonest politician as one who will not stay bought, the Mexican official pocketed the money but failed to perform his part of the bargain. The matter would, however, have domestic repercussions. The following December, Polk received word of it. With a fine show of indignation, he denounced Scott's conduct before the cabinet, which agreed that the incident presented sufficient grounds to recall the general from Mexico.[20]

Polk's source of information was his old friend Gideon Pillow. Now the second-ranking officer in Scott's army, Pillow did his best to undermine his commander's authority by slipping derogatory information directly to the president and the secretary of war. In this case, Pillow claimed that he had initially opposed the bribery scheme but temporarily allowed Scott to persuade him of its merits. Upon reflection, however, he realized its impropriety and succeeded in stopping it—all of which, according to Hitchcock, was "false from first to last."[21]

Meanwhile, at Puebla, Scott's "protracted and irksome" delay was about to come to an end. Reinforcements had been dribbling in for months, and with the arrival in early August of a brigade of 2,500 fresh regulars under New Hampshire's politician-general Franklin Pierce, Scott's army now totaled about 14,000 men. Of that number, however, more than 3,000 were too ill (mainly from diarrhea) to march and had to be left behind, guarded by yet another 600 men.[22] This left Scott with slightly over 10,000 soldiers to deal with the estimated 30,000 troops (of variable quality) Santa Anna had managed to scrape together to defend his capital.

According to a military maxim of the day, an attacking force, to be successful, needed to exceed the defenders by a ratio of three to two. By that standard, Scott's ten thousand was grossly inadequate, but he was confident that the higher caliber of his troops would compensate for their lack of numbers. Even so, he had no men to spare for such mundane duties as guarding his lengthy supply line and garrisoning each of the vulnerable points in his rear. His solution was bold and risky. If he could not secure his supply line, he would simply abandon it and live off the country. Scott justified his decision by invoking a long-distant precedent: "Like Cortez, finding myself isolated and abandoned; and again like him, always afraid that the next ship or messenger might recall or further cripple me—I resolved no longer to depend on Vera Cruz or home, but to render my little army *a self-sustaining machine.*"[23]

Scott was deliberately violating the most sacrosanct rules of "scientific" warfare. Maintenance of supply lines and preservation of lines of retreat were basic principles drummed into every West Point cadet. Even an untutored amateur, such as President Polk (egged on by Gideon Pillow), knew enough to condemn Scott's unorthodox move as "a great military error." More ominously, in far-off London, a greater military authority, the aged Duke of Wellington, sadly shook his head and declared: "Scott is lost. . . . He can't take the city, and he can't fall back upon his base."[24] Scott's audacity, however, did not go wholly unappreciated. Two young American officers, Ulysses S. Grant and William T. Sherman, must have taken careful note of his strategy, which they would later use to such good effect outside of Vicksburg, Mississippi, and when marching through Georgia two decades later.

On August 7, only a day after the arrival of Pierce's brigade, Scott's "self-sustaining machine" renewed its advance along the National Highway. Twiggs's division again led the way, followed by Quitman, Worth, and Pillow. The threat of enemy forces hovering nearby dictated greater caution than had been exercised in the careless days after the fall of Vera Cruz. Each division was always within ten miles of another, ready to come quickly to the aid of their fellows if needed.[25]

Except for the garrison at Vera Cruz and the sick and wounded left under guard at Puebla, Scott massed his entire force for this one decisive blow. He would not look back, nor would he be distracted by guerrilla pinpricks on his flanks. "I steadily held to the policy not to wear out patience and sole leather by running to the right or left in the pursuit of small game," he explained. "I played for the big stakes."[26]

Three days later, the advance guard reached the crest of the Rio Frio range to behold an "enchanted valley." Before being covered by its present-day blanket of smog, the air in the Valley of Mexico was so pure that distant objects—lakes, mountains, villages, perhaps even the outlines of Mexico City itself—stood out with such clarity that it seemed to Scott as if he could almost reach out and touch them. Equally clear in his mind was the prospect of success: "probably, not a man in the column," Scott surmised, "failed to say to his neighbor or himself: *That splendid city soon shall be ours!*"[27]

CHAPTER TWENTY

SUCCESSES

Four routes could carry Scott into Mexico City. None were without difficulties, but one had to be chosen. The most direct route would continue along the National Highway to threaten the city from the east, but because it was the shortest and most obvious approach, it was also the most strongly defended.

In the months since Cerro Gordo, while the American offensive had marked time, Santa Anna had been busy constructing a ring of fortifications around his capital. Even Scott was forced to admit that his opponent's "vigilance and energy were unquestionable, and his powers of creating and organizing worthy of admiration." Rebounding from repeated defeats, Santa Anna had somehow scraped together another army of 35,000 men composed of regulars, National Guardsmen, and patriotic citizens. This force might be ragged, but it was not contemptible. No less an authority than U. S. Grant conceded that "if they were well drilled, well fed and well paid, no doubt they would fight and persist in it," but as it was, though brave, the Mexicans lacked staying power.[1]

Such troops were better employed behind defensive works than in the open field. The most formidable of these works was at El Peñón Viejo, a three-hundred-foot rocky prominence dominating the National Highway eight miles east of Mexico City, boasting over forty cannon, some recently cast from church bells. American scouts reported that the hill could be taken, though at the cost of perhaps three thousand casualties.[2]

Storming a fortified position was not Scott's way. Whenever possible, he preferred to turn an obstacle rather than assault it. But which way should he turn? Lieutenant Grant, in retrospect, thought Scott should have wheeled to the right, skirting Lake Texcoco and threatening the city from the north.[3] Scott,

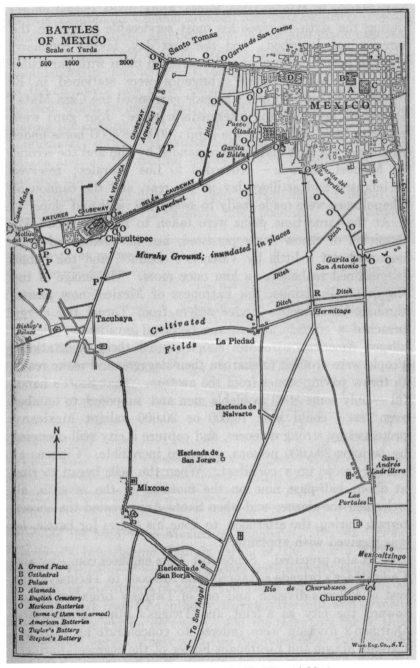

BATTLES
OF MEXICO
Scale of Yards

0   500   1000   2000

Santo Tomás

Garita de San Cosme

MEXICO

CAUSEWAY
Aqueduct

LA VERÓNICA

Paseo
Citadel

Garita
de Belén

BELÉN CAUSEWAY
Aqueduct

Garita del
Niño Perdido

Casa Mata

ANZURES CAUSEWAY

Molino
del Rey

Chapultepec

Marshy Ground; inundated in places

Garita de
San Antonio

Ditch

Ditch

Ditch   Ditch

Bishop's
Palace

Tacubaya

Cultivated

Fields   La Piedad

Hermitage

N

Hacienda de
Nalvarte

Hacienda de
San Jorge

San
Andrés
Ladrillera

Mixcoac

Los
Portales

To
Mexicaltzingo

Hacienda de
San Borja

Río de Churubusco
Churubusco

To San Angel

A Grand Plaza
B Cathedral
C Palace
D Alameda
E English Cemetery
O Mexican Batteries
   (some of them not armed)
P American Batteries
Q Taylor's Battery
R Steptoe's Battery

Wms. Eng. Co., N.Y.

Mexico City and vicinity. Smith, *The War with Mexico*.

however, was reluctant to make a thirty-mile detour through arid country lacking both water and forage only to come up against another well-fortified position.

This left the southern approach, but that too presented hard choices. The more direct road around Lake Chalco passed across a perilously narrow causeway, but the alternate route, around both Lakes Chalco and Xochimilco, was reputed to be impassable for wagon trains and artillery. Scouting reports corrected this misconception, and after feints and countermarches to conceal his intentions, Scott successfully established a fresh base of operations on August 18 at the crossroads village of San Agustín, approximately ten miles due south of Mexico City.

His strategic problem, however, had not been solved, merely transferred to another location. Santa Anna swiftly shifted his troops from El Peñón to San Antonio, again blocking Scott's advance to the capital, and called Gen. Gabriel Valencia from the city's now unthreatened northern gate to Contreras, obstructing any further western movement by the Americans. Colonel Hitchcock was struck by this practical application of what had hitherto seemed merely an academic maxim: the value of interior lines. "We now begin to see that, while we move over the arc of a circle surrounding the city, the enemy moves over a chord, and can concentrate at any point before we can reach it."[4]

Unable to push forward, retreat, or even stay in place (due to lack of provisions for men and beasts), Scott seemed stymied. "Our prospects rather darken every moment," Hitchcock confided to his diary. "Now is the time for the general to keep cool!"[5]

To make matters worse, the terrain seemed to preclude the sort of turning movement that had served Scott so well at Cerro Gordo. Santa Anna's works at San Antonio could be approached only by a narrow causeway flanked by deep ditches. On the east, he was protected by an impassable bog; to the west lay the Pedregal, an old lava bed approximately five miles by three.[6] This was a trackless lunar landscape of volcanic rocks sharp enough to rip apart a horse's hooves and crisscrossed by a labyrinth of gullies and ravines. It stretched all the way to Valencia's position at Padierna, near Contreras, effectively protecting (so Valencia assumed) his right flank.

Reconnaissance parties confirmed the strength of the Mexican lines. The very first cannonball fired from San Antonio carried off Capt. Seth Thornton, the same ill-starred officer whose capture in April 1846 had given Polk his *casus belli*. After that, Worth's division was ordered to remain on the defensive before San Antonio while Scott explored his options to the west.[7] The most promising of these options seemed to be by way of a mule path that cut across the southwest corner of the Pedregal. This had been discovered by Scott's dauntless engineers, Lee, Beauregard, and Zealous Tower. They reported that if this path were widened for artillery, it could lead the Americans somewhat to the rear of Valencia's position.

A work party under Pillow was sent into the Pedregal on the morning of August 19, with Twiggs's division providing additional protection. By three o'clock, the construction crew came under fire from Valencia's heavy battery. Although Twiggs had not been ordered to bring about a general engagement, merely "to brush away the enemy in case he became impertinent," he unlimbered his much lighter artillery and commenced a return fire.[8] This battery, manned by Lt. Thomas J. Jackson (not yet likened to a stone wall), was too badly outgunned to respond effectively.

Pillow, the ranking officer on the field, now took charge. Polk's favorite general threw his units piecemeal into the fray, without coordination, communication, or consistency of purpose. According to Lieutenant Beauregard, the result was "confusion worse confounded, every one seeming to be on his own hook—orders and counter-orders succeeding each other with increased rapidity," creating "the d——dest scatteration" imaginable.[9] First Pillow sent Twiggs to storm Valencia's trenches, then Lt. Col. Bennet Riley was ordered to work his way to the village of San Geronimo in the Mexican rear, so as to cut off the Mexicans' retreat. Valencia, however, held his ground and even drove the Americans back. Reinforcements from Pierce's brigade arrived, but to no avail. Pierce himself, in his first taste of combat, was thrown from his horse, fainted from the injuries, and had to relinquish his command.

With the attack on Valencia stalled, Riley's detachment near San Geronimo was cut off from the main body of the army and faced a further threat from the north. Santa Anna, with perhaps eight thousand men, had been drawn from San Antonio by the sound of gunfire and cautiously approached the battlefield. For some reason, he stopped short, about a thousand yards from Riley's position, close enough for the beleaguered Americans to be entertained by the music from his bands as well as observe the general himself bustling about with his immense staff in tow.[10]

Scott reached the field at about four o'clock and, although wounded slightly in the leg, restored some semblance of order. He realized the futility of further assaults on Valencia's works since, as he explained, "Our infantry unaccompanied by cavalry or artillery could not advance in columns without being mowed down by the grape and canister shot of the batteries, nor advance in line without being ridden over by the enemy's numerous cavalry."[11] He resolved, instead, to strengthen the forces near San Geronimo, which he saw as the key to the situation, by sending Generals Shields and Persifor Smith to their assistance.

Now nearing fifty, Smith was a latecomer to the military trade. A Pennsylvania-born Louisiana lawyer, he had discovered his true vocation during the

Seminole War and was appointed colonel in the regular army at the outset of the Mexican conflict. He served with distinction under Taylor and was brevetted brigadier general. In Scott's army, he won the respect of all ranks for his cool competence under fire and for his refusal to indulge in the backbiting so endemic among his brother officers. To him, more than to anyone else, belongs the credit for turning this battle from disaster into victory.

Smith's first intention was to attack Santa Anna's force to his north, but the gathering darkness rendered this plan impractical.[12] He then turned his attention to Valencia's camp. His engineers had discovered a deep ravine that led close to the Mexican rear. Under its protective cover, the Americans might, if all went well, fall upon the unsuspecting enemy at dawn. To ensure success, a diversionary attack would have to be made simultaneously on Valencia's front. Scott needed to be notified of these plans, but the general had returned to his command post at San Augustín and could be reached only by way of the Pedregal.

After sunset, a tropical storm suddenly burst upon Smith's unsheltered men. Wet, hungry, and sleepless, they endured what Lee would later call the darkest night, in more ways than one, that the American army had ever known. Lee himself volunteered to cross the lava field to contact Scott, who was also in the dark, at least as far as Smith's intentions were concerned. Scott had earlier sent seven scouts stumbling through the Pedregal for information, but each had lost his way. Lee navigated this maze by memory, guided only by occasional flashes of lightning, performing what Scott hailed as "the greatest feat of physical and moral courage" of the campaign. Reaching Scott's quarters about midnight, drenched and exhausted, he was immediately ordered to escort Twiggs to the front to prepare for the morning's assault.[13]

While Lee was making his way through the darkness, General Valencia was celebrating his "victory" of the preceding day, issuing grandiose *pronunciamentoes* and lavishly distributing medals and promotions to his officers. Envisioning himself the savior of Mexico, he acted as if he were already its supreme commander. Such presumption infuriated his blood-rival Santa Anna, who ordered him to spike his guns and abandon what threatened to become a perilous position. Valencia contemptuously defied his commander, insisting that he would easily finish off the "miserable remnant" of the Yankees in the morning. At that, Santa Anna withdrew to safer ground, leaving his insubordinate general on his own.[14]

At three o'clock on the morning of August 20, while the storm was still raging, Smith's troops, with Riley's brigade in the lead, entered the ravine and stealthily moved through waist-deep water toward Valencia's rear. They reached their goal undetected around sunrise, dried their weapons, and awaited the signal.[15]

Valencia was preoccupied with Twiggs's activity in his front when suddenly a horde of screaming Americans swarmed into his rear. All was thrown into confusion: gunners attempted to reverse their cannon to meet this new threat; cavalry trampled the bewildered foot soldiers, still groggy from the previous night's celebration. After half-hearted attempts to improvise resistance, the Mexicans' resolve simply collapsed, as those who could fled for safety while the rest surrendered. At the beginning of the charge, Smith had taken out his watch. Now he put it back in his pocket—only seventeen minutes had elapsed.[16]

Scott reached the field shortly after the fighting ended. Along the way he encountered Lieutenant Beauregard. "Young man," he said, "if I were not on horseback, I would embrace you." Turning to his staff, he declared: "Gentlemen, if West Point had only produced the Corps of Engineers, the country ought to be proud of that institution."[17]

The general himself glowed with understandable pride as he reported the results of the brief Battle of Contreras (or Padierna, as the Mexicans more accurately called it) to the secretary of war. "I doubt whether a more brilliant or decisive victory—taking into view ground, artificial defences, batteries, and the extreme disparity of numbers—without cavalry or artillery on our side—is to be found on record," he claimed. The results seemed to justify the boast. At a cost of sixty dead or wounded, the Americans had killed seven hundred of the enemy; taken over eight hundred prisoners, including four generals (but not the nimble Valencia); and secured over twenty cannon—and it was still morning. Much remained to be done. Perhaps remembering Secretary Armstrong's admonition from an earlier war that "battles are not gained when an inferior and broken army is not destroyed," Scott flagged his men on in hot pursuit. "Make haste my sons," he urged, "or they will be gone before you reach them."[18]

As the shattered remnants of Valencia's command streamed north to the safety of the capital, their panic infected Santa Anna's soldiers at San Antonio. The latter wisely abandoned his camp and ordered a retreat while he still had some control over his men. To impede the advancing Americans, he left behind a garrison to defend the river crossing at Churubusco. The position was well chosen, being on the south bank of the Rio Churubusco where the roads from San Angel and San Antonio converge. A stone church, a stone convent, gardens enclosed by stone walls, and a well-engineered stone fortification at the bridgehead all provided secure cover for the Mexican rear guard. On these rocks, the American wave dashed and broke. For two and half hours, they battered against these defenses and were repeatedly thrown back.[19]

Revisiting the battlefield six months later, even a lowly sergeant was moved to ask: "Why was this battle fought at all?"[20] If he could realize that the position should have been turned instead of assaulted, then surely Scott must have understood that as well. The truth was that in the rush of events, the general lost control of the battle. Unable to follow his usual practice of careful reconnaissance and close supervision, he found himself reacting to situations rather than shaping them. Eventually, he would carry the day, but at a needless cost of men and momentum.

One reason for the unexpectedly tenacious resistance of the Mexican forces at Churubusco was the presence of the San Patricio Battalion, a group of American deserters who had changed flags and now fought for their former foe. Although most were Catholic, they were not, as the battalion's name implied, all Irish. Of the 103 (out of perhaps 260) soldiers whose origins are known, only 40 were from Ireland; 22 were American born, and the rest were from various other countries. Although desertion was not uncommon during the Mexican conflict (more than nine thousand cases occurred during the war, and most went unpunished), the San Patricios compounded the offense by taking up arms against their own comrades, for which the constitutionally prescribed penalty was death. Understanding of the likely fate that awaited them lent desperation to their resistance at Churubusco. When their Mexican colleagues attempted to surrender, the San Patricios would tear down the white flags and continue fighting.[21]

By late afternoon, the Mexican defenders had run low on ammunition, and the Americans had managed to infiltrate from the rear. The stubborn fortress was overrun, and its defenders scattered or made captive. They had succeeded, however, in buying precious time for Santa Anna to prolong a war that, only a few hours earlier, had seemed on the verge of being lost.

The road to Mexico City now lay open, but it was too late for Scott to take it. Even though Worth's advance guard was within a mile and a half of the city limits, the Americans reluctantly drew to a halt. There seemed glory enough for one day: four thousand of the enemy killed or wounded and three thousand taken captive, including eight generals, amounting in all to one-third of Santa Anna's force. The American losses were less severe but irreplaceable: over one thousand killed, wounded, or missing. It was time for a rest, and as evening approached, Scott sounded the recall. One impetuous cavalry officer, Capt. Philip Kearny failed to hear the order (or perhaps deliberately ignored it) and dashed all the way to the city gate. There, he paused to look behind him and realized no one was following. He beat a hasty retreat, but not before losing an arm to Mexican grape shot.[22]

Kearny's close approach convinced many that the City of Mexico could have been taken had Scott not lost his nerve. But to what end? Could a battle-weary army of less than 8,000 men realistically be expected to occupy a hostile city of over 200,000 while a battered but intact enemy army hovered nearby?

Entering the capital under such circumstances was more likely to be a trap than a triumph. Besides, Scott had never believed that the capture of Mexico City was essential to his objective, which, it should be remembered, was not to seize Mexican territory nor even to destroy its army, but rather, as Polk put it, to conquer a peace. As Scott repeatedly explained to the War Department and to his generals, threatening the city was more likely to induce the enemy to make peace than capturing it would. Consequently, he "very cheerfully sacrificed to patriotism . . . the *eclat* that would have followed an entrance—sword in hand—into a great capital" and awaited peace overtures from the enemy.[23]

What he received was a verbal request from Mexican officials for a truce, ostensibly to bury the dead. Scott eagerly (perhaps too eagerly) seized upon this as an opportunity to open more wide-ranging peace negotiations. "Too much blood has already been shed in this unnatural war," he wrote Santa Anna, and he asked for an armistice. Striking the wrong tone, he declared that he awaited the Mexican response "with impatience."[24]

This carelessly drawn note revealed that Scott was too straightforward to be a proper diplomat. Santa Anna seized upon it as a confession of American war guilt, and the phrase "unnatural war," with its unfortunate sexual connotations, evoked snickers. He treated the American request as a desperate plea from a defeated foe, condescendingly granting it as if he were a victor conferring a boon.[25]

Scott ignored the insults, largely on the advice of those same British diplomats who had earlier suggested the bribery scheme and who now warned against unduly humiliating the Mexican authorities. Hitchcock suspected that these "neutrals" were really trying to buy time for a Mexican recovery, and even some captured Mexican officers warned against placing trust in Santa Anna.[26]

The armistice signed on August 22 required both sides to remain in place and refrain from reinforcing their troops or strengthening their fortifications during the peace negotiations. American teamsters were to be allowed unimpeded access into Mexico City in order to purchase food and supplies.[27] All of this rested on Mexican good faith. Some of Scott's generals had suggested demanding more tangible guarantees. They urged that the Americans occupy Chapultepec, a commanding hill overlooking the western approaches to the city, in order to ensure Mexican compliance, but Scott rejected this as an affront to Mexican pride.

The gesture went unrequited. Treating Scott's concessions as signs of weakness, the Mexican peace commissioners raised impossible demands, acting as if the Americans were defeated supplicants. Although Scott scrupulously observed the terms of the armistice, they were regularly violated on the Mexican side. American teamsters, attempting to exercise their right to reprovision in Mexico City, were stoned by a mob and driven off. Curiously, the mob did not shout "Death to the Gringoes," but "Here come the friends of Santa Anna!"—illustrating the treacherous instability of Mexican politics.[28]

Even more disturbing were the many signs that Santa Anna was using the truce to strengthen his military defenses. Now thoroughly disillusioned, Scott realized that he had been snookered.[29] On September 7, he canceled the truce and prepared once again for war.[30]

CHAPTER TWENTY-ONE

TRIUMPH

After the collapse of the truce, Scott pondered his next move from his new headquarters at Tacubaya, only two and a half miles southwest of Mexico City. From this position, he could access a number of the causeways that radiated out from the capital across the otherwise impassable marshes. Each of these roads terminated at a *garita,* or gate, originally designed as customs posts but capable of doing double duty as blockhouses. About a mile to his north loomed Chapultepec, whose two-hundred-foot-high oval-shaped eminence commanded the southwestern approaches to the city. At the western foot of this hill, there was a complex of low buildings, including Casa Mata, a sturdy stone powder magazine, and Molino del Rey, a set of mills that included an old cannon foundry.

On September 7, word reached Scott of unusual enemy activity at these mills. His scouts jumped to the conclusion that the Mexicans were readying the facility to forge fresh cannon. Others, in retrospect, believed Santa Anna was actually setting a cunning trap, but Scott entertained no such suspicions.[1] He ordered Worth's division to make a raid at dawn the next day to brush aside what was assumed to be a small Mexican garrison and carry off their cannon.

Some believed that Scott gave this assignment to Worth as a peace offering to repair their ruptured friendship. If so, it was an expensive gesture. When Worth began his attack, on the morning of September 8, he found more than he had bargained for. Hidden in and around the natural defenses of El Molino, Santa Anna had posted perhaps as many as 17,000 of his best troops to confront Worth's division of less than 3,500.[2]

Worth further divided his command into smaller groups to attack each of the enemy's strongpoints piecemeal. The attack on the mill was spearheaded by a storming party of picked men from various regiments known as a "forlorn hope." (This was not as grim as the term might seem to suggest, but rather a corruption of the Dutch phrase *verloren hoop,* literally a detached troop.) As they approached the foundry, they were suddenly swept by a sheet of enemy fire. Eleven out of fourteen American officers instantly fell, and the leaderless remnant wavered and fled, leaving their wounded comrades to be butchered by Mexican marauders.[3] The Americans regrouped, and in brutal hand-to-hand combat managed to drive the Mexicans from the mills, at heavy cost to both sides. The same story was repeated in other parts of the field, as unexpectedly stubborn Mexican resistance was overcome only by desperate acts of individual courage. The last stronghold to fall was the Casa Mata, but only after a charge across an open field again decimated the attackers.

After two hours, Worth's men prevailed, but the price was exorbitant: 799 killed or wounded, including 58 officers, amounting to over 20 percent of his force. Mexican losses were staggering: perhaps 3,000 killed or wounded, including four dead generals. Another 2,000 dispirited Mexican soldiers made their separate peace and deserted that night.[4]

Even for the victors, the sacrifice proved empty. Scott had been misled: no enemy cannon-making machinery was found at the mill, and the Americans soon withdrew from this dearly bought field where, according to one soldier, "nothing was gained except glory." An officer's assessment was even harsher. "I have seen quite a number of battles in my life," he said, "but I never witnessed one whose management gave such evidence of utter imbecility." The classically educated Colonel Hitchcock drew a disturbing parallel from Roman history. "On Aug. 20," he wrote, "we were like Hannibal after the battle of Cannae: we could have gone into the capital but did not. . . . On Sept. 8th, we were like Pyrrus after the fight with Fabricius—a few more such victories and this army would be destroyed."[5]

The finger pointing began even before the smoke had cleared. Worth had his defenders, who hailed his "soldier-like style, which must forever challenge the admiration of the historian," but they were in the minority. Most officers blamed him for not first softening up the Mexican defenses with artillery and for failing to provide scaling ladders. He was also criticized for mixing regiments in the "forlorn hope," which had the effect of separating men from their officers and forcing them to fight alongside strangers.[6]

Yet even though the fault may have been Worth's, the responsibility was Scott's, and it weighed heavily upon him. He appeared preoccupied and irritable, snapping at his aides and infecting headquarters with a dark mood. He was oppressed by a problem that could no longer be evaded or delayed—how best to enter the enemy's capital. His choices were now reduced to two: an approach from either the south or the west. The southern approach was more direct, but it required advancing along one or more narrow, well-fortified causeways, each a "network of obstacles," while under deadly crossfire from Mexican artillery. The western causeways of Belén and San Cosme were not as strongly fortified, but they passed under the enemy's guns on Chapultepec. If this approach should be taken, that position would first have to be carried by a direct assault.[7]

Scott convened a council of war at Padierna on September 11. The general took the chair and announced that he would not rise from it until a decision had been reached.[8] He himself favored the western approach, but most of the officers in attendance disagreed. With his customary eloquence, Pillow led off with a lengthy argument supporting a southern attack. Quitman modestly deferred to the views of the engineers, most of whom, including Lee, claimed that Chapultepec was too strongly defended to be stormed.

This seemed to convince most of those assembled, and the matter appeared settled until Scott noticed that Beauregard, the most junior officer present, had not yet given his opinion. "You, young man, in that corner," the commanding general asked the lieutenant, "what have you to say on the subject?" Although reluctant to disagree publicly with so many of his seniors, Beauregard observed that the Mexicans evidently expected a southern attack and had been strengthening their defenses to the point that each *garita* could be another Churubusco. Moreover, "they could not by any possibility be taken in flank or rear, which was, after all, our most successful tactic with the Mexicans." Possession of Chapultepec, however, would give the army "a strong pivot" upon which to move in any direction.[9]

After this presentation, "a dead silence ensued." It was broken by Pierce, displaying the same vacillation that would characterize his later presidency, who now declared that he had changed his mind and was in favor of an attack on Chapultepec. Riley concurred, on the grounds that it would entail "less work and more fighting." Scott then drew himself up to his full height and, "with his impressive tone," announced: "Gentlemen, we will attack by the Western gates!"[10]

Not everyone was persuaded. With his usual pessimism, General Worth openly predicted failure. Defeatism could be expected from that quarter, but even Scott privately admitted that he harbored some misgivings.[11] But he put them aside to concentrate on the task at hand.

The first step was deception. Twiggs was ordered to make an ostentatious demonstration before the southern gates, which convinced Santa Anna that the attack would come from that direction. Meanwhile, under cover of darkness, the divisions of Pillow and Quitman were quietly shifted to the west.[12] The next day, September 12, four artillery batteries opened fire on the true objective, Chapultepec, with the intent of pulverizing its defenses.

This bombardment was not as effective as had been hoped, but as it turned out, the defenses of Chapultepec were not as formidable as had been feared. From a distance, the hill may have appeared impregnable. Its northern and eastern faces were protected by unscalable cliffs, while attacks from other directions would require passage through marshes and across drainage ditches. The few open fields could be raked by crossfire and were salted with land mines. The summit was dominated by an imposing "castle," now used as the Mexican military academy.[13] In actuality, Chapultepec was a hollow shell, low on ammunition and defended by less than nine hundred soldiers, some of them mere cadets who had refused to abandon their school. The castle was originally constructed as a summer home for a Spanish viceroy and had been designed for pleasure rather than defense. To the apprehensive Americans assembled at the foot of the hill, however, none of these weaknesses were apparent as they awaited the signal to attack.

That signal was given at eight o'clock on the morning of September 13. Pillow's division charged up the western slope of the hill, and Quitman's troops were launched simultaneously from the southeast. Worth's regulars, still bruised from Molino del Rey, were held in reserve. The attackers raced through an obstacle course of soggy meadows strewn with boulders and blocked by rambling stone walls, across mine fields (which fortunately failed to explode), and over (and often into) muddy ditches, all in the face of enemy fire "so intense and appalling" that it reminded one officer of "a tempest at sea with the wind howling, hissing and whizzing."

Through all this confusion, Quitman remained, according to an admiring soldier, "as cool as any one could have been quietly sitting in a drawing room. . . . He appeared more like a father to his men than a commander, telling all in a kindly tone to obey his orders and he would take care of them." The race to the summit, however, was won by Pillow, or rather by Pillow's men. The general himself was wounded in the ankle by a ricocheting piece of grapeshot and sat out the decisive stage of the battle propped against a tree. Nonetheless, he considered himself the hero of the day. As he told his wife: "I know I am not mistaken when I say it will give my name a place in History which will *live* while our *Republic stands.*"[15]

Clambering up scaling ladders, Pillow's soldiers entered the castle, followed shortly thereafter by Quitman's division from the other side. For a time, they ran wild, looting and hunting down the now defenseless Mexicans in retaliation for the atrocities at Molino del Rey.[16] By 9:30 A.M., their officers had

The Storming of Chapultepec. Author's collection.

restored order, the surviving Mexican prisoners were placed under guard, and the American flag was raised over the castle of Chapultepec, with lusty cheering that could be heard in the city below.

Those cheers sounded the death knell for the remnant of the San Patricio Battalion. After their capture at Churubusco, seventy-two of these turncoats had been tried by a military court, which sentenced all but two to death. Scott agonized over each case, carefully reviewing them to find some legal technicality or extenuating circumstance that might justify clemency. He pardoned two outright because of their youth and reduced the sentences of twenty others. The remaining fifty were hanged in batches: sixteen at San Angel on September 9, and four more at Mixcoac the next day.[17]

The last thirty were scheduled to meet the hangman on September 13. The arrangements were handled by Colonel Harney, who seemed to enjoy that sort of thing. He had a makeshift gallows constructed, consisting of a crossbeam supported by ten-foot-high posts. The prisoners were loaded onto wagons, with their hands tied and a noose around their neck. The wagons were then positioned under the crossbeam, to which were attached the other end of the ropes. There the condemned stood for two hours in the blazing sun, facing Chapultepec while the battle raged. As soon as the American flag was raised over the castle, Harney gave the signal, and the carts pulled away, leaving the prisoners dangling: their last sight, the banner they had deserted; their last sound, the cheers of their former comrades.[18]

Scott did not witness this grisly spectacle. As soon as the battle turned, he dashed to the front, spreading congratulations and encouragement along the way. "The old fellow looked the very personification of happiness," one of his soldiers noted.[19] The general quickly brought order out of confusion and pushed his troops forward while the enemy was still off balance from the loss of Chapultepec. Quitman was sent down the Belén causeway, and Worth's division advanced along the road to the San Cosme *garita*.

The struggles along these causeways were bloodier and more decisive than the better-known battle for Chapultepec. With no room for maneuver, both columns had to slog their way yard by yard, absorbing heavy casualties from Mexican artillery. Scott intended Quitman's thrust as a demonstration designed to divert attention from Worth, to whom he desired to give the honor of conquering the city. Quitman, however, balked at this subordinate role and pressed on, despite Scott's orders to hold back. "The capital is mine," he insisted. "My brave fellows have conquered it, and by God, they shall have it!" By nightfall, both Quitman and Worth had fought their way inside the city gates. There they stopped, and their men shivered through the coldest night they had yet endured in Mexico.[20]

While they lay sleepless and hungry on the cold ground, a group of Mexicans passed through the lines under a flag of truce. It was a delegation from the city council. Ushered into Scott's headquarters at 4:00 A.M., they announced that Santa Anna and his army had fled during the night. The city was now defenseless, and they were prepared to surrender it to the invaders. Scott's Mexican campaign was over.[21]

Six months and five days earlier, Scott and his 10,000 had landed on the beach near Vera Cruz. Since then, as one proud soldier boasted, "the American army has enacted miracles."[22] It had marched almost three hundred miles through the heart of enemy country, cut off from its base and living off the land. It had fought seven battles against larger armies that were entrenched behind positions of their choosing, and the Americans had not lost a single one. Finally, with its numbers reduced to only 7,000, it had occupied an enemy capital of 200,000 from which it dictated terms of peace.

Who deserved credit for what the Duke of Wellington hailed as a campaign "unsurpassed in military annals"? Scott repeatedly insisted that his West Point–trained officers were responsible for its success: "I will say on my dying bed that but for the Military Academy I never could have entered the basin of Mexico."[23] He interpreted his victories as a vindication of that professionalization project to which he had devoted his military career.

Some of his soldiers saw things differently. They attributed the victory to their own fighting spirit, rather than to their officers' military science. "The tactics of the service may be useful in fighting against the soldiers of Europe," one sergeant maintained, "but they cannot be applied in this country." President Polk, who had his own axe to grind, concurred. He claimed that the gallant American army could have won the war "if there was not an officer among them. This proves," he argued, "the injustice of giving all the credit of our victories to the commanding General and none to his inferior officers and men."[24]

Two more-knowledgeable military authorities disagreed with the president. "Credit is due to the troops engaged, it is true," conceded U. S. Grant, "but the plans and the strategy were the general's." The Duke of Wellington offered a simple explanation for American success: Winfield Scott. "He is the greatest living soldier," the Iron Duke magisterially declared. Carping critics might fault this or that aspect of Scott's generalship—the bribery scheme, the truce outside Mexico City, the needless casualties at Churubusco and Molino del Rey—but in the end, they were compelled to agree with Grant that "General Scott's successes are an answer to all criticism."[25]

It is difficult to imagine any of his rival generals overcoming all the obstacles Scott faced—certainly not the plodding Wool, the erratic Gaines, the moody Worth, the impulsive Twiggs, or the half-trained "mushroom generals" of Polk's creation. As Scott would rightly have been blamed had the campaign failed, so he deserved credit for its triumph. In Mexico, he was truly the indispensable man.

One final act in the Mexican drama remained to be played out. With the capital now an open city, the American army moved in to take possession.

Scott entering Mexico City. Mansfield, *The Life and Military Services of Lieut.-General Winfield Scott*, 455.

Early on the morning of September 14, Quitman stole a march on Worth and entered Mexico City at the head of three regiments. They passed in eerie silence through nearly deserted streets lined with barricaded houses, from whose shuttered windows white flags prudently fluttered. Mexicans peering out from behind those shutters saw a scruffy band of conquerors, blood-stained and ragged. Quitman himself, who had fallen into a canal, was splattered with mud and shuffled along less one shoe. Just as the cathedral bells chimed seven o'clock, he reached the Grand Plaza, and as his men stood at attention, the U.S. flag was raised over the National Palace.[26]

An hour later, Scott appeared, astride a magnificent bay charger, so resplendent in his full-dress uniform that even the Mexicans burst into involuntary applause. His aides, fearing snipers, had advised a less conspicuous entry, but the general was not to be denied his moment of glory. This was the realization of that adolescent daydream that all officers shared but hardly any ever achieved—to enter the enemy's capital in triumph like some victorious Roman imperator—and Scott intended to savor it.[27]

The victor dismounted and, after naming Quitman military governor of Mexico City, strode into the Halls of the Montezumas to the strains of "Yankee Doodle" and "Hail to the Chief." He seated himself at Santa Anna's desk, from where he would soon have the satisfaction of sending a long-anticipated dispatch to the secretary of war:

Sir:

At the end of another series of brilliant and arduous operations, of more than forty-eight hours continuance, this glorious army hoisted in the morning of the 14th, the colours of the United States on the walls of this palace.[28]

CHAPTER TWENTY-TWO

PERSECUTIONS

The occupation of Mexico City did not immediately bring peace with Mexico, nor did it end Scott's difficulties with James K. Polk. Both struggles would continue, but as it would turn out, Scott would find the Mexicans easier to deal with than the president.

His immediate task was to restore order. Although Santa Anna and his army had decamped, the capital city was still swarming with freebooters, guerrillas, and aggrieved patriots, augmented by the inhabitants of the local jails, whom Santa Anna had let loose as a parting gift to the Yanquis. For a time they ran wild. Snipers on rooftops and assassins on street corners took a heavy toll of American lives. The Americans then wheeled out their artillery, blasting to rubble houses that harbored snipers. Colonel Hitchcock went before the city council and threatened to "destroy the city and give it up to pillage if the firing does not cease." Within twenty-four hours, order was restored, and Scott could report that the city was now "tranquil and cheerful."[1]

He intended to keep it that way. Continuing with the conciliatory policy he had followed since Vera Cruz, Scott ordered his troops to respect Catholic ceremonies and to pay fair prices for all goods and services. Soldiers were not to be quartered in private homes without the owners' consent, and outrages against civilians would be punished under draconian martial law. "No officer and no man, under my orders, shall be allowed to dishonor me, the army and the U. States with impunity," Scott emphatically insisted.[2]

In effect, Scott had become America's first proconsul, governing Mexico City like some Roman sent to administer a refractory province. Sometimes his actions could seem high-handed, as when he dissolved an uncooperative city council and replaced it with a more amenable body. More often, however, his policies were designed to dampen discontent and promote efficiency. Civilian courts remained open, businesses flourished, corruption decreased, and even a Mexican acknowledged that Scott behaved with "humanity on all occasions." With pardonable exaggeration, Scott boasted, "Mexicans had never before known equal prosperity."[3]

These services carried a price. When he accepted the city's surrender, Scott levied a $150,000 "contribution" in lieu of pillage. From this amount, and another $80,000 from other sources, he earmarked $20,000 for the care of his sick and wounded and $90,000 for the purchase of shoes and blankets for his now ragged soldiers.[4] A further $100,000 was set aside to finance Scott's pet project of an asylum for old soldiers, and in a move that would later cause him embarrassment, $6,400 was pocketed by the general himself.

He justified these last two sums as legitimate under the traditional rules of warfare relating to prize money.[5] What he failed to realize was that these traditional rules had been superseded by the professionalism that Scott himself had labored so hard to bring about. Military commanders were no longer semiautonomous gentleman-adventurers, as in the days of Sir Francis Drake. Thanks in part to Scott's efforts, they were now bureaucratic functionaries of the nation-state. In this instance, Scott apparently failed to understand the full implications of his own life work.

Questions of propriety aside, Polk was disappointed with the meager sums raised by Scott and his fellow commanders. The president hoped that somehow the Mexicans could be made to pay the entire costs of the war. To that end, he and Secretary of War Marcy continually pressed Scott to divert all the customary Mexican taxation to support the American army of occupation, which, he argued, "will constitute powerful motives to induce the Mexican people and their rulers to desire peace."[6]

Scott was willing to take over some of the national revenues, such as import duties and seignorage at the mints, but he balked at siphoning off money needed by local governments, "as that would, in my humble judgment, be to make war on civilization; as no community can escape absolute anarchy without civil government, and all government must have some revenue for its support." He reminded the administration that "the success of our system . . . depends on our powers of conciliation" and warned against "exasperating the inhabitants and rendering the war, on their part, national, interminable and desperate." In any event, despite Polk's prodding, his military commanders were only able to squeeze about $4 million from the Mexicans, a far cry from the $100 million the war was estimated to cost the American treasury.[7]

To add to the expense, the long-awaited reinforcements promised by Marcy finally arrived in Mexico City, too late, of course, to be of help to Scott in his campaign. Veterans disdained these newcomers as "a lot of lousy Dutch and still more worthless natives," but they joined with them in "revelling in the Halls of the Montezumas." Theaters boomed (though boycotted by Mexicans), as did gambling dens, bordellos, and saloons. Officers found diversion in elegant masked balls, and enlisted men flocked to rowdy "fandangoes." Discipline and combat efficiency inevitably slumped. "My daily distress, under this head, weighs me to the earth," Scott moaned. Little wonder that even a sergeant noticed that the old general looked careworn.[8]

With expenses mounting and discipline sagging, an early peace treaty with the Mexicans seemed imperative. "Still," sighed Scott, "such is the obstinacy, or rather infatuation of this people, that it is very doubtful whether the new authorities will dare to sue for peace."[9]

A further obstacle to negotiations was raised by President Polk. His confidence in Commissioner Trist, never great, had now vanished entirely. Initially, Polk had condemned Trist for feuding with Scott; now he was furious because the general and the diplomat had reconciled their differences. The reversal was complete. "I am General Scott's friend for life," Trist gushed, and he now hailed his recent foe as "the soul of honor and probity . . . , affectionate, generous, forgiving, and a lover of justice." Such sentiments confirmed Polk's suspicions that Trist had become Scott's "mere tool and seems to be employed in ministering to his malignant passions."[10]

The president's wrath was fueled by greed. The success of American arms now raised the enticing possibility of acquiring more territory than originally anticipated—perhaps even all of Mexico itself. Trist, however, persisted in adhering to his original instructions, which encompassed only the lightly populated territories of Texas, New Mexico, and Upper California. The diplomat's reasons seemed compelling, though expressed with his customary undiplomatic arrogance that left Polk fuming with rage. To delay the negotiations by transferring them to Washington, as the president desired, would, Trist warned, discredit the Mexican peace party and give the pro-war faction time to mobilize sentiment in its favor. Continuation of the war, moreover, would require, by Scott's estimate, at least 50,000 more U.S. soldiers, vast expenditures, and the permanent military occupation of a hostile country, not to mention the racial and religious complications of trying to absorb millions of Catholic, mixed-race aliens into an already fractious American system.[11]

Polk was unmoved. A man who routinely labeled political opponents as "traitors" and who could wildly accuse the Whigs of "insidiously" plotting to foment a financial panic to undermine his administration would hardly be inclined to credit Trist with good faith.[12] He instantly concluded that the diplomat was in league with Scott to betray both president and country and vowed to rid himself of both men. Trist's authority to negotiate was revoked, and he was ordered to return home at once.

Trist, however, allowed himself to be persuaded that his presence in Mexico was indispensable to the cause of peace.[13] Defying his president's command, he continued to negotiate, and by February 2, 1848, he and the Mexicans finally hammered out a treaty at the suburb of Guadalupe Hidalgo. Since this treaty gave Polk everything he had publicly asked for—California, New Mexico, and Texas to the Rio Grande, all for an indemnity of only $15 million—the president could hardly disavow it, but he did manage to punish its maker. Polk vindictively refused to pay Trist's salary and expenses, leaving the commissioner and his family destitute until restitution was finally made a quarter century later.

Scott could not be dealt with quite so easily, but Polk was willing to wait for an opportunity. He did not have to wait long, for Scott played into the president's hand. His own generals proved to be his undoing. Deprived of further opportunities to fight Mexicans, they fell to quarrelling with each other over the distribution of honors, glory, and public acclaim.

As might have been expected, Worth and Pillow were the chief offenders. Both were ambitious for the fame that could promote their political aspirations, and each was the subject of adulatory letters that appeared in the public press. Although hidden behind pseudonyms, these letters seemed to bear the hallmarks of having been written, or at least encouraged by, the same generals whose heroic deeds they so lavishly extolled. Each also felt it necessary to belittle Scott in order to magnify his own achievements.

The first literary salvo on behalf of Worth appeared in Pittsburgh and was reprinted in a Tampico newspaper. It purported to be a letter from an unnamed army officer who accused Scott of mistreating Worth in order to eliminate a rival to the presidency. In particular, the officer claimed that Scott denied Worth proper credit for supposedly selecting the successful route around Lake Chalco in the army's march to Mexico City. In passing, the author also heaped praise upon Pillow, "bright, keen, and ready as an eagle," and on a certain Col. James Duncan, who, it would turn out, was the secret author of the piece.[14]

This effusion was followed by a series of letters on behalf of General Pillow. The most notorious appeared in the *New Orleans Daily Delta* over the pseudonym "Leonidas." Purporting to be a description of the Battles of Contreras and Churubusco, this letter was actually a hymn in praise of Pillow, who, "Leonidas" claimed, "evinced in this, as he has done on other occasions, that masterly military genius and profound knowledge of the science of war, which has astonished so much the mere martinets of the profession."[15] The chief of these martinets, Winfield Scott, was virtually invisible in this account. According to "Leonidas," he appeared late on the scene and issued only one trivial order. Otherwise, the plan, the execution, and, of course, the credit for these victories belonged exclusively to Pillow.

These letters were not only offensive to Scott personally but also were in violation of a longstanding army regulation that declared: "Private letters or reports, relative to military marches and operations, are frequently mischievous in design, and always disgraceful to the Army. They are therefore strictly forbidden." Officers violating this regulation were subject to dismissal from the service.[16] In early November, Scott officially reminded the army of this regulation and its bearing on the Tampico and "Leonidas" letters:

> It requires not a little charity to believe that the principal heroes of the scandalous letters alluded to, did not write them, or specially procure them to be written, and the intelligent can be at no loss in conjecturing the authors—chiefs, partisans and pet familiars. To the honor of the service, the disease—pruriency of fame *not* earned—cannot have seized upon half a dozen officers . . . all of whom, it is believed, belong to the same two coteries.
>
> False credit, may no doubt, be obtained at home, by such despicable self-puffing and malignant exclusions of others, but at the expense of the just esteem and consideration of all honorable officers who love their country, their profession and the truth of history.[17]

Although Scott's order mentioned no names, Worth leaped to the conclusion that it referred to him. Scott's one-time protégé, according to Hitchcock, had grown increasingly "destitute of both stability and judgment." Even though other officers resented him as the commanding general's pampered pet, Worth felt himself the victim of Scott's envious persecution. He stormed into headquarters demanding an explanation. Not receiving a satisfactory reply, he took his complaint directly to the secretary of war, in clear violation of army regulations and protocol. Worth's letter was so intemperate and insulting that Scott ordered his immediate arrest. When Duncan then stepped forward and admitted that he was the author of the Tampico letter, he received the same punishment. This was not as severe as it may have sounded. Neither officer was clapped in irons but merely confined to Mexico City and its environs.[18] They were soon joined in this confinement by yet another officer—Gideon Pillow.

For months, the master intriguer had been playing a double game: assuring Scott, "I will be his friend as long as I live," while at the same time sending a stream of reports to President Polk designed to undermine his commanding general.[19] Scott was inclined to look the other way rather than offend his politically potent second in command, but as evidence mounted that Pillow was, despite his denials, the only begetter of the "Leonidas" letter, Scott felt he had no choice but to prefer charges.

This was not Pillow's first brush with military justice. Shortly after the capture of Chapultepec, two small Mexican howitzers had been found in his wagon. Souvenirs of this sort were expressly forbidden under army regulations, and at a subsequent court of inquiry, Pillow denied responsibility and shifted the blame, if any, to some young officers. The court acquitted him of wrongdoing but, at the same time, expressed considerable skepticism about the truth of his alibis. Pillow was furious at this implied rebuke. He turned his wrath against his recently proclaimed friend for life, vowing to "blow up Scott. He is a most malignant man." He poured out his grievances to his old friend in the White House, who was predictably outraged. "General Pillow is a gallant and meritorious officer," Polk concluded, "who has been persecuted by Gen'l Scott for no other known reason than that he is a Democrat in his politics and was supposed to be my personal and political friend."[20]

Without waiting to investigate further, Polk blamed Scott's "vanity and tyrannical temper" for the embarrassing dissension within the army's high command and vowed to rid himself of this longstanding irritation. The very next day, December 31, he conferred with Democratic senators Lewis Cass and Jefferson Davis. Neither was a friend of Scott, but Davis was doubly hostile toward him, first as a partisan Democrat, and second as a military comrade and onetime son-in-law of Scott's rival, Zachary Taylor. All agreed that Scott deserved to be relieved of his command. Davis disingenuously suggested that he be replaced by Taylor, but Polk was too shrewd a fox to fall into that trap. He instead chose Maj. Gen. William O. Butler, a dependable Democrat.[21]

Orders went forth from the War Department releasing Scott's high-ranking prisoners from arrest and placing them and Scott, accuser along with the accused, under the scrutiny of a military court of inquiry. "In view of the present state of things in the army," Scott was stripped of his command. With a further twist of the knife, Secretary Marcy pretended that he was obliging Scott by acceding to a long-forgotten request to be relieved that the general had made in a petulant moment the previous spring. And so the axe, which had been long suspended over Scott's head, finally fell. "My poor services with this most gallant army are at length to be requited as I have long been led to expect they would be," Scott declared with understandable bitterness.[22]

The general's stunning fall from power created a universal sensation. Officers of the regular army could scarcely believe that "an idiot monkey" like Pillow "could cause the greatest Captain of the age to be disgraced upon the very theatre of his glory." Pillow himself was filled with "joy *inexpressible*," but some officers outside his small circle of admirers were so dismayed that they threatened to resign their commissions. A few enlisted men were so indignant at this "high-handed, outrageous and shameful act" that they considered mutiny.[23]

Back home, public opinion was divided along party lines: some expected Scott to ride his martyrdom into the White House; others thought he had ruined his political prospects by a display of petty vanity. Europeans were heard to condemn Scott's dismissal "as the result of a low and vulgar intrigue by inferior men." Mexicans were simply baffled. They were accustomed to seeing generals overthrow the government, not the other way around. Despite their hostility to the Yankee invaders, some Mexicans could not help but admire "the moral force of the American government, which, by a simple slip of paper, written at the distance of two thousand leagues, could humble a proud and victorious soldier and make him descend from his exalted position."[24]

That soldier was not surprised at being the victim of "the greatest wrongs ever heaped on a successful commander." To Scott, this latest indignity was merely a "continuation of the Jacksonian persecution" under which he had suffered for so long.[25] The court of inquiry that he now faced would subject him to more of the same.

Unlike a court-martial, a court of inquiry was more in the nature of a preliminary investigation. This meant that even in the unlikely event of a ruling against Pillow, he would be out of the army before the ponderous machinery of military justice could fix punishment. President Polk, however, was taking no chances. He personally intervened to stack the court in Pillow's favor by removing a judge whom he suspected might be sympathetic to Scott.[26]

The court convened on March 16, 1848, in Mexico City. At its outset, Scott asked that the case be dropped, citing the imminent end of the war, the dispersion of witnesses, and the altered circumstances that now made his charges moot. This was agreeable to Worth and Duncan but not to Pillow, who demanded his day (or rather, two months) in court. In the lengthy hearing that, when printed, consumed 635 pages of testimony and documents, Scott served as prosecutor, though at times it seemed as if he were the defendant on trial. Pillow conducted his own defense. Disproving the old saw that a lawyer who represents himself has a fool for a client, Pillow succeeded in tying up the court in legal knots. He fully lived up to Trist's evaluation of his legal talents as sufficient to qualify "for shining at a county court bar, in defence of a fellow charged with horse stealing, particularly if the case were a bad one and required dexterous tampering with witnesses."[27]

The strongest charge against Pillow accused him of responsibility for the "Leonidas" letter. Initially, the case against him had seemed so conclusive that he had considered resigning from the army rather than face an investigation.[28] The war correspondent of the *New Orleans Daily Delta,* James L. Freaner, was prepared to testify that late in August, Pillow had handed him an account of his role in the Battle of Contreras; that he asked it be forwarded to the *Delta;* that Freaner had taken the letter but, after reading it, decided it was too

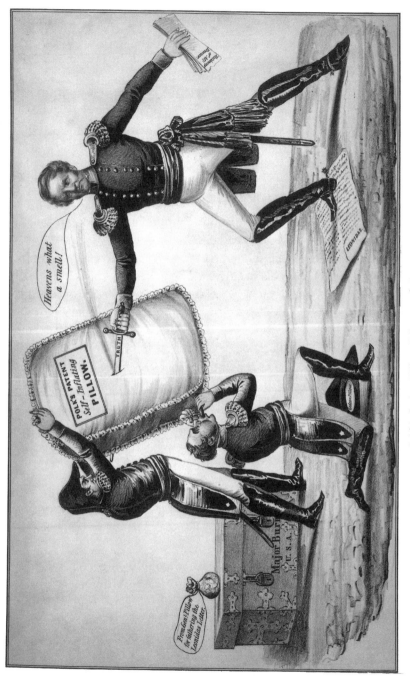

Self-inflating Pillow. Library of Congress.

improbable to publish; that in some manner a copy had been smuggled into his dispatch bag and had found its way into print under the name "Leonidas"; that upon comparison, this document was remarkably similar to Pillow's account; and that Pillow unsuccessfully attempted to retrieve the original.

This testimony could have been devastating, but by the time the court convened, Pillow was able to find an obscure assistant paymaster, Maj. Archibald W. Burns, who was willing to take the blame. Burns swore that he had managed to sneak undetected into Pillow's quarters. For some unexplained reason, he then copied the battle report and, in some unknown fashion, smuggled it into Freaner's dispatch pouch. Cross-examination was unable to shake Burns from his improbable story, and with that, the case against Pillow collapsed. The lesser charges also fell by the wayside. Even though it was shown that Pillow was asleep in the comfort of San Augustín during the decisive stage of the Battle of Contreras, the court indulgently accepted his version of events, as it did for all his other boasts.

Halfway through its deliberations, the court recessed to resume its hearings in the United States. The next day, April 22, Scott left Mexico. Considering his penchant for bombast, his farewell was surprisingly simple and dignified: "In taking official leave of the troops he has so long had the command of in an arduous campaign, a small part of whose glory has been, from position, reflected on the senior officer, Major General Scott is happy to be relieved by a general of established merit and distinction in the service of his country."[29]

The man so often derided as Old Fuss and Feathers would allow no fuss to be made over his departure, no banquets, honors, testimonials, or formal farewells, "on the ground that he is under condemnation of the government." Even his time of departure was kept secret from all but a few close friends. After giving them the keys to his wine cellar, the conqueror of Mexico mounted a small mule-drawn carriage, accompanied by only one servant, and quietly left the scene of his greatest triumph. He did not even have an escort, but as the carriage rolled through the city, it picked up an entourage of mounted officers, who followed it with tears streaming down their cheeks until the general ordered their return.[30]

Even some of his former foes were sorry to see Scott go. After the peace treaty had been agreed upon, a syndicate of wealthy Mexicans approached him with a startling proposition. Become military dictator of the country, they urged. Restore peace and prosperity and pave the way for Mexico's annexation by the United States. As a pledge of good faith, they were prepared to pay him $1.25 million immediately and the usual salary of the Mexican president for six years thereafter. The proposal tickled Scott's ego, but he was not so vain as to accept it. He was well aware that, as an American diplomat put it, "there are parties for any plan that may be proposed however absurd it might be."[31] Besides, he had unfinished business with Gideon Pillow and President Polk that required his immediate return to the United States.

That return by sea was slow and arduous. The broken-down brig he embarked upon, with the sentimental name of *Petersburg,* did not pull into New York harbor until May 20. By that time, Scott had become so incapacitated with what he delicately called "the Mexican disease" that he could scarcely walk, much less mount a vigorous defense at the court of inquiry, which reconvened near Washington on June 5.[32]

It required nearly another month for the mills of justice to grind to their preordained conclusion and wrap up what Scott bitterly called "the whitewashing of Pillow." As soon as he had been officially vindicated, Pillow was invited to dine with the president at the White House, and a promotion to major general soon followed. Brevet promotions were also awarded to two of the court's judges, Nathan Towson and William Belknap, for no other reason, so Scott charged, than "their acceptable services in shielding Pillow and browbeating Scott." Colonel Duncan was rewarded with the choice position of inspector general of the army. Scott tottered back to New Jersey, looking "warworn and Mexico-faded," to regain his health and nurse his grievances.[33]

Scott took little part in that summer's presidential campaign, though in happier circumstances, he might have been cast in the starring role. Before the quarrels with his generals had tarnished Scott's image, he had been considered by some leading Whigs as preferable to the untested Zachary Taylor. Scott at least knew what a tariff was, said Horace Greeley, and was not ashamed to call himself a Whig.[34] But Taylor's inexperience (he had never held public office) only seemed to endear him to the voters, and his nonpolitical stance (he had never even voted) managed to elevate him above mere politicians.

As the Whig nominating convention drew near and Scott still mired in the court of inquiry, Greeley belatedly realized that Taylor was the more serious threat to his preferred candidate, Henry Clay. By then, however, the Taylor bandwagon was unstoppable. At that convention, which met in June at Buffalo, Taylor led from the first ballot. Clay ran a close second, and Scott drew on pockets of support from the Midwest, which increased as Clay's strength faded. Taylor won the nomination with 117 votes on the fourth ballot. Scott had climbed to second place with a respectable 63 votes, but it was too little and too late.[35] The only consolation lay in the selection of Scott's longtime New York supporter Millard Fillmore as Taylor's running mate.

Scott watched quietly from the sidelines as Taylor eked out a narrow victory over the Democrat Lewis Cass. The vindication he might have been expected to feel at this rebuke to Polkism was tempered by the realization that the new president, though a fellow Whig, was no friend. Taylor was still smarting over the "injustice" Scott had committed by stripping him of troops in Mexico and signaled his resentment in numerous petty ways. Scott's official requests went unanswered, and his recommendations were invariably ignored. "My position, therefore, is as bad as it was during the scampism of Tyler or the despicable reign of Polk," he sadly concluded. "My punishments are not over."[36]

Rather than face further humiliation in Washington, Scott transferred army headquarters to New York City, far removed from the "neglect and contumely" he received at the hands of the administration in the capital.[37] There he occupied himself with army business until the sectional crisis of 1850 brought him back into the public eye.

That crisis was precipitated by the territorial expansion that Scott himself had done so much to bring about. As John C. Calhoun had once warned, "Mexico is to us the forbidden fruit, the penalty of eating it [is] to subject our institutions to political death."[38] The problem, as Calhoun had foreseen, was whether slavery would be allowed into these new western lands. At the time they were acquired, that seemed too remote a contingency to worry about, but the subsequent gold rush to California made that territory eligible for statehood far earlier than anyone could have imagined. Its admission had the potential of disrupting the balance between slave and free states and awakened passions that unleashed a whole host of simmering sectional disputes. These passions ran so high that it seemed the Union itself might be torn asunder.

The aging remnants of the Whig party, led by Webster and Clay, came to the rescue with a set of compromise proposals. Like most compromises, that of 1850 satisfied no one completely. In particular, a rigorous fugitive slave bill, thrown in to appease the South, infuriated antislavery elements in the North. Most Americans, including Scott, were prepared to accept the entire package for the sake of peace and union. He lobbied diligently behind the scenes on its behalf, and at a mammoth rally at New York's Castle Garden, he publicly endorsed it to "the most rapturous applause" from the crowd. In an infelicitous phrase, the massive 360-pound general pledged "to throw whatever weight I have into the scale to preserve our glorious Union, for if that should go down, I hope I may not survive it!"[39]

Unexpectedly, the major obstacle to compromise turned out to be President Taylor. Despite his slaveholding background, he revealed himself, once in office, to be a nationalist in the Andrew Jackson tradition, determined to uphold the Union by force rather than concessions. On the morning of July 4, 1850, he was preparing a stern message that could have pushed Southerners over the brink into secession and possibly civil war. That afternoon he attended an Independence Day celebration held under a merciless Washington sun. Returning home parched and woozy, he gobbled a bucket of cherries washed down with iced milk. Four days later, he was dead.

With the accession of the amiable and accommodating Millard Fillmore to the presidency, the sectional crisis was soon resolved. He put the authority of his office behind the compromise measures. They passed, and for the moment at least, sectional strife seemed laid to rest along with Zachary Taylor.

At the late president's state funeral, Scott stood out conspicuously among the mourners. Even a usually hostile newspaper had to concede that the "noble and commanding figure of the General-in-Chief, mounted on a spirited horse and shadowed by the towering plumes of yellow feathers which mark his rank, presented an object well calculated to fill the eye and swell the heart with patriotic pride."[40] At a White House reception shortly after the ceremonies, the new president warmly clasped Scott's hand. "Now, General," Fillmore assured him, "your persecutions are at an end." He spoke too soon. Within a few years, they would start up again.

CHAPTER TWENTY-THREE

CANDIDATE

Restored at last to official favor, Scott returned army headquarters from New York City to the nation's capital. There he conducted business from a cramped suite of rooms whose entrance was decorated with the same captured Mexican howitzers that Gideon Pillow had once tried to appropriate. His cluttered desk was piled high with official papers, which sometimes found their way under the cushions of his capacious armchair.[1]

For a few weeks in the summer of 1850, that office and its occupant were pressed into double duty. When Millard Fillmore assumed the presidency, he had swept away all of his predecessor's cabinet appointees. Until a new secretary of war could take office, Scott served as acting secretary, which made him, in effect, his own superior officer.

He allowed himself to dream of even higher office. It was hardly an accident that the only victorious Whig presidential candidates—William Henry Harrison and Zachary Taylor—had been military heroes, rather than party stalwarts. Their success had been predetermined by the nature of the Whig party. For one thing, the Whigs represented only a minority of the voters. Under normal circumstances, the Democratic majority could be expected to prevail. This compelled Whigs to present a candidate who could reach beyond traditional party ranks and appeal to uncommitted voters. For another thing, the Whigs were a national party, unlike their rival organization, which had been composed of an amalgam of ethnic and sectional interest groups ever since Thomas Jefferson and Aaron Burr first brought Southerners and Northern urban immigrants together to create what would become the Democratic party.

Both of these considerations led to the same conclusion: the Whigs needed a candidate who appeared to rise above party by being associated with some great national cause. In the context of nineteenth-century American society, that meant a military hero and, in turn, pointed to Scott, the last surviving major hero of two wars. This logic seemed compelling to some Whig leaders, too, especially those who had been swept from power and influence by Fillmore's housecleaning. Prominent among this group were William Seward, the New York senator who had been President Taylor's closest advisor, and John M. Clayton of Delaware, Taylor's secretary of state. To these recent insiders, now outsiders, Scott's candidacy represented "a hope of resuscitation," and in December 1851, they opened an official Scott-for-president headquarters in Washington.[2]

Association with Seward would prove a mixed blessing. The wily New Yorker was admired for his political skills, but his antislavery views and opposition to the Compromise of 1850 had rendered his name odious to Southern Whigs and their conservative Northern allies. Scott was warned that he "could not place himself in worse hands." Seward and his friends, it was claimed, "would ruin any patriot," and the general was urged to disassociate himself from their support lest they "drag him down with them."[3]

Despite these mutterings, Scott's path to the nomination seemed clear. "I suppose we must run Scott for President," grumbled Horace Greeley, "and I hate it." As late as December, Fillmore was still insisting that he would not run for reelection, and the perennial candidates of the Whig old guard, Henry Clay and Daniel Webster, were both so feeble that neither would live to see election day.[4] As the Whig nominating convention grew nearer, however, Fillmore allowed his friends to persuade him that his nomination was essential for the well-being of both party and country, while the seventy-year-old Webster, whose ambition overrode his awareness of mortality, refused to withdraw from the race. A bitter three-way contest for the nomination was now assured.

The Democrats seemed equally divided. Old party functionaries such as Lewis Cass, William Marcy, and James Buchanan roused little enthusiasm, and brash newcomer Stephen A. Douglas of Illinois alienated party regulars. They fought each other to a standstill for forty-nine ballots until the exhausted delegates turned in desperation to the darkest of dark horses—Franklin Pierce of New Hampshire. Only forty-seven years old, Pierce had served a few lackluster terms in the U.S. House and Senate before joining Scott's army as a general in the war with Mexico. There his military service had been competent but hardly heroic. He was thrown from his horse at Contreras and fainted from the pain, an experience he repeated at Churubusco, and he had been compelled to sit out the attack on Chapultepec with a bad case of dysentery.

Yet for all of his seeming insignificance, Pierce enjoyed at least two assets that could make him a formidable candidate. For one thing, he was a man of most amiable disposition and pleasing personality, capable, so it was thought, of healing the party divisions that had led to Democratic defeat four years earlier. For another, since he had not publicly committed himself on the great issues of the day, voters were free to write upon this blank slate whatever they pleased. A friend of Scott reluctantly acknowledged as much. "Democracies," he said, "are not over-partial to heroes and great men. . . . Scott's foibles are so many that he's vulnerable and can be made ridiculous, and this galvanized cypher, of whom nothing can be said but that he is a cypher, may very well beat him."[5]

Shortly before noon on June 16, 1852, the "quadrennial Walpurgis Night of the Whigs" was called to order at the Maryland Institute for the Promotion of the Mechanical Arts in Baltimore, the same hall where, just a few weeks earlier, the Democrats had nominated Franklin Pierce. Portraits of Jackson and Polk were now replaced with those of George Washington and Henry Clay, and the interior was lavishly bedecked with flags, bunting, streamers, and patriotic symbols. The city was sweltering under one of its notorious summer heat waves. Not even the generous distribution of fans and ice water could ease the discomfort of the three thousand delegates, reporters, and spectators who packed the steaming hall.[6]

Political passions were as torrid as the temperature. From the convention's opening gavel, it was apparent that the Whigs, once the party of national unity, were now sharply divided along sectional lines. Southern delegates, almost to a man, favored Fillmore because of his open advocacy of the Compromise of 1850 and were leery of Scott because of his association with the hated Seward. The sticking point was the Southern demand that the party commit itself to the "finality" of the 1850 agreement. Since such a pledge would include approval of the Fugitive Slave Law, anathema among some segments of Northern opinion, it was met with resistance from those who warned that the success of their party required avoiding any association with "that obnoxious measure."[7]

Common sense would seem to dictate that such a divisive issue should be evaded, as in 1848, when the Whigs had dispensed with a platform altogether. By a quirk of the rules, however, the Southerners dominated the committees, and in a show of force, they rammed through a platform that specifically and emphatically endorsed the compromise, fugitive slave provision and all. Scott's supporters reluctantly acceded, rather than precipitate an ugly floor fight, but they feared their candidate would "be forced to shoulder the fugitive slave law, and be crushed by it."[8]

Balloting began on the evening of June 20. One hundred and forty-nine votes, a majority of the delegates, were required for nomination. Both Fillmore, with 133 votes, and Scott, with 131, were nail-bitingly close to victory, but the 29 votes cast for Daniel Webster prevented either from claiming the prize.[9] Most of Fillmore's support came from the slaveholding states, few of which were likely to vote for the Whig ticket in November. Scott drew his strength from the populous, vote-rich states of the Old Northwest and Mid-Atlantic regions; Webster's was confined largely to his native New England. This tally remained stubbornly frozen for ballot after ballot throughout Friday night and all day Saturday. Occasionally, a scattered delegate or two might switch sides, but never in large enough numbers to inspire a decisive move in any direction. After forty-six ballots, the weary delegates adjourned until Monday, rather than sully the Lord's Day with worldly matters.

Sunday, however, was largely spent in "intriguing, caucusing, bragging and betting," rather than in prayer. The most frantic negotiations were conducted between the Fillmore and Webster camps. It did not require a mathematician to calculate that their combined votes could constitute a majority if they could be united. Webster seemed the logical choice to withdraw, but his supporters persisted in wishful thinking, acting, so a Fillmore advocate scoffed, "like a parcel of school boys, waiting for the sky to fall, that they might catch larks."[10] Aware that this was his last chance for the prize that had so long eluded him, Webster insisted that the Fillmore men come round to him, but wiser heads realized that the Fillmore votes could not be transferred to Webster in a bloc. Even if Fillmore should withdraw, enough of his Southern supporters would gravitate to Scott to put the general over the top.

When balloting was resumed on Monday, the united Fillmore front began to crumble, as scattered delegates drifted into the Scott column. By the fifty-second ballot, Scott's tally had inched its way to 148 votes, only 1 shy of a majority. The next ballot sealed his victory with 157 votes, which the delegates, in a belated show of unity, then made unanimous.[11] After dinner, the convention wrapped up its business by choosing Secretary of the Navy William A. Graham of North Carolina as Scott's running mate. As a wealthy slaveowner and a loyal member of Fillmore's cabinet, Graham was a satisfactory sop to the defeated factions, and his selection ended this rancorous gathering on a note of harmony.

Could that harmony be sustained throughout the campaign? The signs were not encouraging. In the pages of the most influential Whig newspaper, the *New York Tribune,* Editor Horace Greeley raged against his own party's platform: "We defy it, execrate it, spit upon it." This was not only in questionable taste but also politically awkward, considering that the candidate himself publicly and unconditionally embraced that same platform in his letter of acceptance. Seward attributed Scott's endorsement of that "wretched platform" to political naiveté, but, in fact, Scott's support of the Compromise of

The general in civilian attire. Photo attributed to Matthew Brady, ca. 1848. Courtesy Mead Art Museum, Amherst College.

1850 had been consistent and unequivocal ever since that measure had first been introduced.[12] He could hardly repudiate it now without incurring charges of gross opportunism.

Whigs from the Deep South, however, refused to be placated by Scott's assurances. Seven Southern Whig congressmen, including Alexander Stephens and Robert Toombs of Georgia, publicly rejected their party's nominee, and many other prominent Southern Whigs either sat out the election or openly defected to other candidates. At the same time, some anticompromise Northern Whigs were drawn to the Free Soil party. Four years earlier, that splinter party's candidate, Martin Van Buren, had siphoned off enough votes from the Democrats, especially in New York State, to swing the election to Zachary Taylor. In 1852, however, the Free Soilers chose an avowedly antislavery candidate, John. P. Hale of New Hampshire, who was more likely to make inroads among traditionally Whig voters. To add to Whig disarray, Daniel Webster refused to withdraw from the race. Acting, so Scott charged, "as if he had been cheated out of a rightful inheritance" with his rejection by the Whig convention, Webster allowed his name to be presented as an independent candidate, even though he privately urged his supporters to vote for Pierce.[13]

The Whig party, in short, was falling apart. Originally organized to oppose Andrew Jackson, it had outlived its mission: Jackson was dead. Dead (or dying) also were the party's founders, Calhoun, Webster, and Clay, as was the sense of unified national purpose that had emerged from the War of 1812 and animated the Whigs from their beginning. Now Southerners and Yankees, nativists and immigrants, wets and drys, glowered at each other across seemingly unbridgeable chasms. The traditional remedy of the Whigs—compromise—had proven futile, as their last compromise agreement, that of 1850, had turned on its own makers. Nor could the party fall back on its old program of promoting economic growth through tariffs, banks, and internal improvements, for the nation's gold rush–fueled prosperity had made these measures unnecessary.

Lacking a clearly defined set of issues, Whigs were compelled to emphasize their candidate's personal qualities. Here they found themselves at a disadvantage. Even a fellow Whig was compelled to concede that Scott lacked, "in his personal character, those attributes and qualities which make the people love him as they loved Jackson, Taylor and Harrison." Burdened with what a friend described as "the conceit and absurdity which have gained Scott the epithet of Fuss and Feathers," the candidate was unlikely to rouse much popular enthusiasm.[14] Whig publicists attempted to humanize their stuffy standard bearer with a slew of laudatory campaign biographies but found themselves outgunned on the literary front when Pierce enlisted his old college chum, Nathaniel Hawthorne, to write his life story.

On a somewhat less exalted literary level, both sides indulged in ridicule and personal vilification. Pierce's less-than-glorious military record made him fair game for derision. Although Scott himself chivalrously defended his recent subordinate's military service, his supporters had no such compunctions.[15] They gleefully circulated a mocking ditty:

> Two generals are in the field,
> Frank Pierce and Winfield Scott.

> Some think that Frank's a fighting man,
>   And some think he is not.
> 'Tis said that when in Mexico,
>   While leading on his force,
> He took a sudden fainting fit,
>   And tumbled off his horse.[16]

In Illinois, the prairie humorist Abraham Lincoln made fun of Pierce's meager civilian record. "He has *stood* in Congress," Lincoln observed. "If this make a man of him, then standing in a stable would make a man a horse."[17]

Two could play at that game, and Scott, with his long record of pompous pronouncements and verbal gaffes, was more vulnerable to mockery than the relatively unknown Pierce. The notorious "hasty plate of soup" and the dreaded "fire in the rear," of course, came in for their share of derision, as did Scott's alleged vanity and avarice. It was calculated that the general had, over his career, drawn more than $350,000 from the public trough but, like Oliver Twist, was "always asking for more."[18]

His earlier flirtation with nativism was dredged up to discredit him with immigrant voters, though, at the same time, he was accused of being a closet Papist on the basis of his daughter's conversion and his own toleration of Mexican Catholicism during the recent war. Scott's clumsy efforts to repudiate his earlier nativism only backfired. "Perhaps no man, certainly no American, owes so much to the valor and blood of Irishmen as myself. Many of them marched and fought under my command . . . , not one of whom was ever known to turn his back upon the enemy or a friend," he now insisted, forgetting for the moment the unfortunate San Patricio deserters he had ordered hanged.[19]

Even Scott's military exploits were denigrated. A widely circulated pamphlet raked over every incident of his army career, from the quarrel with Wilkinson to the controversy with Pillow, in order to demonstrate a pattern of vanity, contentiousness, self-serving ambition, and downright incompetence that rendered him unfit for the presidency. The anonymous pamphleteer concluded that Scott, unlike such revered citizen-soldiers as Washington and Jackson, "began life in command of a company of Regulars, a rank and file accustomed to black his boots and dress his horse and walk in silence in his presence, touching their caps with the fore-finger. It was in this school that he acquired the habit of indulging an overbearing, arrogant, insolent temper. . . . The result is, a character which may manage a regular soldierly . . . but is not one to be trusted with the management of the civil concerns of a free people."[20]

Democratic stump speakers across the nation joined the attack. In New York, Lewis Cass linked Whiggery to socialism and free love. In Pennsylvania, James Buchanan warned against Caesarism and asked rhetorically whether Scott, "in self-control, temper and disposition, is fit to become the successor to General Washington, in the presidential chair." Mississippi's Jefferson Davis, still fuming over "the heartless selfishness" with which Scott had stripped General Taylor's army of its best troops, assailed the Whig candidate as an out-and-out abolitionist and warned fellow Southerners that Seward "and his higher-law gang, steeped in slime of treasonable designs, have folded themselves about Gen. Scott with the tenacious hug of the anaconda."[21]

These shrill warnings seemed to have little effect on a largely indifferent electorate. Neither General Pierce nor General Scott, but rather "Gen'l. Apathy is the strongest candidate out here," reported a Cincinnati Whig. In an effort to inject some life into what was turning into a "horribly dull and stupid" election campaign, Scott's managers tried a bold experiment: they would send Scott himself on the campaign trail.[22]

This was an unprecedented step. Unlike candidates for lesser officers, presidential aspirants were expected to maintain a statesmanlike silence while allowing others to speak on their behalf. As Henry Clay had discovered, to his sorrow, Americans distrusted politicians who lusted too openly for the presidency, preferring what has been called "the reluctant tribune" on the model of that noble Roman, Cincinnatus. Scott could not, therefore, afford to appear too eager: he needed some respectable pretext to justify his campaign swing. President Fillmore obliged by sending his commanding general off on an inspection tour, ostensibly to evaluate sites for an old soldiers' home.

Scott's little train meandered through New York, Pennsylvania, and Ohio, stopping briefly at any village where Whig advancemen could assemble an audience. The crowds were enthusiastic, but unfortunately, the general had almost nothing to say to them. Discussing the issues would be a breach of propriety, and begging for votes would be unseemly. Instead, he spoke of the weather, greeted veterans, praised each city, hailed the rich Irish brogues or the hearty German accents he heard from the crowd, and then moved on to repeat the performance. The speeches, sneered a Democratic paper, were "as alike as eggs," and even a friend conceded that they appeared "awkward, strained, vapid and egotistical."[23]

When Scott's train reached Columbus, Ohio, farce turned to tragedy. The whistlestop began badly when some local Germans asked the general to comment on rumors that he had punished German deserters far more severely than Irishmen or natives. At that, Scott flew into an incoherent rage, flailing his arms "like a wild man," as he shouted: "It's a devilish invention! An infamous lie! A damned falsehood! . . . This is wicked, atrocious, horrible! You see me excited! I have a right to be excited! I carried on war as a Christian, and not as a fiend!" The intimidated Germans hastily withdrew, while the crowd sang:

> Hurrah for General Scott,
> The hero brave and true.
> We'll place him there,
> In the presidential chair,
> For he's our nominee.[24]

The candidate was then hailed with a twenty-one-gun salute. Unfortunately, one of the gunners carelessly overloaded his cannon, which blew up in his face and killed him. This sad news was concealed from Scott, but at the banquet that evening, word leaked out. The old general was so deeply affected that he had to be led, weeping "like a child," to his hotel room. "It is one thing to lose an arm in battle," he sobbed, "but, by God, no office in this world is worth a limb, much less a life!"[25]

Even without this incident, which Scott later declared was the most distressing he had ever experienced, his "nonpolitical" campaign tour had to be judged a failure. The candidate's efforts to strike the common touch came across as condescending, and his speeches evoked ridicule for their empty bombast.[26] Future presidential aspirants would draw a lesson from his example: not until 1872, with Horace Greeley, and 1896, with William Jennings Bryan, would major-party nominees attempt similar campaign swings, and with similar results.

The lesson was lost, however, on Scott himself. Surrounded by sycophantic advisors and wrapped in a cocoon of self-satisfaction, he floated serenely above unpleasant reality, so supremely confident of success that he was already distributing offices to deserving friends. "Gentlemen," he assured them, "I can count on my election with the same certainty that I can count the fingers on my hand and the toes on my feet."[27]

Scott was not alone in his delusion. Throughout October, predictions of a sweeping victory flowed into Whig headquarters, and even President Fillmore was encouraged by his party's prospects. November's election results brought a rude awakening. Scott and his party were not only defeated, they were overwhelmed. "Till the day when Babylon the Great shall be cast into the sea as a millstone," reflected a stunned Whig, "there will not be such another smash and collapse and catastrophe as yesterday befell the Whig party."[28]

Four years earlier, the Whigs had captured the presidency for Zachary Taylor by winning fifteen states with 163 electoral votes. In the election of 1852, Scott was able to carry only four states—Kentucky, Tennessee, Massachusetts, and Vermont—with a meager 42 electoral votes, while Pierce and the Democrats were racking up the 254 votes of the remaining twenty-seven states. Scott lost both his home state of Virginia and his adopted state of New Jersey.[29] Even Scott County, Virginia, named in his honor, voted for Pierce.

The defeat was not Scott's alone. His entire party was dragged down with him. In 1848, the Whigs had won control of Congress with 57 percent of the seats; after the deluge of 1852, they were reduced to 29 percent. Only five governors' chairs were now occupied by Whigs, three of them precariously. These results seemed to fulfill the prophecy of a disgruntled Tennessee Whig who had warned that should Scott be nominated, "he will prove to be the weakest man ever run of the Presidency. He will be more overwhelmingly defeated . . . than any man who has ever been placed in that position by any considerable political organization."[30] The future was even bleaker. By the time the next presidential election would roll around, the Whig party would no longer exist: Scott was the last Whig.

Could a disaster of this magnitude be blamed on any one candidate, no matter how inept he may have been? Even if Scott had possessed Webster's eloquence and Clay's cunning, could he have overcome the obstacles his party faced? Some have suggested that a forthright repudiation of the Fugitive Slave Law might have salvaged the campaign by preventing the Free Soil defection.[31] Yet even on the unlikely assumption that every Free Soil vote would have been cast for Scott, he would have carried only three additional states—Ohio, Connecticut, and Delaware (the latter two by paper-thin margins)—for a total of thirty-two additional electoral votes, not nearly enough to prevent a resounding defeat. The sad truth was that the Whig party was a sinking ship, and Scott could no more have prevented its wreck than could a passenger on the deck.

Scott himself professed relief over his political defeats, which he regarded as "blessings in disguise" for him personally. "Have they," he asked, "been as much to the country?" Or to put it another way, would Scott have made a good president? The obvious answer is no. His administrative and personal shortcomings were apparent: he was vain, pompous, inflexible, naive about men, and out of touch with the currents of his time. But the American people in 1852 were not voting in a vacuum, they were choosing between two men. They chose Franklin Pierce, and his presidency would lead straight to Civil War and over half a million American deaths. It is hard to imagine that Scott could have done worse, and his brief experience in governing Mexico gave some indication that he might have done better.[32]

Whether for good or ill, Scott's long presidential quest was over. "That hope is now gone forever; for even if I were twenty years younger," he vowed, "nothing would induce me again to place myself in the political arena. Five months' experience has made me heartily sick of that."[33] Now at age sixty-seven, he intended to devote his remaining years to the profession he knew best.

CHAPTER TWENTY-FOUR

EXILE

The army with which Scott fought the Mexican War was not all that different from the one he had commanded in the War of 1812. Its essential elements had changed so little that, had the young Scott been magically transported three decades into the future, he would have felt at home. The army was still a small force, composed of regulars augmented in wartime by volunteers; its basic weapon remained the muzzle-loaded musket; and its tactics (except for the innovative employment of light artillery to screen the infantry) could have come straight out of Scott's original handbooks. The Mexican War was hardly over, however, before the army's role began to be transformed by two elements: geography and technology.

During the 1840s, almost 1.25 million square miles of territory had been added to the United States, thanks in large part to Scott's Mexican campaign. Much of this increase, which amounted to an expansion of nearly 70 percent, encompassed remote and forbidding deserts and plains populated largely by roving Indian tribes, whose mastery of horsemanship made them some of the most formidable mounted warriors the world had seen since the days of the Mongol Horde.

Bringing these vast expanses under the sway of U.S. authority would, as Scott realized, require fundamental changes in the mission and organization of the army. For one thing, the American practice of allowing its army to melt away once a war was over would have to be modified, given the new responsibilities that patrolling this vast domain imposed. A year after the Treaty of Guadalupe Hidalgo, the authorized size of the army had dwindled to fewer than 9,500 men, or about 25 percent less than in 1815. Yet as Scott pointed out, even that number was misleading, since death, disability, and desertion could be counted on to reduce the ranks by a further 25–33 percent. This would leave only about 7,000 actual effectives to guard the augmented border, protect settlers, escort emigrant wagon trains, and overawe hostile Indians, all the while conducting the normal business of the military establishment.[1]

Rather than shrink the army to a "peace establishment," Scott proposed to double its size to 18,000 men. Part of this increase would come from adding a few additional regiments, but most of it could be achieved by doubling the number of enlisted men in each company, from forty-two to eighty-four, along the lines suggested by Calhoun's old plan of an "expansible army."[2] This argument was sufficiently persuasive to convince Congress to authorize a somewhat scaled-down version of Scott's plan in 1850.

The new territories required not merely a larger army but also a more mobile one. Cavalry had long been the neglected stepchild of American arms, scorned for its high expense and tainted by its association with suspect European aristocratic values.[3] It was of so little use in dealing with the woodland Indians east of the Mississippi that the branch virtually disappeared from the American order of battle during the twenty years following the War of 1812. Expansion of settlement onto the Great Plains restored its utility. In these wide-open spaces, Indian horsemen could literally ride rings around the lumbering American foot soldiers, whom they mockingly called "walk-a-heaps."

To redress this imbalance, Scott called in the early 1850s for more cavalry regiments, arguing, "Experience has shown that small bodies of horse traversing the prairies . . . exert a greater pacific influence over the wild Indians, than would, perhaps, ten times the number of troops tied down . . . to a few fixed points." He insisted on professionally trained cavalrymen, rather than the "mongrel force" of mounted infantry often adopted as an economical makeshift. Putting foot soldiers in the saddle, he argued, "can only result in disorganizing them as infantry, and converting them into extremely indifferent horsemen," whose inexperience would ruin both horses and equipment, "thus making this non-descript force the most expensive and the least efficient ever known to the service."[4]

Scott's recommendations on this matter would be adopted during the Pierce administration. Pierce's secretary of war, Jefferson Davis, is usually given credit for this as well as for the expansion of the army, but the record shows that he was anticipated on both points by Scott.[5] Davis's bizarre experiment with a camel corps to patrol the New Mexico desert, however, appears to have been entirely his own idea.

When it came to the military implications of the new technology, however, Scott's vision was less keen. By the mid–nineteenth century, the United States was in the throes of a technological upheaval. Railroads, steamships, the telegraph, cheap and abundant steel, and efficient techniques of mass production not only transformed civilian life but also held the potential of altering the nature of war. Although Scott was not averse to technological innovations (he was an early and persistent advocate of replacing flintlock muskets with percussion caps), he did not fully grasp their consequences.[6] Mass production, for example, made mass armies possible, not only by its capacity to produce more weapons for more soldiers but also by increasing economic output so that nations could afford the productivity drain these large armies imposed. Improved farm machinery, to take another example, allowed farmers to be withdrawn from their fields to fight without creating massive food shortages. Mass literacy and mass politics encouraged them to become motivated by a cause, rather than by dreams of glory or fear of discipline.

War, in short, was on the verge of becoming industrialized and democratized, which spelled an end to Scott's cherished professionalism. Future wars might be led by a professional officer corps, but the mass armies they commanded would be composed, by necessity, largely of hastily trained citizen-soldiers, rather than Scott's "rascally regulars."

A seemingly minor innovation epitomized the revolutionary effect of new technology. This was the introduction of the minié ball rifle, which, in the mid-1850s, replaced the smoothbore musket as the standard infantry weapon. A simple, machine-produced bullet, the minié "ball" was actually a dimpled conical projectile of lead designed to expand under the heat of exploding gunpowder so that it would fit snugly into the rifled grooves of the barrel. The spin imparted as it traveled along these spiral grooves focused its energy and gave it a killing range of up to one thousand yards, ten times that of the old musket. And the simplicity of the rifle's operation allowed it to be fired two or three times within a minute.[7]

At one stroke, the lessons Scott had so carefully imparted at his 1814 training camp at Flint Hill were now rendered obsolete. Close-order drill, rigid discipline, automaton-like precision, the "touch of the elbow"—all of which were based on the requirements of the short-range, inaccurate musket—were now useless skills.

Swept away also was the foundation stone of Scott's life work—the faith that wars must be fought by a small, rigorously trained, professional force. Scott did not realize this, but then neither did Jefferson Davis nor anyone else. It would require a year or more of Civil War before the tactical problems posed by the new weaponry would even be addressed, and by that war's end, they had not yet been satisfactorily solved.

With the army at such a critical juncture, it needed, more than ever, firm, coordinated guidance from its high command. That command appeared ideally suited by background and ability to meet the challenges of this new era: a general, ripe with the accumulated wisdom of four decades experience; a young, vigorous president; and a secretary of war who boasted a unique set of qualifications. As a graduate of the U.S. Military Academy; a genuine Mexican War hero, whose Mississippi Rifles had saved the day at Buena Vista; and as a former chairman of the Senate Committee on Military Affairs, Jefferson Davis brought to the War Department a rare combination of theoretical, practical, and political knowledge and experience.

But appearances were deceptive. Despite their credentials, all three men wasted the opportunity before them. As with so much else in that dismal decade, the military leadership descended into pettiness, bickering, and vituperation. There was ample blame to go around. As Scott aged, he grew even more querulous and testy. President Pierce revealed himself as both indecisive and stubborn, dependent upon a small circle of advisers, mostly Southern, of whom Davis was the most influential. Davis, despite his manifest abilities, was wrapped in an impenetrable mantle of self-righteousness. Even more than Henry Clay, Jefferson Davis would rather be right than president. Unfortunately for the Confederacy, he would be president and, in that office, would display the same smug pedantry, vindictiveness, and obsessive micromanagement that he exhibited in his dealings with Scott, foreshadowing one of the reasons the Lost Cause would be lost.

Scott could read the signs. Rather than deal face to face with a president who had recently been his political rival and a secretary of war who was on record as declaring Scott to be "peevish, proud, petulant, vain and presumptuous," he packed his bags and returned army headquarters to New York City. There he rented office space on West 11th Street, only a block from the handsome townhouse a consortium of wealthy Whig admirers had given him as consolation for his recent political disappointment. The location was convenient, but the quarters were chilly and uncomfortable, since a stingy War Department would only authorize fuel for two rooms, hardly enough to accommodate the general and his staff of seven.[8]

From this cramped suite, Scott conducted what amounted to a command post in exile. Although he continued to supervise the day-to-day business of the army and to advocate for such favorite measures as pay raises for officers and the establishment of an old soldiers' home, his suggestions for promotions and appointments often went unheeded, and his policy advice was seldom solicited. In 1855, he complained to the War Department that, even though he stood ready to return to Washington at any time for consultation, "I have not, in more than two years, been once summoned and I do not remember to have been consulted by mail or wire more than once."[9] He did make occasional forays to inspect army posts or to testify before congressional committees, but in important matters, he was largely ignored.

These side trips touched off the first round of what would prove the most vitriolic feud of a career that had been marked by feuds. Scott had been in the habit of billing the War Department for trips taken on official business. In May 1853, Secretary Davis discovered a regulation permitting reimbursements only to those officers "who travel under written and special orders from their proper superiors," and he disallowed seven expense vouchers totaling $577.60.[10]

Scott objected on the grounds that, as commanding general, he had no superior officer. The secretary responded that the president was Scott's superior, and he had to approve of any voucher, be it only for ten cents (as if the president of the United States had nothing better to do than act as a glorified disbursing clerk). Davis was probably trying to make two points: first, that the military was under civilian control; second, that Scott had lost the recent presidential election. Having made both, he then, two years later, approved Scott's disputed vouchers.[11] By that time, however, the original quarrel had been swallowed up in the next round of the controversy.

Round two began when Davis dredged up Scott's old Mexican War accounts and challenged the commission of over $6,000 that Scott had retained according to "the laws and usages of war." The general appealed to the president directly and persuaded him to approve his claim. As he left the White House, Scott ran into Secretary Davis, who had evidently been forewarned of his mission. No sooner had he returned to his lodgings than a messenger appeared, summoning him back to the White House, where Pierce explained that he had changed his mind after talking to the secretary of war. Scott offered counterarguments, and the malleable president again reversed his stand, ruling once more in Scott's favor. Davis did not take defeat lightly. With a tenacity worthy of Inspector Javert, he burrowed into the department accounts and came up with sums allegedly owed by Scott that more than offset the amount Pierce had authorized. Scott not only lost his promised commission but also wound up owing the government money. Round two for Davis.[12]

The next round was touched off by Scott's promotion to brevet lieutenant general, an honor Davis had opposed from its inception, but which Scott had pursued with what some regarded as almost indecent eagerness. "At my time of life," he admitted, "a man requires compliments."[13] A few years earlier, the award of an honorary doctorate by Columbia College had so pleased him that he would later append the initials "LL.D." to the title page of his *Memoirs*. To occupy the rank last held by George Washington would be an even greater honor, confirming the title with which his admirers liked to describe him: "The Greatest Captain of the Age."

It was a long, drawn-out process. Congress considered the matter first in February 1849 and regularly thereafter. Scott closely watched every step of its progress, though he insisted he did not lobby for its passage. Technically, that disclaimer may have been truthful, but he was hardly a passive observer. He mobilized his friends in and out of Congress, had General Hitchcock write a puff piece for the press, and even contributed some anonymous squibs himself.[14]

On March 7, 1855, the coveted promotion was finally granted, backdated to March 29, 1847, the day Scott received the surrender of Vera Cruz. It was not an empty honor: by some constructions, it also carried with it a retroactive increase in salary and perquisites. Scott certainly thought it did, and on the very next day, he submitted a bill for $26,661.72 for eight years of back pay. The paymaster general cautiously passed the request on to Secretary Davis, who, having failed to block the measure, now tried to negate it by disallowing the claim.

To buttress his position, Davis appealed to Attorney General Caleb Cushing for a definitive legal ruling. Scott was prepared for battle. He submitted a massive brief of thirty-three printed pages, containing six attachments and eight endorsements, including three from former attorneys general, to buttress his case. Living up to his reputation as the most learned man in America, Cushing responded with a ruling of twenty-five closely packed pages that drew upon Roman law, English precedent, and American history to support Scott's position.[15]

This was not the answer Davis had expected. He coldly replied that Cushing's "reasoning does not carry conviction to my mind" and brushed aside a relevant federal court decision on the grounds that civilians could not understand military procedure. He made his case to the president in a rambling, monstrously long memo, the thrust of which seemed to be that, despite the recent act of Congress, the office of lieutenant general did not exist; and that if it did, it had no duties; and even if it did have duties, they would not warrant extra pay. Forced to chose between two of his own cabinet officers, President Pierce sided with the attorney general, even though Davis threatened to resign. The payment to Scott was scaled down to $10,465.67 by eliminating some perquisites, but even so, Davis sulked over his defeat. He endorsed the president's order with a sullen disclaimer: "The opinion of the Department, as heretofore expressed, remains unchanged."[16] Round three to Scott.

The various controversies involving Scott were so extensive that the relevant correspondence filled a 254-page compendium. One wonders how the Pierce administration found time to do anything else, but, in fact, it was simultaneously involved in the most serious sectional crisis since Jackson's day: the Kansas-Nebraska imbroglio.

In January 1854, Senator Stephen A. Douglas introduced a measure that would permit slavery in the newly organized Kansas Territory if the settlers so desired. This raised the possibility of slavery being extended into those western lands that the Missouri Compromise of 1820 had declared forever free. The repeal of this hitherto-sacred sectional compact was, ironically, supported by those same Southerners who, two years earlier, had insisted upon the "finality" of the Compromise of 1850. In the North, however, the measure raised a storm of protest that led, among other consequences, to the formation of a new political party, the Republican, to fill the void left by the collapse of the Whigs.

Kansas itself was thrown into chaos, as guerrilla warfare erupted between rival factions. Since the Pierce administration, which had supported Douglas's measure, was unable to control the violence the proposal spawned, some suggested that the Kansas frontier might be pacified by the same man who had brought peace to the northern frontier a generation earlier—Winfield Scott. "His great name would speak trumpet-tongued for peace," claimed Whig senator John J. Crittenden, "his words of reproof would be sharper than the sword to the refractory and rebellious, and his words of cheer would comfort and strengthen good men. . . . Those who are lost to a sense of duty will know that they will be made to feel the power of the sword of this great people in his hands."[17]

Other Whigs, such as Horace Greeley, objected that sending Scott to Kansas only "to obey the instructions of Jeff Davis and enforce the acts of the tyrannical bogus Legislature would be to lacerate his feelings, tarnish his proud fame and probably hasten his descent to the tomb." Scott, who had been opposed to the Kansas-Nebraska Act from the first, had no desire to involve himself in its enforcement.[18] More to the point, neither Davis nor Pierce had any intention of allowing him to do so. Bleeding Kansas would continue to bleed.

And Davis and Scott would continue to feud. Up to this point, the tone of their correspondence had been frosty but relatively civil. It now degenerated into an ill-tempered slanging match. The nerves of both principals had grown increasingly frayed. Scott was aging, ill, and bitter over being shunted aside. Davis was still reeling from the loss of his infant son to measles and was beginning to show signs of that painful neuralgia that would torment his latter years. Always pugnacious—he had once engaged in a knockdown, drag-out fistfight with a fellow senator—Davis now vented his anger upon all who opposed him, picking quarrels with Generals Wool and Hitchcock that were almost as fierce as the one he conducted with Scott.[19] His treatment of Hitchcock set off the fourth and most rancorous round of his dispute with the commanding general.

In July 1855, Scott granted Hitchcock a leave of absence to attend to personal business. Seeing an opportunity to strike two foes with one stone, Davis revoked it. Scott protested on the somewhat dubious legal grounds that the secretary's orders were invalid unless made specifically in the name of the president, but his real grievance was with Davis's long train of provocations, designed, so he charged, "to crush me into a servile dependence to your self-will." The general professed reluctance to answer Davis in kind, "for at my time of life all angry discussions are painful," but as he enumerated his griev-ances at length, his relish for this style of verbal conflict could not be dis-guised. "I know your obstinacy," Scott concluded, "and I know also what is due to myself as a man and a soldier, and if I am to be crushed I prefer it at the hands of my military peers," rather than by Davis's band of "mercenaries and sycophants."[20]

Poor Hitchcock, the original casus belli, was now quite forgotten as the war of words escalated. The principal antagonists were no longer writing to each other, nor were they even addressing the public or posterity. They had passed beyond those considerations into that purer realm where the author writes solely for the joy of seeing his words emerge upon the page. They were engaged in art for art's sake.

Scott: "I shall treat your communications, whether designed as private and scurrilous, or public missives of arrogance and superciliousness, as equally official. There are beauties in them which ought not to be lost; and it shall not be my fault if I do not render your part of this correspondence as memorable examples to be shunned by your successors."[21]

Davis: "Your petulance, characteristic egotism, and recklessness of ac-cusation, have imposed on me the task of unveiling some of your defor-mities . . . , and if I have succeeded in making you see yourself as others see you, it may prove a useful service."[22]

Scott: "My silence under the new provocation, has been the result, first, of pity, and next, forgetfulness. Compassion is always due to an enraged imbecile, who lays about him in blows which hurt only himself, or who, at the worst, seeks to stifle his opponent by the dint of naughty words."[23]

Davis (unable to resist getting in the last word): "The delay for which you make a hypocritical apology has strengthened you to resume the labor of vituperation; but, having early in this correspondence stamped you with falsehood, . . . I am gratified to be relieved from the necessity of further exposing your malignity and depravity."[24]

And there the matter rested, with the combatants exhausted. Hitchcock was driven out of the army, retiring to the quiet of his library to immerse himself in Swedenborgian mysticism. Davis, in his subsequent career as president of the Confederacy, would refuse to appoint a commanding general until the waning days of the Civil War, perhaps fearing a replay of his 1850s difficulties. Scott would be driven further into his self-imposed exile. As a final humilia-tion, Davis issued a new edition of the army's regulations without bothering to consult Scott, its original author. Article 10, which defined the duties of the commanding general, was pointedly omitted.[25]

This was Davis's parting shot. President Pierce had made himself so controversial by his espousal of the Kansas-Nebraska Act that he was passed over by his party for renomination. His successor, James Buchanan, was no friend to Scott, whom he regarded as vain, stubborn, and lacking in sound judgment. Even so, Scott eagerly looked forward to the new administration. After suffering four years under Pierce, "the meanest creature that ever aspired to be President," any change, he allowed himself to hope, was bound to be a change for the better.[26]

CHAPTER TWENTY-FIVE

RETURN

The new administration had scarcely settled in before Winfield Scott paid his respects and declared his willingness to return army headquarters to Washington if the president so desired.[1] Despite their political differences, President Buchanan received the general with his characteristic courtliness. Now in his mid-sixties, Buchanan, in contrast to his youthful predecessor, brought an impressive resume and a cautious disposition to his high office. Their political views, however, were cut from the same cloth. Both Pierce and Buchanan were what the political slang of the day called "Doughfaces"—that is, Northern men with Southern principles. Both surrounded themselves with Southern partisans and leaned heavily upon them for advice.

Prominent among this circle was former Virginia governor John B. Floyd, Buchanan's choice to head the War Department. A proslavery advocate of such intense zeal that he had once proposed that Virginia levy a tax on goods produced by states that refused to return fugitive slaves, Floyd was totally devoid of military experience, and he was considered venal and lazy to boot. His first interview with Scott was brief but friendly, and the general was sufficiently encouraged to bombard the new secretary with proposals to undo some of his predecessor's "acts of injustice." None of these suggestions were acted upon, the secretary being, so Scott complained, "perfectly green as well as dilatory."[2] The frustrated commanding general took up again his post of exile at army headquarters in New York.

One military project did arouse Secretary Floyd's enthusiasm, though it was not one of Scott's suggestions. This was an expedition into the Territory of Utah. Only a few years earlier, the Mormons had been driven out of the

United States by the hostility of the Gentiles (as they called all non-Mormons). The Saints (as the Mormons called themselves) settled in the isolated desert region around the Great Salt Lake, established a theocracy under the tight control of Brigham Young and his Twelve Apostles, and prospered mightily. Now, by terms of the Treaty of Guadalupe Hidalgo, they found themselves back within the borders of the United States, and what was even worse, their home lay smack across the main emigrant trail to California.

Inevitably, friction between Saints and Gentiles struck sparks that threatened to produce a general conflagration. Lurid tales of emigrants harassed, judges defied, federal officials intimidated, and dissidents murdered were splashed across eastern newspapers, raising a demand for some assertion of national authority over this refractory territory. The newly installed Buchanan administration proposed a massive punitive expedition, ultimately involving over one-third of the army, making it the most ambitious military project between the Mexican War and the Civil War.

This response seemed so disproportionate to the provocation that it invited conspiracy theories among the skeptical.[3] Some, with the advantage of hindsight, would later suggest that the expedition was a pretext to send the army to intimidate Kansas or perhaps to disperse it in the event of a civil war. Others, conversely, suspected that the expedition was an attempt to divert public attention from the looming sectional crisis. A prominent Democrat urged President Buchanan to "supersede the Negro-Mania with the almost universal excitement of an Anti-Mormon Crusade," in which "the pipings of Abolitionism will hardly be heard amidst the thunder of the storm we shall raise."[4]

Such a crusade might well prove popular, especially considering the public outrage over the Mormon practice of polygamy. The newly organized Republican party condemned the practice, linking it with slavery as "twin relics of barbarism." Many regarded it with prurient fascination, and a few with amusement (such as Mark Twain, who wrote, "In Utah, the girls mostly marry Young"), but it was unlikely that they would support a full-scale war to eradicate the practice, however odious it might seem.[5]

Some cynics thought they detected a more sordid motive lurking behind Floyd's proposed expedition. "Who has this enormous expenditure of public funds benefitted," asked a Mormon newspaper, "except it be army contractors, speculators and depraved politicians?" Considering the high level of corruption that permeated the Buchanan administration, including scandals that smirched Floyd's conduct of the War Department, such a suspicion was not unwarranted, though subsequent investigations have found no evidence linking the Mormon expedition to corrupt schemes. Scott did not need direct evidence. By observing "the desperate characters who frequented the Secretary," he was convinced that the expedition was nothing more than an excuse for "frauds and peculation."[6]

The old general threw cold water on Floyd's pet project from the first. A mere token expedition, he advised, would not suffice to overawe the undisciplined but "fanatical" Mormons, and it could well find itself under siege for six months or a year until reinforcements arrived. He estimated that 4,000 troops would be required to do the job properly, but Scott was willing to risk a minimum detachment of 2,500. He sternly warned "that if the occupation be attempted with an inadequate force, and consequently, be cut off or destroyed, the U. States, after suffering the deep mortification, would be obliged to employ double the force that would, originally, have been necessary. This disgrace ought not to be risked by too great a parsimony in the means first employed."[7]

How could the tiny American army, already stretched to the limit by Kansas and Indian troubles, spare such a large force, and how could it arrive at its destination in time to be of use? Scott tried to explain the daunting logistical difficulties to the untutored secretary of war. The expedition, he explained, had to reach Utah and establish its camp before the winter frosts set in, say by early November. Since the 1,150-mile march from Fort Leavenworth would require at least ninety days, this set a limit of mid-July for its departure. If the available troops had to be drawn from bases farther east, an even earlier date would be required, yet it was already late in May. For all these reasons, Scott gravely concluded, "we cannot make an orderly or safe movement upon the Utah valley, before the beginning of the summer of 1858."[8]

The general's advice was ignored, and his misgivings proved well-founded. As he had feared, the expeditionary force was too little and too late. Unable to reach Utah before the onset of winter, it was forced to hole up in the mountains, awaiting springtime and fresh supplies. While the soldiers were suffering under half rations necessitated by Brigham Young's scorched-earth policy, the government did what it should have done in the first place—it sent civilian negotiators to Utah to iron out the difficulties with the Mormons. By the time fresh reinforcements arrived, the crisis had passed, and the soldiers were no longer needed. The entire project, as Scott had feared, turned out to be a needless drain on army resources.

Scott harbored equally grave reservations over the War Department's initial choice of commander for this futile expedition, Brig. Gen. William S. Harney. Bad blood had festered between the two for decades. In Mexico, Harney's rash, insubordinate, and self-serving course had been partially redeemed in Scott's eyes by his gallantry at Cerro Gordo, but to some disgruntled brother officers, he continued to be regarded as "notorious for profanity, brutality, incompetence, peculation, recklessness, insubordination, tyranny and mendacity."[9]

For these reasons, Scott attempted to keep Harney on a tight leash, insisting that he work in full cooperation with civil authorities and under no circumstances "attack any body of citizens whatever except in self-defence." Self-restraint, however, was not Harney's strong suit, and soon he was breathing fire and threatening to hang Brigham Young and his Twelve Apostles on Temple Square. Nor was Harney known for docile submission to authority. His habitual bypassing of Scott's office drew repeated reprimands, which he just as repeatedly ignored. The last straw was the loss of a vital supply train of beef cattle, directly attributable to Harney's flagrant disregard of Scott's specific orders.[10] His command was turned over to Col. Albert Sidney Johnston, and Harney was sent off to the distant reaches of the Pacific Northwest, where it was hoped that he would have less opportunity to exercise his capacity for mischief.

Scott had toyed with the idea of taking control of the expedition into his own hands, but age and infirmities kept him at home. He was now over seventy years old, and it showed. Scott could no longer mount a horse without the aid of a stepladder, and he complained of sore knees, sore throat, sore back, and other assorted ills his aging flesh was heir to. In winter, he found comfort basking in the Louisiana sunshine, and in summer, he sought relief in the refreshing breezes of West Point. Otherwise, he maintained his headquarters in New York City, where he was a fixture on the social circuit and a familiar figure in the market stalls of Greenwich Village.[11] In this semiretirement, the reins of army control gradually slipped from his hands. He seemed to be drifting into irrelevancy until, in the summer of 1859, a crisis in far-off Oregon thrust him suddenly back onto center stage.

It started with a pig. That unfortunate animal was, indirectly, a victim of an ambiguity in the Oregon Treaty of 1846. This agreement had established the forty-ninth parallel as the boundary between the United States and British Canada except for its westernmost end, which was to run through the main channel of Puget Sound. Left unresolved, however, was the question of just which channel was the main one. By one interpretation, the San Juan Islands belonged to England; by another, to the United States. Until a boundary commission could settle the matter, the tiny archipelago lay in limbo, with a handful of settlers from both nations living there in uneasy coexistence.

That relative peace was shattered when an American farmer shot a prize British pig found rooting in his garden. When British officials demanded compensation, the farmer threatened to shoot them as well; backed by a man-of-war, they then threatened his arrest. American reaction was swift and decisive, as was to be expected, considering the impulsive nature of the general in command—William S. Harney. He ordered a company of infantry under Capt.

George Pickett to land on the disputed island. The British retaliated by sending more warships, and Harney then sent more soldiers, almost seven hundred in all.[12]

For official consumption, Harney pretended that he was only acting to protect American settlers from Indian attacks, but the British were not deceived. They thought they detected the opening gun of a campaign to snatch western Canada from their grasp. Harney added fuel to this suspicion by publicly calling for the American annexation of Vancouver Island. Some Americans, Scott included, suspected that Harney was trying to promote his improbable quest for the presidency, but whatever his motive, Harney had plunged his country into an unnecessary crisis.[13] It would take only one hotheaded soldier or another errant pig to spark a war.

The confrontation on San Juan Island began in late June 1859, but the news did not officially reach Washington until September. When it did, President Buchanan decided at once that a cooler head than Harney's was needed on the scene. Who more appropriate to send than the seasoned Pacificator of the Northern Border? Scott needed no persuasion. The seventy-three-year-old general put aside his aches and pains and promptly boarded the steamer *Star of the West* for the first leg of a tedious, month-long, seven-thousand-mile journey. From far-off Paris, Maria Scott bade her husband Godspeed with a graceful *l'envoi*, which concluded:

> Sail on gallant Scott! true disciple of virtue!
> Whose justice and faith every danger will breast.
> Nor swerve in the conflict. Heaven will not desert you,
> There are angels on guard 'round the "Star of the West."[14]

During the long voyage, Scott had ample time to mull over his instructions from the War Department, which were vague but flattering. The president, who had once in the heat of the campaign of 1852 denounced Scott's judgment as perverse and unsound, now gave him carte blanche. "It is impossible, at this distance from the scene, and in ignorance of what may have already transpired on the spot, to give you positive instructions as to your course of action. Much, very much, must be left to your own discretion, and the President is happy to believe that discretion could not be entrusted to more competent hands."[15]

The preferred outcome of his mission, Scott was advised, would be the maintenance of peace and the status quo until the boundary could be settled by diplomacy. In the meantime, he was to press for a joint occupation of the islands by a limited number of troops from both nations. "But what shall be your course should the forces of the two Governments have come into collision before your arrival?" In that case, Scott was urged to restore calm and good order, if that could be managed on honorable terms. "It would be a shocking event if the two nations should be precipitated into war respecting the possession of a small island." But, in the unlikely event that the crisis should escalate into war, "the President feels a just confidence, from the whole tenor of your past life, that you will not suffer the national honor to be tarnished."[16]

When Scott arrived at Puget Sound (after a tumultuously enthusiastic reception in San Francisco), he found, to his relief, that "nothing of interest" had occurred during his voyage and that the much-feared collision had not yet taken place. Wasting no time, he immediately approached Vice Adm. James Douglas, the British governor of Vancouver, with a proposal for joint military occupation of the island, with each nation limited to a token force of one hundred soldiers. Preserving the fiction devised by Harney, Scott claimed that these troops were needed "to repel any descent on the part of hostile Indians."[17]

Douglas could not go along with this subterfuge, especially in view of Harney's admission that the sole reason for his occupation of San Juan was to protect American citizens from British "insults and indignities." Nor would he accept Scott's proposal for a joint military occupation. Instead, he proposed the immediate withdrawal of American troops to be followed by discussions leading to a joint *civil* administration.[18]

Scott, of course, could not agree to any proposal that could be interpreted as an American retreat. He offered a counterproposal that, when stripped of its verbiage, was essentially a rewording of his earlier plan. In the next step of this diplomatic dance, Douglas rejected Scott's suggestions and offered a compromise that was, in essence, merely a restatement of his own earlier proposal. He concluded with assurances that the British would not disturb the status quo "by taking possession of the Island or by assuming any jurisdiction there."[19]

Scott seized upon this assurance as an opportunity to withdraw all American soldiers except for Pickett's original company. Douglas could do no less. As a gesture of reciprocity, he pulled out all British troops except for a token detachment. The wily old general had maneuvered the British into the very settlement he had urged from the beginning: a joint military occupation. This arrangement would continue without further incident until 1872, when an arbitration panel, headed by the kaiser of Germany, awarded the islands to the United States, ending the dispute forever.[20]

Retracing his arduous voyage, Scott returned to Washington in December 1859, in time to bask in the praise President Buchanan lavished upon his mission of peace in his annual message to Congress.[21] It seemed a fitting conclusion to a long and active career, but, in fact, that career was not yet over: there were ominous signs that Scott's services might be needed again.

While Scott had been preoccupied with averting a war over a dead pig, John Brown had launched his raid against Harpers Ferry, Virginia, an act that raised sectional tension to a new high. The forthcoming presidential election held the potential for even greater disruption. Many Southerners looked upon the purely Northern Republican party as illegitimate and vowed to leave the Union if it should ever come to power. Since the Republicans, like the Whigs before them, could command the allegiance of only a minority of the voters, such an outcome seemed unlikely, unless the dominant Democrats should commit some act of self-destructive folly.

That was precisely what they did. At their convention in the summer of 1860, the Democrats were so divided along sectional lines that they were unable to agree upon a candidate. Reassembling later, they split into segments, with the Southerners choosing John J. Breckenridge of Kentucky and the rest of the party nominating Stephen A. Douglas of Illinois. With two Democrats in the field, the door was now open for a victory by the Republican candidate, Abraham Lincoln.

Even before the conventions, there were some who found all of these presidential alternatives equally unpalatable. A loose coalition of old Whigs, former Know Nothings, and Southern unionists planned yet another political organization, which eventually took the name Constitutional Union party. Some of its organizers sounded out Scott on his willingness to be their standard bearer.

After his humiliation in 1852, Scott had renounced further political ambitions, but old dreams die hard. He gently rebuffed the Constitutional Unionists' overtures but admitted, "The state of the country almost deprives me of sleep and sometimes I *dream* that I might possibly be of some service were I at the centre of agitation." Despite his disavowals, Scott took pains to dispel the objection that he was too old and sickly for the presidency. "In bright weather, I read and write without spectacles," he boasted. "I dine, sup, drink, and sleep *like a young man.*" He even speculated on what might be his policies, "*if* nominated and *if* elected—*two tall gates* to be leaped by an *old horse.*"[22]

As it turned out, these gates were indeed too tall for Scott to hurdle. When "the sanhedrin of the undeveloped Third Party" convened, it chose John Bell of Tennessee as its candidate.[23] Scott gave Bell his blessing but otherwise remained passively on the sidelines during the presidential campaign. As both feared and expected, Lincoln was able to eke out a victory in the four-way contest. His popular vote, however, was less than 40 percent of the electorate, even smaller than Scott's 44 percent in 1852.

True to its vow, South Carolina withdrew from the Union as soon as the Republican victory was announced. Other states of the Deep South soon followed. In the face of this crisis, the gravest the nation had yet known, Scott felt that his proper place was at the capital. As soon as his recently injured right foot could bear his weight, he closed up headquarters in New York and, in response to President Buchanan's urgent summons, returned at last to Washington, where he belonged.

CHAPTER TWENTY-SIX

SECESSION

In order to understand Scott's course during the secession crisis, it is necessary to wipe one's mind clean of all awareness of what actually happened later. We know, but he did not, that the secession impulse was genuine and not a bluff, that it would be put down only by a long and bloody war, and that out of this war would ultimately emerge a unified nation, purged of slavery. None of these outcomes was foreordained, and in the confused winter of 1860–1861, it was possible to envision entirely different scenarios.

Along with so many others, Scott peered through a clouded crystal ball. For one thing, he could not see that the secession threat was serious. "I know your little South Carolina," he told the wife of one of the state's U.S. senators. "I lived there once. It is about as big as Long Island, and two-thirds of the population are negroes. Are you mad?" Nor did he appreciate the depth of sectional discontent. He was persuaded that the crisis was manipulated by a handful of extremists on either side of the Mason-Dixon Line and that "if it had pleased God . . . to have taken away some ten or fifteen of those zealots from one half of the Union, and as many of the hot-headed Southerners," all agitation would have ceased.[1] Scott had lived through other sectional crises, and each had been resolved by some sort of compromise. Given time for tempers to cool, he saw no reason why this latest difficulty could not be settled just as peacefully.

As it turned out, none of these assumptions were valid, but Scott could not be expected to read the future; he could only be guided by the past. The most relevant experience from his own past was the nullification crisis of thirty years before. As President Jackson's emissary to South Carolina, he had been required to combine conciliation with an implicit threat of force. On the one hand, he had to avoid any provocative actions, and, on the other, he had quietly strengthened government forts and property so that extremists would think twice before risking a confrontation. His strategy had been to play for time while cooler heads fashioned a compromise plan. Above all, he sought to avoid violence, convinced that "the first drop of blood shed . . . would prove an immedicable wound," leading straight to civil war and the disintegration of the Union into at least three separate nations organized along sectional lines.[2]

Not surprisingly, when Scott came to offer President Buchanan advice during the early days of the secession crisis, he harkened back to his prior success with President Jackson during the nullification episode. Even before the 1860 election, he sent the president an unsolicited exposition of his "Views Suggested by the Imminent Danger . . . of a Disruption of the Union, etc."[3] Based on his familiarity with the volatile Southern temperament, Scott warned that there existed "some danger of an early act of rashness," most likely an attack on the lightly defended federal forts and property within the Southern states. To avert such a premature clash of arms, he recommended that immediate reinforcements be sent south so as "to make any attempt to take any one of them by surprise or *coup de main* ridiculous." In a later memo, he reminded the president that Jackson himself had not hesitated to reinforce South Carolina's forts with trustworthy soldiers during the early stages of the nullification troubles.[4]

Unfortunately, the force of this advice was diluted by being embedded within a long, rambling memo cluttered with extraneous digressions and political speculations, some of which were just plain silly. As he had thirty years earlier, Scott predicted that the secession impulse would not be confined to the South but would lead to four new nations on the ruins of the old, whose possible boundaries and capitals he described in minute detail. He also proposed the bizarre theory that the federal government had the right to put down the secession of an *interior* state, such as South Carolina, but not one on the periphery, such as Texas.[5]

Buchanan later seized upon some of the weak points in Scott's "strange and inconsistent" memo to justify his own inaction during the secession crisis. In particular, he argued that the advice to strengthen the Southern forts was unrealistic, for even Scott admitted that there were not nearly enough readily available troops to do the job. This was true. On the eve of the Civil War, the regular army could muster only 16,367 men, organized into 198 companies. Of these companies, all but 15 were scattered throughout the Far West, too distant to be of use in an eastern emergency. Perhaps five hundred or, in a pinch, a thousand soldiers were on hand to reinforce the garrisons of nine Southern forts. To augment those posts with such feeble numbers, scoffed

Buchanan, "would have been a confession of weakness, instead of an exhibition of imposing and overpowering strength."[6]

But Scott did not expect to make these forts invulnerable. At this early stage of the crisis, he was concerned that the forts' glaring weaknesses might tempt some hotheaded Southrons into a rash, perhaps unauthorized, attack that could present the government with an unwelcome fait accompli. "The great aim and object of this plan," he explained, "was to gain time . . . to await expected measures of conciliation on the part of the North and the subsidence of angry feelings in the opposite quarter," just as had been done in 1831.[7]

Scott's advice was ignored; 1861 was not 1831, and Buchanan was certainly not Jackson. Buchanan's loyalty was to the Union, but his political ties and sympathies were with the South. He believed that secession was illegal, but that it was equally illegal for the federal government to "coerce" a seceding state back into the Union, which William Seward paraphrased as meaning "that no state has a right to go out of the Union—unless it wants to."[8]

Fearful of giving offence, he retained within his cabinet three Southerners who actively sought to destroy the government for which they worked: Secretary of Treasury Howell Cobb, who circulated an inflammatory pamphlet urging his fellow Georgians to secede; Secretary of the Interior Jacob Thompson, who plotted to disrupt Lincoln's inauguration, by force if necessary; and Secretary of War John Floyd, who tried (unsuccessfully) to transfer heavy artillery from Northern to Southern armories. With such advisors, it was hardly surprising that Buchanan was cool to Scott's plans to reinforce the Southern forts. When the general at last arrived in Washington in mid-December to make his case in person, the president told him that the time was not ripe, that he was awaiting the arrival of commissioners from South Carolina, and that, in any event, such a decision was up to Congress, not the executive.[9]

While Buchanan dithered, events were spinning out of control. On December 20, South Carolina officially withdrew from the Union, followed in January 1861 by a string of other states from the Deep South. Early in February, they proclaimed themselves the Confederate States of America and selected Jefferson Davis as their president. In response, Buchanan remade his cabinet at the end of 1860, replacing the three Southerners with staunchly loyal Northern Democrats.

This revamped administration was likely to prove more receptive to Scott's urgings in regard to the Southern forts than the previous cabinet. Additional support for Scott's policies came from Abraham Lincoln. Scott had never met the president-elect, but he sounded out a mutual friend, Congressman Elihu Washburne. Is Lincoln "a *firm* man?" he asked. Washburne assured him that Lincoln would do his duty "in the sight of the furnace seven times heated." In that case, the old general sighed with relief, "All is not lost." Washburne, of course, reported the conversation to Lincoln, who responded by return mail: "Please present my respects to the general, and tell him, confidentially, I shall be obliged to him to be as well prepared as he can to either hold or retake the forts, as the case may require, at and after the inauguration."[10]

Thus doubly encouraged, Scott renewed his efforts to strengthen the forts in a more hopeful frame of mind than he had enjoyed for weeks. Buchanan, however, suffered another attack of cold feet. He had just met with the self-styled "commissioners" from South Carolina and argued that "common courtesy" required that he abstain from any act they might consider provocative. After considerable backing and filing, and under pressure from his new cabinet appointees, he recovered his nerve and finally agreed to relieve the beleaguered forts.

It was too late. The situation in Charleston Harbor had deteriorated since Scott had first suggested a relief expedition. With only sixty-five men at his disposal to garrison three Federal forts, Maj. Robert Anderson had abandoned the two most vulnerable positions and consolidated his tiny force on Fort Sumter, a half-finished pile of masonry on an island in the middle of the harbor.[11] South Carolinians responded by constructing batteries that controlled the approaches to the fort.

The warship *Brooklyn* was initially selected to carry provisions and reinforcements to Anderson's men, but it was feared that she drew too deep a draft to clear the harbor's sandbars. A swifter, lighter-draft merchant vessel was substituted—the same *Star of the West* that had carried Scott to Panama the previous year. Had it left a few weeks earlier, the vessel might have landed unopposed, but some warning shots from the recently emplaced Southern battery convinced the civilian captain to turn back within sight of his goal. Fort Sumter was left in limbo: it could not be defended, but as one of the last remaining symbols of Union presence in the seceded states, neither could it be abandoned. It would remain a ticking time bomb, ready to explode at the pleasure of the Confederacy.

In dealing with this crisis, Scott consistently advocated a policy of force tempered with conciliation. The first attempt at force at Charleston Harbor had failed. Conciliation would fare no better, though not for want of effort on Scott's part. "I have not rested supine during this alarming state of the Union," he assured his friends. Always an indefatigable correspondent, he now outdid himself, sending a stream of letters to acquaintances in every Southern state, warning of the dangerous path upon which they were about to embark.[12] He lent his support to the various compromise schemes then floating around the capital, especially the plan proposed by his good friend John J. Crittenden.

Another old political ally, William Seward, was working toward the same goal as Scott. While President-elect Lincoln was maintaining a discreet silence in Springfield, Illinois, Seward, his secretary of state–designate, filled the power vacuum, becoming, for a time, according to the admiring young Henry Adams, "virtually the ruler of the country." Despite his reputation as a foe of slavery, Seward's was actually a voice for caution and moderation during this crisis. Convinced that the majority of Southerners were still loyal Americans at heart, his policy was to avoid confrontation and allow the secession frenzy to burn itself out. Then the erring sisters would return in peace.[13] All this, of course, was wishful thinking, but it corresponded so closely to Scott's views that the two were able to work in close harmony.

The way of the peacemaker is hard. Both Seward and Scott were showered with abuse for their pacific efforts. "God damn you, Seward," growled an exasperated Republican senator, "you've betrayed your principles and your party; we've followed your lead long enough." Scott fared even worse at the hands of Southerners who had long considered him one of their own. Death threats bearing Southern postmarks clogged his mailbox, and he was denounced on the floor of Congress as a traitor to his native state. Southerners in the gallery jeered at the "Superannuated old dotard!" and the "Free-state pimp!" whom they had once delighted to honor.[14]

Yet at the same time, some influential unionists feared that Scott's Virginia upbringing and his alleged preference for Southern officers gave grounds to question his loyalty.[15] Salmon P. Chase, soon to be secretary of the Treasury, required assurance that the general intended to stand by the old flag, and Lincoln himself was sufficiently concerned to send an emissary to feel out Scott's stand.[16] The president-elect instructed, "Listen to the old man, and look him in the face, note carefully what he says and how he says it," and report back to Springfield. Lincoln's friend found Scott ill:

Propped up in bed by an embankment of pillows, lay the hero of Lundy's Lane, grizzly, wrinkled and pale. His hair and beard were disordered, and his flesh lay in rolls across his warty neck. His breathing was labored and difficult. In his trembling hand lay Lincoln's letter.

"You may present my compliments to Mr. Lincoln when you reach Springfield," he said in a wheezy voice. " . . . Say to him also that, when once here, I shall consider myself responsible for his safety. If necessary, I shall plant cannon at both ends of Pennsylvania Avenue, and if any of the Maryland and Virginia gentlemen who have become so threatening or troublesome of late show their heads or even venture to raise a finger, I shall blow them to hell!"[17]

This was not mere bravado. In the months preceding Lincoln's inauguration, Washington was buzzing with rumors of plots, uprisings, and coup d'états.

Scott himself had received over fifty letters, some quite credible, warning that Lincoln's inauguration would be opposed by violence. Tension ran so high that, according to Scott, "a dog-fight might cause the gutters of the capital to run red with blood." Faced with what he regarded as "the most critical and hazardous event" with which he had ever been connected, the general was determined to do his duty, even if it required that he lash any troublemaker to the muzzle of a cannon and "manure the hills of Arlington with fragments of his body." "The old warrior is aroused and he will be equal to the occasion," reported Simon Cameron, soon to be Lincoln's secretary of war.[18]

The old warrior, however, was almost toothless. The only regular troops at his disposal were a few hundred marines and a handful of artillerymen, while the local militia was so riddled with secessionists that it could not be relied upon.[19] With the help of Col. Charles P. Stone, Scott purged the militia of its unreliable elements, organized and drilled loyal volunteers, and unobtrusively moved in a few companies of regulars from West Point and Carlisle Barracks. By March 4, 1861, he at last felt prepared to meet any emergency.

On inauguration day, all elements of an elaborate military operation were in place to ensure a peaceful transition of power. Sharpshooters were posted on rooftops along the Pennsylvania Avenue parade route and behind windows on the wings of the Capitol, flanking the inaugural stand. Bomb squads scoured the space underneath the stands, searching for rumored infernal machines, and armed guards carefully restricted access to the platform. Side streets were blocked by cavalry, and the presidential carriage was flanked by a double row of mounted men, with more soldiers marching in front of and behind it. Plainclothesmen infiltrated the crowd, ready to pounce at the first sign of any suspicious movement.[20]

Scott himself was not part of that crowd. He had chosen a strategic spot overlooking the ceremonies, where he sat in his carriage while supervising the operation. From that distance, he could see, but not hear, the new president as he assured his "dissatisfied fellow-countrymen" in the South that the government would not assail them but fully intended to "hold, occupy and possess" (but not retake) Federal forts and property. After the speech, the new president took his oath of office, kissed the Bible, and the crowd dispersed peacefully. Thanks to Scott's vigilance, the first crisis of the new administration had passed without incident. From his vantage point, the general allowed himself to breathe a prayer of relief. "God be praised!" he sighed.[21]

Now that the new administration was safely installed, Scott wasted no time before dispensing advice. In a letter addressed to (and probably inspired by) Seward, he outlined what he considered the four options the government could pursue to repair "the highly disordered condition of our (so late) happy and glorious Union." The first, which Scott clearly favored, was conciliation.

Adopt some soothing compromise measure, such as the one proposed by his friend Crittenden, and, "my life upon it," he guaranteed that the secession movement would collapse, and the refractory states would return to a reconstructed Union. The second choice was watchful waiting: make no overt move, but collect the customs duties offshore of the Southern ports and wait for a favorable reaction to set in. The third option was to restore the Union by force of arms. He estimated that this would require three years, 300,000 soldiers, and $250 million "and *Cui bono?* Fifteen devastated provinces! . . . to be followed for generations by heavy garrisons . . . followed by a Protector or an Emperor." Finally, option number four: "Say to the seceded States—*Wayward Sisters, depart in peace!*"[22]

This was not the sort of advice the new cabinet wanted. They expected the commanding general of the United States Army to give them the benefit of his military wisdom, not comment on political matters. The most pressing military problem was the still-unresolved question posed by the Southern forts, particularly Fort Sumter as well as Fort Pickens in Florida, the last remaining outposts of Federal presence in the seceded states. When President Lincoln asked Scott whether these forts could be maintained, he received an unpleasant surprise.[23]

Up to now, Scott had vigorously urged reinforcing Major Anderson's beleaguered garrison. Now he had undergone a change of heart and threw cold water on any such project. Until about mid-February, Scott had thought it would have been relatively easy to relieve Fort Sumter, but since then, he now feared, the defenses of Charleston Harbor had been so greatly strengthened that the difficulties facing a relief expedition were increased "ten or twelve fold." He now estimated that it would take four months to assemble the required fleet and six to eight months to prepare the 25,000 troops needed for the expedition. "As a practical military question," he concluded, "the time for securing Fort Sumter with any means at hand had passed away nearly a month ago. Since then, a surrender under assault or from starvation has been merely a question of time."[24] He therefore advised that the forts be evacuated.

Scott's bombshell presented the new administration with an awkward dilemma. Having entered office with a pledge to hold these forts, could it now abandon them without sacrificing its credibility? But could it risk bearing the onus of commencing a war over an objective (Fort Sumter) that was probably unattainable? The cabinet was divided. Seward, of course, supported Scott, but Montgomery Blair, the firebrand postmaster general, was hot for any action that would uphold national honor. "As regards General Scott," Blair said, "I have no confidence in his judgment on the questions of the day. . . . whilst no one will question his patriotism, the results are the same is if he was in fact traitorous."[25]

Blair thought he had a better plan. His brother-in-law, Gustavus Vasa Fox, a bold and experienced former naval officer, was convinced that warships could successfully run the South Carolina batteries under cover of darkness and land small boats laden with provisions onto Sumter's beach. Despite Scott's reservations, this plan was approved by the government, and Fox proceeded to New York to assemble his flotilla.[26]

At the same time, an expedition to Fort Pickens was also set in motion. Scott feared that this mission was impractical from a military standpoint, and on Easter morning, he sent his secretary, Col. Erasmus Keyes, to explain the difficulties to Seward. "I don't care about the difficulties," snapped Seward, who, under pressure, had now changed his mind in favor of reinforcing Pickens. He ordered Keyes to confer with Capt. Montgomery Meigs and draw up a detailed plan of operation to present to the president by three o'clock. Forgoing church, the two officers worked frantically in the deserted War Department office. By the time they finished, it was too late, or so Keyes claimed, to notify Scott of their activities. At the White House, they found Seward and the president waiting impatiently. Lincoln was fidgety: coiling and uncoiling his long legs in an unsuccessful attempt to find a comfortable spot to rest them. Keyes thought he had never seen a man "who could scatter his limbs more than he." The president brushed aside Keyes's objection that Scott had not yet been consulted, heard the officers out, and ordered them to execute their plan without delay.[27]

Scott was predictably furious at being bypassed. Behind his chief's wrath, Keyes thought he could detect a "gloomy sadness" at this first hint that the authority he had so long enjoyed was beginning to slip from his grasp. But when Seward officially informed him that the president had overruled his advice against relieving the forts, Scott put his best face on the matter. "Well, Mr. Secretary," he said, "the great Frederick used to say that 'when the King commands, nothing is impossible!' Sir, the President's orders shall be obeyed!"[28]

The relief expeditions went forward, but as Scott had feared from the beginning, with mixed results. Fort Pickens was successfully reinforced on April 12 and would remain securely in Union hands throughout the war that followed. On that same day, however, as Fox's flotilla came within sight of Charleston, Confederate batteries opened fire upon Fort Sumter, lobbing some four thousand shells over the next twenty-two hours until Major Anderson hauled down his flag. Miraculously, there were no casualties, except for two soldiers accidentally killed during the surrender ceremony, but this near-bloodless bombardment would inaugurate the bloodiest war in American history.

Fox offered a host of excuses for the failure of his mission—bad weather, bureaucratic mix-ups, even deliberate sabotage by "that timid traitor" Seward—but subsequent events would prove that it was Fox's plan itself that was flawed.[29] During the Civil War, Union naval forces would repeatedly attempt to force their way into Charleston Harbor and would be repulsed each time, vindicating Scott's military judgment that its defenses were too strong to be overcome by naval assault alone.

The fate of Fort Sumter was soon dwarfed by the magnitude of the events its fall precipitated. President Lincoln immediately called for 75,000 ninety-day volunteers to quell the uprising in South Carolina. The states of the Upper South, including Scott's native Virginia, responded to this act of "coercion" by withdrawing from the Union to join the Confederacy. The war Winfield Scott had dreaded, but not really expected, had now begun.

CHAPTER TWENTY-SEVEN

CIVIL WAR

Once more, and for the last time, the now nearly seventy-five-year-old general was called upon to prepare for war. Unlike his first such experience, Scott took up his sword with a heavy heart. He was faced with two daunting tasks: to restore the unity of the Republic, which he had served for half a century; and to maintain the integrity of the army, to which he had devoted his professional life. These goals were not always compatible, but Scott would attempt, during this, the last year of his active career, to reconcile them.

Like the nation itself, the army was divided along sectional lines. Many of the career soldiers Scott himself had trained chose to join with their states in rebellion. These defections were confined largely to the officer class; although only twenty-six enlisted men changed their uniform, 313 officers, almost one-third of the corps, put on Confederate gray.[1]

Notable among these turncoats were former Mexican War generals Gideon Pillow and David Twiggs. Scott could, no doubt, accept the loss of Pillow with equanimity, but the defection of Twiggs was an unexpected blow. Twiggs, who was in charge of the government forces in Texas, proved unworthy of Scott's oft-repeated confidence in his "discretion, firmness and patriotism." A secret Southern sympathizer, he surrendered his entire command even before the Texas Ordinance of Secession was ratified, and he promptly accepted a commission in the Confederate army. "If an old woman with a broomstick would come with full authority from the State of Texas to demand the public property," he said, "I would give it up to her."[2]

This was bad enough, but the disloyalty of the "little cabinet" of junior officers, upon whom Scott had relied so heavily during the Mexican War, was even more disheartening. After much soul-searching, Joseph E. Johnston left his desk at the Quartermaster's Bureau to put on the stars of a major general of Virginia. With considerably less anguish, P. G. T. Beauregard abandoned his post as superintendent of West Point (where he had been counseling Southern cadets to join the Confederacy) in order to supervise the bombardment of Fort Sumter.

The greatest disappointment came from Scott's favorite soldier, Robert E. Lee. Scott had hoped that Lee would take command of all Union forces in the field, and there is reason to believe that he and other members of the Lincoln administration urged him to accept that position. This was not as unlikely a possibility as it might appear in retrospect. Lee disapproved of slavery and opposed secession, but in the end, loyalty to his native state overrode these qualms. Rather than draw his sword against Virginia, he rejected Scott's offer and took up that sword against his old flag.[3]

Was it possible that Scott, a fellow Virginian, might follow Lee's example? Rumors to that effect swept the South. In Virginia, former president John Tyler, now an ardent Confederate, rejoiced at a report that Scott had resigned, and in Mobile, Alabama, a one-hundred-gun salute was fired in celebration. When the rumors proved false, disappointed Southerners turned on their former hero with fury. "It is a sight to see the drivelling old fop, with his skinny hands and bony fingers, undo, at one dash, the labors of a long and active life," a Virginia paper fumed. "With the red-hot pencil of infamy, he has written upon his wrinkled brow, the terrible, damning word, 'Traitor.'"[4] Regretting now the ceremonial sword the Virginia legislature had given its once-favorite son, a local rhymester urged Scott to "Give Back Thy Sword":

> Oh! Chief among ten thousand,
> Thou whom I loved so well,
> Star that has set, as never yet,
> Since Son of Morning fell
>
> . . . . . .
>
> Yea! by thy mother's honor
> And by thy father's grave,
> By hell beneath, and heaven above,
> Give back the sword I gave![5]

Southerners need not have been so surprised that Scott should "prove false to the mother which gave him birth." Could they really have expected Scott to join any movement led by Jefferson Davis? "There is contamination in his touch," said Scott of his old foe. "If secession was 'the holiest cause that tongue or sword of mortal ever lost or gained,' he would ruin it!"[6]

But even putting his personal prejudices aside, Scott's long-held political convictions would have placed him firmly with the Union. He was, and always had been, a nationalist. As early as 1815, when Connecticut had opposed the war with Great Britain, Scott had advocated the use of force to "lash her into obedience." The issue, he then maintained, was "whether one of the most inconsiderable states in the Union can, at pleasure, put the acts of the federal government at disobedience." The passage of time did nothing to weaken that conviction. In April 1861, when a delegation of old Virginia friends tried to tempt him with a lucrative offer to command the state's armed forces, Scott indignantly spurned such a "mortal insult." "I have served my country, under the flag of the Union, for more than fifty years," he insisted, "and so long as God permits me to live, I will defend that flag with my sword, even if my own native State assails it!"[7]

At a time when treason seemed to have infected the highest levels of government, when the nation appeared helpless and confused, such unswerving loyalty made Scott a symbol of patriotic determination and a reminder of the age of giants. The last of the generation of Clay, Webster, Jackson, and John Quincy Adams, Scott was, by 1861, a living fossil bearing the imprint of an earlier, happier day, and as such, he became for a time a venerable icon around whom defenders of the Union could rally. To them, it was "an inexpressible source of consolation and pride . . . to know that the General-in-Chief of the Army remains like an impregnable fortress at the post of duty and glory."[8]

As a symbol, Scott filled an important psychological need during these dark early months of the Civil War. It was a comfort to imagine that the nation's fate rested securely in the hands of "the wily old Lieutenant General, who lies there like a great spider in the center of his net, throwing out cords that will entangle his buzzing blue-bottle of an antagonist." To Edwin Stanton, Scott seemed to have been given a free hand. "He is, in fact, the Government," Stanton reported to former president Buchanan, "and if his health continues, vigorous measures are anticipated."[9]

That, of course, was a very large "if." Under the strain of the crisis, Scott's advanced years were beginning to tell. Sometimes he would doze off at his desk if unwelcome visitors overstayed their welcome, and at meetings with political dignitaries, he might seem rambling and confused. "My God, the country is at the mercy of a dotard!" exclaimed Pennsylvania's governor, Andrew Curtin, after an embarrassingly inconclusive conference.[10]

Yet, for a dotard, Scott was accomplishing an enormous amount of work under uniquely difficult circumstances. The War Department, like the rest of the army, had been gutted by resignations and defections. Of the ninety civilians employed by the War Department at the beginning of the war, only fifty-six were still at their posts half a year later. Their places were too often filled by untrained replacements, many of whom happened to be Pennsylvania cronies of Secretary of War Cameron.

The semiautonomous bureaus were in equal disarray. Both the quartermaster general and the adjutant general resigned to join the Confederacy, and most of the other bureau chiefs were antiquated veterans, some older than Scott himself. Living testimonials to the inexorable workings of seniority, they were physically and psychologically incapable of meeting the extraordinary demands that the crisis imposed.[11]

Even Scott's personal staff was scattered. His military secretary, George W. Lay, had departed for his native North Carolina and his longtime aide, Erasmus Keyes, was banished from headquarters for his apparent insubordination in planning the Fort Pickens relief expedition. Other aides were seeking the glory of field commands in the expanded army. In their absence, Scott made do with whatever assistance he could scrape together. A visitor to the modest three-story house that served as army headquarters was not impressed. "There are a few plodding pedants, with maps and rulers and compasses," he noted, "and there are some ignorant, and not very active young men, who loiter about the head-quarters' halls and strut up the street with brass spurs on their heels and kepis raked over their eyes as though they were soldiers, but I see no system, no order, no knowledge, no dash!" Scott had to train this new team while shouldering the burdens of mobilization, which sometimes kept him at his desk around the clock. Little wonder that he acted increasingly irritable, snapping at aides who fidgeted during the recitation of his familiar stories, or that he would doze off during meetings with longwinded congressmen.[12]

With his limited resources, Scott had three formidable tasks to perform. The first, and most pressing, was to defend Washington. The next was to oversee an unprecedented expansion of the nation's armed forces. Finally, he had to decide what to do with that army once it was assembled. These three missions would occupy Scott during what remained of his military career.

Defending the capital was the general's first priority in the days immediately following the fall of Fort Sumter. Located entirely within slaveholding territory, the District of Columbia was in danger of being cut off from the free states. With the secession of Virginia, access via the Potomac was jeopardized, and the hills of Arlington, just across the river, provided high ground should Rebel artillery choose to begin a bombardment. The only railroad link to the North ran through the city of Baltimore, where pro-Southern sentiment ran so high that a mob of its "plug-uglies" attacked the train carrying the 6th Massachusetts Regiment to Washington, leaving a trail of dead and wounded. Following the riot, enraged Marylanders ripped up railroad tracks, burned bridges, and cut telegraph lines, effectively isolating the capital from the outside world. The city was, in effect, under siege, and there was reason to fear that it could be starved into submission within a few days unless help arrived.[13]

Wild rumors flew through Washington telling of mobs marching from Baltimore to burn down the city or of forty thousand Virginians armed with Bowie knives preparing to storm the bridges across the Potomac. Nervous congressmen packed their families off to the relative safety of the Maryland countryside, and even President Lincoln paced the White House, staring out the window for signs of reinforcements. "Why don't they come!" he asked plaintively, "Why don't they come!"[14]

Scott remained uninfected by this unseemly panic. Sitting at his desk, "placid as a summer morning," he calmly mobilized the meager forces at his disposal. Two companies of superannuated congressmen and government clerks guarded the public buildings. The district militia patrolled the streets, and the handful of available regulars defended the vulnerable bridges and wharves. To ward off starvation, seven thousand barrels of flour were stored in the basement of the Capitol and other public buildings. The War Department seized control of telegraph lines and railroad rolling stock and hastily repaired the bridges and tracks the Marylanders had sabotaged.[15]

This was impressively vigorous activity for a man some dismissed as senile, but Scott harbored no illusions that he had secured the safety of the city against a determined Confederate assault. When asked whether Fort Washington, across the river from Mount Vernon, could be held, he replied with mock gravity: "I think sir, that Fort Washington could now be taken with a bottle of whisky. At last account, it was in the charge of a single old soldier, who is entirely reliable when he is sober."[16]

Scott's goal was to buy time until the anticipated reinforcements could arrive. To that end, he even devised a desperate plan for the last-ditch defense of the capital, with the Treasury Building as his final redoubt.[17] It did not come to that, of course. Within days, the first of a flood of Union regiments arrived. The siege was broken, normal contact with the outside world was restored, and the capital was saved. Scott could now turn his attention to his next task, building an army.

Precisely what kind of army was needed, however, no one, including Scott, could foresee. Its size, composition, and organization all depended on what sort of war was to be fought. A beginning had already been made with Lincoln's April call for 75,000 volunteers to serve for ninety days, but that was merely a stopgap measure that would, in retrospect, appear laughably inadequate. By war's end, perhaps two million men would have served, at one time or another, in the Union army, a number equivalent to the entire male population of the United States when Scott had been born. Two thousand of these would become generals, almost as many men as the total force Scott had commanded at Chippewa.

The organizational structure of the army, created in simpler times for entirely different purposes, was inadequate to handle these numbers. Provost Marshall James Fry catalogued some its deficiencies: "The law required that vacancies should as a rule be filled by seniority. There was no retired list for the disabled, and the army was weighed down by longevity; by venerated traditions; by prerogatives of services rendered in former wars; by the firmly tied red-tape of military bureauism, and by the deep-seated and well-founded fear of auditors and comptrollers of the treasury."[18]

The Confederate army, in contrast, was free, as Lincoln put it in another context, to "think anew and act anew," unhobbled by tradition or outmoded regulations. There was no crushing weight of seniority preventing the rise of young, vigorous officers to high command. And there was no any reluctance to mingle volunteers with regulars, since there was, strictly speaking, no regular army. U. S. Grant thought that this practice of assigning professionally trained officers to command volunteers gave the Confederacy an initial advantage: "what there was of military education and training was distributed throughout their whole army. The whole loaf was leavened."[19]

Should the Union have followed the Confederate example and utilized regular officers to lead its volunteer troops? This was the most contentious question Scott faced during the early stages of Northern mobilization. It was argued that the officers, and even some of the sergeants, of the regular army constituted an invaluable pool of professional knowledge. They could become the captains, colonels, and even generals of the vast volunteer force that would be required to put down the rebellion. "In other words," explained John Schofield, "by a judicious use of the small body of officers whom the country had educated at so great expence, a fine army of 500,000 men or more could have been called into service, organized, disciplined and put into the field [by] August 1, 1861."[20]

Scott instinctively rejected this suggestion. His long-nurtured distrust of volunteer soldiers had by now hardened into dogma. Ignoring the respectable performance of volunteer troops in Mexico, he hearkened back to the memory of Queenston Heights and continually warned of the dire consequences of relying on enthusiastic amateur soldiers.[21] He seems to have believed that the volunteers should be relegated to the role of an auxiliary force acting in support of the regular army's "iron column," which would bear the brunt of whatever hard fighting needed to be done. This required that the regular army remain intact so as "to give steadiness and confidence to the volunteers or militia." Consequently, he rejected all requests to detach army officers to command volunteers on the grounds that "no officer of the regular army can be spared."[22]

Until overruled late in 1861, Scott stubbornly stuck to this position, even in the face of pressure from influential politicians such as Senator John Sherman, with whom he conducted a raucous shouting match, and, it must be admitted, in the face of common sense. In the aftermath of Fort Sumter, Northern recruiting stations were so swamped with eager volunteers that many had to be turned away. A more sensible policy, many urged, would have been to take all comers and worry about their efficiency later. "What was demanded by the necessities of the country in 1861," argued Schofield, himself a career soldier, "was the best large army that could be made in the shortest time, not a better small army to be made in a much longer time."[23] Such a policy would not only tap Northern enthusiasm but also play to another potential strength of the Union, its larger population, which would prove so useful in the new age of mass armies the technological revolution required.

Without competent commanders, such a *levée en masse* could, as Scott feared, degenerate into an armed mob. Yet the officers assigned to these early regiments were often elected by the men themselves or chosen by state governors for reasons of political patronage. Many of them had to be weeded out after an expensive process of trial and error. Fortunately, there existed a substantial body of West Point graduates who had already resigned to follow civilian pursuits. Many of these dropouts, including Grant, William T. Sherman, George B. McClellan, and William S. Rosecrans, would find their way to high command, while career officers who had loyally stuck by their posts vegetated in junior positions because of what seemed to be Scott's rigid adherence to an outmoded prejudice.

Contrary to appearances, Scott was not merely a crabby old man mired in the ways of the past. He was, in some respects, a precursor of a type that would become increasingly common in the next century—the technocrat whose chief loyalty is given to his profession. Protecting the integrity of that profession had become to Scott an end in itself, and he would not allow a temporary emergency, however grave, to endanger it.

Winfield Scott had not become commanding general to preside over the dissolution of his army and undo the work of a lifetime. He would have shuddered had he known of Grant's proposal to disband the regular army, except for the staff corps, and force all of its officers into the volunteers on pain of being dropped from the service at war's end.[24] Scott feared that once the army had been that thoroughly scrambled, it could not be unscrambled but would have to be created anew. This realization was one consideration, though far from the only one, that shaped the strategy he proposed for the conduct of the war.

CHAPTER TWENTY-EIGHT

ANACONDA

Grand strategy was not a subject taught at West Point. Cadets studied how to maneuver companies and regiments, not armies. They learned how to fight battles, not how to win wars. In the upper reaches of the army, there was no general staff to coordinate war plans, no "think tanks," no war games against hypothetical enemies, and even if there had been, it would have been unthinkable to consider military measures against fellow Americans rather than foreign foes. It was hardly surprising, therefore, that with so much energy being devoted to raising, equipping, and transporting immense armies, almost no attention was given to the inevitable next question—what to do with these armies once they were assembled.

Scott was an exception. Virtually alone among Northern policymakers, he had a plan. In later years, his plan would be dismissed as unrealistic and overly timid, but at the time, it made sense, given certain premises. The first was the conviction, which Scott shared with Seward, that Southern nationalism was a temporary enthusiasm. There would be no fighting, Seward insisted. If left alone, "the South would collapse and everything be serenely adjusted." Scott was not quite as sanguine as Seward. He knew Southerners far better than did the New Yorker. As he had earlier told South Carolina's Mary Chesnut, Southern soldiers possessed "élan, courage, woodcraft, consummate horsemanship, endurance of pain equal to the Indians, but [they] will not submit to discipline." They were bold, brave, and could "bear pain without a murmur, but . . . will not submit to be bored."[1]

Scott intended to bore the Rebels into submission. Fearful that a massive invasion would only solidify Southern resistance, he proposed to cut off the rebel states from the rest of the world and let them stew in their own juice. He advised President Lincoln to maintain a strict naval blockade along the sea-coast and to send a military column down the Mississippi to control that waterway and isolate the South from the West. He assured the president that "when they feel this pressure, not having been exasperated by attacks made on them within their respective States, the Union spirit will assert itself . . . , and I will guarantee that in one year from this time all difficulties will be settled. But, if you invade the South at any point," he gravely warned, "I will guarantee that at the end of a year you will be further from a settlement than you are now."[2]

Contemporaries derisively dubbed this the "Anaconda Plan," after the snake that squeezes its prey to death, though Scott never used that term himself. Subsequent commentators, aware that the actual course of the Civil War did not follow the path foreseen by Scott, have been equally critical. The elderly general, they argue, was living in the past. His strategy, they claim, was not suited to the crisis of 1861 but was drawn from two irrelevant sources: outdated European military texts and the inappropriate lessons Scott had learned from his Mexican experience.[3]

Neither of these suggested influences is persuasive. True, Scott did love to parade his book learning, but it was more in the spirit of a debater than a true scholar. In this instance, it seems significant that Scott, who was never reticent when it came to citing European authorities, did not mention any to bolster his arguments for the Anaconda. Nor was his Mexican War experience germane to the later situation. Quite the contrary, his strategy in 1847 had been to strike directly for the Mexican capital and end the war with one blow, a very different plan than the slow economic strangulation he advocated in 1861.

The inspiration for Scott's strategic conception was not derived from any single source, but rather seems to have been the distillation of the lessons of a lifetime. One such lesson was his reliance on regulars rather than volunteers. The advance down the Mississippi was to be led by regulars, who would inspire the volunteers by their steadiness and professionalism. These volunteers should not be rushed into battle but kept in training camps similar to the one Scott conducted at Flint Hill in 1814. There they should "*drill* and *drill* and *drill*" for four or five months until ready.[4] This, of course, would require the North to stand on the defensive until late fall 1861, but that did not disturb Scott, for it would delay operations in the South past the sickly summer season. Leery of diseases ever since Terre aux Boeufs, the cholera epidemic of 1832, and the threat of yellow fever at Vera Cruz, he was in no hurry to rush soldiers into tropical pestholes.

Another lesson Scott applied from his long experience was the importance of interservice cooperation. On Lake Erie during the War of 1812, on the Great Lakes during the Black Hawk expedition, and, most notably, in his

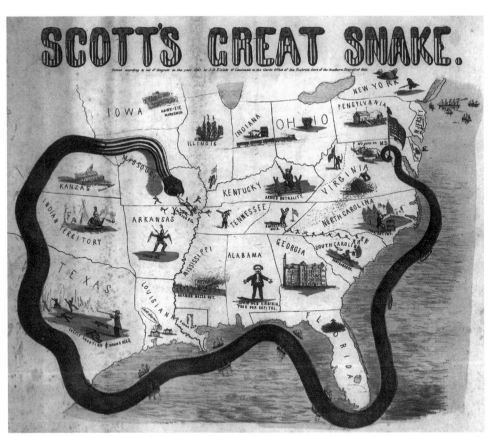

Scott's Great Snake. Library of Congress.

amphibious invasion of Mexico, Scott had become accustomed to conducting combined operations with the navy. He now envisioned a fleet of gunboats steaming down the Mississippi in tandem with the foot soldiers, providing transport, artillery cover, and an unbreakable supply line. As with the surfboats at Vera Cruz, Scott took a personal interest in the gunboats' design. When Secretary Cameron offered to supply rented steamboats for the expedition, Scott replied testily: "Mr. Secretary, I do not want even *one* rotten contract steamboat. I want *gunboats*, built to draw just as many feet of water as I say, to carry just as many guns as I say, and of just such caliber as I say." The secretary hastily agreed.[5]

After the bloodbath at Lundy's Lane, Scott had developed an aversion to needless casualties among his troops. In Mexico, he had resisted the temptation to rack up the large "butcher's bill" of killed and wounded that had led other commanders to fame and glory. In 1861, it was noted that he still "expends lives as reluctantly as a miser parts with dollars," which further inclined him to favor a strategy designed to minimize casualties on both sides. This inclination was not merely the outgrowth of a humanitarian impulse. Scott feared that bloody battles fought on Southern soil would only solidify Southern nationalism and create bitter memories that could impede sectional reconciliation for generations to come. Looking ahead to postwar America, he wryly predicted that even after a Union victory, "for a long time thereafter it will require the exercise of the full powers of the Federal Government to restrain the fury of the noncombatants."[6]

In many ways, therefore, the Anaconda Plan was consistent with the major themes of Scott's lifework. Was it also appropriate to the needs of the hour? That depended, to a large extent, on whether or not the strategy's underlying premise was valid. If, as Scott seemed to assume, secession were merely a passing fancy, then a policy of delay would allow the sober second thoughts of Southerners to assert themselves. If, however, it was a genuine revolutionary movement, then time was on the Southern side, for it would allow the Confederacy to consolidate its institutions and establish habits of loyalty.

With the retrospective awareness of how intensely Southerners would fight to preserve their new nation, it would seem that Scott's major premise was based on unsubstantiated wishful thinking. Yet it could also be argued that Southern nationalism might have been forged in that very armed conflict that Scott had sought to avoid. But could the Union afford to risk its existence on such a will-o'-the-wisp? That uncertainty alone doomed Scott's plan, though major elements of it, such as the coastal blockade and the control of the Mississippi, would be retained as elements of a more aggressive military strategy.

From a military point of view, the Anaconda Plan had grave defects. It took no account of possible Southern initiatives and assumed that they would remain passive while the great snake's coils contracted around them. In Mexico, such neglect of the enemy's intentions had been forgivable, since the Mexicans tended to remain in static positions awaiting Scott's moves. Confederate generals, many of whom had learned their trade under Scott, were not likely to be so obliging. They could be expected to concentrate their forces to break out of the cordon. Since Scott's 85,000-man column was insufficient to hold a thousand-mile frontier, Federal forces would have to concentrate to meet the Rebels, which would then bring about the armed struggle that Scott's strategy had been designed to forestall.

The major weakness of the Anaconda was political. Scott himself acknowledged that "the greatest obstacle in the way of this plan—the great danger now pressing upon us—[is] the impatience of our patriotic and loyal Union friends. They will urge instant and vigorous action, regardless, I fear of consequences." Scott's apprehensions were soon confirmed by the impatient rumblings emanating from Horace Greeley's influential *New York Tribune*. In late

June, that journal began running an inflammatory standing headline: "Forward to Richmond! Forward to Richmond! The rebel Congress must not be allowed to meet there on the 20th of July."[7]

Although Greeley was certainly not a military authority, his bellicose demand was not entirely unreasonable. The enlistment term of the ninety-day volunteers would soon draw to a close. If they should be sent home without having struck a single blow, Northern morale would undoubtedly plummet. Furthermore, the recent relocation of the Confederate capital from Montgomery, Alabama, to Richmond, Virginia, scarcely one hundred miles from Washington, was not only an affront but also an opportunity. A bold strike at the enemy's capital, it was hoped, might settle the rebellion at one blow. This was, in fact, the preferred strategy employed in contemporary wars. Scott himself had followed it in Mexico, and in the succeeding decade, the Prussians would utilize it successfully in their wars against Austria and France.

Scott was not persuaded. He knew that Southerners were not Mexicans and that his own soldiers were not Prussians. He continued to urge caution, warning the administration: "If you push these three-month men into battle just as they are all thinking of going home; if you push the two or three years men into battle just before they shall be organized, you will be beaten in the first general action of this war! You will consolidate what is now an insurrection, and make of it a rebellious government—which . . . you may be able to put down in two or three years, but I doubt it!"[8]

He tried to instruct the impatient politicians in the elements of his craft, carefully explaining the difficulties such an advance would face in the way of supplies and terrain. All supplies, he insisted, would have to be laboriously hauled by wagons, since the invaders "would find every house deserted; not a cow, or a chicken, or an accidental pig on the entire route."[9] The broken terrain of the Virginia countryside, which he knew from his boyhood, would present even greater obstacles.

One evening, near the end of May, after a dinner party for administration dignitaries, including Treasury Secretary Chase, who had tried to pressure Scott into approving an immediate advance, the general staged a little colloquy to drive home his objections. After the table had been cleared, he called on Colonel Stone. How many men would you require to march on Richmond, he asked. Stone instantly replied that he would not undertake it with fewer than forty thousand men and with fifteen thousand more in reserve. "How fast could you advance," Scott continued.

"Having all prepared, general, the advance guard of my force might be on the Rappahannock in three days, and—"

"Rappahannock! What is that?" the general broke in. The Rappahannock River, Stone replied.

"Oh, there is a *river* there, is there? . . . I wish everybody knew that! Well, sir, what then?"

"Should the bridge be burned—"

"Eh! there is a bridge over that river, and that bridge might be burned! I wish everybody knew *that* too. Well, sir! if the bridges are burned?" In that case, Stone replied, he would lose two or three days in forcing a passage. He then detailed, step by step, every stage of the proposed advance. "Why, Colonel Stone," exclaimed Scott in mock surprise, "you are taking forty or fifty days to get to Richmond!" He then sent for the aged Brig. Gen. Joseph Totten, chief of the Corps of Engineers, put to him the same questions he had asked Stone, and received similar answers.

Scott turned to his guests, who now included Secretaries Seward and Cameron. "Really, gentlemen," he gloated, "here is a most extraordinary unanimity of opinion." The youngest colonel and the oldest general in the army were in total agreement. How could that be explained? "Gentlemen, the only way I can explain it . . . is *that it must be of their trade* that they have been speaking, and they speak from its principles!"

"Gentlemen," Scott triumphantly concluded, "this matter has now, unfortunately, gone beyond politics, and has become a military question. . . . Such being the case, since, unfortunately, soldiers must settle it, you must allow the soldiers to do what they know they ought to do; and you must be careful not to force them to do what they know they ought not to do."[10]

Scott failed to realize that civil wars are not merely tactical exercises to be conducted by military professionals. This war was, by its very nature, intensely political in its origins, aims, and management—a classic illustration of the maxim that war is a continuation of politics by other means. In such a conflict, it was unrealistic of Scott to expect that political leaders would defer to his professional judgment.

That became clear at a meeting of civil and military leaders held at the White House on June 29. The question at hand was whether or not to make an advance into Virginia to dislodge the Rebel army under Beauregard, which had concentrated at the rail center of Manassas Junction, halfway between Richmond and Washington. Scott spoke against the move, repeating his arguments against waging "a little war by piecemeal."[11] The civilians warned that the public demanded immediate action and that, without it, enlistments could dry up, bond sales falter, and voters turn against the administration at the polls. Scott was overruled, and with that, his Anaconda was buried. Political considerations had scotched that snake, and Scott had no choice but to acquiesce.

He had already prepared a contingency plan. Brig. Gen. Irvin McDowell, recently promoted from Scott's staff to commander of Union forces south of the Potomac, was to march on Manassas with 30,000 men. This force should have been sufficient to dislodge the 23,000 Confederate troops Beauregard had assembled, provided that the 8,000 Southerners under Joseph Johnston were kept bottled up in the Shenandoah Valley.[12] The crucial mission of preventing a linkup of the two Confederate armies was given to Maj. Gen. Robert Patterson.

Patterson was a poor choice for such an important assignment. A wealthy sixty-nine-year-old Pennsylvania businessman and part-time soldier with experience in both the War of 1812 and the war with Mexico, Patterson was noted for his caution. In the Mexican War, that caution had proved a valuable corrective to the rashness of Scott's other generals, but in 1861, boldness was required. Patterson, however, jumped at shadows. Magnifying both the enemy's strength and his own weakness, he seemed paralyzed by indecision, and while he pondered on what course to take, Johnston slipped out of the valley and joined his force with that of Beauregard. The fault was not entirely Patterson's: Scott's orders had been ambiguous, and the experienced regulars on Patterson's staff, Fitz-John Porter and George H. Thomas, should have given him better advice. Nevertheless, the damage had been done, and Beauregard now faced his old West Point classmate McDowell with almost equal numbers.[13]

Had McDowell been able to move more quickly, Patterson's ineptitude would not have mattered, but shortages of transport and supplies compelled him to delay his projected advance. When he finally was able to march, many of his half-trained volunteers, plucked straight from their farms and offices, lay gasping by the roadside under the strain of their unaccustomed exertions. Nonetheless, when they encountered the main Confederate force entrenched behind Bull Run on July 21, they acquitted themselves well against Beauregard's equally green soldiers. By early afternoon, it appeared that the field would be theirs, but the unexpected arrival of additional Confederate reinforcements from the valley created a panic that, as Scott had feared from the very first, turned into a rout.

Unable to take the field himself, the general in chief followed the course of the battle from the fragmentary and often contradictory rumors and telegraph dispatches that flowed into Washington. From what he learned, Scott was so confident of victory that he allowed himself the indulgence of a midafternoon nap, which was how President Lincoln found him when he dropped by the general's office to discuss the news. Scott assured him that all was well and went back to sleep, and the president enjoyed a leisurely carriage ride through the Maryland countryside.

While they were thus pleasantly engaged, disturbing reports reached the capital telling first of a reverse, then of a retreat, then of the rout. "The day is lost," announced one telegram. "Save Washington and the remnants of this army."[14] These alarming reports were confirmed by eyewitness accounts from defeated Union soldiers. By dawn, the streets of Washington were filled with dazed battlefield survivors begging for food and collapsing in an exhausted stupor on doorsills. Could Beauregard be far behind? The city's defenses were hastily strengthened, and reinforcements urgently summoned, but many feared that nothing could stop the victorious Confederates in their pursuit.

In the face of this despair, Scott remained as "firm and unwavering as a rock." He scoffed at reports that the Rebel advance guard had reached the Potomac and was preparing to cross the bridge into the city. "It is impossible, sir!" he assured the president. "We are now tasting the first fruits of a war, and learning what a panic is. We must be prepared for all kinds of rumors. Why sir, we should soon hear that Jefferson Davis has crossed the Long Bridge at the head of a brigade of elephants, and is trampling our citizens under foot. He has no brigade of elephants," Scott explained, perhaps unnecessarily, "he cannot by any possibility get a brigade of elephants."[15]

The old general's instincts were sound. The Confederates were, as he suspected, just as demoralized by victory as their opponents had been by defeat and were unable to follow up their battlefield success with a vigorous pursuit. The capital was secure; the Union, however, was in graver peril than before. As Scott had repeatedly warned, a failed invasion of the South would only solidify Southern nationalism, inflate Southern arrogance, and feed Southern dreams of imperial domination.

At a postmortem following the defeat, Scott could not resist reminding the president and his advisors that he had told them so. "Sir, I am the greatest coward in America," he burst out in agitation. "I have fought this battle, sir, against my judgment. . . . As God is my judge, after my superiors had determined to fight it, I did all in my power to make the army efficient. I deserve removal because I did not stand up, when the army was not in a condition for fighting, and resist it to the last." Lincoln coldly replied, "Your conversation seems to imply that I forced you to fight this battle." Realizing he had gone too far, Scott backpedaled. "I have never served a President who has been kinder to me than you have been," he said contritely.[16]

Lincoln's rebuke was a harbinger of Scott's waning influence. It was not merely that his leadership had (for reasons admittedly beyond his control) failed to bring success. More significantly, the defeat at Bull Run had created an entirely new war, one that Scott was not equipped to wage. The illusion (which Scott had never shared) that the rebellion could be put down cheaply and quickly was now shattered. It was painfully clear that the Union would have to gird itself for a long struggle requiring all of its resources. Scott was too old and too set in his ways to conduct such a struggle and would have to give way to younger and more innovative leadership.

Ominously, when Secretary of War Cameron wired Maj. Gen. George B. McClellan on July 22 to hasten to Washington, he did not bother to inform the commanding general.[17] Scott's star was fading.

CHAPTER TWENTY-NINE

FADING AWAY

"The first condition of successful leadership in war is youth," declared Alexis de Tocqueville. Unfortunately, as he further observed, "when a democratic people does at last take up arms after a long peace, all the leaders of the army are found to be old men." To Tocqueville, this paradox explained why democracies so often suffered defeats in the early stages of their wars. This is, however, only a temporary condition, for he was convinced that "great generals always emerge in the end. A long war has the same effect on a democratic army as a revolution has on the people themselves. It breaks down rules and makes outstanding men come forward. Officers whose minds and bodies have grown old in peacetime are eliminated, retire or die. In their place a multitude of young men, already toughened by war, press forward with ambitious hopes aflame."[1]

Scott himself bore witness to the prescient Frenchman's observations both at the beginning and at the end of his military career. During the War of 1812, he often had been heard to complain that the fifty-seven-year-old General Wilkinson "was too old for the active duties of the field; that he hoped never again to see him, or any other general officer of his age, at the head of the army."[2] Now Scott's own turn had come.

The executor of Wilkinson's belated revenge was Maj. Gen. George Brinton McClellan. Only thirty-five years old, the well-born McClellan had been something of a prodigy, entering West Point at the age of fifteen and graduating second in the class of 1846, just in time to serve in Scott's army in Mexico. Too impatient to endure the slow pace of promotion in the peacetime army, he resigned his commission in 1857 to become a railroad executive. At the outbreak of the rebellion, McClellan was appointed by the governor of Ohio to command that state's troops, with the rank of major general of volunteers. In that capacity, he conducted a successful campaign in the mountains of western Virginia that brought one of the few early rays of sunshine to brighten the prevailing Northern gloom. "Little Mac," the "Young Napoleon," became the Union's first hero.

With an eye on even higher things, McClellan began a correspondence with the commanding general. Knowing the surest way to Scott's heart, he larded his letters with flattery: "All that I know of war I have learned from you. . . . It is my ambition to merit your praise & never to deserve your censure." And again: "Next to maintaining the honor of my country, General, the first aim of my life is to justify the good opinion you have expressed concerning me. . . . I do not expect your mantle to fall upon my shoulders, for no man is worthy to wear it, but I hope that it may be said hereafter that I was no unworthy disciple of your school." Little wonder that Scott declared himself "charmed" by his fawning protégé's "activity, enterprise and success."[3]

Emboldened, the Young Napoleon offered his old commander advice on how to win the war. The road to victory, he argued, lay in the West, where, by no coincidence, McClellan happened to be in command. He urged the government to "strain every nerve" to augment his department so that he could either move on Richmond via the Kanawha Valley or march on Kentucky, Tennessee, and points south, "according to circumstances."[4]

Scott easily poked apart McClellan's half-baked plans, but he could not help but be pleased to find that at least one of his generals was thinking in larger strategic terms. He congratulated his young disciple on his "intelligence, zeal, science and energy" and hinted that the young general would play "an important if not the principal part" in Scott's plans for the future. He hailed McClellan's arrival at his headquarters as "an event of happy consequence to the country and to the army" and warmly welcomed into his official family this talented and promising subordinate.[5]

Subordination, however, was not what McClellan had in mind. He had been in Washington scarcely a week before he was confiding to his wife that Scott had grown "very slow and very old. He cannot long retain command I think—when he retires I am sure to succeed him." Basking in the attention he received from lawmakers and cabinet ministers, as well as in the adulation displayed by soldiers (whose stage-managed cheers at his every appearance never failed to lift his spirits), McClellan was carried away by his sense of self-importance. "I find myself in a new & strange position here—President, Cabinet, Genl Scott & all deferring to me—by some strange operation of magic I seem to have become *the* power of the land." He proudly asked his wife,

"Who would have thought when we were married that I should so soon be called upon to save my country?"[6]

Only one obstacle stood in McClellan's way—the old general to whom he had pledged eternal fealty just a few weeks earlier. How can I be expected to save this country, he asked, "when stopped by General Scott. . . . If he cannot be taken out of my path I . . . will resign & let the admn. take care of itself." Although the young general tried to maintain a respectful face in public, in private, he raged furiously against his onetime mentor: "I do not know whether he is a *dotard* or a *traitor!* . . . he is a perfect imbecile. He understands nothing, appreciates nothing & is ever in my way."[7]

Unwilling to let events take their natural course, McClellan tried to force the issue by manufacturing a crisis. From rumors, guesswork, and out of the depths of his own troubled psyche, the Young Napoleon had become convinced that Beauregard commanded 100,000 men poised to attack Washington at any moment. To meet this emergency, he demanded that all other theaters be stripped of troops so that the entire Union army could be concentrated under his command at the capital.[8]

Scott dismissed these hysterical fears. He was convinced (correctly) that the Union troops already stationed around Washington far outnumbered whatever force the enemy could assemble. He was, however, concerned about his own position. Recognizing that McClellan's demands constituted a naked power play and resentful of the irregular manner in which his own office was being bypassed, Scott countered with a move of his own: he offered to resign. Citing the numerous infirmities that made him "an incumbrance to the army," he proposed to retire "and then quietly to lay myself up—probably forever—somewhere in or about New York. But, wherever I may spend my little remainder of life," he concluded with well-calculated pathos, "my frequent and latest prayer will be 'God save the Union.'"[9]

Alarmed at the prospect of open warfare between his two leading generals, President Lincoln stepped in to make peace. At his insistence, Scott withdrew his resignation, and McClellan issued a public apology, which oozed respect for his senior officer. At the same time, Little Mac privately indicated that his war with Scott was far from over. "I have to fight against him," he told his wife. "I suppose it will result in a mortal enmity on his part against me, but I have no choice—the people call upon me to save the country—I *must* save it & cannot respect anything that is in the way."[10]

Unable to sleep nights for fear of a Confederate surprise attack, the exhausted young general's nerves frayed to the breaking point. As he tossed and turned, he was kept awake by the tramp of Jeff Davis's elephants. By mid-August, he was convinced that Beauregard's strength had swollen to 150,000 men, outnumbering his own force by three or four to one. A month later, McClellan's newly christened Army of the Potomac had increased to 80,000 soldiers, but by that time, Beauregard had somehow acquired an additional twenty thousand phantom soldiers.[11]

In fact, the Confederates never numbered more than 45,000 and were in no condition to launch the offensive that McClellan so greatly feared. Mere facts, however, could not shake the Young Napoleon from his delusions. He claimed that he needed 300,000 men, including the entire regular army, in order to protect the capital. All other theaters would have to stand on the defensive. Now that he had been transferred to the East, McClellan quite forgot his earlier argument that the West should be the crucial battleground. The real fighting must be in Virginia, he insisted; everything else would be "a mere bagatelle."[12]

Such a strategy, of course, was completely contrary to Scott's own Anaconda Plan, and it was hardly surprising that the old general resisted McClellan's proposals. McClellan retaliated with a campaign calculated to drive his aged commander out of office. Scott's orders were ignored, his letters went unanswered, and the young general, in open defiance of army regulations, communicated directly with the president and cabinet, bypassing the required channels and leaving the commanding general in the dark.[13]

It did not take long for McClellan's contempt for his commander to seep down into the ranks. Officers who passed Scott on the street failed to salute him and jeered within his hearing, "Old fuss-&-feathers don't look first-rate today." A British journalist bearing a pass issued by Scott was turned back by an officer who refused to recognize its validity. "I guess the General's a dead man, sir," the officer explained. "Is he not Commander-in-Chief of the United States army?" the journalist asked. "Well, I believe that's a fact sir; but you had better argue that point with McClellan." Two months earlier, the Englishman reflected, Scott's was "the most honored name in the States[,] ... 'now none so poor to do him reverence.' Hard is the fate of those who serve republics."[14]

Things came to a head at a stormy cabinet meeting in late September, attended by both Scott and McClellan. The question arose as to how many troops were stationed in the Washington area. Neither Scott nor the secretary of war knew the answer, but Secretary of State Seward, who could never resist an opportunity to demonstrate his importance, pulled out a slip of paper on which he had jotted down the position of every regiment in the vicinity. It was evident that he had been in consultation with McClellan outside the proper channels. It was also clear that Seward, unaware that McClellan considered him "a meddling, officious incompetent little puppy," had abandoned his former ally Scott in order to hitch his wagon to the young general's rising star.[15]

Scott's face clouded. This, he said, "is a remarkable state of things. I am in command of the armies of the United States, but have been wholly unable to get any reports, any statement of the actual forces, but . . . this civilian is possessed of facts which are withheld from me. . . . Am I Mr. President to apply to the Secretary of State for the necessary military information to discharge my duties?" Seward tried to explain that he obtained his information by vigilant observation, but Scott, "with a grim smile," easily demolished that clumsy lie. Cameron defused the tension with a jest at Seward's expense, and the meeting broke up. Scott detained McClellan for a parting word: you were called to Washington at my suggestion, he reminded him. "When I proposed that you should come here to aid, not supersede me, you had my friendship and confidence. You still have my confidence." The young general bowed and said nothing, but to his wife he gloated: "As he threw down the glove & I took it up, I presume war is declared—so be it. I do not fear him."[16]

For Scott, the end was at hand. Abandoned by his sycophants, mocked by his subordinates, and reviled by his successor, he had outlived his usefulness. More than fifty years earlier he had entered his country's service as Hotspur; he departed as King Lear.

The old general tried to cling to office a bit longer, awaiting the arrival from the West of Maj. Gen. Henry Wager Halleck, a pedantic fussbudget whom Scott barely knew but whose scholarship he admired. Scott had hoped that Halleck, rather than the ungrateful McClellan, might be installed as his successor, but even that consolation would be denied him. McClellan forced the government's hand by telling a group of influential senators that only Scott's foot dragging prevented him from embarking on an immediate advance. The impression he conveyed of an impetuous young general being restrained by the palsied hand of his doddering commander was effective in persuading the senators to pressure the administration into forcing Scott out. But considering that even an unfettered McClellan would remain inactive until the following spring, his argument was highly misleading. It was also unnecessary. Scott had already signaled his intention to retire, and the cabinet had agreed to let him go.[17]

On October 31, 1861, Scott officially requested that his name be placed on the army's retired list. His stated reason was ill health: "For more than three years I have been unable, from a hurt, to mount a horse or to walk more than a few paces at a time, and that with much pain. Other and new infirmities— dropsy and vertigo—admonish me that repose of mind and body, with the appliance of surgery and medicine, are necessary to add a little more to a life already protracted beyond the usual span of man." Grateful to be relieved of an embarrassment, the administration allowed the deposed warrior to exit public life with his dignity intact. At four o'clock on the afternoon of November 1, the entire cabinet trooped into Scott's quarters to pay their final respects. The president made what Scott called "a neat and affecting address,"

A very old Fuss and Feathers, ca. 1865. National Archives.

and the general responded in kind, though his unsteady legs forced him to cut his remarks uncharacteristically short.[18]

Press and public realized that Scott's passage marked the end of an era, and tributes poured in from all quarters. In his annual message, President Lincoln would call attention to Scott's retirement as one of the year's notable events. "During his long life the nation has not been unmindful of his merit, yet on calling to mind how fruitfully, ably, and brilliantly he has served the country, from a time far back in our history when few of the now living had been born, and thenceforth continually, I can not but think we are still his debtors."[19] Poets echoed the sentiment:

> Not when his country needs his arms no more
> Quits he the field, but when she needs it most;
> Too worn, and old, to head her patriot host,
> And lead it on to victory as before![20]

Even McClellan weighed in with such lavish praise that Scott was ready to forget the insults and indignities Little Mac had heaped upon him. He may not have been so forgiving had he known of McClellan's cynical admission that his tribute to Scott "*was* a little rhetorical—but I wrote it *at* him—for a particular market."[21]

In the predawn darkness of November 2, while a fierce storm was raging, the old soldier made his final exit from the nation's capital. A gratifyingly large assemblage of dignitaries gathered at the depot to see him off. They were soon joined by McClellan and his staff, whose entrance in black rain slickers reminded observers of "the black knights of old." The two generals exchanged small talk, and the younger was momentarily humbled by the thought "that at some distant day I too shall totter away from Washn—a worn out soldier with naught to do but make my peace with God."[22]

Scott was bundled into a private car, placed at his disposal by wealthy admirers, and carried back to New York City. From there, he planned to sail for Europe to consult with what a skeptical friend called "some quack in France" recommended by Mrs. Scott. The crossing proved more eventful than anticipated. As the steamer *Arago* neared Europe, a Confederate commerce raider was spotted hovering nearby. Scott took command of his ship's meager defenses and drilled the crew and all able-bodied passengers on the main deck. The Confederate ship passed by, in search of bigger game, but the event was notable in at least one respect: it marked the last time Winfield Scott would command troops for battle.[23]

A much more serious naval encounter took place off the coast of Cuba while Scott was on the high seas. An impetuous American captain seized two Confederate diplomats from off the British ship *Trent*. When similar highhanded outrages had been committed by the English in 1812, they had been considered acts of war. Now, with the tables turned, some voices in England were raised for war, or at least in favor of greater support for the Confederacy.

Upon his arrival in France, Scott was enlisted to calm this crisis. Since the U.S. government could not issue an official apology without appearing weak, Scott, now a private citizen, was persuaded to issue a statement appealing for calm. The general's hands, however, were too swollen with gout to grasp a pen, so a statement was drafted in his name by Thurlow Weed, a fellow passenger on the *Arago,* with the help of some American diplomats stationed in France. Aware of the general's vanity in matters literary, Weed feared that his temerity might ignite Scott's wrath. To his surprise, the touchy general docilely approved the statement in toto, even to the punctuation, a subject "in regard to which he was known to be particularly tenacious and sensitive." Scott laboriously affixed his signature to the letter, which had a soothing effect on the crisis when it appeared in newspapers throughout England.[24]

While the *Trent* excitement was still raging, Scott decided to cut his European stay short in case a war with England required his services at home. He left on the next boat without even seeing the doctors he had come so far to consult. It is not clear whether he even saw his wife during his brief stay in France. If he did, it would have been for the last time. Maria Mayo Scott died at Rome in June 1862, an expatriate to the end. Her remains were returned to the cemetery at West Point, where they were laid beside those of her daughter Maria. A plot next to her was reserved for her husband. So often separated in life, the couple would at last be united.

In 1862, Scott also mourned the loss of one whom he cherished as "the oldest friend I have in the world"—Martin Van Buren.[25] As the general had outlived his professional usefulness, so he also outlived his friends. Like the old soldier of the barracks-room ballad, there was little left for him but to fade away.

As he gradually withdrew from the world, Scott's public appearances became less frequent. In June 1862, he held his last conference with President Lincoln. The substance of their meeting was not recorded, but as it was followed by the selection of Halleck as general in chief and John Pope as commander of the Army of the Potomac, it can be assumed that these unfortunate appointments were made at Scott's suggestion. Three years later, the old general, "pale and feeble, but resolute," paid his respects to Lincoln's coffin as it lay in state at New York's City Hall.[26]

Scott's last major activity was the completion of the *Memoirs,* on which he had labored so long. It was too late. The two volumes bore all too clearly the marks of an old man, rambling, cranky, and self-serving, with the events of the distant past more vivid in the memory than those of his last few years. Some reviewers were needlessly cruel. "This is one of the most unsatisfactory books ever published," complained the anonymous reviewer for *Harper's Weekly,* who seemed almost personally offended by the work's shortcomings.

If such hostile criticism disturbed Scott, he did not show it. He proudly presented copies to friends and colleagues, inscribing the one to Grant, "From the oldest to the greatest general."[27]

After this, the oldest general's public appearances became even less frequent. "Quietness," he insisted, "is the great necessity of my little remainder of life." He was increasingly absorbed in the aches and pains of his ever-weakening body, complaining of gravel in the kidneys, paralysis in the spine, dropsy in his legs, and vertigo, dilating at length on his annoying suppression of urine to any sympathetic listener. He spent the winter of 1865–66 in the sunny South, returning in May to his favorite summer home, West Point. As he checked into Roe's Hotel, he announced with his customary decisiveness, "Roe, I have come here to die."[28]

He was as good as his word. Within days, his appetite began to fail, his skin turned yellow, and he experienced difficulty in swallowing. For a time, he continued to play whist and take drives in the countryside, but chills, vomiting, and muscle weakness confined him to his bed, where the doctors were compelled to "manage him exactly as we would a child."[29]

On the morning of May 29, just two weeks short of his eightieth birthday, the patient took a turn for the worse. His daughter Camilla was hurriedly sent for, but before she could arrive, the post's Episcopal chaplain began to administer the last rites of his church. Without his false teeth, the dying man was unable to respond vocally, but he signified his understanding by squeezing the chaplain's hand. During this ceremony, at about 11 o'clock in the morning, Winfield Scott passed away, "so quietly and calmly that it was impossible to note the exact moment."[30]

The funeral was held on Friday, June 1, 1866, in the Cadets' Chapel, which was draped in black for the occasion. Prominent among the mourners was a dazzling list of military guests and pallbearers, headed by Generals Grant and George Meade, which read like a roster of the army's high command. The ceremony itself, conducted in the high-church Episcopalian manner, was deemed "cold and formal," with the only note of sentiment being sounded by the mournful strain of "Taps," which accompanied the coffin to its final resting place.[31]

President Andrew Johnson declared a day of national mourning.[32] Government offices were closed, and flags everywhere fluttered at half-staff. Eulogists across the nation remembered Scott's long service, from the victories in Canada, which helped restore America's tarnished military honor, to the campaign in Mexico, which added such vast amounts of territory to the American domain at such a relatively small cost.

Scarcely noted among the flowery tributes was the project closest to Scott's heart, the creation of a wholly professional U. S. Army, perhaps because its effects were less tangible and its results less clear-cut. Although he had waged

Scott on his deathbed. *Harper's Magazine,* courtesy Western Reserve Historical Society.

a long-running war with the likes of Jefferson, Jackson, Gaines, and Taylor, who all advocated a people's army, Scott's victory was short-lived: his vision of an elite, professional army could not survive into the age of total war. An offshoot of this project—the establishment of a professional military management structure—would, however, endure as his major monument.

Friends recalled Scott's quirks with affection, his accomplishments with pride. "Did ever a man with foibles so many and so ridiculous do his country so much service?" The late hero's "bad French and flat jokes, his tedious egotism, his agonizing pedantries" seemed, in retrospect, endearing rather than irritating. They were overshadowed by the memory of "a brave, prudent, skillful, brilliant, and humane commander, and a warmhearted and excellent man," who was "as strong in great things" as he was "weak in little things." That Scott was "prone to vanity there is no denying," another friend conceded, but he acknowledged that the general had "much to be vain of."[33]

A "silly giant" perhaps, but nonetheless a giant.[34]

NOTES

PREFACE

1.Winfield Scott, *Memoirs of Lieut.-General Scott, LL.D., Written by Himself,* 2 vols. (New York: Sheldon, 1864), 1:xxi.

2. Memory F. Mitchell, "Publishing in State Historical Journals," *Wisconsin Magazine of History* 59 (Winter 1976–77), 135–42.

3. John S. D. Eisenhower, *Agent of Destiny: The Life and Times of General Winfield Scott* (New York: Free Press, 1997), xiv; Timothy D. Johnson, *Winfield Scott: The Quest for Military Glory* (Lawrence: Univ. Press of Kansas, 1998), 4.

1. Russell F. Weigley, *History of the United States Army* (New York: Macmillan, 1967), 560–67; Leonard D. White, *The Jeffersonians: A Study in Administrative History, 1801–1829* (New York: Free Press, 1965), 264; "Army of the United States," *North American Review* 8 (n.s. 23, no. 53; Oct. 1826): 246–50.

2. Scott, *Memoirs,* 1:1–2.

3. Ibid., 3; General Marcus J. Wright, *General Scott* (New York: Appleton, 1897), 3.

4. Scott, *Memoirs,* 1:2; E[rasmus] D[arwin] Keyes, *Fifty Years Observation of Men and Events, Civil and Military* (New York: Scribner's, 1884), 19–34.

5. Scott, *Memoirs,* 1:2–3; Wright, *General Scott,* 2–3.

6. Scott, *Memoirs,* 1:6–9; Fayette Robinson, *An Account of the Organization of the Army of the United States,* 2 vols. (Philadelphia: Butler, 1848), 1:110.

7. Scott, *Memoirs,* 1:6.

8. Ibid., 8; Keyes, *Fifty Years Observation,* 36–47.

9. Diary, Sept. 21, 1857, Edmund Ruffin Papers, LC; journal, Mar. 4, 1841, Benjamin Tappan Papers, LC (microfilm, Ohio Historical Society, Columbus).

10. Scott, *Memoirs,* 1:13; Charles Winslow Elliott, *Winfield Scott: The Soldier and the Man* (New York: Macmillan, 1937), 143–44.

11. Burr cited in Elliott, *Winfield Scott,* 11; Keyes, *Fifty Years Observation,* 9–10; Thurlow Weed, *Life of Thurlow Weed,* 2 vols. (Boston, 1883–84; reprint, New York: Da Capo, 1970), 1:663.

12. One of the midshipmen later recalled his captor as "a great overgrown, clumsy country fellow." William Howard Russell, *My Diary North and South* (Boston: Burnham, 1863), 76.

13. Scott, *Memoirs,* 1:19–21; Elliott, *Winfield Scott,* 16 n.

14. See Report of Secretary of War Henry Dearborn, Dec. 2, 1807, *ASP:MA,* 1:227.

15. Scott, *Memoirs,* 1:22–23.

16. Ibid. 1:22–26. Although grateful for the presidential favor, Scott did not become a supporter of Jefferson. He conceded that the Sage of Monticello was "a man of genius, of literary culture and with a fine turn for philosophic inquiry," but he blamed him for setting in motion that pernicious doctrine of states rights, which in Scott's view, had led directly to secession and the Civil War. Ibid., 182.

17. WS to Secretary of War Dearborn, May 19, 1808, Charles Winslow Elliott Collection, NYPL (typescript).

18. Keyes, *Fifty Years Observation,* 9.

2. CAPTAIN

1. WS to Secretary of War Dearborn, June 1, 1808, Charles Winslow Elliott Collection, NYPL (typescript).

2. WS to Secretary of War Dearborn, Nov. 25, 1808, Elliot Collection (typescript); Francis Paul Prucha, "The United States Army as Viewed by British Travelers, 1825–1860," *Military Affairs* 17 (Fall 1953): 115.

3. Gen. James Wilkinson, *Memoirs of My Own Times,* 3 vols. (Philadelphia: Abraham Small, 1816), 1:798–99; Elliott, *Winfield Scott,* 25–26.

4. Alexis de Tocqueville, *Democracy in America,* ed. J. P. Mayer (New York: Harper-Collins, 1969), 622; WS to Secretary of War William Eustis, Jan. 15, 1811, Letters Received by the Secretary of War, Main Series, RG 107, NA (M221).

5. Elliott, *Winfield Scott,* 26–27. To add to his other difficulties, Scott almost caused the *Nancy*'s skipper to lose his vessel. Apparently, Scott had been asked to transport a slave boy from Virginia to new owners in Louisiana. Because of the *Nancy*'s detour to Cuba, federal officials suspected that he was smuggling the boy illegally into the country and threatened to seize the entire ship. The matter was finally cleared up, but Scott had to dispose of the young slave. The incident demonstrates that, whatever may have been his later reservations about slavery, Scott had no moral qualms about the institution in his youth. See WS to A. Jordan, Aug. 5, 1809, Feb. 27, 1810, Charles Chaille-Long Papers, LC.

6. Weigley, *United States Army,* 113.

7. For evidence that Wilkinson's underhanded activities were suspected by other army officers, see Col. Alexander Smyth to William Eustis, Aug. 16, 1810, Letters Received by the Secretary of War, Unregistered Series, RG 107, NA (M222).

8. The Terre aux Bouefs disaster deserves, but has not yet received, a full-scale examination, either in the form of a monograph or a historical novel. Ample sources exist for such an investigation, including "Mortality in the Troops at New Orleans" (a report communicated to the House of Representatives on April 27, 1810), *ASP:MA,* vol. 1; Wilkinson, *Memoirs,* 2:341–521 (apps. 103–17); Jabez Wiggins Heustis, *Physical Observations and Medical Tracts and Researches on the Topography and Diseases of Louisiana* (New York: T. and J. Swords, 1817), 89–108; and John Duffy, ed., *The Rudolph Matas History of Medicine in Louisiana,* 2 vols. (Baton Rouge: Louisiana State Univ. Press, 1957), 1:464–75.

9. Scott, *Memoirs,* 1:31, 34–35.

10. Wilkinson, *Memoirs,* 1:807, 2:14, 1:799–800.

11. George Templeton Strong, *The Diary of George Templeton Strong,* ed. Allan Nevins and Milton Halsey Thomas, 4 vols. (New York: Macmillan, 1952), 3:144. See also Richard M. McMurry, "Marse Robert and the Fevers: A Note on the General as Strategist and on Medical Ideas as a Factor in Civil War Decision Making," *Civil War History* 35 (Sept. 1989): 203.

12. WS to Secretary of War Eustis, July 14, 1809, Elliott Collection (typescript).

13. WS to Secretary of War Eustis, July 23, 1809, Elliott Collection (typescript).

14. Wilkinson, *Memoirs,* 1:802–3.

15. WS to Secretary of War Eustis, July 29, 1809, Elliott Collection (typescript).

16. Memorandum by WS on charges brought by Lt. Bingham against Col. Brown, June 8, 1859, Letters Sent by the Headquarters of the Army, RG 108, NA (M857).

17. WS to Jordan, Aug. 5, 1809. Chaille-Long Papers.

18. A copy of the trial's transcript can be found in Letters Received by the AGO, RG 94, NA (M566). It is filed, however, for the year 1865, which was when Scott, after a long search, discovered a copy among his personal papers. The original was missing, and the old general suspected that it was removed around 1855 by Secretary of War Jefferson Davis to be used as ammunition in their feud. See also Robinson, *Organization of the Army,* 1:116–20; Wilkinson, *Memoirs,* 1:802; and Edward D. Mansfield, *The Life and Military Services of Lieut.-General Winfield Scott* (New York: N. C. Miller, 1862), 29.

19. *(Natchez) Weekly Chronicle*, Feb. 5, 1810, Elliott Collection; Wilkinson, *Memoirs*, 1:802. Wilkinson also claimed that Scott fought an earlier duel while in New Orleans with a Dr. Claude, in which he displayed cowardice.

20. John M. Hallahan, "No Doubt Blameable: The Transformation of Captain Winfield Scott," *Virginia Cavalcade* 40 (1991): 160–71; Elliott, *Winfield Scott,* 36–37.

21. WS to Lewis Edwards, June 11, 1811, in Scott, *Memoirs,* 1:42–43.

22. WS to Secretary of War William Eustis, Jan. 15, 1811, Letters Received by Secretary of War, Main Series.

23. Scott, *Memoirs,* 1:50–52. Scott's admiration for Hampton was not universally shared. Col. Alexander Smyth (later a general) had a less charitable view of the South Carolina general, accusing him of incompetence, lechery, and being "liable to mental disease." Col. Alexander Smyth to Secretary of War William Eustis, Aug. 16, 1810, Letters Received by Secretary of War, Unregistered Series.

24. WS to William Eustis, Oct. 10, 1811, Letters Received by Secretary of War, Unregistered Series.

25. Elliott, *Winfield Scott,* 40–41.

26. Scott, *Memoirs,* 1:48–52.

3. DEFEAT

1. "Military Force in June, 1812," *ASP:MA,* 1:319.

2. James D. Richardson, *A Compilation of the Messages and Papers of the Presidents, 1789–1897,* 9 vols. (Washington, D.C., 1896–97), 1:322.

3. Patrick McDonogh, "A Hero of Fort Erie: Letters Relating to the Military Service . . . of Lieutenant Patrick McDonogh," ed. Frank H. Severance, *Publications of the Buffalo Historical Society* 5 (1902): 74, 72.

4. WS to Secretary of War John C. Calhoun, Apr. 18, 1822, Letters Received by the Secretary of War, RG 107, NA (M221). Unless otherwise specified, all subsequent references are to the Main Series.

5. Isaac Roach, "Journal of Major Isaac Roach, 1812–1824," *Pennsylvania Magazine of History and Biography* 17 (1893): 132–33.

6. George D. Emerson, "The Episode of the *Adams* and *Caledonia*," *Publications of the Buffalo Historical Society* 8 (1905): 405–9; Mrs. James Hoskins, "Exploits of John Dickson," *Publications of the Buffalo Historical Society* 8 (1905): 415–17; Elliott, *Winfield Scott,* 50–53.

7. Emerson, "*Adams* and *Caledonia*," 407; Scott, *Memoirs,* 1:56.

8. Elliott, *Winfield Scott,* 49–50, 54–56.

9. Henry Adams, *History of the United States of America during the Administration of James Madison* (New York: Library of America, 1986), 546–47.

10. Benson J. Lossing, *The Pictorial Field Book of the War of 1812* (New York: Harper and Brothers, 1868), 392.

11. Ibid., 393 n.

12. Ibid., 393–94; Scott, *Memoirs,* 1:56–57; Report of WS to the Secretary of War, Dec. 29, 1812, Charles Winslow Elliott Collection, NYPL (typescript).

13. Elliott, *Winfield Scott,* 62 n. In the conclusion of his report, Scott not only neglected to give credit to Wool but also omitted mentioning any other officer by name.

The regular troops, he explained, "conscious of having done their duty, think not of particular honors or distinction. I have, therefore, no names to enumerate." Report of WS to the Secretary of War, Dec. 29, 1812, Elliott Collection (typescript).

14. John E. Wool to Sen. I. Harris, Nov. 6, 1865, NYSL.

15. Report of WS to the Secretary of War, Dec. 29, 1812, Elliott Collection (typescript).

16. For an account of the battle from the Indian point of view, see John Norton, *The Journal of Major John Norton, 1816,* ed. Carl F. Klink and James J. Talugo (Toronto: Champlain Society, 1970), 304–10. The son of a Cherokee father and a Scottish mother, equally at home in both worlds, Norton commanded the Indian auxiliaries at Queenston Heights.

17. Report of WS to the Secretary of War, Dec. 29, 1812, Elliot collection (typescript).

18. Report of WS to the Secretary of War, Dec. 29, 1812; *Niles' Register* 3 (Nov. 14, 1812): 170; Scott, *Memoirs,* 1:60.

19. Mansfield, *Lieut.-General Winfield Scott,* 43; Lossing, *Pictorial Field Book,* 402. For the balladeer's version, see Elliott, *Winfield Scott,* 54.

20. Lossing, *Pictorial Field Book,* 403; Elliott, *Winfield Scott,* 67–68.

21. Report of WS to Secretary of War, Dec. 29, 1812, Elliot collection (typescript).

22. Elliott, *Winfield Scott,* 69–71.

23. McDonogh, "Hero of Fort Erie," 76.

24. Scott, *Memoirs,* 1:63.

4. ROCKET

1. Scott, *Memoirs,* 1:64–66. Although it is tempting to dismiss this swashbuckling tale as a romantic embroidery by Scott in his old age, it was confirmed by Edward Mansfield, who claimed to have heard it from Captain Coffin, the British officer involved. *Lieut.-General Winfield Scott,* 46–48.

2. Scott, *Memoirs,* 67–68; Elliott, *Winfield Scott,* 75.

3. Scott, *Memoirs,* 1:72–74; WS to Secretary of War, Jan. 30, 1813, *ASP:MA,* 1:346.

4. WS to Charles Kitchell Gardner, Dec. 25, 1812, Charles Kitchell Gardner Papers, NYSL.

5. Technically speaking, the Presidential Palace, or Executive Mansion, was not yet called "The White House," a nickname it would acquire only after it had been whitewashed to cover the soot left by the 1814 British burning of Washington.

6. Elliott, *Winfield Scott,* 81–84.

7. WS to Charles Kitchell Gardner, Feb. 16, 1813, Gardner Papers.

8. Gen. Henry Dearborn to Secretary of War John Armstrong, May 13, 1813, *ASP:MA,* 1:443–44; WS to Lieutenant Colonel Lamb, Mar. 22, 1813, Elliott Collection, NYPL (typescript).

9. WS to Charles Kitchell Gardner, July 16, 1813, Gardner Papers; Scott, *Memoirs,* 1:87.

10. For the 1813 Fort George campaign, see Scott, *Memoirs,* 87–98; WS to Charles Kitchell Gardner, June 4, July 16, 1813, Gardner Papers; Henry Dearborn to Secretary of War John Armstrong, May 27, 1813, *ASP:MA,* 1:444–45; and Elliott, *Winfield Scott,*

85–91. Although the Fort George campaign was officially commanded by Maj. Gen. Morgan Lewis, it was universally agreed that Scott was its moving spirit. Lewis himself handsomely acknowledged that Scott "fought nine-tenths of the battle." Adams, *History of the United States,* 729.

11. Scott, *Memoirs,* 1:88.

12. The officer, Lt. Col. Christopher Myers, had been one of Scott's captors at Newark. One evening, over the dinner table, Scott mentioned that he had never seen the falls from the Canadian side. Myers teasingly remarked that he would first have to win a battle. The hot-blooded Scott had taken offense at the remark, but now, with their situations reversed, Myers, though seriously wounded, chivalrously apologized. Ibid., 91 n.

13. Later, as a gesture of respect, he sent the flag to General Dearborn. "Why does he trouble me *with this bit of bunting?*" the confused old general was heard to ask. WS to Col. W. J. Worth, Feb. 12, 1838, WS Papers, HSP.

14. WS to Maj. Charles K. Gardner, June 4, 1813, Gardner Papers.

15. WS to Maj. Charles K. Gardner, June 4, 1813; Armstrong to Dearborn, June 19, 1813, in Elliott, *Winfield Scott,* 101.

16. *ASP:MA,* 1:445. See also the confused series of orders and counterorders Dearborn issued to General Lewis on June 6, 1813, in ibid., 446–47.

17. WS to Charles K. Gardner, July 16, 1813, Gardner Papers; Scott, *Memoirs,* 1:93.

18. Scott, *Memoirs,* 1:94; WS to Charles Kitchell Gardner, July 16, 1813, and WS to Charles Kitchell Gardner, June 4, 1813, both in Gardner Papers; WS to Brigadier General Boyd, July 18, 1813, Letters Received by the AGO, RG 94, NA (M567).

19. WS to Capt. James N. Barber, Aug. 18, 1813, WS Papers, HSP.

20. Lt. Col. John Harvey to Brig. Gen. Morgan Lewis, June 13, 1813, quoted in Elliott, *Winfield Scott,* 107–8; Capt. Talbott Chambers (Scott's ADC) to Col. John Harvey, June 17, 1813, quoted ibid., 108.

21. Brig. Gen. John P. Boyd to Secretary of War Armstrong, Aug. 3, 1813, *ASP:MA,* 1:450.

22. Ibid.; Scott, *Memoirs,* 1:98–99; *Niles' Register* 5 (Aug. 13, 1813).

23. Scott, *Memoirs,* 1:95.

24. Ibid., 94 n, 100; Wilkinson, *Memoirs,* 1:815–16.

25. *Niles' Register* 5 (Oct. 25, 1813): 116; Lossing, *Pictorial Field Book,* 631; Scott, *Memoirs,* 1:100.

26. WS to Wilkinson, Oct. 11, 1813, in Scott, *Memoirs,* 1:103.

27. WS to Secretary of War Armstrong, Dec. 31, 1813, in Scott, *Memoirs,* 1:104–6; Lossing, *Pictorial Field Book,* 631–32; Scott, *Memoirs,* 1:107.

28. Also known variously as Hoop-hoole's, Hooppole's, or Uphold's Creek.

29. Scott, *Memoirs,* 1:108; WS to John Armstrong, Nov. 26, 1835, Elliott Collection (typescript).

30. Scott, *Memoirs,* 1:110.

31. Ibid., 109; WS to Armstrong, Nov. 26, 1835; Elliott Collection (typescript); Mansfield, *Lieut.-General Winfield Scott,* 84; Adams, *History of the United States,* 157–58.

32. WS to Charles K. Gardner, July 16, 1813, Gardner Papers.

33. Scott, *Memoirs,* 1:115–16.

34. Elliott, *Winfield Scott,* 142–44.

35. WS to Wilkinson, Jan. 22, 1814, and Wilkinson to Governor Tomkpins, Jan. 23, 1814, both in Wilkenson, *Memoirs,* 1:612–14, 616–17; WS to Jacob Brown, May 23, 1814, Jacob Brown Papers, William L. Clements Library, University of Michigan, Ann Arbor.

36. WS to Secretary Armstrong, Jan. 25, 1814, Letters Received by Secretary of War, RG 107, NA (M221); WS to Swift, Jan. 24, 1814, Elliott Collection (typescript).

5. VICTORY

1. John C. Fredriksen, *Officers of the War of 1812 with Portraits and Anecdotes: The United States Army Left Division, Gallery of Honor,* with an introduction by Donald E. Graves (Lewiston, N.Y.: Edwin Mellon Press, 1989), 25–26; Scott, *Memoirs,* 1:118; John D. Morris, *Sword of the Border: Major General Jacob Jennings Brown, 1775–1828* (Kent, Ohio: Kent State Univ. Press, 2000).

2. Fredriksen, *Officers of the War of 1812,* 4; WS to John Armstrong, May 17, 1814, Charles Winslow Elliott Collection, NYPL (typescript).

3. Scott, *Memoirs,* 1:119. Regarding U.S. camps of instruction, see Donald E. Graves, "'I Have a Handsome Little Army. . . . ': A Reexamination of Winfield Scott's Camp at Buffalo in 1814," in *War along the Niagara: Essays on the War of 1812 and Its Legacy,* ed. R. Arthur Bowler (Youngstown, N.Y.: Old Fort Niagara Association, 1991), 45–46.

4. [John Armstrong], *Hints to Young Generals. By an Old Soldier* (Kingston, [1812]), 7. See J. C. A. Stagg, "Enlisted Men in the United States Army, 1812–1815: A Preliminary Survey," *William and Mary Quarterly* 43 (1986): 615–45.

5. Col. Alexander Smyth to Secretary of War William Eustis, Aug. 16, 1810, Letters Received by the Secretary of War, Unregistered Series, RG 107, NA (M222); John S. Hare, "Military Punishments in the War of 1812," *Journal of the American Military Institute* 4 (1940): 225–39; Frank H. Severance, ed., "Militia Service of 1813–14: Correspondence of Maj.-Gen. Amos Hall," *Publications of the Buffalo Historical Society* 5 (1902): 55–58.

6. Donald E. Graves, *The Battle of Lundy's Lane: On the Niagara in 1814* (Baltimore: Nautical and Aviation Publishing, 1993), 23. Scott was harder on his officers than on enlisted men. In late June, nine officers were under arrest compared to only seventeen enlisted men. (Elliott, *Winfield Scott,* 150.) One officer, whom he observed passing a sentinel without returning his salute, was ordered by Scott to repair the oversight within twenty minutes or face court-martial. Mansfield, *Lieut.-General Winfield Scott,* 101 n.

7. WS to Jacob Brown, May 4, 1814, Jacob Brown Papers, William L. Clements Library, University of Michigan, Ann Arbor; Lester W. Smith, ed., "A Drummer Boy in the War of 1812: The Memoir of Jarvis Frary Hanks," *Niagara Frontier* 7 (Summer 1950): 55.

8. WS to Jacob Brown, May 23, 1814, Brown Papers; Graves, "Handsome Little Army," 46; Elliott, *Winfield Scott,* 147.

9. WS to Jacob Brown, May 17, 1814, Brown Papers; WS to C. Irvine, Apr. 27, 1814, Buffalo and Erie County Historical Society, Buffalo, N.Y.; WS to Secretary of War Armstrong, May 17, 1814, Elliott Collection (typescript); René Chartand, "The U.S. Army's Uniform Supply 'Crisis' during the War of 1812," *The Military Collector and Historian* 40 (Summer 1988): 63–64.

10. Smith, "Drummer Boy," 59; Graves, *Lundy's Lane,* 31–32.

11. R. Alan Douglas, "Weapons of the War of 1812," *Michigan History* 47 (Dec. 1963): 324; Graves, *Lundy's Lane,* 23–25.

12. Douglas, "Weapons of the War of 1812," 323–24.

13. See Jeffrey Kimball, "The Battle of Chippewa: Infantry Tactics in the War of 1812," *Military Affairs* 8 (1949): 172–74.

14. [Armstrong], *Hints to Young Generals.* This manual of about seventy pages, small enough to slip into a pocket, included instruction on such elementary matters as the superiority of interior over exterior lines of operation and advice on such highly practical matters as how to conduct a retreat.

15. See the illuminating discussions in Donald E. Graves, "'Dry Books of Tactics': U.S. Infantry Manuals of the War of 1812 and After," *Military Collector and Historian* 38 (1986): 50–61; and Theodore J. Crackel, "The Battle of Queenston Heights, 13 October 1812," in *America's First Battles, 1776–1865,* ed. Charles E. Heller and William A. Stofft (Lawrence: Univ. Press of Kansas, 1986), 49–56.

16. WS to Secretary of War Lewis Cass, Mar. 21, 1835, Letters Received by the AGO, RG 94, NA (M567); WS to Col. S. B. Walbach, Feb. 14, 1814, Daniel Parker Papers, HSP; Scott *Memoirs,* 1:119–20; WS to Col. S. B. Walbach, Apr. 20, 1814, Letters Received by the AGO. Scott's recollection of his training procedure at Flint Hill is gently debunked by Donald Graves. "Handsome Little Army," 46–49.

17. WS to John Armstrong, May 17, 1814, and WS to Gen. Wm. H. Winder, May 6, 1814, both in Elliott Collection (typescript).

18. John D. Morris, "General Jacob Brown and the Problem of Command in 1814," in *War along the Niagara: Essays on the War of 1812 and Its Legacy,* edited by R. Arthur Bowler (Youngstown, N.Y.: Old Fort Niagara Association, 1991), 30; Kimball, "Battle of Chippewa," 170–71.

19. Armstrong to Jacob Brown, June 10, 1814, in Elliott, *Winfield Scott,* 155; Scott, *Memoirs,* 1:121.

20. Scott, *Memoirs,* 1:121–22; Elliott, *Winfield Scott,* 156.

21. Scott, *Memoirs,* 1:123.

22. Scott was spared another potential peril by the conclusion of the prisoner exchange agreement in mid-May. This meant that, if captured, he would no longer need fear facing a firing squad.

23. Lossing, *Pictorial Field Book,* 405.

24. Ibid., 805; Riall to Sir Gordon Drummond, July 6, 1814, in James L. Babcock, ed., "The Campaign of 1814 on the Niagara Frontier," *Niagara Frontier* 10 (Winter 1963): 131.

25. Scott, *Memoirs,* 1:124–26; Lossing, *Pictorial Field Book,* 806.

26. Weed, *Life,* 1:651–53.

27. Scott, *Memoirs,* 1:127.

28. Peter B. Porter to W. J. Stone, May 26, 1840, in Babcock, "Campaign of 1814," 127–30.

29. Ibid., 130; Scott, *Memoirs,* 1:128; Lossing, *Pictorial Field Book,* 808.

30. Smith, "Drummer Boy," 56; Scott, *Memoirs,* 1:129. Recent investigation has cast doubt on this remark, for its only source is Scott's memoirs, and he was hardly in a

position to overhear Riall's statement. Graves, *Lundy's Lane,* 269 n. But after Lundy's Lane, Scott and Riall became acquainted while they were recovering from their wounds, and it is not impossible that Scott learned of this remark from Riall himself.

31. Mansfield, *Lieut.-General Winfield Scott,* 111.

32. Randolph C. Randall, *James Hall, Spokesman of the New West* (Columbus: Ohio State Univ. Press, 1964), 27.

33. Scott, *Memoirs,* 1:131; Lossing, *Pictorial Field Book,* 809–10; Mansfield, *Lieut.-General Winfield Scott,* 108–10.

34. Kimball, "Battle of Chippewa," 184–86; Mansfield, *Lieut.-General Winfield Scott,* 114–15 n; Lossing, *Pictorial Field Book,* 810–11; Graves, *Lundy's Lane,* 72. None of these authorities agree on the numbers and losses involved in the Battle of Chippewa.

35. Thomas S. Jesup, quoted in Kimball, "Battle of Chippewa," 185.

36. Col. Hercules Scott to his brother, Aug. 12, 1814, in Babcock, "Campaign of 1814," 158; and Riall to Sir Gordon Drummond, June 6, 1814, in "Campaign of 1814," 158, 132; Kimball, "Battle of Chippewa," 180.

37. Quoted in Mansfield, *Lieut.-General Winfield Scott,* 114–15. Mansfield gives no source for this quotation.

38. Scott, *Memoirs,* 1:134, 129; Chartand, "Uniform Supply Crisis," 54.

39. Maj. Gen. Jacob Brown to Secretary of War Armstrong, July 7, 1814, in *Niles' Register* 6 (July 26, 1814): 355.

6. HERO

1. WS to Jacob Brown, July 10, 1814 (two letters of same date), and Brown to WS, July 10, 1814, both in Jacob Brown Papers, William L. Clements Library, University of Michigan, Ann Arbor.

2. "Jesup's Narrative," in Charles J. Ingersoll, *Historical Sketch of the Second War between the United States of America and Great Britain . . . ,* 2 vols. (Philadelphia: Lea and Blanchard, 1849), 2:106; Scott, *Memoirs,* 1:136.

3. Smith, "Drummer Boy," 56–57.

4. [David Bates Douglass], "An Original Narrative of the Niagara Campaign of 1814," ed. John T. Horton. *Niagara Frontier* 11 (Spring 1964): 10.

5. Drummond to Sir George Prevost, July 27, 1814, in Babcock, "Campaign of 1814," 137.

6. Lossing, *Pictorial Field Book,* 815; Chauncey to Brown, Aug. 10, 1814, in Wilkinson, *Memoirs,* 1:667 n.

7. Scott, *Memoirs,* 1:137; Maj. Gen. Brown to Secretary of War, Aug. 7, 1814, in Babcock, "Campaign of 1814," 139; Lossing, *Pictorial Field Book,* 816. Scott had earlier boasted of his spy network, but in this campaign, its effectiveness was negligible. See WS to Jacob Brown, Apr. 13, May 14, 1814, Brown Papers.

8. "Brown's Diary," in Ingersoll, *Historical Sketch,* 2:102; Brown to Secretary of War, Aug. 7, 1814, in Babcock, "Campaign of 1814," 139; [Douglass], "Original Narrative," 13.

9. Scott, *Memoirs,* 1:138–39; Lossing, *Pictorial Field Book,* 816–17; [Douglass], "Original Narrative," 15.

10. Mansfield, *Lieut.-General Winfield Scott,* 125.

11. Scott, *Memoirs,* 1:140.

12. Ibid., 141; Graves, *Lundy's Lane,* 101.

13. Graves, *Lundy's Lane,* 112.

14. Fredriksen, *Officers of the War of 1812,* 153, 73.

15. [Douglass], "Original Narrative," 21 n.

16. Graves, *Lundy's Lane,* 114–15.

17. Scott, *Memoirs,* 1:143; Graves, *Lundy's Lane,* 154.

18. Scott, *Memoirs,* 1:145. Lundy's Lane is also known as the Battle of Bridgewater or the Battle of Niagara.

19. Drummond to Sir George Prevost, July 27, 1814, in Babcock, "Campaign of 1814," 137–38.

20. Mansfield, *Lieut.-General Winfield Scott,* 131 n; Graves, *Lundy's Lane,* 174–75. For an example of public praise over Lundy's Lane, see *Buffalo Gazette,* Aug. 2, 1814, in Elliott, *Winfield Scott,* 182.

21. Col. Hercules Scott to his brother, Aug. 21, 1814, in Babcock, "Campaign of 1814," 158.

22. Eber Howe cited in Fredriksen, *Officers of the War of 1812,* 49; Wilkinson, *Memoirs,* vol. 1, chaps. 14–15.

23. Scott, *Memoirs,* 1:150–51.

24. See WS to James Monroe, Nov. 6, 16, 1814, and WS to Martin Van Buren, Oct. 22, 1814, (typescripts) both in Elliott Collection; WS to James Monroe, Oct. 15, 1814, U.S. Military Academy Library, West Point, N.Y., Nov. 28, 1814, Letters Received by the Secretary of War, RG 107, NA (M221), Jan. 10, 1815, James Monroe Papers, NYPL; WS to General Cadwalader, Oct. 27, 1814, Cadwalader Family Papers, HSP; "Remarks on Subsisting the Army," *NASP:MA,* 5:522–53.

25. WS to James Monroe, Jan. 31, 1815, Elliott Collection (typescript); Scott, *Memoirs,* 1:154.

26. James Monroe to WS, Feb. 21, 1815, Confidential and Unofficial Letters Sent by the Secretary of War, 1814–47, RG 107, NA (M7); Scott, *Memoirs,* 1:154.

27. WS to James Monroe, Feb. 4, 1815, Elliott Collection (typescript).

7. PROFESSIONAL

1. Charles P. Stone, "Washington in March and April, 1861," *Magazine of American History* 14 (July 1883): 21. For an extended discussion of professionalization in a military context, see William B. Skelton, *An American Profession of Arms: The Army Officer Corps, 1784–1861* (Lawrence: Univ. Press of Kansas, 1992).

2. WS to Maj. Gen. Jacob Brown, Feb. 8, 1815, Letters Received by the Secretary of War, RG 107, NA (M221); WS to Brigadier General Cadwalader, Oct. 27, 1814, Cadwalader Family Papers, HSP.

3. Scott, *Memoirs,* 1:155–56; George Graham (chief clerk) to Major Generals Gaines, Scott, and Macomb, Mar. 21, 1815, and A. J. Dallas to Majors General Brown, Scott, and Macomb, Apr. 8, 1815, both in Confidential and Unofficial Letters Sent by the Secretary of War, 1814–47, RG 107, NA (M7).

4. WS to James Monroe, Nov. 6, 1814, Charles Winslow Elliott Collection, NYPL (typescript); Ethan Allen Hitchcock, *Fifty Years in Camp and Field: Diary of Major-General Ethan Allen Hitchcock, U.S.A.,* ed. A. A. Croffut (New York: G. P. Putnam's Sons, 1909), 42; Dallas to Generals Brown, Scott, and Macomb, Apr. 8, 1815.

5. A. J. Dallas to Generals Brown, Scott, and Macomb, Apr. 28, May 10, 1815, Jacob Brown Papers, William L. Clements Library, University of Michigan, Ann Arbor; Hitchcock, *Fifty Years,* 42.

6. Charles Fisher of North Carolina cited in Carlton Smith, "Congressional Attitudes towards Military Preparedness during the Monroe Administration," *Military Affairs* 40 (Feb. 1976): 24.

7. Roger J. Spiller, "Calhoun's Expansible Army: The History of a Military Idea," *South Atlantic Quarterly* 79 (Spring 1980): 189–91.

8. James Monroe to Sen. William. B. Giles (confidential), Feb. 22, 1815, *NASP:MA,* 1:80–81; Spiller, "Calhoun's Expansible Army," 193–95.

9. Skelton, *American Profession of Arms,* 126–30; Weigley, *United States Army,* 566–67.

10. See Graves, "'Dry Books of Tactics.'"

11. WS to Secretary of War James Monroe, Feb. 10, 1815, Letters Received by the Secretary of War, RG 107, NA (M221).

12. Charles F. O'Connell Jr., "The Corps of Engineers and the Rise of Modern Management, 1827–1856," in *Military Enterprise and Technological Change,* ed. Merritt Rose Smith (Cambridge: MIT Press, 1958), 97–102.

13. General Scott's Remarks on Subsisting the Army, *NASP:MA,* 5:52–53. See also White, *Jeffersonians,* 227–32.

14. Scott, *Memoirs,* 1:157.

15. WS to Maj. William. J. Worth, May 24, 1815, Solomon Gratz Collection, HSP; A. J. Dallas to WS, June 16, 1815, Confidential and Unofficial Letters Sent by the Secretary of War.

16. WS to A. J. Dallas, June 13, 1815, Elliott Collection (typescript); A. J. Dallas to WS, June 16,19, 1815, Confidential and Unofficial Letters Sent by the Secretary of War.

17. *Niles' Register* 8 (June 10, 1815): 253.

18. Scott, *Memoirs,* 1:158–59, 164–67; Lafayette to Henry Clay, Dec. 26, 1815, Henry Clay, *The Papers of Henry Clay,* ed. James F. Hopkins et al., 10 vols. (Lexington: Univ. Press of Kentucky, 1959–91), 2:114.

19. WS to James Monroe, Nov. 18, 1815, Elliott Collection (typescript); WS to Daniel Parker [c. Mar. 20, 1816], Daniel Parker Papers, HSP; James Monroe to WS, Mar. 20, 1816, James Monroe Papers, NYPL; WS to John Howard Payne, Sept. 14, Dec. 24, 1815, Special Manuscript Collection, Columbia University Library, New York; WS to Daniel Parker, Nov. 19, 1815, Parker Papers. On the possibility of war with Spain, see Maury Baker, "The Spanish War Scare of 1816," *Mid-America* 45 (Apr. 1963).

20. Jacob Brown to WS, June 8, 1816, Brown Papers, LC; WS to Daniel Parker, Nov. 5, 1816, Parker Papers.

21. "Some Richmond Portraits," *Harper's Magazine* 70 (1884–85): 713–15; Samuel Cortland to Andrew Mack, Mar. 16, 1817, Coles Collection, University of Virginia Library, Charlottesville.

22. Elliott, *Winfield Scott,* 214; Marian Gouverneur, *As I Remember: Recollections of American Society during the Nineteenth Century* (New York: Appleton, 1911), 181.

23. WS to Parker, Nov. 5, 1816; WS to Jacob Brown, Nov. 12, 1816, Brown Papers.

24. WS to [Daniel Parker], Feb. 9, 1817, Parker Papers; Jane G. R. Bernard to John H. Bernard, Feb. 11, 1817, William and Mary College Library (typescript, Virginia Historical Society, Richmond); Mary Buchanan Robertson to John H. Barnard, Mar. 17, 1817, William and Mary College Library (typescript, Virginia Historical Society, Richmond).

25. *Niles' Register* 8 (Sept. 6, 27, 1817): 29, 79.

26. WS to Jacob Brown, June 4, 1817, Brown Papers.

27. "Army of the United States," 254; WS to John C. Calhoun, Sept. 2, 1818, *ASP:MA,* 2:200; Scott, *Memoirs,* 1:205–206.

28. WS to Daniel Parker, [1821], Parker Papers; WS to Christopher Van Deventer, Feb. 6, 1819, Christopher Van Deventer Collection, William L. Clements Library, University of Michigan, Ann Arbor. Under the title *General Regulations for the Army,* the work can be found in *ASP:MA,* 2:199–268.

29. *ASP:MA,* 2:210, 233.

30. Scott, *Memoirs,* 1:206.

31. *ASP:MA,* 2:201.

32. Ibid., 216–17, 250.

33. O'Connell, "Corps of Engineers," 93.

8. MIDLIFE CRISIS

1. WS to James Monroe, Apr. 12, 1822, Solomon Gratz Collection, HSP; WS to Christopher Van Deventer, Sept. 24, 1822, Christopher Van Deventer Collection, William L. Clements Library, University of Michigan, Ann Arbor.

2. Johnson, *Winfield Scott,* 75; WS to Maj. Christopher Van Deventer, Dec. 27, 1822, Van Deventer Collection.

3. *ASP:MA,* 2:673–74; WS to James Monroe, Apr. 12, 1822, Gratz Collection. For examples of Scott's requests, see WS to John Calhoun, Nov. 26, Mar. 27, 1822, Letters Received by the Secretary of War, RG 107, NA (M221); William Wirt to Calhoun, Dec. 29, 1821, *ASP:MA,* 2:356–60; and WS to Sen. James Barbour, Feb. 23, 1821, Charles Winslow Elliott Collection, NYPL (typescript).

4. Gouverneur, *As I Remember,* 201; Henry Heth, *The Memoirs of Henry Heth,* ed. James L. Morrison Jr. (Westport, Conn.: Greenwood, 1974), 76.

5. Mary Boykin Miller Chesnut, *Mary Chesnut's Civil War,* ed. C. Vann Woodward (New Haven: Yale Univ. Press, 1981), 126; Gouverneur, *As I Remember,* 201.

6. Elliott, *Winfield Scott,* 765; WS to H. Dearborn, June 3, 1822, U.S. Military Academy Library, West Point.

7. WS to Monroe, Apr. 12, 1822. Gratz Collection, HSP.

8. WS to Monroe, Apr. 12, 1822; John Quincy Adams, *Memoirs of John Quincy Adams, Comprising Portions of His Diary from 1795 to 1848,* ed. Charles Francis Adams, 12 vols. (Philadelphia, 1874–77; reprint, New York: AMS Press, 1970), 5:496. On Scott's requests for overseas duties, see also WS to Monroe, July 19, 1823, James Monroe Papers, NYPL.

9. WS to Col. B. Peyton, Oct. 30, 1822, University of Virginia Library, Charlottesville; Adams, *Memoirs,* 6:7, 21–22; WS to James Monroe, Apr. 12, 1822, Gratz Collection; WS to Van Deventer, Dec. 27, 1822.

10. See Thomas Robson Hay, "John C. Calhoun and the Presidential Campaign of 1824," *North Carolina Historical Review* 12 (Jan. 1935).

11. WS to Samuel Gouverneur, Apr. 21, 1823, Elliott Collection (typescript); WS to Charles Kitchel Gardner, Apr. 8, May 7, 1823, and WS to "Dear Sir" [C. K. Gardner?], Aug. 7, [1823], both in Charles Kitchel Gardner Papers, NYSL, Albany; WS to Samuel Gouverneur, Apr. 8, 1823, Elliott Collection (typescript).

12. WS to James Monroe, Apr. 12, 1822, Gratz Collection; WS to Van Deventer, Sept. 24, 1822.

13. WS to Jacob Brown, Aug. 21, 1816, Jacob Brown Papers, William L. Clements Library, University of Michigan, Ann Arbor.

14. Scott, *Memoirs,* 1:196–98.

15. Jackson to WS, Sept. 8, 1817, Andrew Jackson, *Correspondence of Andrew Jackson,* ed. John Spenser Bassett, 7 vols. (Washington, D.C., 1928–35; reprint, Millwood, N.Y.: Kraus, 1969), 2:325; Adams, *Memoirs,* 4:434; WS to Jackson, Oct. 4, 1817, "Correspondence between Major General Jackson and Brevet Major General Scott on the Subject of an Order Bearing Date the 22d of April, 1817," *Army and Navy Life* 9 (Aug. 1906): 88.

16. WS to Jackson, Oct. 4, 1817, 88; Jackson to WS, Dec. 3, 1817, "Correspondence between Major General Jackson and Brevet Major General Scott," 89.

17. WS to Jackson, Jan. 2, 1818, "Correspondence between Major General Jackson and Brevet Major General Scott," 91; Jackson to A. J. Donelson, July 14, 1818, Jackson, *Correspondence,* 2:382; Scott, *Memoirs,* 1:200.

18. "Governor Clinton to the Public," a card in the *Columbian,* Apr. 6, 1819, Elliott Collection (typescript); WS to Clinton, Apr. 14, 1819, NYSL, Albany; Clinton to WS, Apr. 26, 1819, Special Manuscript Collection, Columbia University Library, New York. Among other things, Clinton called Scott "degraded," "a shallow coxcomb," "cowardly," "a bully," and "a ruffian."
    Scott was almost embroiled in yet another duel in the spring of 1822, when Congressman John Floyd of Virginia charged him with forgery in the reprinting of the army regulations. This accusation was based on a misunderstanding and was quickly retracted, but not before Scott had sent his seconds to demand satisfaction of the congressman. *Niles' Register* 23 (May 11, 1822): 158, 176; Adams, *Memoirs,* 5:510–11, 517; *ASP:MA,* 2:422–25.

19. Adams, *Memoirs,* 4:332.

20. WS to Calhoun, Feb. 22, 1819, Elliott Collection (typescript); Calhoun to WS, Mar. 5, 11, 1819, Confidential and Unofficial Letters Sent by the Secretary of War, RG 107, NA (M7); WS to Calhoun, Mar. 8, 1819, [Monroe] to WS (draft), Mar. 30, 1819, Monroe Papers, NYPL.

21. Adams, *Memoirs,* 4:323–24; James Monroe to Jackson, May 31, 1819, Jackson, *Correspondence,* 2:419.

22. Scott, *Memoirs,* 1:200; WS to Jackson, Dec. 11, 1823, and Jackson to WS, Dec. 11, 1823, both in Scott, *Memoirs,* 201, 202; WS to Jefferson Davis, Mar. 20, 1856, *NASP:MA,* 12:482–83.

23. Elliott, *Winfield Scott,* 237; Jackson to Maj. George W. Martin, Jan. 24, 1824, Jackson, *Correspondence,* 3:222.

24. Scott, *Memoirs,* 1:300; WS to Gen. Joseph G. Swift, Oct. 24, 1825, Elliott Collection (typescript). For Scott's attempt to come to grips with the pros and cons of Jackson's personality and career, see *Memoirs,* 265–69, 284–300.

25. William B. Skelton, "The Commanding General and the Problem of Command in the United States Army, 1821–1891," *Military Affairs* 31 (Dec. 1970): 118.

26. Gaines to Joel R. Poinsett, May 6, 1839, cited in Skelton, *American Profession of Arms,* 240; E. P. Gaines to William Marcy, June 28, 1845, copy in Durrett Miscellaneous Manuscripts, University of Chicago Library.

27. Gaines to Calhoun, Mar. 25, 1822, Letters Received by the Secretary of War, Unregistered Series, RG 107, NA (M222).

28. See James Barbour to J. Q. Adams, July 18, 1825, *NASP:MA,* 12:119; and Adams, *Memoirs,* 6:547, 7:205–6. Calhoun's letter, dated September 14, 1822, being private correspondence, was not retained in the War Department files and was apparently lost.

29. WS to Swift, Oct. 24, 1825, Elliott Collection.

30. WS to Calhoun, Dec. 14, 1821, Letters Received by the Secretary of War, NA (M221).

31. WS to AG, Jan. 21, 1825, Letters Received by the Secretary of War, Unregistered Series.

32. Robinson, *Organization of the Army,* 1:109.

33. See WS letter of Jan. 18, 1827, and Gaines letter of Mar. 8, 1828, both in Letters Received by the Secretary of War, Unregistered Series.

34. WS to Col. William Hamilton, Sept. 30, 1825, Elliott Collection (typescript); WS to AG, Jan. 10, 1827, Letters Received by the AGO, RG 94, NA (M566); Gaines to Secretary of War Calhoun, Aug. 24, 1824, Letters Received by the Secretary of War, Unregistered Series.

35. "Any commissioned officer of the army of the United States who shall send or accept a challenge to fight a duel, or who, knowing that any other officer has sent or accepted, or is about to send or accept a challenge to fight a duel, and who does not immediately arrest and bring to trial the offenders in this case, shall be dismissed from the service of the United States." *General Regulations for the Army, ASP:MA,* 2:263.

36. WS to Jacob Brown, Feb. 4, 1825, Letters Received by the Secretary of War, Unregistered Series; WS to AG, Jan. 10, 1827.

37. Scott, *Memoirs,* 1:211; Adams, *Memoirs,* 7:205.

38. "Proceedings of a Board of Officers . . . ," Feb. 25, 1825, Letters Received by the Secretary of War, Unregistered Series; Adams, *Memoirs,* 6:537; 7:23, 391–92; James Barbour to J. Q. Adams, July 18, 1825, *NASP:MA,* 12:123–25.

39. Adams, *Memoirs,* 7:251, 252–53.

40. Ibid., 449–50, 457.

41. Ibid., 506–7; James K. Polk, *The Diary of James K. Polk,* ed. Milo Milton Quaife, 4 vols. (Chicago: A. C. McClurg, 1910), 1:342–44. Scott attributed Rush's support of Macomb to a petticoat intrigue plotted by Mrs. Rush, but however comforting that interpretation might have been to Scott's self-esteem, it flies in the face of all the evidence. Scott, *Memoirs,* 1:209–11.

42. Adams, *Memoirs,* 7:507.

43. WS to Secretary of War Peter B. Porter, Sept. 23, 1828, Letters Received by the Secretary of War, Unregistered Series; WS to Acting Secretary of War Samuel Southard, May 30, 1828, Elliott Collection (typescript).

44. Adams, *Memoirs*, 8:42–43, 75. For an example of Scott's rationalizations, see WS to Secretary of War Peter Porter, Aug. 29, 1828, Winfield Scott Papers, HSP.

45. Adams, *Memoirs*, 8:33; *ASP:MA*, 4:53–59; *Niles' Register* 35 (Dec. 6, 1828): 226.

46. Despite their differences, Scott and Adams would remain on good terms. Scott would later praise the former president as "a statesman of great learning and abilities, of high patriotism and conscientiousness—an unostentatious Christian—honest, and as obstinately brave as any Puritan in Cromwell's time." Scott, *Memoirs*, 1:208.

47. Adams, *Memoirs*, 9:81–82.

48. WS to Thomas Cadwalader, Feb. 7, 1829, Cadwalader Family Papers, HSP; memorandum, WS to Secretary of War, [Feb. 2, 1829], Letters Received by the Secretary of War, Unregistered Series.

49. WS to Thomas Cadwalader, July 7, 1828, Feb. 7, 1829, Cadwalader Family Papers.

50. John Eaton to WS, Apr. 22, 1829, Elliott Collection (typescript); Mary Mayo Crenshaw, ed., *An American Lady in Paris, 1828–1829: The Diary of Mrs. John Mayo* (Boston: Houghton Mifflin, 1927), 99; *Niles' Register* 37 (Dec. 5, 1829): 238.

51. WS to Secretary of War John Eaton, Nov. 10, 1829, in Mansfield, *Lieut.-General Winfield Scott*, 194–95.

9. TROUBLESHOOTER

1. Andrew Jackson, First Annual Message, Dec. 8, 1829, in Richardson, *Messages and Papers*, 2:449.

2. Andrew Jackson, First Inaugural Address, Mar. 4, 1829, in Richardson, *Messages and Papers*, 2:437–38.

3. Alden Partridge, quoted in *NASP:MA*, 2:78; Ulysses S. Grant, *Memoirs and Selected Letters* (New York: Library of America, 1990), 32; Report of WS to War Department "Relative to a Modification of the U.S. Military Academy," Nov. 13, 1831, Manuscript Collection, U.S. Military Academy Library, West Point (photocopy).

4. For a brief survey of the Blackhawk War, see George W. Balogh, "The Regular Army in the Blackhawk War," *Order of the Indian Wars Journal* 1 (Fall 1980): 18–27.

5. Macomb cited in Emory Upton, *The Military Policy of the United States* (1904; reprint, New York: Greenwood, 1968), 160; WS to Lewis Cass, June 20, 1832, Letters Received by the AGO, RG 94, NA (M566).

6. WS to Col. R. Jones, July 2, 1832, and WS to ?, July 5, 1832, both in Letters Received by the AGO.

7. Mansfield, *Lieut.-General Winfield Scott*, 204.

8. Ibid., 183–84; Scott, *Memoirs*, 1:204–205; Scott's order quoted in Elliott, *Winfield Scott*, 270.

9. Scott, *Memoirs*, 1:218; junior officer quoted in Mansfield, *Lieut.-General Winfield Scott*, 210.

10. *Niles' Register* 42 (Aug. 11, 1832): 423, 390–91; Augustus Walker, "Early Days on the Lakes," *Publications of the Buffalo Historical Society* 5 (1902): 311.

11. Walker, "Early Days," 311–12.

12. WS to Brig. Gen. H. Atkinson, July 18, 1832, WS Collection, Chicago Historical Society; *Niles' Register* 42 (Aug. 11, 1832): 423.

13. WS to Lewis Cass, July 19, 22, 1832, Letters Received by the AGO.

14. Address of WS to Warriors of the Sac and Fox, Sept. 7, 1832, Letters Received by the AGO.

15. WS to General Macomb, Sept. 10, 1832, Charles Winslow Elliott Collection, NYPL (typescript).

16. Macomb to WS, Aug. 16, 1832, *NASP:MA,* 4:68–69; WS to Macomb, Sept. 10, 1832.

17. Elliott, *Winfield Scott,* 273; Scott, *Memoirs,* 1:230; Andrew Jackson, Fourth Annual Message, Dec. 4, 1832, in Richardson, *Messages and Papers,* 2:603.

18. WS to [William C. Preston], Dec. 14, 1832, Preston Family Papers, LC; Secretary of War Cass to WS, Nov. 18, 1832, Confidential and Unofficial Letters Sent by the Secretary of War, 1814–47, RG 107, NA (M7). For Secretary Cass's "confidential" instructions of November 18, 1832, see *Niles' Register* 43 (Feb. 23, 1833): 437.

19. William W. Freehling, *Prelude to Civil War: The Nullification Controversy in South Carolina, 1816–1836* (New York: Harper and Row Torchbooks, 1968), 253; "Brutus," cited in David Franklin Houston, *A Critical Study of Nullification in South Carolina* (Cambridge: Harvard Univ. Press, 1896), 72.

20. Scott, *Memoirs,* 1:236–37, 248; WS to Lieutenant Colonel Fanning, Dec. 7, 1832, Letters Received by the AGO; Lewis Cass to WS, Jan. 26, 1833, Confidential and Unofficial Letters Sent by the Secretary of War; WS to Col. R. Jones, Feb. 23, 1833, Letters Received by AGO.

21. Richard N. Current, *Lincoln and the First Shot* (Philadelphia: J. B. Lippincott, 1963), 73; WS to [William C. Preston], Dec. 14, 1832.

22. Thomas Hart Benton, *Thirty Years View; or, a History of the Workings of the American Government for Thirty Years, from 1820 to 1850,* 2 vols. (New York: Appleton 1858), 1:311.

23. WS to [William C. Preston], Dec. 14, 1832.

24. Scott, *Memoirs,* 1:255.

25. WS to Thomas Cadwalader, Dec. 2, 1833, Cadwalader Family Papers, HSP; WS to Major General Macomb, July 2, 1835, Manuscript Collection, U.S. Military Academy Library.

26. Philip Hone, *The Diary of Philip Hone, 1828–1851,* ed. Allan Nevins, 2 vols. (New York, 1927; reprint [2 vols. in 1], Kraus, 1969), 2:674; Keyes, *Fifty Years Observation,* 29, 34.

27. WS to Cadwalader, Dec. 2, 1833. See Daniel Walker Howe, *The Political Culture of the American Whigs* (Chicago: Univ. of Chicago Press, 1976).

28. WS to Cadwalader, Dec. 2, 1833.

29. Scott, *Memoirs,* 1:260.

10. FAILURE

1. See John K. Mahon, *History of the Second Seminole War, 1835–1842* (Gainesville: Univ. Press of Florida, 1991), 103–6.

2. Mansfield, *Lieut.-General Winfield Scott,* 264.

3. Lewis Cass to WS, Jan. 21, 1836, *ASP:MA,* 7:215–17; Cass to WS, Feb. 25, Confidential and Unofficial Letters Sent by the Secretary of War, 1814–47, RG 107, NA (M7).

4. WS to Brig. Gen. Roger Jones, Apr. 30, 1836, and WS to Secretary of War Lewis Cass, June 14, 1836, Letters Received by the AGO, RG 94, NA (M566).

5. Scott, *Memoirs,* 1:95.

6. E. P. Gaines to Editor of *New Orleans Bee,* in *Niles' Register* 56 (June 22, 1839): 27. See Elliott, *Winfield Scott,* 300 n.

7. WS to Brig. Gen. Roger Jones, Jan. 31, Feb. 16, 20, Mar. 9, 6, 1836, and WS to Brig. Gen. Duncan Clinch, Mar. 1, 1836, all in Letters Received by the AGO.

8. E. P. Gaines to General Clinch, Feb. 22, 1836, Letters Received by the AGO; *ASP:MA,* 7:302–5.

9. E. P. Gaines to Brigadier General Clinch, Feb. 29, 1836, Letters Received by the AGO.

10. Order No. 7, Mar. 9, 1836, *ASP:MA,* 7:428.

11. *Niles' Register* 50 (Apr. 9, 1836): 97; WS to Brig. Gen. R. Jones, Feb. 26, 1836, and WS to Brigadier General Clinch, Feb. 25, 26, Mar. 1, 4, 1836, all in Letters Received by the AGO. For a strongly argued defense of Gaines's Florida campaign, see James W. Silver, *Edmund Pendleton Gaines: Frontier General* (Baton Rouge: Louisiana State Univ. Press, 1949), 176–79, 190 n. See also Gaines's lengthy defense at the subsequent court of inquiry, *ASP:MA,* 7:395–418. Gaines's own inspector general, Ethan Allen Hitchcock, however, concluded: "The Truth is, that the whole difficulty resulted from General Gaines having made an injudicious movement and placed himself and his command out of position." Hitchcock, *Fifty Years,* 95.

12. WS to Clinch, Mar. 1, 4, 1836.

13. Thomas Jesup to Secretary of War Poinsett, Apr. 9, 1837, *ASP:MA,* 7:867; Mahon, *Second Seminole War,* 156; John Bemrose, *Reminiscences of the Second Seminole War,* ed. John K. Mahon (Gainesville: Univ. Press of Florida, 1966), 88.

14. *Niles' Register* 50 (May 7, 1836): 161; WS to Brig. Gen. Roger Jones, Apr. 12, 30, 1836, Letters Received by the AGO.

15. WS to Jones, Apr. 12, 30, 1836.

16. Upton, *Military Policy,* 172; WS to Brig. Gen. Roger Jones, May 11, 1836, Letters Received by the AGO.

17. *Niles' Register* 50 (May 28, 1836): 217; General Orders No. 48, May 17, 1836, ibid. (June 4, 1836): 239.

18. Joseph M. White to A. Jackson, May 28, 1836, in *Niles' Register* 50 (July 2, 1836): 309.

19. WS to "a friend," May 27, 1836, in *Niles' Register* 50 (June 4, 1836): 257; Gov. William Schley to Lewis Cass, May 12, 1836, Letters Received by the AGO; Gov. Clement C. Clay to WS, May 18, 1836, *ASP:MA,* 7:311.

20. WS to Brig. Gen. R. Jones, June 17, 1836, WS to Brig. Gen. R. Jones, May 22, June 2, 12, 14, 17, 1836, ibid.; WS to Maj. Gen. T. S. Jesup, June 1, 1836, and WS to Gov. R. K. Call, June 17, 1836, all in Letters Received by the AGO. WS Papers, William L. Clements Library, University of Michigan, Ann Arbor; WS to C. C. Clay, May 21, 1836, WS Papers, HSP; WS to "a friend," May 22, 1836, in *Niles' Register* 50 (June 11, 1836): 257.

21. WS to Call, June 17, 1836.

22. WS to Maj. Gen. Thomas Jesup, June 17, 1836, and Maj. Gen. Thomas Jesup to WS, June 15, 16, 1836, Letters Received by the AGO.

23. WS to Maj. Gen. Thomas Jesup, June 16, 17, 1836, Letters Received by the AGO.

24. Maj. Gen. Thomas Jesup to WS, June 17, 19, 1836, Letters Received by the AGO.

25. WS to Maj. Gen. Thomas Jesup, June 19, 1836, Letters Received by the AGO.

26. WS to Maj. Gen. Thomas Jesup, June 19, 1836, Letters Received by the AGO.

27. Thomas S. Jesup to Francis P. Blair, June 20, 1836, *ASP:MA,* 7:336.

28. Maj. Gen. Thomas Jesup to WS, June 22, 1836, and WS to Maj. Gen. Thomas Jesup, June 22, 1836, Letters Received by the AGO.

29. WS to Brig. Gen. R. Jones, June 23, 24, 1836, Letters Received by the AGO.

30. Maj. Gen. Thomas Jesup to Lewis Cass, June 25, 1836, *ASP:MA,* 7:347–48 (emphasis added).

31. Jackson to Francis P. Blair, Aug. 12, 1836, Jackson, *Correspondence,* 5:419; *ASP:MA,* 7:357; *Niles' Register* 50 (Aug. 13, 1836): 400.

32. Major General Macomb to WS, June 28, 1836, *ASP:MA,* 7:355; Order No. 29, July 7, 1836, in *Niles' Register* 50 (July 23, 1836): 349; ibid., (Aug. 13, 1836): 401.

33. *New York American,* July 29, 1836, in Elliott, *Winfield Scott,* 323–24; *National Intelligencer,* July 29, 1836, ibid., 324.

34. *Niles' Register* 50 (Aug. 13, 1836): 401; WS to Gales and Seaton, Jan. 13, 1837, Charles Winslow Elliott Collection, NYPL (typescript); WS to Brig. Gen. R. Jones, May 20, 1836, Letters Received by the AGO.

35. *Niles' Register* 51 (Dec. 10, 1836): 227; *ASP:MA,* 7:160, 179–80.

36. Scott, *Memoirs,* 1:271–73; Jackson to Blair, Aug. 12, 1836, 5:419; *ASP:MA,* 7:328–29, 811–12, 838–39.

37. Jackson, "Memo of the Florida Campaign," Apr. (?), 1837, Jackson, *Correspondence,* 5:471.

38. *Niles' Register* 56 (Apr. 27, 1839): 132.

11. PACIFICATOR

1. Scott, *Memoirs,* 1:305; WS to Col. William. J. Worth, Dec. 18, 1837, Charles Winslow Elliott Collection, NYPL (typescript).

2. WS to Joel Poinsett, Jan. 12, 1839, Poinsett Papers, HSP.

3. WS to Alexander Macomb, Nov. 14, 1837, Letters Received by the AGO, RG 94, NA (M566); WS to Poinsett, Jan. 12, 1839.

4. General Macomb to WS, Oct. 18, 1837, *NASP:MA,* 1:68–69; WS to Joel R. Poinsett, Nov. 5, Apr. 25, 1837, Poinsett Papers.

5. Scott, *Memoirs,* 1:301–4.

6. Ibid., 306–7.

7. Edmund C. Guillet, *The Life and Times of the Patriots: An Account of the Rebellion in Upper Canada, 1837–1838.* . . . (1938; reprint, Toronto: University of Toronto Press, 1968), 75; Howard Jones, "The *Caroline* Affair," *The Historian* 38 (May 1976): 490–91, 492 n; Kenneth R. Stevens, *Border Diplomacy: The* Caroline *and McCleod Affairs in Anglo-American-Canadian Relations, 1837–1842* (Tuscaloosa: Univ. of Alabama Press, 1989), 15.

On the life of Drew, see John Ireland, "Andrew Drew: The Man Who Burned the *Caroline," Ontario Historical Society* 59 (Sept. 1967).

8. Quoted in Henry Kurtz, "The Undeclared War between Britain and America," *History Today* 12 (1962): 779.

9. *New York Herald,* Jan. 11. 1838, in Howard Jones, *To the Webster-Ashburton Treaty: A Study in Anglo-American Relations, 1783–1843* (Chapel Hill: Univ. of North Carolina Press, 1977), 30; Secretary of War Joel R. Poinsett to WS, Jan. 5, 1838, *NASP:MA,* 1:153–54.

10. Scott, *Memoirs,* 1:308; Mansfield, *Lieut.-General Winfield Scott,* 293.

11. WS to Secretary of War Joel R. Poinsett, Jan. 16, 1838, and Lieutenant Colonel Hughes to WS, Jan. 14, 1838, 10:00 P.M., both in Letters Received by the AGO; R. Van Rensselaer, "Military Notes," in Catherine V. R. Bonney, *A Legacy of Historical Gleanings,* 2 vols. (Albany, 1875), 2:90.

12. Scott, *Memoirs,* 1:316.

13. WS to Joel R. Poinsett, Feb. 3, 1838, Poinsett Papers.

14. R. Van Rensselaer to William L. Mckenzie, Jan. 21, 1838, in Bonney, *Historical Gleanings,* 2:91.

15. WS to Brig. Gen. Hugh Brady, Jan. 30, 1838, Letters Received by the AGO; Joel R. Poinsett to WS, Feb. 5, 1838, Poinsett Papers; Keyes, *Fifty Years Observation,* 124.

16. Keyes, *Fifty Years Observation,* 50, 124.

17. Ibid.

18. Scott, *Memoirs,* 1:310; Brig. Gen. John Wool to WS, Mar. 19, 1838, and WS to Joel. R. Poinsett, Mar. 7, 1838, both in Letters Received by the AGO.

19. Lt. G. H. Talcott to Brig. Gen. R. Jones, Mar. 13, 1838, Letters Received by the AGO; *Niles' Register* 54 (Mar. 24, 1838): 49; WS to Joel R. Poinsett, Feb. 18, 1838, Letters Received by the AGO.

20. Maj. Gen. Alexander Macomb to WS, Apr. 6, 1838, Letters Sent by the Headquarters of the Army, RG 108, NA (M857).

21. Unnumbered Order, May 17, 1838, in Mansfield, *Lieut.-General Winfield Scott,* 304.

22. Scott, *Memoirs,* 1:323–25; *Niles' Register* 54 (Mar. 24, 1838): 385.

23. WS to Col. William J. Worth, June 2, 1835, WS Papers, William L. Clements Library, University of Michigan, Ann Arbor; *Niles' Register* 54 (Mar. 24, 1838): 385; Georgia officer quoted in Grant Foreman, *Indian Removal: The Emigration of the Five Civilized Tribes of the Indians* (Norman: Univ. of Oklahoma Press, 1953), 287.

24. Scott, *Memoirs,* 1:326; WS to Gen. Nathaniel Smith, June 8, 1838, Elliott Collection (typescript).

25. *Niles' Register* 54 (Aug. 28, 1838): 407; Mansfield, *Lieut.-General Winfield Scott,* 308–13; WS to Governor Gilmer of Georgia, Oct. 15, 1838, Elliott Collection (typescript).

26. Jackson to Felix Grundy, Aug. 23, 1838, in John P. Brown, *Old Frontiers: The Story of the Cherokee Indians from Earliest Times to the Date of Their Removal to the West* (Kingsport, Tenn.: Southern Publishing, 1938), 511–12.

27. WS to Joel R. Poinsett, Oct. 23, 1838, Poinsett Papers; Scott, *Memoirs,* 1:331–32.

28. WS to Brig. Gen. R. Jones, Feb. 18, 1839, Letters Received by the AGO; WS to Joel R. Poinsett, Jan. 12, 1839, Poinsett Papers.

29. Jones, *To the Webster-Ashburton Treaty,* 40.

30. Elliott, *Winfield Scott,* 360, 358.

31. Col. William J. Worth to WS, Feb. 9 1839, Letters Received by the AGO.

32. Scott, *Memoirs,* 2:333; Mansfield, *Lieut.-General Winfield Scott,* 326–27.

33. Scott, *Memoirs,* 2:334. See memorandum, Forsyth to Fox, Feb. 27, 1839, in Mansfield, *Lieut.-General Winfield Scott,* 329.

34. Joel R. Poinsett to WS (draft), [Feb. 1839], Poinsett Papers.

35. Portland *Argus,* cited in *Niles' Register* 56 (Mar. 16, 1839): 34; Scott, *Memoirs,* 2:336.

36. Marginal note, WS to Secretary Poinsett, Mar. 17, 1839, on draft of WS to Sir John Harvey, n.d., Poinsett Papers; Scott, *Memoirs,* 2:345.

37. WS to Sir John Harvey, Mar. 9, 1839, Letters Received by the Secretary of War, NA (M221).

38. WS to Harvey, Mar. 9, 1839.

12. POLITICIAN

1. *New York American,* Mar. 30, 1839, in Elliott, *Winfield Scott,* 368; Jones, *To the Webster-Ashburton Treaty,* 47; Hone, *Diary,* 391.

2. WS to Henry Clay, Feb. 5, 1839, Charles Winslow Elliott Collection, NYPL (typescript); Gouverneur Kemble to Joel Poinsett, June 7, 1839, in Marcus Cunliffe, *Soldiers and Civilians. The Martial Spirit in America, 1775–1865* (Boston: Little, Brown, 1968), 304; WS to Joel R. Poinsett, Feb. 4, 1839, Poinsett Papers, HSP.

3. Fillmore to Weed, June 5, 1839, Millard Fillmore, *Papers,* ed. Frank H. Severance, 2 vols., *Publications of the Buffalo Historical Society* 10–11 (1907), 2:192.

4. M. Bradley to Thurlow Weed, Aug. 27, 1839, in Robert Gray Gunderson, *The Log Cabin Campaign* (Lexington: Univ. of Kentucky Press, 1957), 52.

5. William Henry Harrison to Gen. Solomon Van Rensselaer, Nov. 19, 1839, in Bonney, *Historical Gleanings,* 2:114; WS to Henry Clay, Feb. 5, 1839, Elliott Collection (typescript); Peter Porter to Clay, Aug. 9, 1839, Clay, *Papers,* 9:334.

6. Fillmore to Thurlow Weed, Dec. 26, 1838, Gunderson, *Log Cabin Campaign,* 44; WS to William Seward, Nov. 9, 1839, WS Papers, HSP. For a "stalking horse" interpretation, see *New York Courier and Enquirer,* June 15, 1839, in Elliott, *Winfield Scott,* 375–76.

7. For a brief historiographic review, see William Nesbit Chambers, "Election of 1840," in *History of American Presidential Elections, 1789–1968,* edited by Arthur M. Schlesinger Jr. and Fred L. Israel, 12 vols. (New York: Chelsea House, 1985), 2:661. For interpretations supporting the New Yorkers' sincerity, see, for example, Glyndon G. Van Deusen, *Thurlow Weed, Wizard of the Lobby* (Boston: Little, Brown, 1947); and Gunderson, *Log Cabin Campaign.*

8. WS to Brig. Gen. R. Jones, May 14, 1839, and WS to Major Mackay, quartermaster, Apr. 15, 1839, both in Letters Received by the AGO, RG 94, NA (M566); WS to Joel Poinsett, May 22, 1839, Poinsett Papers.

9. *Wisconsin Enquirer,* Madison, July 27, 1839, in Elliott, *Winfield Scott,* 372.

10. *New York American,* Sept. 19, 1839, in Elliott, *Winfield Scott,* 377; *Army and Navy Chronicle,* Nov. 7, 1839, ibid., 377–78.

11. WS to Col. William J. Worth, Nov. 17, 1839, WS Papers, HSP; Peter B. Porter to Henry Clay, Aug. 9, 1839, Clay, *Papers,* 9:334; Keyes, *Fifty Years Observation,* 139.

12. For the Whig nominating convention of 1839, see Chambers, "Election of 1840," 661–64; Michael F. Holt, *The Rise and Fall of the American Whig Party: Jacksonian Politics and the Onset of the Civil War* (New York: Oxford Univ. Press, 1999), 101–5; and Gunderson, *Log Cabin Campaign,* 57–66.

13. Gunderson, *Log Cabin Campaign,* 60.

14. Keyes, *Fifty Years Observation,* 11; Scott, *Memoirs,* 2:356–58. According to journalist Alexander McLure, Virginia's failure to support Scott was due to a trick played by Thaddeus Stevens, who thought he had a promise to be appointed to the cabinet should Harrison be elected. Supposedly, Stevens had obtained a letter by Scott expressing antislavery views, which the Pennsylvanian casually dropped onto the floor of the headquarters of the Virginia delegation. Appalled by this revelation of Scott's unsoundness on their peculiar institution, the Virginians withdrew their support. McClure claimed to have heard this from Stevens himself. *Our Presidents and How We Make Them* (New York: Harper and Brothers, 1902), 68.

This charming tale has beguiled almost all subsequent commentators, but it seems improbable for a number of reasons. For one thing, Leigh was a longtime confidant of Scott, well acquainted with all his views without Stevens's prodding. Scott continued on close terms with Leigh and other Virginia delegates, but none of them apparently saw fit to mention Stevens's alleged intrigue to him, even though the story would seem to have been too good to suppress. Moreover, though McClure claimed that Stevens "disliked Scott on general principles," Stevens would be the leading advocate of Scott's presidential candidacy in the next election, and the two would collaborate as if nothing untoward had ever happened between them. It strains credulity to imagine that, in the gossip-loving world of politics, not one of the many people who would have known of the alleged incident would have tattled to Scott.

15. Henry A. Wise, *Seven Decades of the Union* (Philadelphia: Lippincott, 1872), 171–72.

16. Schuyler Hamilton, "Anecdotes of General Winfield Scott," *Southern History Association Publications* 4 (May 1900): 192–94.

17. Of course, it is also possible that if Scott had been elected president in 1840 that there would have been no war with Mexico. Once one enters the labyrinth of historical "what ifs," there is no easy escape.

18. Gouverneur, *As I Remember,* 201–2; Bonney, *Historical Gleanings,* 2:164.

19. WS to Secretary of War John Bell, June 27, 1841, Letters Received by the AGO.

20. Hitchcock, *Fifty Years,* 133; John Bell to John Tyler, June 29, 1841, *NASP:MA,* 12:255–57.

13. COMMANDER

1. See Skelton, "Commanding General"; and Leonard D. White, *The Jacksonians: A Study in Administrative History, 1829–1861* (New York: Free Press, 1965), 191–93.

2. Report of Sen. William Henry Harrison, Mar. 19, 1828, *NASP:MA,* 11:151.

3. Ibid., 149–51. See also Secretary of War J. C. Spencer to E. Stanley, Feb. 16, 1843, in U.S. Congress, House, *On Military Districts,* 27th Cong., 3d sess., 1843, H. Doc. 147.

4. WS to Z. Pratt, Dec. 30, 1844; WS to Secretary of War Spencer, Dec. 7, 1841,

Letters Sent by Headquarters of the Army, RG 108, NA (M857); Keyes, *Fifty Years Observation,* 48.

5. Maj. Gen. Alexander Macomb to "Sirs," July 25, 1831, *NASP:MA,* 11:166–67.

6. WS to Secretary of War G. W. Crawford, July 18, 1849, Letters Sent by Headquarters of the Army; Secretary of War C. M. Conrad to Chairman of House Military Affairs Committee, Apr. 5, 1852, *NASP:MA,* 11:289–294. See Leonard D. White, *The Republican Era: A Study in Administrative History, 1869–1901* (New York: Free Press, 1965), 140–46.

7. WS to Col. R. Jones, Oct. 15, 1830, *ASP:MA,* 4:649. For Scott's views on the proper division of authority between the secretary of war and the commanding general, see memorandum, WS to Secretary of War, Apr. 3, 1857, Letters Sent by the Headquarters of the Army.

8. Mansfield, *Lieut.-General Winfield Scott,* 180–82.

9. "Remarks . . ." by WS, Nov. 3, 1842, Letters Received by the Secretary of War, RG 107, NA (M221).

10. J. C. Spencer to E. Stanley, Feb. 16, 1843, *NASP:MA,* 11:244–48.

11. WS to Secretary of War John C. Calhoun, Dec. 16, 1817, Letters Received by the AGO, RG 94, NA (M566); "Remarks of Genl. Scott on the Proceedings of a Public Meeting at Memphis, Aug. 30, 1842," Nov. 3, 1842, Letters Received by the Secretary of War, NA (M221); Silver, *Gaines,* 161–62; Maj. Gen. E. P. Gaines to Sen. J. J. Crittenden, Feb. 19, 1844, *NASP:MA,* 11:275; Memorial of William A. Whitney to Congress, ibid., 260; Scott, *Memoirs,* 2:368–69.

12. Keyes, *Fifty Years Observation,* 172; Remarks of WS, Dec. 6, 1842, endorsed on Gaines to Secretary of War Spencer, Nov. 26, 1842, Letters Received by the Secretary of War (Main); Lt. Henry Smith (ADC to WS) to AG, Jan. 16, 1842, Letters Received by the AGO; Secretary of War John C. Spencer to Pres. John Tyler, Dec. 13, 1841, *NASP:MA,* 12:268–71; WS to Pres. John Tyler, Apr. 21, 1843, ibid., 290–91.

13. Edward M. Coffman, *The Old Army: A Portrait of the American Army in Peacetime, 1784–1898* (New York: Oxford Univ. Press, 1986), 193–94; White, *Jacksonians,* 202–3. The quote is from Coffman, *Old Army,* 138.

14. Skelton, *American Profession of Arms,* 267–73; WS to Colonel Pinckney, Sept. 23, Letters Received by the AGO.

15. WS to Secretary of War William Marcy, Apr. 23, 1845, Letters Sent by the Headquarters of the Army; General Orders No. 53, Aug. 20, 1842, in Scott, *Memoirs,* 2:361–66.

16. Memorandum by WS, Nov. 4, 1842, Letters Received by the AGO; Hitchcock, *Fifty Years,* 182–84; WS to Secretary of War J. M. Porter, Nov. 24, 1843, Letters Sent by the Headquarters of the Army.

17. WS to Secretary of War Jefferson Davis, Nov. 18, 1854, and Irwin McDowell, AAG, to Col. John Magruder, Sept. 9, 1858, Letters Sent by the Headquarters of the Army; Irwin McDowell, AAG, to Col. David T. Chandler, Oct. 7, 1857, Letters Sent by the Headquarters of the Army. For examples of Scott's mercy toward enlisted men, see Lorenzo Thomas, AAG, to Maj. Francis O. Wayne, Mar. 31, 1853, to Col. A. S. Johnston, Jan. 17, 1857, and to Lt. Dabney H. Maury, Feb. 2, 1857, all in Letters Sent by the Headquarters of the Army.

18. Lt. Col. G. W. Lay, AAG, to Maj. Jonathan Barnard, Nov. 25, 1858, ibid.; Irwin McDowell, AAG, to Col. Samuel Cooper, Jan. 11, 1854, ibid.; WS to Porter, Nov. 24, 1843.

19. See, for example, WS to the Secretary of War, Nov. 22, 1841, Nov. 14, 1842, Nov. 20, 1845, all in Letters Sent by the Headquarters of the Army.

14. MIDDLE AGE

1. Keyes, *Fifty Years Observation,* 7; Grant, *Memoirs,* 1:33.

2. Charles Wilkes autobiography, 370–71, Wilkes Family Papers, LC (typescript); "A Subaltern" [Braxton Bragg], "Notes on Our Army," *Southern Literary Messenger* 10 (Mar. 1844): 157.

3. Heth, *Memoirs,* 24; E. Parker Scammon, "A Chapter of the Mexican War," *Magazine of American History* 14 (Dec. 1885): 573.

4. Keyes, *Fifty Years Observation,* 8, 65; WS to William Marcy, Jan. 10, 1847, *NASP:MA,* 6:362.

5. Heth, *Memoirs,* 75–77.

6. Keyes, *Fifty Years Observation,* 3–6; Robert Anderson to his wife, Feb. 15, 1847, Robert Anderson, *An Artillery Officer in the Mexican War, 1846–7: Letters of Robert Anderson, Captain 3rd Artillery, U.S.A.* (New York: G. P. Putnam's Sons, 1911), 45.

7. Keyes, *Fifty Years Observation,* 38; Hitchcock, *Fifty Years,* 241–42.

8. Wright, *General Scott,* 333–34.

9. Buchanan and Greeley quoted in William E. Gienapp, "The Whig Party, the Compromise of 1850, and the Nomination of Winfield Scott," *Presidential Studies Quarterly* 14 (Summer 1984): 405; Keyes, *Fifty Years Observation,* 8; Scammon, "Chapter of the Mexican War," 576.

10. Keyes, *Fifty Years Observation,* 55–58; Wright, *General Scott,* 331–32; Hamilton, "Anecdotes," 191–92; WS to General Clinch, July 10, 18[46], Robert Anderson Papers, LC.

11. Gouverneur, *As I Remember,* 170; Maria Scott to Mrs. John H. Bernard, Apr. 13, 1843, William and Mary College Library (typescript, Virginia Historical Society, Richmond).

12. Manuscript Collection, U.S. Military Academy Library.

13. Keyes, *Fifty Years Observation,* 202; Strong, *Diary,* 2:66, 100; Gouverneur, *As I Remember,* 186.

14. Strong, *Diary,* 2:104; Gouverneur, *As I Remember,* 103–6.

15. Gouverneur, *As I Remember,* 61–62; Hone, *Diary,* 694; Mrs. Philip Thornton to Mrs. John H. Bernard, July 23, 1844, and Mrs. Winfield Scott to Mrs. John H. Bernard, Apr. 13, 1845, both in William and Mary College Library (typescript, Virginia Historical Society, Richmond).

16. Mrs. Scott to Mrs. Bernard, Apr. 13, 1845; Strong, *Diary,* 2:103–4.

17. Keyes, *Fifty Years Observation,* 58.

18. WS to Sen. J. J. Crittenden, Jan. 25, 1843, Mrs. Chapman Coleman, *The Life of John J. Crittenden, with Selections from his Correspondence and Speeches,* 2 vols. (Philadelphia, 1871; reprint, New York: Da Capo, 1970), 1:203.

19. Thaddeus Stevens to WS, Oct. 20, 1841, Thaddeus Stevens Papers, LC.

20. WS to "A Group of Querists," Oct. 25, 1841, Charles Winslow Elliott Collection, NYPL (typescript).

21. WS to Thomas Henry Burrows, Oct. 19, 1841, WS Papers, William L. Clements Library, University of Michigan, Ann Arbor; WS to Thaddeus Stevens, Nov. 4, 1841, May 5, 1842 [first of two letters so dated], Elliott Collection (typescripts); WS to T. H. Barrows, Nov. 13, 1841, WS Papers, NYPL; WS to R. P. Maclay et al., July 15, 1842, Elliott Collection (typescript).

22. WS to Maclay et al., July 15, 1842; WS to Thaddeus Stevens, May 5, 1842 [second of two letters so dated], and WS to "A Group of Querists," Oct. 25, 1841, both in Elliott Collection (typescripts); WS to "My Dear Sir," Feb. 17, 1842, WS Papers, Clements Library; Mansfield, *Lieut.-General Winfield Scott*, 183–89; Scott, *Memoirs*, 1:204–5.

23. WS to T. P. Atkinson, Feb. 9, 1843, Scott, *Memoirs*, 2:373.

24. Ibid., 374. "I own, myself, no slaves," Scott said in a cautiously guarded formulation, which left open the possibility that his wife might own some in her name. Ibid., 373.

25. WS to Thaddeus Stevens, Nov. 21, 1841, Elliott Collection (typescript); Daniel F. Webster to Sen. Daniel Webster, Nov. 7, 1841, Daniel Webster, *The Papers of Daniel Webster: Correspondence*, ed. Charles M. Wiltse, 7 vols. (Hanover, Hanover, N.H.: Univ. Press of New England, 1971–74), 5:170; Andrew Jackson to William B. Lewis, Jan. 1, 1842, Jackson, *Correspondence*, 6:133; Henry Clay to Peter Porter, Feb. 7, 1842, Clay, *Papers*, 9:647.

26. Nathan Sargent to Henry Clay, Aug. 6, 1842, Clay, *Papers*, 9:751; WS to Thaddeus Stevens, May 5, 1842 [second letter of same date], Elliott Collection (typescript); WS to Gen. Duncan Clinch, Dec. 14, 1842, Anderson Papers; WS to Gen. Duncan Clinch, July 7, 1843, Elliott Collection (typescript).

27. Scott, *Memoirs*, 2:380; WS to Benjamin Silliman, Nov. 12, 1844, Elliott Collection (typescript).

15. WAR

1. James K. Polk, First Annual Message, Dec. 21, 1845, in Richardson, *Messages and Papers*, 4:413; Eugene Irving McCormac, *James K. Polk: A Political Biography* (New York: Russell and Russell, 1965), 471 n.

2. John J. Crittenden to R. P. Letcher, Mar. 9, 1846, in Coleman, *Life of John J. Crittenden*, 1:235.

3. WS to Gen. Duncan Clinch, June 28, 1845, WS Papers, William L. Clements Library, University of Michigan, Ann Arbor.

4. The label did not connote ignorance but was derived from the secretive nature of their organization. When questioned about their movement, they were instructed to reply "I know nothing."

5. Although Scott later played down his involvement with nativism, his advocacy was extensive and well documented. See, for example, WS to G. W. Reed et al., Nov. 10, 1844, and WS to Benjamin Silliman, Nov. 12, Dec. 17, 1844 (typescripts), both in Charles Winslow Elliott Collection, NYPL; WS to John Cozzens, Nov. 15, 1844, WS Papers, Clements Library; WS to Alexander Kelsey, Nov. 17, 1844, in "General Winfield Scott on *Native Americanism* in 1844 . . . ," *American Catholic Historical Research*, n.s., 7 (Jan. 1911): 10; and *Niles' Register* 67 (Nov. 18, 1848): 162.

6. *New York Herald*, Nov. 6, 1844, in Elliott, *Winfield Scott*, 412.

7. Benton, *Thirty Years View*, 2:680.

8. Richard Bruce Winders, *Mr. Polk's Army: The American Military Experience in the Mexican War* (College Station: Texas A&M Univ. Press, 1997), 9; Upton, *Military Policy*, 206; Hitchcock, *Fifty Years*, 215.

9. WS to Secretary of War William Marcy, Dec. 24, 1845, *NASP:MA*, 3:264–67; WS to Gen. Zachary Taylor, Jan. 1846, *NASP:MA*, 6:40–41.

10. Grant, *Memoirs*, 94–95.

11. WS to Secretary of War William Marcy, Mar. 25, 1844, Letters Received by the AGO, RG 94, NA (M566); Scott, *Memoirs*, 2:382. "General Taylor knows nothing of army movement," reported Ethan Allen Hitchcock of the inspector general's staff. Hitchcock, *Fifty Years*, 215.

12. Scott, *Memoirs*, 2:382–84.

13. Pres. James K. Polk, Message of May 11, 1846, in Richardson, *Messages and Papers*, 4:442.

14. Grant, *Memoirs*, 41.

15. *Niles' Register* 69 (Nov. 19, 1845): 197; Scott, *Memoirs*, 1:53.

16. Justin H. Smith, *The War with Mexico*, 2 vols. (New York: Macmillan, 1919), 1:157; WS to James Monroe, Apr. 12, 1822, Elliott Collection (typescript).

17. Polk, *Diary*, 1:401. At the beginning of hostilities, Gaines flew into a panic and, as he had earlier done in Florida, issued an unauthorized call for volunteers to assist Taylor. Since their term of enlistment was for only three months, these unwanted reinforcements did nothing for Taylor except consume his supplies. This was the last straw for Scott, who persuaded the War Department that the "deranged" general should be shunted off to some harmless post until "the recovery of his mental sanity." WS to James Watson Webb, June 9, 1846, Clements Library; WS to William L. Marcy, May 23, 1846, *NASP:MA*, 6:63–64.

18. Polk, *Diary*, 1:418. Polk apparently forgot, for the moment, that Wool was a Democrat.

19. John Fairfield to his wife, May 24, 1846, in Elliott, *Winfield Scott*, 426; Polk, *Diary*, 1:396.

20. WS to James Watson Webb, June 11, 1846, WS Papers, Clements Library.

21. "Memo for Chiefs of the General Staff . . . ," May 18, 1846, and memorandum, WS to the Secretary of War, June 19, 1845, both in Letters Sent by the Headquarters of the Army, RG 108, NA (M857); WS to R. P. Letcher, June 5, 1846, Coleman, *Life of John J. Crittenden*, 1:244–45.

22. Polk, *Diary*, 1:408, 385.

23. During the Mexican War, Polk appointed thirteen generals of volunteers: Majors General William Butler, Robert Patterson, Gideon Pillow, and John Quitman; and Brigadiers General Thomas Marshall, Thomas Hamer, Joseph Lane, James Shields, Franklin Pierce, George Cadwalader, Enos Hopping, Caleb Cushing, and Sterling Price. Winders, *Mr. Polk's Army*, 75–76.

24. WS to R. P. Letcher, June 5, 1846, in Coleman, *Life of John J. Crittenden*, 1:245.

25. WS to Secretary of War Marcy, Mar. 25, 1854, Letters Sent by the Headquarters of the Army; WS to R .P. Letcher, June 5, 1846, 1:246.

26. WS to R .P. Letcher, June 5, 1846, 1:246.

27. Ibid.

28. WS to Secretary William Marcy, May 21, 1846, Letters Received by the AGO.

29. WS to Secretary William Marcy, May 21, 1846.

30. WS to William S. Archer, Feb. 6, 1846, in Polk, *Diary,* 1:414 n, 414–15.

31. Ibid., 419–21.

32. William L. Marcy to WS, May 25, 1846, *NASP:MA,* 6:65–70.

33. WS to William Marcy, May 25, 1846, *NASP:MA,* 6:65–70.

34. Polk, *Diary,* 1:428.

35. Anthony Butler to J. J. Crittenden, June 15, 1846, Coleman, *Life of John J. Crittenden,* 1:247.

36. Scott, *Memoirs,* 2:391; WS to William L. Marcy, Sept. 12, 1846, Letters Received by the AGO; William L. Marcy to WS, Sept. 14, 1846, WS to J. J. Crittenden, Sept. 17, 1846, Coleman, *Life of John J. Crittenden,* 1:249–50.

37. WS, "Vera Cruz and its Castle," Oct. 27, 1846 [filed in 1847], Letters Received by the Secretary of War, NA (M221).

38. Polk, *Diary,* 2:205, 249–50.

39. Ibid., 242, 328, 250.

40. Ibid., 245.

41. Scott, *Memoirs,* 1:95.

42. Ibid., 399, 349; WS to William L. Marcy, Dec. 26, 1846, Elliott Collection (typescript); WS to William Marcy, Jan. 16, 1847, William Marcy Papers, LC.

43. Polk, *Diary,* 2:394, 272, 242–43.

44. Scott, *Memoirs,* 2:401, 402.

45. Scammon, "Chapter of the Mexican War," 564–65.

46. WS to William Marcy, Jan. 27, 1847, *NASP:MA,* 6:386.

47. WS to William Marcy, Feb. 24, 1848, Letters Received by the Secretary of War, NA (M221).

48. WS to Zachary Taylor, Jan. 3, 1847. Letters Received by the AGO.

16. INVASION

1. Scott, *Memoirs,* 2:403, 404.

2. Gen. E. P. Gaines to Joel R. Poinsett, May 6, 1839, cited in Skelton, *American Profession of Arms,* 240; WS to Secretary of War William Marcy, Jan. 16, 1847 [1848], *NASP:MA,* 6:358.

3. WS to Gen. Duncan Clinch, July 10 [1846], Robert Anderson Papers, LC; WS to Senators Benton, Crittenden, and Morehead, June 4, 1846, *NASP:MA,* 6:98; WS to J. J. Crittenden, June 4, Sept 30, 1846; to R. P. Letcher, June 5, 1846; and to Zachary Taylor, Sept. 26, 1846, all in Coleman, *Life of John J. Crittenden,* 1:243–44, 256, 256–58.

4. Hitchcock, *Fifty Years,* 366; Zachary Taylor to J. J. Crittenden, Jan. 26, 1847, in Coleman, *Life of John J. Crittenden,* 1:270–76; Col. J. T. Taylor to Thurlow Weed, Apr. 24, 1847, in Weed, *Life,* 1:574.

5. WS to William Marcy, Jan. 23, 1847, *NASP:MA,* 6:380; WS to Zachary Taylor, Nov. 25, 1846, *NASP:MA,* 6:312.

6. WS to Zachary Taylor, Jan. 26, 1847, Letters Received by the AGO, RG 94, NA (M566); WS to William Marcy, Jan. 16, 1847, Charles Winslow Elliott Collection, NYPL (typescript). Regarding captured dispatches, see WS to General Taylor (confidential), Dec. 20, 1846, WS to William Marcy, Jan. 24, 1847, and Charges and Specifications

against Captain William R. Montgomery . . . , [1847], all in Letters Received by the AGO; and Scott, *Memoirs,* 2:401–2.

7. WS to Gen. Duncan Clinch, July 10, 18[46], Anderson Papers; WS to William Marcy, "Private," Jan. 23, 1847, *NASP:MA,* 6:380; Zachary Taylor to J. J. Crittenden, Jan. 26, 1847, in Coleman, *Life of John J. Crittenden,* 1:273.

8. WS, *Memoirs,* 2:401; WS to William L. Marcy, Feb. 24, 1848, Letters Received by the AGO.

9. WS to William L. Marcy, Jan. 12, 1847, Letters Received by the AGO.

10. See WS to Lt. C. Tompkins, June 20, 1846, Letters Sent by the Headquarters of the Army, RG 108, NA (M857); WS to Commodore David Conner, Dec. 23, 1845, Letters Received by the AGO.

Conner was the son-in-law of the Dr. Physick who had tended Scott's wounds after Lundy's Lane. His successor as commander of the naval squadron would be Matthew C. Perry, brother of Scott's War of 1812 colleague, Oliver H. Perry. The world of mid–nineteenth-century America was a small one, with most members of the elite acquainted with each other and often related.

11. For detailed specifications of the surfboats, see Philip Syng Physick Conner, *The Home Squadron under Commodore Conner in the War with Mexico* (Philadelphia, 1896), 60–63.

12. E. Kirby Smith to wife, Feb. 23, 1847, in E. Kirby Smith, *To Mexico with Scott: Letters of Captain E. Kirby Smith to His Wife* (Cambridge: Harvard Univ. Press, 1917), 108; Allan Peskin, ed., *Volunteers: The Mexican War Journals of Private Richard Coulter and Sergeant Thomas Barclay, Company E, Second Pennsylvania Infantry* (Kent, Ohio: Kent State Univ. Press, 1991), 31–32.

13. Smith, *War with Mexico,* 2:186.

14. James B. Frost, *The Mexican War and Its Warriors* (New Haven and Philadelphia: H. Mansfield 1848), 263; Peskin, *Volunteers,* 141.

15. Nathaniel Cheairs Hughes and Roy P. Stonesifer, *The Life and Wars of Gideon J. Pillow* (Chapel Hill: Univ. of North Carolina Press, 1993), 47–48. In a less publicized gaffe, Pillow would position soldiers on both sides of a road to ambush Mexicans. If any of the enemy had stumbled into his trap, they would likely have suffered less than the Americans, who would have had to fire in each other's direction. Peskin, *Volunteers,* 47–48.

16. Smith, *War with Mexico,* 2:377 n. 8; Scott, *Memoirs,* 2:416.

17. Anderson, *Artillery Officer,* 32; George T. M. Davis, *Autobiography of the Late Col. Geo. T. M. Davis. . . .* (New York: [Jenkins and McCowan], 1891), 123.

18. *General Scott and His Staff. . . .* (Philadelphia: Grigg, Elliot, and Co., 1848), 24.

19. K. Jack Bauer, *Surfboats and Horse Marines: U.S. Naval Operations in the Mexican War, 1846–48* (Annapolis: U.S. Naval Institute, 1964), 83–84; Richard Berg and Joe Bulkoski, "Veracruz—U.S. Invasion of Mexico, 1847," *Strategy and Tactics* 63 (1977): 9; [Daniel H. Hill], "The Siege of Vera Cruz," *Southern Quarterly Review* 20 (1851): 26–27.

20. Scammon, "Chapter of the Mexican War," 567; Hitchcock, *Fifty Years,* 237.

21. Conner, *Home Squadron,* 64–65.

22. Pierre Gustave Toutant Beauregard, *With Beauregard in Mexico: The Mexican War Reminiscences of P. G. T. Beauregard,* ed. T. Harry Williams (New York: Da Capo, 1969), 25; *Scott and His Staff,* 24; Peskin, *Volunteers,* 39–40.

23. *Scott and His Staff,* 25.

24. Anderson, *Artillery Officer,* 66; Bauer, *Surfboats,* 81–82.

25. Scott, *Memoirs,* 2:421.

26. Scott says it was thirty years—not the only place in his memoirs where his memory betrays him. Ibid., 2:418.

17. SIEGE

1. See Peskin, *Volunteers,* 46–54.

2. Beauregard, *With Beauregard in Mexico,* 26; Scott, *Memoirs,* 2:424.

3. Scott, *Memoirs,* 2:423.

4. Lt. Isaac Ingalls Stevens to wife, Aug. 22, 1847, in Grady McWhiney and Sue McWhiney, *To Mexico with Scott and Taylor, 1845–1847* (Waltham, Mass.: Blaisdell, 1968), 196; Scott, *Memoirs,* 2:423.

5. Scott, *Memoirs,* 2:423–25.

6. Ibid., 426.

7. Albert C. Ramsey, trans. and ed., *The Other Side: Or Notes for the History of the War between Mexico and the United States. . . .* (1850; reprint, New York: Burt Franklin, 1970), 180; Smith, *War with Mexico,* 2:1–16.

8. Hitchcock, *Fifty Years,* 243; Beauregard, *With Beauregard in Mexico,* 27.

9. WS to William L. Marcy, Mar. 12, 18, 1847, and WS to the Governor of Vera Cruz, Mar. 22, 1847 (copy), both in Letters Received by the Secretary of War, RG 107, NA (M221).

10. Scammon, "Chapter of the Mexican War," 568; Gen. Juan Morales to WS, Mar. 22, 1847 (translation), Letters Received by the Secretary of War.

11. Scammon, "Chapter of the Mexican War," 568.

12. *Scott and His Staff,* 27.

13. William Elliott Griffis, *Matthew Calbraith Perry: A Typical American Naval Officer* (Boston: Cupples and Hurd, 1887), 226–27; Peskin, *Volunteers,* 57.

14. Griffis, *Perry,* 231, 238–37; Scott, *Memoirs,* 2:424.

15. WS to Messrs. Gifford, Gloux, et al., Mar. 25, 1847 (copy), Letters Received by the Secretary of War, NA; Scammon, "Chapter of the Mexican War," 568–69; Scott, *Memoirs,* 2:436–37. See Matthew C. Perry to WS; to Secretary of the Navy; and WS to Perry, all Mar. 25, 1847, Letters Received by the Secretary of War.

16. Peskin, *Volunteers,* 59.

17. Scammon, "Chapter of the Mexican War," 569–70; Propositions from the Mexican Commissioners, [Mar. 26, 1847], Letters Received by the Secretary of War, NA.

18. Reply to Proposals of Mexican Commissioners, Mar. 27, 1847, and Articles of Capitulation, Mar. 27, 1847, Letters Received by the Secretary of War; Anderson, *Artillery Officer,* 98; Scott, *Memoirs,* 2:427–28.

19. Raphael Semmes, *The Campaign of General Scott, in the Valley of Mexico* (Cincinnati: Moore and Anderson, 1852), 29–30; Smith, *War with Mexico,* 2:33; Scott, *Memoirs,* 2:425 n.

20. Peskin, *Volunteers,* 61–62.

21. Ibid., 64–65.

22. Major General Worth, Orders No. 3, Mar. 30, 1847, Letters Received by the

AGO, RG 94, NA (M566); Henry O. Whiteside, "Winfield Scott and the Mexican Occupation: Policy and Practice," *Mid-America* 52 (1970): 107.

23. Whiteside, "Scott and the Mexican Occupation," 104–6; General Orders No. 101, Apr. 9, 1847, Letters Received by the AGO.

24. James K. Polk, Third Annual Message, Dec. 7, 1847, in Richardson, *Messages and Papers,* 4:547.

25. Scammon, "Chapter of the Mexican War," 572; J. Jacob Oswandel, *Notes of the Mexican War, 1846–48* (Philadelphia: [s.n.], 1885), 104.

26. Davis, *Autobiography,* 141.

18. ADVANCE

1. Hitchcock, *Fifty Years,* 130; Scammon, "Chapter of the Mexican War," 573–74.

2. WS to General Twiggs, Apr. 6, 1847, and WS to Secretary of War William Marcy, Apr. 5, 1847, both in Letters Received by the AGO, RG 94, NA (M566); Beauregard, *With Beauregard in Mexico,* 33; Grant, *Memoirs,* 113–14.

3. Peskin, *Volunteers,* 69.

4. Smith, *War with Mexico,* 2:41–42, 47; WS to William L. Marcy, Apr. 5, 15, 1847, Letters Received by the Secretary of War, NA (M221).

5. Beauregard, *With Beauregard in Mexico,* 34–37; Davis, *Autobiography,* 146.

6. Ramsey, *Other Side,* 200; WS to William Marcy, Apr. 23, 1847, Letters Received by the Secretary of War, NA.

7. Grant, *Memoirs,* 91.

8. Smith, *War with Mexico,* 2:52.

9. General Orders No. 111, Apr. 17, 1847, in Scott, *Memoirs,* 2:433–36.

10. Hitchcock, *Fifty Years,* 250–51.

11. See, for example, Grant, *Memoirs,* 91; and Mansfield, *Lieut.-General Winfield Scott,* 383.

12. [Daniel H. Hill], "Battle of Cerro Gordo," *Southern Quarterly Review* 21 (1852): 142–43; Smith, *War with Mexico,* 2:53–55; George B. McClellan, *The Mexican War Diary of George B. McClellan,* ed. William Starr Myers (Princeton, N.J.: Princeton Univ. Press, 1917), 87.

13. Davis, *Autobiography,* 152.

14. General Orders No. 111, Apr. 17, 1847, in Scott, *Memoirs,* 2:434.

15. Hughes and Stonesifer, *Gideon J. Pillow,* 70–72; Peskin, *Volunteers,* 81.

16. Peskin, *Volunteers,* 78–79.

17. McClellan, *Mexican War Diary,* 86. In his official report, however, Scott diplomatically glossed over Pillow's failings and even found some kind words for President Polk's favorite general. WS to William Marcy, Apr. 19, 1847, Letters Received by the Secretary of War. In this, he was ignoring his own regulations of a quarter century earlier that advised, "reports of military affairs are highly defective which do not notice faults committed as well as strokes of extraordinary courage or genius exhibited." *General Regulations for the Army, ASP:MA,* 2:232.

18. WS to William L. Marcy, Apr. 19, 23, 1847, Letters Received by the Secretary of War, NA.

19. WS to William L. Marcy, Apr. 19, 1847; Smith, *War with Mexico,* 2:58.

20. John P. Bloom, "With the American Army in Mexico, 1848–1849" (Ph.D. diss., Emory University, 1956), 98; Peskin, *Volunteers,* 98–99.

21. Hitchcock, *Fifty Years,* 255; Ramsey, *Other Side,* 223–25.

22. Hitchcock, *Fifty Years,* 258–59; Grant, *Memoirs,* 93.

23. Scott, *Memoirs,* 2:452.

19. HALT

1. WS to Zachary Taylor, Apr. 24, 1847, and WS to Col. Henry Wilson, Apr. 23, 1847, both in Letters Received by the AGO, RG 94, NA (M566).

2. General Orders No. 135, May 4, 1847, and WS to William Marcy, June 4, 1847, both in Letters Received by the AGO; WS to William Marcy, Jan. 16, 1847, *NASP:MA,* 6:364.

3. WS to Marcy, Jan. 16, 1847, 362–64.

4. Robert W. Johannsen, *To the Halls of the Montezumas: The Mexican War in the American Imagination* (New York: Oxford Univ. Press, 1985), 41; Smith, *To Mexico with Scott,* 151–52.

5. Peskin, *Volunteers,* 48, 120; Smith, *War with Mexico,* 2:318–19. Smith draws different conclusions from these figures.

6. WS to William Marcy, Jan. 16, 1847, 358–59; Smith, *War with Mexico,* 2:318–19; Robert Ryal Miller, *Shamrock and Sword: The Saint Patrick's Battalion in the U.S.-Mexican War* (Norman: Univ. of Oklahoma Press, 1989), 175.

7. Ramsey, *Other Side,* 417.

8. Peskin, *Volunteers,* 323–27.

9. WS to William Marcy, Jan. 16, 1847, in Elliott, *Winfield Scott,* 476.

10. Polk, *Diary,* 2:468.

11. William Marcy to WS, Apr. 14, 1847, *NASP:MA,* 7:6–9.

12. WS to Marcy, May 20, 1847, WS to William Marcy, June 4, 1847, and WS to N. P. Trist, May 7, 1847, all in Letters Received by the AGO.

13. N. P. Trist to WS, May 9, 1847, in Elliott, *Winfield Scott,* 479, 480–81.

14. WS to N. P. Trist, May 29, 1847, Letters Received by the AGO.

15. WS to William Marcy, July 25, 1847, Letters Received by the AGO; Scott, *Memoirs,* 2:579–80.

16. Polk, *Diary,* 3:76, 89–90, 75–79.

17. William Marcy to WS, May 31, 1847, *NASP:MA,* 7:39–40; WS to Marcy, July 25, 1847, Letters Received by the AGO.

18. WS to Nicolas P. Trist, July 17, 1847, Charles Winslow Elliott Collection, NYPL (typescript).

19. Memorandum on the bribe question, [1848], Ethan Allen Hitchcock Papers, LC; Hitchcock, *Fifty Years,* 266–68; Davis, *Autobiography,* 178–80. Hitchcock was at the meeting; Davis was not but apparently received his information from Shields. His account differs somewhat from Hitchcock's, but both agree on Pillow's enthusiastic advocacy of the scheme.

20. Polk, *Diary,* 3:245–46.

21. Memorandum on the bribe question, [1848].

22. Scott, *Memoirs,* 2:453, 459–60.

23. WS to William Marcy, Feb. 24, 1848, Letters Received by the Secretary of War, NA.

24. Polk, *Diary,* 3:84; Scott, *Memoirs,* 2:466 n.

25. Scott, *Memoirs,* 2:465.

26. Ibid., 454.

27. Peskin, *Volunteers,* 136; Scott, *Memoirs,* 2:467.

20. SUCCESSES

1. Scott. *Memoirs,* 2:466; Grant to ?, [Aug. 22, 1847], *The Papers of Ulysses S. Grant:* Vol. 1, *1837–1861,* ed. John Y. Simon (Carbondale: Southern Illinois Univ. Press, 1967), 1:144.

2. WS to William Marcy, Aug. 19, 1847, Letters Received by the Secretary of War, RG107, NA (M221).

3. Grant, *Memoirs,* 112–13.

4. Hitchcock, *Fifty Years,* 276.

5. Ibid., 275–76.

6. It is now the site of the University of Mexico.

7. WS, Report No. 31, Aug. 19, 1847, in *Memoirs,* 2:470–71.

8. George H. Gordon, "The Battles of Contreras and Churubusco," *Papers of the Military Historical Society of Massachusetts* 13 (1913): 575.

9. Beauregard, *With Beauregard in Mexico,* 48.

10. Ibid., 49–51.

11. WS to William Marcy, Aug. 19, 1847, Letters Received by the Secretary of War.

12. Beauregard, *With Beauregard in Mexico,* 51–53.

13. Gordon, "Contreras and Churubusco," 581; U.S. House, Senate, *Message from the President of the United States Communicating . . . the Proceedings of the Two Courts of Inquiry in the Case of Major General Pillow,* 30th Cong., 1st sess., 1848. S. Exec. Doc. 65, 65; WS to William Marcy, Aug. 19, 1847, Letters Received by the Secretary of War.

14. Gordon, "Contreras and Churubusco," 582–83; Smith, *War with Mexico,* 2:106–7.

15. Beauregard, *With Beauregard in Mexico,* 54–55.

16. Smith, *War with Mexico,* 2:108–10; [Daniel H. Hill], "The Battle of Contreras," *Southern Quarterly Review* 21 (1852): 419–21.

17. Beauregard, *With Beauregard in Mexico,* 55–56.

18. WS to William Marcy, Report No. 32, Aug. 28, 1847, Letters Received by the Secretary of War; Secretary of War Armstrong to General Dearborn, June 19, 1813, in Elliott, *Winfield Scott,* 101; Smith, *War with Mexico,* 2:114.

19. For fuller accounts of the Battle of Churubusco, see Smith, *War with Mexico,* 2:110–18, 382–85; and Gordon, "Contreras and Churubusco."

20. Peskin, *Volunteers,* 262.

21. Miller, *Shamrock and Sword,* 175, 87.

22. WS to Marcy, Report No. 32, Aug. 28, 1847; Report of Maj. Gen. William J. Worth, Aug. 23, 1847, Letters Received by the AGO, RG 94, NA (M566).

23. Grant, *Memoirs,* 99; WS to Zachary Taylor, Apr. 24, 1847, and WS to William Marcy, June 4, 1847, both in Letters Received by the AGO; Davis, *Autobiography,* 189; Scott, *Memoirs,* 2:488–89.

24. WS to Santa Anna, Aug. 21, 1847, Charles Winslow Elliott Collection, NYPL (typescript).

25. Gen. L. J. Alcorta to WS, Aug. 27, 1847, in Elliott, *Winfield Scott,* 523–24.

26. Hitchcock, *Fifty Years,* 299; Davis, *Autobiography,* 208–9.

27. General Orders No. 262, Aug. 24, 1847, Letters Received by the AGO.

28. Davis, *Autobiography,* 211.

29. For a contrary view, see [Daniel H. Hill], "Battle of Molino del Rey," *Southern Quarterly Review* 22 (1852).

30. WS to William Marcy, Report No. 33, Sept. 11, 1847, Letters Received by the Secretary of War.

21. TRIUMPH

1. [Hill], "Molino del Rey," 301–2.

2. Grant, *Memoirs,* 102; [Hill], "Molino del Rey," 301 n.

3. George H. Gordon, "The Battles of Molino del Rey and Chapultepec," *Papers of the Military Historical Society of Massachusetts* 13 (1913): 608–9.

4. Report of WS, Sept. 18, 1847, Letters Received by the AGO, RG 94, NA (M566); [Hill], "Molino del Rey," 311.

5. Peskin, *Volunteers,* 156; Hamilton, "Anecdotes," 81; Hitchcock, *Fifty Years,* 298.

6. Semmes, *General Scott's Campaign,* 322; Hitchcock, *Fifty Years,* 297–98; Beauregard, *With Beauregard in Mexico,* 64; Davis, *Autobiography,* 221–22.

7. Hitchcock, *Fifty Years,* 299–300; WS to William Marcy, Report No. 34, Sept. 18, 1847, Letters Received by the AGO.

8. U.S. Senate, Exec. Doc. 65, 30 Cong., 1 sess. *[Case of Major General Pillow],* 121.

9. Beauregard, *With Beauregard in Mexico,* 68–72.

10. Ibid., 72.

11. Hitchcock, *Fifty Years,* 302.

12. WS to Marcy, Report No. 34, Sept. 18, 1847.

13. For more complete descriptions of Chapultepec, see Gordon, "Molino del Rey and Chapultepec," 617–20; [Daniel H. Hill], "Chapultepec and the Garitas of Mexico," *Southern Quarterly Review* 23 (1853): 21–24; and Smith, *War with Mexico,* 2:149–51, 405–11.

14. Beauregard, *With Beauregard in Mexico,* 80.

15. Peskin, *Volunteers,* 176–77; Pillow to wife, Oct. 18, 1847, in Hughes and Stonesifer, *Gideon J. Pillow,* 104.

16. Beauregard, *With Beauregard in Mexico,* 82–83.

17. Miller, *Shamrock and Sword,* 92–112.

18. Hamilton, "Anecdotes," 82.

19. Peskin, *Volunteers,* 172.

20. WS to Marcy, Report No. 34, Sept. 18, 1847; Elliott, *Winfield Scott,* 549; Peskin, *Volunteers,* 176. Beauregard, who was with Quitman, claimed that Scott's orders to fall back never reached the front. Beauregard, *With Beauregard in Mexico,* 99–100.

21. WS to Marcy, Report No. 34, Sept. 18, 1847.

22. Peskin, *Volunteers,* 180.

23. *New York Times,* June 22, 1852, cited in Arthur D. Howden Smith, *Old Fuss and Feathers: The Life and Exploits of Lt. General Winfield Scott* (New York: Greystone, 1937), 250 n; William Wallace Burns, "Gen'l Winfield Scott," Manuscript Collection, U.S. Military Academy Library, West Point.

24. Peskin, *Volunteers,* 170; Polk, *Diary,* 2:492–93.

25. Grant, *Memoirs,* 113; *New York Times,* June 22, 1852, cited in Smith, *Old Fuss and Feathers,* 250 n; Beauregard, *With Beauregard in Mexico,* 104–5.

26. Beauregard, *With Beauregard in Mexico,* 100–102.

27. Weed, *Life,* 1:656–67; Scott, *Memoirs,* 2:535.

28. WS to William Marcy, Sept. 18, 1847, Letters Received by the AGO.

22. PERSECUTIONS

1. Hitchcock, *Fifty Years,* 305; WS to William Marcy, Report No. 34, Sept. 18, 1847, RG 94, NA (M566).

2. WS to Col. Henry Wilson, Oct. 13, 1847, and General Orders Nos. 287, 289, 297, Sept. 17, 18, 24, 1897, all in Letters Received by the AGO.

3. Justin H. Smith, "American Rule in Mexico," *American Historical Review* 23 (1918): 297, 289 (Mexican quoted); Scott, *Memoirs,* 2:580.

4. General Orders No. 287, Sept. 17, 1847, Letters Received by the AGO.

5. WS to William Marcy, Feb. 6, 1848, ibid.; WS to Secretary of War Jefferson Davis, Jan. 30, 1856, *NASP:MA,* 12:470–71.

6. William Marcy to General Butler, Jan. 13, 1848, *NASP:MA,* 7:197; Marcy to WS, Oct. 6, 1847, *NASP:MA,* 7:114–15.

7. WS to William Marcy, Report No. 41, Dec. 25, 1847, Letters Received by the AGO; Thomas M. Davies Jr., "Assessments during the Mexican War: An Exercise in Futility," *New Mexico Historical Review* 41 (1966): 212.

8. Peskin, *Volunteers,* 226, 227; Edward S. Wallace, "The United States Army in Mexico City," *Military Affairs* 13 (1949); WS to William Marcy, Dec. 25, 1847, Letters Received by the AGO.

9. WS to Marcy, Report No. 34, Sept. 18, 1847.

10. Nicholas Trist to wife, Oct. 18, 1847, Charles Winslow Elliott Collection, NYPL (typescript); Polk, *Diary,* 3:267.

11. Polk, *Diary,* 3:300–301; WS to Marcy, Reports No. 34, 41, Sept. 18, Dec. 25, 1847.

12. Polk, *Diary,* 3:322.

13. Nicholas Trist to wife, Dec. 4, 1847, in Elliott, *Winfield Scott,* 560.

14. Anonymous letter, Oct. 26, 1847, U.S. Senate, *Case of Major General Pillow,* 521–22.

15. Ibid., 388.

16. General Regulations for the Army, *ASP:MA,* 2:232.

17. General Orders No. 349, Nov. 12, 1847, Letters Received by the AGO.

18. U.S. Senate, *Case of Major General Pillow,* 527; Davis, *Autobiography,* 269–70; Gen. William Worth to Marcy, Nov. 16, 1847, in Elliott, *Winfield Scott,* 571–72; Scott, *Memoirs,* 2:584 n.

19. Scammon, "Chapter of the Mexican War," 574. See also Gideon Pillow to WS, Oct. 3, 1847, in U.S. Senate, *Case of Major General Pillow,* 631.

20. General Orders No. 305, Oct. 1, 1847, Letters Received by the AGO; Senate, *Case of Major General Pillow,* 361–62; Gideon Pillow to wife, Dec. 8, 1847, University of Virginia Library, Charlottesville; Polk, *Diary,* 4:17.

21. Polk, *Diary,* 3:266, 269–70.

22. William Marcy to WS, Jan. 13, 1848 (two letters of same date), *NASP:MA,* 7:179–194; WS to Marcy, Feb. 19, 1848, Letters Received by the AGO.

23. D. H. Hill, diary, Feb. [?], 1848, in Hughes and Stonesifer *Gideon J. Pillow,* 115; Oswandel, *Notes of the Mexican War,* 481.

24. Hitchcock, *Fifty Years,* 321; Ramsey, *Other Side,* 421.

25. Scott, *Memoirs,* 2:584.

26. Polk, *Diary,* 3:301–2.

27. U.S. Senate, *Case of Major General Pillow,* 23.

28. Smith, *War with Mexico,* 435 n. 31.

29. General Orders No. 56, Feb. 18, 1848. Letters Received by the AGO.

30. Hitchcock, *Fifty Years,* 328. See Theodore Laidley to his father, May 13, 1848, *"Surrounded by Dangers of All Kinds": The Mexican War Letters of Lieutenant Theodore Laidley,* ed. James McCaffrey (Denton: Univ. of North Texas Press, 1997), 159–61.

31. WS to John W. Clayton, Mar. 4, 1852, Elliott Collection (typescript); John Parrot to William Marcy, Dec. 20, 1847, *NASP:MA,* 7:165.

32. Scott, *Memoirs,* 2:584.

33. Ibid., 584, 584 n; Hone, *Diary,* 853.

34. Horace Greeley to Henry Clay, Nov. 30, 1847, Clay, *Papers,* 10:381.

35. Elliott, *Winfield Scott,* 595–96.

36. WS to Duncan L. Clinch, March 26, 1849, Manuscript Collection, U.S. Military Academy Library, West Point.

37. WS to Persifor Smith, Mar. 13, 1850, Manuscript Collection, U.S. Military Academy Library, West Point. After Scott's recall from Mexico, he was reduced from commanding general to head of the Eastern Division. He served in that capacity from August 31, 1847, to May 10, 1849, when he was restored to his former position. W. G. Freeman, memorandum, Jan. 22. 1856, Letters Sent by the Headquarters of the Army, RG 108, NA (M857).

38. Calhoun quoted in Merrill D. Peterson, *The Great Triumvirate: Webster, Clay, and Calhoun* (New York: Oxford Univ. Press, 1987), 423.

39. Hone, *Diary,* 885; *New York Morning Courier and Enquirer,* Feb. 26, 1856, in Elliott, *Winfield Scott,* 601.

40. *Washington Union,* July 16, 1850, in Elliott, *Winfield Scott,* 602; Hone, *Diary,* 901.

23. CANDIDATE

1. Hamilton, "Anecdotes," 189–90; WS to Secretary of War Conrad, Dec. 23, 1850, Letters Sent by the Headquarters of the Army, RG 108, NA (M857).

2. *New York Herald,* Dec. 19, 1850, in Elliott, *Winfield Scott,* 608.

3. Ibid.

4. Horace Greeley to Schuyler Colfax, Feb. 12, 1851, in Allan Nevins, *Ordeal of the Union,* 2 vols. (New York: Charles Scribner's Sons, 1947), 2:26, 25 n.

5. Strong, *Diary,* 2:96.

6. Ibid., 95; Charles R. Schultz, "The Last Great Conclave of the Whigs," *Maryland Historical Magazine* 63 (Dec. 1968): 385–86; Holt, *American Whig Party,* 712–13.

7. Seth C. Hawley to William Seward, June 4, 1852, in Holt, *American Whig Party,* 706.

8. The platform can be found in Schlesinger and Israel, *American Presidential Elections,* 3:956–57; Horace Greeley to Thurlow Weed, Apr. 18, 1852, Weed, *Life,* 2:217.

9. For a detailed account of the balloting, see Schultz, "Last Great Conclave," 393–97; and Holt, *American Whig Party,* 720–24.

10. Strong, *Diary,* 2:96–97; Francis Granger to Millard Fillmore, June 30, 1852, in Gienapp, "Whig Party," 409.

11. Holt, *American Whig Party,* 723. Schultz calculates Scott's total on the last ballot as 159 votes. "Last Great Conclave," 395.

12. Greeley quoted in Gienapp, "Whig Party," 41; WS to J. G. Chapman, June 24, 1852, Charles Winslow Elliott Collection, NYPL (typescript); William Seward to ?, June 25, 1852, in Frederick W. Seward, *Seward at Washington, as Senator and Secretary of State: A Memoir of His Life, with Selections from His Letters, 1846–1861* (New York: Derby and Miller, 1891), 188.

13. Arthur Charles Cole, *The Whig Party in the South* (1914; reprint, Gloucester, Mass.: Peter Smith, 1962), 259–76; Scott, *Memoirs,* 2:596.

14. Meridith Gentry cited in Elliott, *Winfield Scott,* 613; Strong, *Diary,* 2:98.

15. WS to Marcellus Eels, Aug. 7, 1852, Letters Sent by the Headquarters of the Army.

16. James Ford Rhodes, *History of the United States from the Compromise of 1850,* 5 vols. (New York: Harper, 1896), 1:271–72 n.

17. Memorandum of speech made in Peoria, Ill., Sept. 17, 1852, Chicago Historical Society (typescript).

18. Elliott, *Winfield Scott,* 641.

19. WS to R. Tyler et al., Mar. 11, 1852, Elliott Collection (typescript).

20. *Memoir of General Scott, from Records Contemporaneous with the Events* (Washington, D.C., 1852), 31.

21. Roy Nichols and Jeanette Nichols, "Election of 1852," in Schlesinger and Israel, *Presidential Elections,* 3:947; Speech at Greensburgh, Penn., Oct. 7, 1852, in ibid., 998; Jefferson Davis, *The Papers of Jefferson Davis,* ed. Lynda Lasswell Crist, 7 vols. (Baton Rouge: Louisiana State Univ. Press, 1971–92), 4:306, 267–68; Speech at Memphis, Tennessee, July 24, 1852, ibid., 398–99.

22. Holt, *American Whig Party,* 751; *New York Herald,* Aug. 17, 1852, in Elliott, *Winfield Scott,* 633.

23. *New York Herald,* Sept. 30, 1852; Elliot, *Winfield Scott,* 640; Strong, *Diary,* 2:106.

24. Gen. H. B. Carrington, "Winfield Scott's Visit to Columbus," *Ohio Archaeological Society and Historical Quarterly* 19 (July 1910): 280–81.

25. Ibid., 275–85.

26. Strong, *Diary,* 2:106; Keyes. *Fifty Years Observation,* 141–42.

27. Heth, *Memoirs,* 112–13; Weed, *Life,* 2:218–19.

28. Holt, *American Whig Party,* 751; Elliott, *Winfield Scott,* 641; Strong, *Diary,* 2:98, 108.

29. Whig campaign ribbons identified their candidate as "Winfield Scott of New Jersey."

30. Holt, *American Whig Party,* 754; Meridith Gentry cited in Elliott, *Winfield Scott,* 613.

31. Gienapp, "Whig Party," 407.

32. Scott, *Memoirs*, 2:391, 598. With the benefit of hindsight, historians have come to agree that Scott would have been preferable to Pierce. In 1995, a poll conducted by William J. Riddings Jr. and Stuart B. McIver asked professional historians to state their preferences for presidential elections from 1788 to 1988. For the election of 1852, 132 of the historians polled preferred Pierce, but 203 declared that they would have voted for Scott.

33. WS to Hamilton Fish, Nov. 16, 1852, Hamilton Fish Papers, LC.

24. EXILE

1. WS to Secretary of War Charles Conrad, Nov. 3, 1849. Letters Sent by the Headquarters of the Army, RG 108, NA (M857).

2. WS to Secretary of War Charles Conrad, Nov. 3, 1849.

3. See Michael E. Bryant, "An Army in Search of a Mission: The U.S. Army to the Civil War" (master's thesis, Cleveland State University, 1986), 95.

4. WS to Secretary of War Conrad, ca. Nov. 25, 1851, WS endorsement on Col. James Monroe to Major General Twiggs, May 21, 1850, cited in W. H. Freeman to Monroe, May 27, 1850, and WS to Secretary of War Conrad, Nov. 30, 1850, all in Letters Sent by the Headquarters of the Army.

5. See, for example, Weigley, *United States Army*, 189–90.

6. See, for example, WS to AG, Oct. 21, Dec. 11, 1848, Letters Received by the AGO, RG 94, NA (M566).

7. Grady McWhiney, "Who Whipped Whom? Confederate Defeat Reexamined," *Civil War History* 12 (Mar. 1965): 8–9. For a perceptive analysis of the effect of the minié-ball revolution and other mid–nineteenth-century technological developments on warfare, see Bryant, "Army in Search of a Mission," 172–205.

8. Davis, *Papers,* 4:305; Gouverneur, *As I Remember,* 103; Lorenzo Thomas, AAG, to Robert Atkinson, 3d Auditor of the Treasury, Dec. 24, 1855, and Lorenzo Thomas, AAG, to Gen. Thomas Jesup, quartermaster general, July 25, 1856, both in Letters Sent by the Headquarters of the Army.

9. WS to Jefferson Davis, Sept. 29, 1855, *NASP:MA,* 12:415.

10. Jefferson Davis to WS, May 11, 1853, in U.S. Senate, *Pay and Emoluments of Lt. Gen. Scott,* 34th Cong., 3d sess., 1857, S. Exec. Doc. 34, 14.

11. Jefferson Davis to WS, Sept. 7, 1855, and memorandum by Jefferson Davis, Feb. 9, 1855, both in U.S. Senate, *Pay and Emoluments of Lt. Gen. Scott,* 169.

12. WS to Secretary of War John Floyd, Apr. 19, 1858, Letters Sent by the Headquarters of the Army. See U.S. Senate, *Pay and Emoluments of Lt. Gen. Scott,* 19–53.

13. Keyes, *Fifty Years Observation,* 318.

14. WS to Jefferson Davis, Jan. 30, 1856, *NASP:MA,* 12:463–65; Elliott, *Winfield Scott,* 598, 603–4, 647–48, 653–54; WS to Hamilton Fish, Feb. 27, Dec. 29, 1855, Manuscript Collection, Virginia Historical Society, Richmond.

15. U.S. Senate, *Pay and Emoluments of Lt. Gen. Scott,* 71–131.

16. Jefferson Davis to President Pierce, Oct. 12, 1855, in U.S. Senate, *Pay and Emoluments of Lt. Gen. Scott*, 131–43, 144.

17. Remarks in the Senate, June 10, 1855, in Coleman, *Life of John J. Crittenden,* 2:125–26.

18. *New York Tribune,* June 12, 1856, in Scott, *Memoirs,* 2:600; WS to J. J. Crittenden, March, 21, 1854, in Coleman, *Life of John J. Crittenden,* 2:106.

19. William C. Davis, *Jefferson Davis: The Man and His Hour* (New York: Harper Collins, 1991), 226–28.

20. WS to Jefferson Davis, Sept. 29, 1855, in U.S. Senate, *Pay and Emouluments of Lt. Gen. Scott,* 203–14.

21. WS to Jefferson Davis, Aug. 6, 1855, in U.S. Senate, *Pay and Emouluments of Lt. Gen. Scott,* 165.

22. Jefferson Davis to WS, Aug. 6, 1855, in U.S. Senate, *Pay and Emouluments of Lt. Gen. Scott,* 239–40.

23. WS to Jefferson Davis, May 21, 1856, in U.S. Senate, *Pay and Emouluments of Lt. Gen. Scott,* 251–52.

24. Jefferson Davis to WS, May 23, 1856, in U.S. Senate, *Pay and Emouluments of Lt. Gen. Scott,* 254.

25. Remarks, WS to Secretary of War Floyd, Mar. 28, 1857, Letters Sent by the Headquarters of the Army.

26. Ben: Perley Poore, *Perley's Reminiscences of Sixty Years in the National Metropolis,* 2 vols. (Philadelphia: Hubbard Brothers, 1886), 2:419–20; Keyes, *Fifty Years Observation,* 11.

25. RETURN

1. WS to Col. Samuel Cooper, AG, Mar. 7, 1857, Letters Sent by the Headquarters of the Army, RG 108, NA (M857).

2. WS to Maj. Irvin McDowell, Apr. 11, 1857, WS Papers, William L. Clements Library, University of Michigan, Ann Arbor.

3. See William P. MacKinnon, "125 Years of Conspiracy Theories: Origin of the Utah Expedition of 1857–58," *Utah Historical Quarterly* 52 (summer 1984); and Norman F. Furniss, *The Mormon Conflict, 1850–1859* (New Haven: Yale Univ. Press, 1960), 62–94. I am grateful to Mr. MacKinnon for calling these and other sources to my attention.

4. Robert Tyler to President Buchanan, Apr. 27, 1857, cited in Furniss, *Mormon Conflict,* 75. Furniss mistakenly identifies the correspondent as Robert "Taylor."

5. See David Brion Davis, "Some Themes of Counter-Subversion: An Analysis of Anti-Masonic, Anti-Catholic, and Anti-Mormon Literature," *Mississippi Valley Historical Review* 67 (1960): 205–24.

6. Furniss, *Mormon Conflict,* 72–73; Scott, *Memoirs,* 2:604. For an examination of prewar scandals, including Floyd's, see Mark W. Summers, *The Plundering Generation: Corruption and the Crisis of the Union, 1849–1861* (New York: Oxford Univ. Press, 1987).

7. WS to Secretary of War Floyd, May 26, 1857, Letters Sent by the Headquarters of the Army.

8. WS to Secretary of War Floyd, May 26, 1857.

9. WS to Col. R. Jones, AG, Sept. 15, 1831, Letters Received by the AGO, RG 94, NA (M566); Lt. George P. Ihrie, cited in Wifford Hill LeCheminant, "A Crisis Averted?

General Harney and the Change in Command of the Utah Expedition," *Utah Historical Society* 61 (1983): 43.

10. Lt. Col. George W. Lay, ADC, to Harney, June 29, 1857, Letters Sent by the Headquarters of the Army; LeCheminant, "A Crisis Averted?" 30; Lorenzo Thomas, AAG, to Harney, July 17, 1857, Letters Sent by the Headquarters of the Army; H. L. Scott, ADC, to Harney, May 28, 1858, *NASP:MA,* 10:358–59; WS to John Floyd, Aug. 19, 1857, Letters Sent by Headquarters of the Army.

11. WS to Col. William S. Hamilton, Feb. 21, 1859, in Elliott, *Winfield Scott,* 664; "General Winfield Scott in Greenwich Village," *New York Mercury,* Mar. 9, 1859 (transcript), WS Papers, NYPL.

12. Gen. Edwin C. Mason, "How We Won the San Juan Archipelago," *Collections of the Minnesota Historical Society* 9 (Apr. 1901): 36–40.

13. William S. Harney to AAG, Aug. 1, 1859, Letters Received by the AGO; LeCheminant, "A Crisis Averted?" 42; Scott, *Memoirs,* 2:605.

14. Scott, *Memoirs,* 2:606–7.

15. W. R. Drinkard, acting secretary of war, to WS, Sept. 16, 1859, James Buchanan Papers, HSP.

16. W. R. Drinkard, acting secretary of war, to WS, Sept. 16, 1859.

17. Lorenzo Thomas, AAG, to Col. Samuel Cooper, AG, Oct. 22, 1859, *NASP:MA,* 10:260; WS to Gov. James Douglas, Oct. 25, 1859, *NASP:MA,* 10:261–62.

18. James Douglas to WS, Oct. 29, 1859, Letters Received by the AGO.

19. WS to Gov. James Douglas, Nov. 2, 1859, *NASP:MA,* 10:265–69; James Douglas to WS, Nov. 3, 1859, Letters Received by the AGO.

20. WS to James Douglas, Nov. 5, 1859, *NASP:MA,* 10:269–70; James Douglas to WS, Nov. 7, 1859, Letters Received by the AGO. Before wrapping up his business in Oregon, Scott dealt with the officers who had precipitated the crisis. Pickett was slapped with an official reprimand for his "offensive, if not wanton," recklessness. WS to John B. Floyd, Feb. 27, 1860, *NASP:MA,* 10:281. Harney was more difficult to deal with. Scott suggested that he be transferred to St. Louis to forestall any British demands that he be removed from his Oregon command (WS to William Harney, Nov. 15, 1859, Letters Sent by the Headquarters of the Army), but a deeper reason lay in Scott's doubts about whether Harney's impulsive nature could be trusted to carry out the agreement with the British. Scott gave Harney permission to throw the transfer to St. Louis into the fire if he pleased, and apparently Harney did just that. He remained in Oregon until the eve of the Civil War, despite Scott's complaints of the "ignorance, passion, and caprice" he displayed while at that post. Cited in LeCheminant, "A Crisis Averted?" 44.

21. James Buchanan, Third Annual Message, Dec. 15, 1859, in Richardson, *Messages and Papers,* 5:563.

22. WS to Henry Wilson, [Jan. 1860], in Coleman, *Life of John J. Crittenden,* 2:165; WS to J. J. Crittenden, Jan. 6, 1860, ibid., 182–83; WS to J. J. Crittenden, Jan. 27, 1860, ibid., 184. Coleman mistakenly reads "toll" for "tall."

23. Strong, *Diary,* 3:2.

1. Chesnut, *Mary Chesnut's Civil War,* 232; Scott, *Memoirs,* 1:180.

2. Benjamin Watkins Leigh to Edward Mansfield, n.d., in Mansfield, *Lieut.-General Winfield Scott,* 251; WS to [W. C. Preston], Dec. 14, 1832, Preston Family Papers, LC.

3. The version of this Oct. 29, 1860, letter that Scott printed in the *Memoirs* (1:609–11) was substantially abridged to remove some of his more foolish speculations that subsequent events had proven embarrassingly off the mark. An unbowdlerized version is WS, "Views Suggested by the Imminent Danger . . . of a Disruption of the Union, etc.," in James Buchanan, *The Works of James Buchanan, Comprising His Speeches, State Papers, and Private Correspondence,* ed. John Bassett Moore, 12 vols. (Philadelphia: J. B. Lippincott, 1910), 11:301–3.

4. WS, "Views," Oct. 29, 1860, in Buchanan, *Works,* 11:303; WS to James Buchanan, Dec. 15, 1860 (night), Buchanan Papers, HSP.

5. WS to Secretary of War Floyd, Oct. 30, 1860, in Buchanan, *Works,* 11:304.

6. [James Buchanan], *Mr. Buchanan's Administration on the Eve of the Rebellion* (New York, 1866), 103–6; Philip Gerald Auchampaugh, *James Buchanan and His Cabinet on the Eve of Secession* (n.p., 1926), 63–64; Upton, *Military Policy,* 275. See the maps in Francis Paul Prucha, "Distribution of Regular Army Troops before the Civil War," *Military Affairs* 16 (Winter 1952): 169–73.

7. WS, "Views," 11:303 n.

8. Rhodes, *History of the United States,* 3:137.

9. Memorandum by Lorenzo Thomas, Dec. 17, 1860, Samuel L. Crawford Papers, LC.

10. John G. Nicolay and John Hay, *Abraham Lincoln: A History,* 10 vols. (New York: Century, 1890), 3:250; Lincoln to E. B. Washburne, Dec. 21, 1860, Abraham Lincoln, *Complete Works of Abraham Lincoln,* ed. John G. Nicolay and John Hay, 12 vols. (n.p., 1894), 6:84–85.

11. Robert Underwood Johnson and Clarence Clough Buel, eds., *Battles and Leaders of the Civil War,* 4 vols. (New York: Century, 1887–88), 1:50.

12. Charles P. Stone, "Washington on the Eve of the War," *Century Illustrated Monthly Magazine* 24 (July 1883): 459; WS to J. J. Crittenden, Nov. 12, 1860, Coleman, *Life of James J. Crittenden,* 2:219; Joseph Gardner Swift, *The Memoirs of Gen. Joseph Gardner Swift, LL.D., U.S.A., First Graduate of the United States Military Academy. . . .* (n.p., 1890), 285–86.

13. Henry Adams, *The Great Secession Winter of 1860–61 and Other Essays,* ed. George Hochfield (New York: A. S. Barnes, 1963), 22; Charles Francis Adams, *Charles Francis Adams, 1835–1915: An Autobiography* (New York: Houghton Mifflin, 1916), 73, 104.

14. Adams, *Great Secession Winter,* 29; Keyes, *Fifty Years Observation,* 361, 410–11; E. D. Townsend, *Anecdotes of the Civil War in the United States* (New York: Appleton, 1884), 22–27; Elliott, *Winfield Scott,* 690–92.

15. This charge of preferring Southern officers was made by his longtime aide Erasmus Keyes and convincingly refuted by James B. Fry. See Keyes, *Fifty Years Observation,* 318–19; and Fry, *Military Miscellanies* (New York: Brentano's, 1889), 480–83.

16. WS to S. P. Chase, Jan. 16, 1861, Dreer Collection, HSP.

17. Jesse W. Weik, "How Lincoln Was Convinced of General Scott's Loyalty," *Century Magazine* 81 (Feb. 1911): 594.

18. Stone, "Washington on the Eve of War," 461; Elliott, *Winfield Scott,* 691; Simon Cameron to Lincoln, Jan. 3, 1861, Nicolay and Hay, *Abraham Lincoln,* 3:250.

19. Johnson and Buel, *Battles and Leaders,* 1:7.

20. Stone, "Washington on the Eve of the War," 466.

21. Elliott, *Winfield Scott,* 696.

22. WS to William Seward, Mar. 3, 1861, in Scott, *Memoirs,* 2:625–28.

23. Lincoln to WS, Mar. 9, 1861, Lincoln, *Complete Works,* 6:188–89.

24. Memorandum on Southern forts, Mar. 12, 1861, in Scott, *Memoirs,* 2:620; WS quoted in Lincoln, *Complete Works,* 6:204–205. See Gideon Welles, *Diary of Gideon Welles, Secretary of the Navy under Lincoln and Johnson,* ed. Howard K. Beale, 3 vols. (New York: W. W. Norton, 1960), 1:4–10, 2:515–16; and Edward Bates, *The Diary of Edward Bates, 1859–1866,* ed. Howard K. Beale (1933; reprint, New York: Da Capo, 1971), 177–78.

25. Lincoln, *Complete Works,* 6:230.

26. Gustavus Fox, "Memo for the relief of Fort Sumter," *Confidential Correspondence of Gustavus Vasa Fox, Assistant Secretary of the Navy, 1861–1865,* ed. Robert Means Thompson and Richard Wainwright, 2 vols. (1920; reprint, Freeport, N.Y.: Books for Libraries, 1972), 1:8–9; WS to Col. H. L. Scott, Apr. 4, 1861, *NASP:MA,* 19:151.

27. Keyes, *Fifty Years Observation,* 377–84.

28. Ibid., 384; Seward, *Seward at Washington,* 534.

29. Ari Hoogenboom, "Gustavus Fox and the Relief of Fort Sumter," *Civil War History* 9 (1963): 392–96.

27. CIVIL WAR

1. B. Howard Meneely, *The War Department, 1861: A Study in Mobilization and Administration* (New York: Columbia Univ. Press, 1928), 106.

2. Johnson and Buel, *Battles and Leaders,* 1:38.

3. Seward, *Seward at Washington,* 560–61; Keyes, *Fifty Years Observation,* 205–7; Nicolay and Hay, *Abraham Lincoln,* 4:97–102.

4. John Tyler to wife, Apr. 16, 18, 1861, Lyon G. Tyler, ed., *The Letters and Times of the Tylers,* 3 vols. (Richmond, 1885; reprint, New York: Da Capo, 1970), 2:640–41; Frank Moore, ed., *The Rebellion Record: A Diary of American Events,* 12 vols. (1861–68; reprint, New York: Arno, 1977), 1:D33, P57. See Francis MacDonnell, "The Confederate Spin on Winfield Scott and George Thomas," *Civil War History* 44 (1998): 255–66.

5. H. M. Wharton, ed., *War Songs and Poems of the Southern Confederacy. . . .* (n.p., [1904]), 286–87. I am indebted to Frank Byrne for calling this item to my attention.

6. Moore, *Rebellion Record,* 1:D53; Elliott, *Winfield Scott.* 712.

7. WS to James Monroe, Feb. 13, 1815, Charles Winslow Elliott Collection, NYPL (typescript); Nicolay and Hay, *Abraham Lincoln,* 4:103–4.

8. Moore, *Rebellion Record,* vol. 1, doc. 179.

9. Strong, *Diary,* 3:151; Edwin Stanton to James Buchanan, May 16, 1861, in Elliott, *Winfield Scott,* 724.

10. A. K. McClure, *Alexander K. McClure's Recollections of Half a Century* (Salem, Mass.: Salem Press, 1902), 206.

11. Meneely, *War Department, 1861,* 106–9.

12. Russell, *My Diary*, 424; Townsend, *Anecdotes*, 43–44; Elliott, *Winfield Scott*, 724.

13. Seward, *Seward at Washington*, 550–52; Nicolay and Hay, *Abraham Lincoln*, 3:109–30; F. J. Porter to Col. H. L. Scott, Apr. 24, 1861, Letters Sent by the Headquarters of the Army, RG 108, NA (M857).

14. Seward, *Seward at Washington*, 550–51; Nicolay and Hay, *Abraham Lincoln*, 4:152.

15. Seward, *Seward at Washington*, 550–52; Wright, *General Scott*, 305–6; Stone, "Washington in March and April, 1861"; Eldon E. Billings, "Military Activities in Washington in 1861," *Records of the Columbia Historical Society of Washington, D.C., 1960–62*, 123–22.

16. Seward, *Seward at Washington*, 553.

17. Charles P. Stone, "A Dinner with General Scott in 1861," *Magazine of American History* 14 (July 1885): 528–32; Townsend, *Anecdotes*, 257–58.

18. Johnson and Buel, *Battles and Leaders*, 1:169.

19. Grant, *Memoirs*, 1:187.

20. John M. Schofield, *Forty-Six Years in the Army* (New York: Century, 1897), 515.

21. See, for example, WS to Secretary of War Conrad [c. Nov. 25, 1851], Letters Sent by the Headquarters of the Army.

22. William Tecumseh Sherman, *Memoirs of General W. T. Sherman* (New York: Library of America, 1990), 196; Johnson and Buel, *Battles and Leaders*, 1:94; Schofield, *Forty-Six Years*, 513; Col. Edward D. Townsend, AAG, to Col. A. J. Pleasonton, Apr. 30, 1861, Letters Sent by the Headquarters of the Army.

23. John Sherman, *John Sherman's Recollections of Forty Years in the House, Senate, and Cabinet: An Autobiography*, 2 vols. (Chicago: Werner, 1895), 1:265; Schofield, *Forty-Six Years*, 514.

24. Grant, *Memoirs*, 188.

28. ANACONDA

1. Strong, *Diary*, 3:144; Chesnut, *Mary Chesnut's Civil War*, 376.

2. Townsend, *Anecdotes*, 55–56.

3. John F. Marszalek, "Where Did Winfield Scott Find His Anaconda?" *Lincoln Herald* 89 (Summer 1987): 77–81; Theodore Rupp, "Anacondas Anyone?" *Military Affairs* 27 (Summer 1963): 71–76. Scott never reduced the so-called Anaconda Plan to writing, but its essential elements can be found in letters sent to Maj. Gen. George B. McClellan, especially those of May 3 and May 21, 1861, which can be found in *OR*, 51(1):369–70, 386–87. The original draft of the May 3 letter, along with Scott's corrections and revisions, can be found in Townsend, *Anecdotes*, 260–62. Scott did, however, frequently discuss his strategic plans in conversations. See, for example, Townsend, *Anecdotes*, 55–56; Strong, *Diary*, 3:144; and Charles P. Stone, "Washington in 1861," *Magazine of American History* 12 (July 1884): 59–60.

4. Stone, "Washington in 1861," 60.

5. Ibid.

6. Strong, *Diary*. 3:148; Wright, *General Scott*, 330.

7. WS to Maj. Gen. George B. McClellan, May 3, 1861,
OR, 51(1):370; *New York Tribune*, June 26, 1861, in Nicolay and Hay, *Abraham Lincoln*, 4:321.

8. Stone, "Washington in 1861," 61.

9. Townsend, *Anecdotes,* 56.

10. Stone, "Washington in 1861," 57–60.

11. Nicolay and Hay, *Abraham Lincoln,* 4:323.

12. Johnson and Buel, *Battles and Leaders,* 1:175 n.

13. Ibid., 172–75, 181–82; Jeffry D. Wert, "Duped in the Mountains of Virginia," *Civil War Times Illustrated* 17 (1978): 4–11, 41–44.

14. Nicolay and Hay, *Abraham Lincoln,* 4:354.

15. Townsend, *Anecdotes,* 58–59.

16. Nicolay and Hay, *Abraham Lincoln,* 4:358–59.

17. Townsend, *Anecdotes,* 62.

29. FADING AWAY

1. Tocqueville, *Democracy in America,* 655, 657.

2. Wilkinson, *Memoirs,* 1:612.

3. McClellan to WS, July 18, 1861, in McClellan, *The Civil War Papers of George B. McClellan: Selected Correspondence, 1860–1865,* ed. Stephen W. Sears (New York: Ticknor and Fields, 1989), 60; McClellan to WS, May 9, 1861, ibid., 17–18; E. P. Townsend to McClellan, July 6, 1861 (telegram), ibid., 49.

4. McClellan to WS, Apr. 27, 1861, *OR,* 51(1):338–39.

5. Endorsement of above to President Lincoln by WS, May 2, 1861, ibid., 339; WS to McClellan, ibid., 386–87; WS to McClellan, May 21, 1861, ibid., 387; WS to Simon Cameron, Oct. 4, 1861, Townsend, *Anecdotes,* 63.

6. McClellan to wife, Aug. 2, 1861, in McClellan, *Civil War Papers,* 75; McClellan to wife, July 27, 1861, ibid., 70; McClellan to wife, July 30, 1861, ibid., 71.

7. McClellan to wife, Aug. 8, 1861, in McClellan, *Civil War Papers,* 81.

8. McClellan to WS, Aug. 8, 1861, ibid., 79–80.

9. WS to Simon Cameron, Aug. 9, 1861, Charles Winslow Elliott Collection, NYPL (typescript).

10. McClellan to Lincoln, Aug. 10, 1861, in McClellan, *Civil War Papers,* 82–82; McClellan to wife, Aug. 9 [10], 1861, ibid., 81–82.

11. McClellan to wife, Aug. 8, 15 [14], 1861, in McClellan, *Civil War Papers,* 81, 84; McClellan to wife, Aug. 16, 19, 1861, ibid., 85–87; McClellan to Secretary of War Cameron, Sept. 13, 1861, ibid., 100.

12. Stephen W. Sears, *George B. McClellan: The Young Napoleon* (New York: Ticknor and Fields, 1989), 101–6; McClellan to wife, Oct. 6, 1861, McClellan, *Civil War Papers,* 106.

13. WS to Simon Cameron, Oct. 4, 1861, Townsend, *Anecdotes,* 63–65. See memorandum, "Respecting the Routine of Army Correspondence," by L. Thomas, ADC, Apr. 1, 1857, Letters Sent by the Headquarters of the Army, RG 108, NA (M857).

14. Russell, *My Diary,* 519–22.

15. McClellan to wife, Oct. 10, 1861, in McClellan, *Civil War Papers,* 106. This contempt extended to the entire Lincoln administration. The president, according to McClellan, was "nothing more than a well meaning baboon." The cabinet contained "some of the greatest geese" the general had ever seen, including the cowardly Seward;

"that garrulous old woman" Secretary of the Navy Gideon Welles; the rascally Simon Cameron; and that "old fool" Attorney General Edward Bates. He conceded that Postmaster General Montgomery Blair possessed some courage and sense, but, he added, "I do not altogether fancy him." McClellan to wife, Oct. 31, 1846, ibid., 114.

16. Welles, *Diary*, 241–42; McClellan to wife, Sept. 27, 1861, in McClellan, *Civil War Papers*, 103–4.

17. McClellan to wife, Oct. 26, 1861, McClellan, *Civil War Papers*, 112; WS to Simon Cameron, Oct. 4, 1861; Townsend, *Anecdotes*, 62–65; Bates, *Diary*, 196–97.

18. Nicolay and Hay, *Abraham Lincoln*, 4:464–65; Scott, *Memoirs*, 2:629; *Harper's Weekly*, Nov. 16, 1861, 722; Bates, *Diary*, 199.

19. Abraham Lincoln, First Annual Message, Dec. 3, 1861, in Richardson, *Messages and Papers*, 6:56.

20. R. H. Stoddard, "Winfield Scott: Nov. 1st, 1861," from *Vanity Fair*, reprinted in *Littel's Living Age* 71 (1861): 471.

21. McClellan to wife, Nov. 7, 1861, McClellan, *Civil War Papers*, 126.

22. "General Scott's Departure from Washington," *Littel's Living Age* 71 (1861): 470; McClellan to wife, Nov. 3 [2], 1861, in McClellan, *Civil War Papers*, 123.

23. Gouverneur Kemble to Gen. B. Howard, Nov. 10, 1861, Bayard Papers, Maryland Historical Society, Baltimore; Weed, *Life*, 1:654.

24. Weed, *Life*, 1:654–56.

25. WS to Martin Van Buren, Oct. 28, 1861, Elliott Collection (typescript).

26. McClure, *Recollections*, 183–84; Nicolay and Hay, *Abraham Lincoln*, 10:321.

27. *Harper's Weekly*, Dec. 17, 1864, p. 803; Elliott, *Winfield Scott*, 757.

28. WS to J. M. Drake, Nov. 1, 1865, Clinton H. Haskell Collection, William L. Clements Library, University of Michigan, Ann Arbor; WS to Martin Van Buren, Oct. 29, 1861, Elliott Collection (typescript); Strong, *Diary*, 3:493; "Lt. Gen. Scott," *Hours at Home* 3 (1866): 279.

29. Asst. Surgeon E. J. Marsh diary, in Elliott, *Winfield Scott*, 760–62.

30. Ibid.

31. *Harper's Weekly*, June 16, 1866, 375.

32. Richardson, *Messages and Papers*, 6:388.

33. Strong, *Diary*, 4:87, 2:21; Hone, *Diary*, 826.

34. Strong, *Diary*, 2:21.

SOURCES CITED

MANUSCRIPTS AND ARCHIVAL MATERIAL

Since no centralized, comprehensive collection of Scott manuscripts exists, largely due to an 1841 fire that destroyed many of his personal papers, a biographer is compelled to search out scattered items at various libraries. Fortunately, Scott's first modern biographer, Charles Winslow Elliott, has already done some of the spadework. For his 1937 study, *Winfield Scott: The Soldier and the Man,* Elliott tracked down hundreds of Scott items, many in out-of-the-way locations, and then generously deposited typed copies at the New York Public Library. The Charles Winslow Elliott Collection should be the starting point for any investigation of the general's life. Among the other valuable collections at the New York Public Library are the James Monroe and the Winfield Scott Papers.

Two other very useful libraries are the Historical Society of Pennsylvania at Philadelphia and the William L. Clements Library at the University of Michigan in Ann Arbor. The most valuable collections at the former are the Winfield Scott Papers, the Daniel Parker Papers, the Cadwalader Family Papers, the Solomon Gratz Collection, the Dreer Collection, and the James Buchanan Papers. The Clements Library holds the Christopher Van Deventer Collection and the Jacob Brown Papers as well as the substantial Winfield Scott Papers.

Various Scott items can be found in literally dozens of collections at the Library of Congress. I have cited those from the papers of Robert Anderson, Charles Chaille-Long, Samuel L. Crawford, Hamilton Fish, Ethan Allen Hitchcock, William Marcy, Edmund Ruffin, Thaddeus Stevens, and Benjamin Tappan, as well as those in the Preston Family and the Wilkes Family Papers.

Other libraries that provided miscellaneous items of interest include:

The Buffalo and Erie County Historical Society, Buffalo, N.Y.
The Chicago Historical Society

The Maryland Historical Society, Baltimore
The New York State Library, Albany (especially its Charles Kitchel Gardner Papers)
The Special Manuscript Collection, Columbia University Library, New York, N.Y.
The U.S. Military Academy Library, West Point, N.Y.
The University of Chicago Library
The University of Virginia Library, Charlottesville
The Virginia Historical Society, Richmond

The most valuable resource for this study was found in the day-to-day records of army routine preserved in the National Archives. No one who has plowed through these records can fail to be continually delighted by the buried jewels that can be uncovered from the archival sludge, nor can they fail to be surprised at how few researchers have had the patience to dig through the muck of routine correspondence to find them. For my purposes, the most useful record groups have been:

Confidential and Unofficial Letters Sent by the Secretary of War, 1814–47, Record Group 107 (M7)
Letters Received by the Office of the Adjutant General, Record Group 94 (M566)
Letters Received by the Secretary of War, Main Series, Record Group 107 (M221)
Letters Received by the Secretary of War, Unregistered Series, Record Group 107 (M222)
Letters Sent by the Headquarters of the Army, Record Group 108 (M857)

OTHER SOURCES

Adams, Charles Francis. *Charles Francis Adams, 1835–1915: An Autobiography.* New York: Houghton Mifflin, 1916.
Adams, Henry. *The Great Secession Winter of 1860–61 and Other Essays.* Ed. George Hochfield. New York: A. S. Barnes, 1963.
———. *History of the United States of America during the Administration of James Madison.* New York: Library of America, 1986.
Adams, John Quincy. *Memoirs of John Quincy Adams, Comprising Portions of His Diary from 1795 to 1848.* Ed. Charles Francis Adams. 12 vols. Philadelphia, 1874–77. Reprint, New York: AMS Press, 1970.
American State Papers: Military Affairs. 7 vols. Washington, D.C., 1832–61.
Anderson, Robert. *An Artillery Officer in the Mexican War, 1846–7: Letters of Robert Anderson, Captain 3rd Artillery, U.S.A.* New York: G. P. Putnam's Sons, 1911.
[Armstrong, John]. *Hints to Young Generals. By an Old Soldier.* Kingston, [1812].
"Army of the United States." *North American Review* 8 (n.s. 23, no. 53; October 1826): 245–74.
Auchampaugh, Philip Gerald. *James Buchanan and His Cabinet on the Eve of Secession.* N.p., 1926.
Babcock, James L., ed. "The Campaign of 1814 on the Niagara Frontier." *Niagara Frontier* 10 (Winter 1963): 12–78.
Baker, Maury. "The Spanish War Scare of 1816." *Mid-America* 45 (April 1963): 67–78.

Balogh, George W. "The Regular Army in the Blackhawk War." *Order of the Indian Wars Journal* 1 (Fall 1980): 18–27.

Bates, Edward. *The Diary of Edward Bates, 1859–1866.* Ed. Howard K. Beale. 1933. Reprint, New York: Da Capo, 1971.

Bauer, K. Jack. *Surfboats and Horse Marines: U.S. Naval Operations in the Mexican War, 1846–48.* Annapolis: U.S. Naval Institute, 1964.

Beauregard, Pierre Gustave Toutant. *With Beauregard in Mexico: The Mexican War Reminiscences of P. G. T. Beauregard.* Ed. T. Harry Williams. New York: Da Capo, 1969.

Bemrose, John. *Reminiscences of the Second Seminole War.* Ed. John K. Mahon. Gainesville: Univ. Press of Florida, 1966.

Benton, Thomas Hart. *Thirty Years View; or, a History of the Workings of the American Government for Thirty Years, from 1820 to 1850.* 2 vols. New York: Appleton, 1858.

Berg, Richard, and Joe Bulkoski. "Veracruz—U.S. Invasion of Mexico, 1847." *Strategy and Tactics* 63 (1977): 4–18.

Billings, Elden E. "Military Activities in Washington in 1861." *Records of the Columbia Historical Society of Washington, D.C., 1960–62,* 123–33.

Bloom, John P. "With the American Army in Mexico, 1848–1849." Ph.D. diss., Emory University, 1956.

Bonney, Catherine V. R. *A Legacy of Historical Gleanings.* 2 vols. Albany, 1875.

Brown, John P. *Old Frontiers: The Story of the Cherokee Indians from Earliest Times to the Date of their Removal to the West, 1838.* Kingsport, Tenn.: Southern Publishing, 1938.

Bryant, Michael E. "An Army in Search of a Mission: The U.S. Army to the Civil War." Master's thesis, Cleveland State University, 1986.

[Buchanan, James]. *Mr. Buchanan's Administration on the Eve of the Rebellion.* New York, 1866.

———. *The Works of James Buchanan, Comprising His Speeches, State Papers, and Private Correspondence.* Ed. John Bassett Moore. 12 vols. Philadelphia: J. B. Lippincott, 1910.

Carrington, Gen. H. B. "Winfield Scott's Visit to Columbus." *Ohio Archaeological Society and Historical Quarterly* 19 (July 1910): 278–91.

Chartand, René. "The U.S. Army's Uniform Supply 'Crisis' during the War of 1812." *The Military Collector and Historian* 40 (Summer 1988): 62–65.

Chesnut, Mary Boykin Miller. *Mary Chesnut's Civil War.* Ed. C. Vann Woodward. New Haven: Yale Univ. Press, 1981.

Clay, Henry. *The Papers of Henry Clay.* Ed. James F. Hopkins et al. 10 vols. Lexington: Univ. Press of Kentucky, 1959–91.

Coffman, Edward M. *The Old Army: A Portrait of the American Army in Peacetime, 1784–1898.* New York: Oxford Univ. Press, 1986.

Cole, Arthur Charles. *The Whig Party in the South.* 1914. Reprint, Gloucester, Mass.: Peter Smith, 1962.

Coleman, Mrs. Chapman. *The Life of John J. Crittenden, with Selections from his Correspondence and Speeches.* 2 vols. Philadelphia, 1871. Reprint, New York: Da Capo, 1970.

Conner, Philip Syng Physick. *The Home Squadron under Commodore Conner in the War with Mexico.* Philadelphia: [n.p.], 1896.

"Correspondence between Major General Jackson and Brevet Major General Scott on the Subject of an Order Bearing Date the 22d of April, 1817." *Army and Navy Life* 9 (August 1906): 83–92.

Crackel, Theodore J. "The Battle of Queenston Heights, 13 October 1812." In *America's First Battles, 1776–1965,* edited by Charles E. Heller and William A. Stofft. Lawrence: Univ. Press of Kansas, 1986. 33–56.

Crenshaw, Mary Mayo, ed. *An American Lady in Paris, 1828–1829: The Diary of Mrs. John Mayo.* Boston: Houghton Mifflin, 1927.

Cunfiffe, Marcus. *Soldiers and Civilians: The Martial Spirit in America, 1775–1865.* Boston: Little, Brown, 1968.

Current, Richard N. *Lincoln and the First Shot.* Philadelphia: J. B. Lippincott, 1963.

Davies, Thomas M., Jr. "Assessments during the Mexican War: An Exercise in Futility." *New Mexico Historical Review* 41 (1966): 197–216.

Davis, David Brion. "Some Themes of Counter-Subversion: An Analysis of Anti-Masonic, Anti-Catholic, and Anti-Mormon Literature." *Mississippi Valley Historical Review* 67 (1960): 205–24.

Davis, George T. M. *Autobiography of the Late Col. Geo. T. M. Davis. . . .* New York: [Jenkins and McCowan], 1891.

Davis, Jefferson. *The Papers of Jefferson Davis.* Edited by Lynda Lasswell Crist. 7 vols. Baton Rouge: Louisiana State Univ. Press, 1971–92.

Davis, William C. *Jefferson Davis: The Man and His Hour.* New York: HarperCollins, 1991.

Douglas, R. Alan. "Weapons of the War of 1812." *Michigan History* 47 (December 1963): 321–26.

[Douglass, David Bates]. "An Original Narrative of the Niagara Campaign of 1814." Ed. John T. Horton. *Niagara Frontier* 11 (Spring 1964): 1–36.

Duffy, John, ed. *The Rudolph Matas History of Medicine in Louisiana.* 2 vols. Baton Rouge: Louisiana State Univ. Press, 1957.

Eisenhower, John S. D. *Agent of Destiny: The Life and Times of General Winfield Scott.* New York: Free Press, 1997.

Elliott, Charles Winslow. *Winfield Scott: The Soldier and the Man.* New York: Macmillan, 1937.

Emerson, George D. "The Episode of the *Adams* and *Caledonia.*" *Publications of the Buffalo Historical Society* 8 (1905): 405–9.

Fillmore, Millard. *Papers.* Ed. Frank H. Severance. 2 vols. Publications of the Buffalo Historical Society 10–11 (1907).

Foreman, Grant. *Indian Removal: The Emigration of the Five Civilized Tribes of the Indians.* Norman: Univ. of Oklahoma Press, 1953.

Fox, Gustavus Vasa. *Confidential Correspondence of Gustavus Vasa Fox, Assistant Secretary of the Navy, 1861–1865.* Ed. Robert Means Thompson and Richard Wainwright. 2 vols. 1920. Reprint, Freeport, N.Y.: Books for Libraries, 1972.

Fredriksen, John C. *Officers of the War of 1812 with Portraits and Anecdotes: The United States Army Left Division, Gallery of Honor.* Introd. Donald E. Graves. Lewiston, N.Y.: Edwin Mellon Press, 1989.

Freehling, William W. *Prelude to Civil War: The Nullification Controversy in South Carolina, 1816–1836.* New York: Harper and Row Torchbooks, 1968.

Frost, J. *The Mexican War and Its Warriors.* New Haven and Philadelphia: H. Mansfield, 1848.

Fry, James B. *Military Miscellanies.* New York: Brentano's, 1889.

Furniss, Norman F. *The Mormon Conflict, 1850–1859.* New Haven: Yale University Press, 1960.

General Scott and His Staff. . . . Philadelphia: Grigg, Elliot, and Co., 1848.

"General Winfield Scott on *Native Americanism* in 1844. . . ." *American Catholic Historical Research,* n.s., 7 (January 1911): 10–12.

Gienapp, William E. "The Whig Party, the Compromise of 1850, and the Nomination of Winfield Scott." *Presidential Studies Quarterly* 14 (Summer 1984): 399–415.

Gordon, George H. "The Battles of Contreras and Churubusco." *Papers of the Military Historical Society of Massachusetts* 13 (1913): 561–98.

———. "Battles of Molino del Rey and Chapultepec." *Papers of the Military Historical Society of Massachusetts* 13 (1913): 601–39.

Gouverneur, Marian. *As I Remember: Recollections of American Society during the Nineteenth Century.* New York: Appleton, 1911.

Grant, Ulysses S. *Memoirs and Selected Letters.* New York: Library of America, 1990.

———. *The Papers of Ulysses S. Grant.* Vol. 1, *1837–1861.* Ed. John Y. Simon. Carbondale: Southern Illinois Univ. Press, 1967.

Graves, Donald E. *The Battle of Lundy's Lane: On the Niagara in 1814.* Baltimore: Nautical and Aviation Publishing, 1993.

———. "'Dry Books of Tactics': U.S. Infantry Manuals of the War of 1812 and After." *Military Collector and Historian* 38 (1986): 50–61.

———. "'I Have a Handsome Little Army. . . .': A Reexamination of Winfield Scott's Camp at Buffalo in 1814." In *War along the Niagara: Essays on the War of 1812 and Its Legacy,* edited by R. Arthur Bowler, 43–52. Youngstown, N.Y.: Old Fort Niagara Association, 1991.

Griffis, William Elliott. *Matthew Calbraith Perry: A Typical American Naval Officer.* Boston: Cupples and Hurd, 1887.

Guillet, Edwin C. *The Life and Times of the Patriots: An Account of the Rebellion in Upper Canada, 1837–1838.* . . . 1938. Reprint, Toronto: Univ. of Toronto Press, 1968.

Gunderson, Robert Gray. *The Log Cabin Campaign.* Lexington: Univ. of Kentucky Press, 1957.

Hallahan, John M. "No Doubt Blameable: The Transformation of Captain Winfield Scott." *Virginia Cavalcade* 40 (1991): 160–71.

Hamilton, Charles S. "Memoirs of the Mexican War." *Wisconsin Magazine of History* 14 (1930): 63–92.

Hamilton, Schuyler. "Anecdotes of General Winfield Scott." *Southern History Association Publications* 4 (May 1900): 187–98.

Hare, John S. "Military Punishments in the War of 1812." *Journal of the American Military Institute* 4 (1940): 225–39.

Harper's Weekly, 1861, 1864–66.

Hay, Thomas Robson. "John C. Calhoun and the Presidential Campaign of 1824." *North Carolina Historical Review* 12 (January 1935): 20–44.

Heth, Henry. *The Memoirs of Henry Heth.* Ed. James L. Morrison Jr. Westport, Conn.: Greenwood, 1974.

Heustis, Jabez Wiggins. *Physical Observations and Medical Tracts and Researches on the Topography and Diseases of Louisiana.* New York: T. and J. Swords, 1817.

[Hill, Daniel H.]. "Battle of Cerro Gordo." *Southern Quarterly Review* 21 (1852): 121–53.

———. "The Battle of Contreras." *Southern Quarterly Review* 21 (1852): 373–426.

————. "Battle of El Molino del Rey." *Southern Quarterly Review* 22 (1852): 281–315.

————. "Chapultepec and the Garitas of Mexico."*Southern Quarterly Review* 23 (1853): 1–52.

————. "The Siege of Vera Cruz." *Southern Quarterly Review* 20 (1851): 1–40.

Hitchcock, Ethan Allen. *Fifty Years in Camp and Field: Diary of Major-General Ethan Allen Hitchcock, U.S.A.* Ed. A. A. Croffut. New York: G. P. Putnam's Sons, 1909.

Holt, Michael F. *The Rise and Fall of the American Whig Party: Jacksonian Politics and the Onset of the Civil War.* New York: Oxford Univ. Press, 1999.

Hone, Philip. *The Diary of Philip Hone, 1828–1851.* Ed. Allan Nevins. 2 vols. New York, 1927. Reprint (2 vols. in 1), New York: Kraus, 1969.

Hoogenboom, Ari. "Gustavus Fox and the Relief of Fort Sumter." *Civil War History* 9 (1963): 383–98.

Hoskins, Mrs. James. "Exploits of John Dickson." *Publications of the Buffalo Historical Society* 8 (1905): 411–17.

Houston, David Franklin. *A Critical Study of Nullification in South Carolina.* Cambridge: Harvard Univ. Press, 1896.

Howe, Daniel Walker. *The Political Culture of the American Whigs.* Chicago: Univ. of Chicago Press, 1976.

Hughes, Nathaniel Cheairs, and Roy P. Stonesifer. *The Life and Wars of Gideon J. Pillow.* Chapel Hill: Univ. of North Carolina Press, 1993.

Ingersoll, Charles J. *Historical Sketch of the Second War between the United States of America and Great Britain. . . .* 2 vols. Philadelphia: Lea and Blanchard, 1849.

Ireland, John. "Andrew Drew: The Man Who Burned the *Caroline.*" *Ontario Historical Society* 59 (September 1967): 137–56.

Jackson, Andrew. *Correspondence of Andrew Jackson.* Ed. John Spencer Bassett. 7 vols. Washington, D.C., 1926–35. Reprint, New York: Kraus, 1969.

Johannsen, Robert W. *To the Halls of the Montezumas: The Mexican War in the American Imagination.* New York: Oxford Univ. Press, 1985.

Johnson, Robert Underwood and Clarence Clough Buel, eds. *Battles and Leaders of the Civil War.* 4 vols. New York: Century, 1887–88.

Johnson, Timothy D. *Winfield Scott: The Quest for Military Glory.* Lawrence: Univ. Press of Kansas, 1998.

Jones, Howard. "The *Caroline* Affair." *The Historian* 38 (May 1976): 241–62.

————. *To the Webster-Ashburton Treaty: A Study in Anglo-American Relations, 1783–1843.* Chapel Hill: Univ. of North Carolina Press, 1977.

Keyes, E[rasmus] D[arwin]. *Fifty Years Observation of Men and Events, Civil and Military.* New York: Brentano's, 1884.

Kimball, Jeffrey. "The Battle of Chippewa: Infantry Tactics in the War of 1812." *Military Affairs* 8 (1949): 169–86.

Kurtz, Henry. "The Undeclared War between Britain and America." *History Today* 12 (1962): 777–83, 872–82.

LeCheminant, Wifford Hill. "A Crisis Averted? General Harney and the Change in Command of the Utah Expedition." *Utah Historical Society* 61 (1983): 30–45.

Lincoln, Abraham. *Complete Works of Abraham Lincoln.* Ed. John G. Nicolay and John Hay. 12 vols. N.p., 1894.

"Lieutenant-General Scott." *Hours at Home* 3 (1866): 273–80.

"Lieut.-General Scott." *Littel's Living Age* 71 (1861): 468–71.

Lossing, Benson J. *The Pictorial Field Book of the War of 1812.* New York: Harper and Brothers, 1868.

MacDonnell, Francis. "The Confederate Spin on Winfield Scott and George Thomas." *Civil War History* 44 (1998): 255–66.

MacKinnon, William P. "125 Years of Conspiracy Theories: Origin of the Utah Expedition of 1857–58." *Utah Historical Quarterly* 52 (Summer 1984): 212–30.

McCaffrey, James, ed. *"Surrounded by Dangers of All Kinds": The Mexican War Letters of Lieutenant Theodore Laidley.* Denton: Univ. of North Texas Press, 1997.

McClellan, George B. *The Civil War Papers of George B. McClellan: Selected Correspondence, 1860–1865.* Ed. Stephen W. Sears. New York: Ticknor and Fields, 1989.

———. *The Mexican War Diary of George B. McClellan.* Ed. William Starr Myers. Princeton, N.J.: Princeton Univ. Press, 1917.

McClure, A. K. *Colonel Alexander K. McClure's Recollections of Half a Century.* Salem, Mass.: Salem Press, 1902.

———. *Our Presidents and How We Make Them.* New York: Harper and Brothers, 1902.

McCormac, Eugene Irving. *James K. Polk: A Political Biography.* New York: Russell and Russell, 1965.

McDonogh, Patrick. "A Hero of Fort Erie: Letters Relating to the Military Service . . . of Lieutenant Patrick McDonogh." Ed. Frank H. Severance. *Publications of the Buffalo Historical Society* 5 (1902): 63–93.

McMurry, Richard M. "Marse Robert and the Fevers: A Note on the General as Strategist and on Medical Ideas as a Factor in Civil War Decision Making." *Civil War History* 35 (September 1989): 197–207.

McWhiney, Grady. "Who Whipped Whom? Confederate Defeat Reexamined." *Civil War History* 12 (March 1965): 5–26.

McWhiney, Grady, and Sue McWhiney. *To Mexico with Scott and Taylor, 1845–1847.* Waltham, Mass.: Blaisdell, 1968.

Mahon, John K. *History of the Second Seminole War, 1835–1842.* Gainesville: Univ. Press of Florida, 1991.

Mansfield, Edward D. *The Life and Military Services of Lieut.-General Winfield Scott.* New York: N. C. Miller, 1862.

Marszalek, John F. "Where Did Winfield Scott Find His Anaconda?" *Lincoln Herald* 89 (Summer 1987): 77–81.

Mason, Gen. Edwin C. "How We Won the San Juan Archipelago." *Collections of the Minnesota Historical Society* 9 (April 1901): 34–54.

Memoir of General Scott, from Records Contemporaneous with the Events. Washington, D.C., 1852.

Meneely, B. Howard. *The War Department, 1861: A Study in Mobilization and Administration.* New York: Columbia Univ. Press, 1928.

Miller, Robert Ryal. *Shamrock and Sword: The Saint Patrick's Battalion in the U.S.-Mexican War.* Norman: Univ. of Oklahoma Press, 1989.

Moore, Frank, ed. *The Rebellion Record: A Diary of American Events.* 12 vols. 1861–68. Reprint, New York: Arno, 1977.

Morris, John D. "General Jacob Brown and the Problem of Command in 1814." In

War along the Niagara: Essays on the War of 1812 and Its Legacy, edited by R. Arthur Bowler. Youngstown, N.Y.: Old Fort Niagara Association, 1991.

———. *Sword of the Border: Major General Jacob Jennings Brown, 1775–1828.* Kent, Ohio: Kent State Univ. Press, 2000.

Nevins, Allan. *Ordeal of the Union.* 2 vols. New York: Charles Scribner's Sons, 1947.

New American State Papers: Military Affairs. Ed. Benjamin Franklin Cooling. 19 vols. Wilmington, Del.: Scholarly Resources, 1979.

Nicolay, John G., and John Hay. *Abraham Lincoln: A History.* 10 vols. New York: Century, 1890.

Niles' Register 3–75 (1812–49). [To 1814 it is called *The Weekly Register;* from 1814 to 1838, *Niles' Weekly Register;* and from 1838 to 1849, *Niles' National Register.*]

Norton, John. *The Journal of Major John Norton, 1816.* Ed. Carl F. Klink and James J. Talugo. Toronto: Champlain Society, 1970.

O'Connell, Charles F., Jr. "The Corps of Engineers and the Rise of Modern Management, 1827–1856." In *Military Enterprise and Technological Change,* edited by Merritt Roe Smith. Cambridge, Mass.: MIT Press, 1985.

———. "The United States Army and the Origins of Modern Management, 1818–1860." Ph.D. diss., Ohio State University, 1982.

Oswandel, J. Jacob. *Notes of the Mexican War.* Philadelphia: [n.p.], 1885.

Peskin, Allan, ed. *Volunteers: The Mexican War Journals of Private Richard Coulter and Sergeant Thomas Barclay, Company E, Second Pennsylvania Infantry.* Kent, Ohio: Kent State Univ. Press, 1991.

Peterson, Merrill D. *The Great Triumvirate: Webster, Clay, and Calhoun.* New York: Oxford Univ. Press, 1987.

Polk, James K. *The Diary of James K. Polk.* Edited by Milo Milton Quaife. 4 vols. Chicago: A. C. McClurg, 1910.

Poore, Ben Perley. *Perley's Reminiscences of Sixty Years in the National Metropolis.* 2 vols. Philadelphia: Hubbard Brothers, 1886.

Prucha, Francis Paul. "Distribution of Regular Army Troops before the Civil War." *Military Affairs* 16 (Winter 1952): 169–73.

———. "The United States Army as Viewed by British Travelers, 1825–1860." *Military Affairs* 17 (Fall 1953): 113–24.

Ramsey, Albert C., trans. and ed. *The Other Side; or, Notes for the History of the War between Mexico and the United States. . . .* 1850. Reprint, New York: Burt Franklin, 1970.

Randall, Randolph C. *James Hall, Spokesman of the New West.* Columbus: Ohio State Univ. Press, 1964.

Rhodes, James Ford. *History of the United States from the Compromise of 1850.* 5 vols. New York: Harper, 1896.

Richardson, James D., ed. *A Compilation of the Messages and Papers of the Presidents, 1789–1897.* 9 vols. Washington, D.C., 1896–97.

Roach, Isaac. "Journal of Major Isaac Roach, 1812–1824." *Pennsylvania Magazine of History and Biography* 17 (1893): 129–58, 281–315.

Robinson, Fayette. *An Account of the Organization of the Army of the United States.* 2 vols. Philadelphia: Butler, 1848.

Rupp, Theodore. "Anacondas Anyone?" *Military Affairs* 27 (Summer 1963): 71–76.

Russell, William Howard. *My Diary North and South.* Boston: Burnham, 1863.

Scammon, E. Parker. "A Chapter of the Mexican War." *Magazine of American History* 14 (December 1885): 562–76.

Schlesinger, Arthur M., Jr. and Fred L. Israel, eds. *History of American Presidential Elections, 1789–1968.* 12 vols. New York: Chelsea House, 1985.

Schofield, John M. *Forty-Six Years in the Army.* New York: Century, 1897.

Schultz, Charles R. "The Last Great Conclave of the Whigs." *Maryland Historical Magazine* 63 (December 1968): 379–400

Scott, Winfield. *Memoirs of Lieut.-General Scott, LL.D., Written by Himself.* 2 vols. New York: Sheldon, 1864.

Sears, Stephen W. *George B. McClellan: The Young Napoleon.* New York: Ticknor and Fields, 1989.

Semmes, Raphael. *The Campaign of General Scott in the Valley of Mexico.* Cincinnati: Moore and Anderson, 1852.

Severance, Frank H., ed. "Militia Service of 1813–14: Correspondence of Maj.-Gen. Amos Hall." *Publications of the Buffalo Historical Society* 5 (1902): 27–59.

Seward, Frederick W. *Seward at Washington, as Senator and Secretary of State: A Memoir of His Life, with Selections from His Letters, 1846–1861.* New York: Derby and Miller, 1891.

Sherman, John. *John Sherman's Recollections of Forty Years in the House, Senate, and Cabinet: An Autobiography.* 2 vols. Chicago: Werner, 1895.

Sherman, William Tecumseh. *Memoirs of General W. T. Sherman.* New York: Library of America, 1990.

Silver, James W. *Edmund Pendleton Gaines: Frontier General.* Baton Rouge: Louisiana State Univ. Press, 1949.

Skelton, William B. *An American Profession of Arms. The Army Officer Corps, 1784–1861.* Lawrence: Univ. Press of Kansas, 1992.

———. "The Commanding General and the Problem of Command in the United States Army, 1821–1891." *Military Affairs* 31 (December 1970): 117–22.

Smith, Arthur D. Howden. *Old Fuss and Feathers: The Life and Exploits of Lt. General Winfield Scott.* New York: Greystone, 1937.

Smith, Carlton. "Congressional Attitudes towards Military Preparedness during the Monroe Administration." *Military Affairs* 40 (February 1976): 22–25.

Smith, E. Kirby. *To Mexico with Scott: Letters of Captain E. Kirby Smith to His Wife.* Cambridge: Harvard Univ. Press, 1917.

Smith, Justin H. "American Rule in Mexico." *American Historical Review* 23 (1918): 287–302.

———. *The War with Mexico.* 2 vols. New York: Macmillan, 1919.

Smith, Lester W., ed. "A Drummer Boy in the War of 1812: The Memoir of Jarvis Frary Hanks." *Niagara Frontier* 7 (Summer 1950): 53–62.

"Some Richmond Portraits." *Harper's Magazine* 70 (1884–85): 712–23.

Spiller, Roger J. "Calhoun's Expansible Army: The History of a Military Idea." *South Atlantic Quarterly* 79 (Spring 1980): 189–203.

Stagg, J. C. A. "Enlisted Men in the United States Army, 1812–1815: A Preliminary Survey." *William and Mary Quarterly* 43 (1986): 615–45.

Stevens, Kenneth R. *Border Diplomacy: The* Caroline *and* McLeod *Affairs in Anglo-American-Canadian Relations, 1837–1842.* Tuscaloosa: Univ. of Alabama Press, 1989.

Stone, Charles P. "A Dinner with General Scott in 1861." *Magazine of American History* 11 (June 1884): 528–32.

———. "Washington in 1861." *Magazine of American History* 12 (July 1884): 55–61.

———. "Washington in March and April, 1861." *Magazine of American History* 14 (July 1885): 1–24.

———. "Washington on the Eve of the War." *Century Illustrated Monthly Magazine* 24 (July 1883): 458–66.

Strong, George Templeton. *The Diary of George Templeton Strong.* Ed. Allan Nevins and Milton Halsey Thomas. 4 vols. New York: Macmillan, 1952.

"A Subaltern" [Braxton Bragg]. "Notes on Our Army." *The Southern Literary Messenger* 10 (1844): 80–88, 155–57, 246–51, 283–87, 372–77, 510–12, 750–53; 11 (1845): 39–47, 104–9.

Summers, Mark W. *The Plundering Generation: Corruption and the Crisis of the Union, 1849–1861.* New York: Oxford Univ. Press, 1987.

Swift, Joseph Gardner. *The Memoirs of Gen. Joseph Gardner Swift, LL.D., U.S.A., First Graduate of the United States Military Academy. . . .* N.p., 1890.

Tocqueville, Alexis de. *Democracy in America.* Ed. J. P. Mayer. New York: HarperCollins, 1969.

Townsend, E. D. *Anecdotes of the Civil War in the United States.* New York: Appleton, 1884.

Tyler, Lyon G. *The Letters and Times of the Tylers.* 3 vols. Richmond, 1885. Reprint, New York: Da Capo, 1970.

Upton, Emory. *The Military Policy of the United States.* 1904. Reprint, New York: Greenwood, 1968.

U.S. Congress. House. *On Military Districts.* 27th Cong., 3d sess., 1843, H. Doc. 147.

———. Senate. *Message from the President of the United States Communicating . . . the Proceedings of the Two Courts of Inquiry in the Case of Major General Pillow.* 30th Cong., 1st sess., 1848. S. Exec. Doc. 65.

———. *Pay and Emoluments of Lt. Gen. Scott.* 34th Cong., 3d sess., 1857. S. Exec. Doc. 34.

Van Deusen, Glyndon G. *Thurlow Weed, Wizard of the Lobby.* Boston: Little, Brown, 1947.

Walker, Augustus. "Early Days on the Lakes." *Publications of the Buffalo Historical Society* 5 (1902): 287–317.

Wallace, Edward S. *General William Jenkins Worth, Monterey's Forgotten Hero.* Dallas: Southern Methodist Univ. Press, 1953.

———. "The United States Army in Mexico City." *Military Affairs* 13 (1949): 158–66.

The War of the Rebellion: A Compilation of the Official Records of the Union and Confederate Armies. 128 vols. Washington, D.C.: GPO, 1880–1901.

Webster, Daniel. *The Papers of Daniel Webster: Correspondence.* Ed. Charles M. Wiltse. 7 vols. Hanover, N.H.: Univ. Press of New England, 1971–74.

Weed, Thurlow. *Life of Thurlow Weed.* 2 vols. Boston, 1883–84. Reprint, New York: Da Capo, 1970.

Weigley, Russell F. *History of the United States Army.* New York: Macmillan, 1967.

Weik, Jesse W. "How Lincoln Was Convinced of General Scott's Loyalty." *Century Magazine* 81 (Feb. 1911): 593–94.

Welles, Gideon. *Diary of Gideon Welles, Secretary of the Navy Under Lincoln and Johnson.* Edited by Howard K. Beale. 3 vols. New York: W. W. Norton, 1960.

Wert, Jeffry D. "Duped in the Mountains of Virginia." *Civil War Times Illustrated* 17 (1978): 4–11, 41–44.

Wharton, H. M., ed. *War Songs and Poems of the Southern Confederacy. . . .* N.p., [1904].

White, Leonard D. *The Jacksonians: A Study in Administrative History, 1829–1861.* New York: Free Press, 1965.

———. *The Jeffersonians: A Study in Administrative History, 1801–1829.* New York: Free Press, 1965.

———. *The Republican Era: A Study in Administrative History, 1869–1901.* New York: Free Press, 1965.

Whiteside, Henry O. "Winfield Scott and the Mexican Occupation: Policy and Practice." *Mid-America* 52 (1970): 102–18.

Wilkinson, Gen. James. *Memoirs of My Own Times.* 3 vols. Philadelphia: Abraham Small, 1816.

Winders, Richard Bruce. *Mr. Polk's Army: The American Military Experience in the Mexican War.* College Station: Texas A&M Univ. Press, 1997.

Wise, Henry A. *Seven Decades of the Union.* Philadelphia: Lippincott, 1872.

Wright, Gen. Marcus J. *General Scott.* New York: Appleton, 1897.

INDEX

Adams, Henry, 237

Adams, John Quincy, 72, 74, 75, 80, 109, 117, 282n46

Alexander I, czar, 64

Algeria, French invasion of, 152

"Anaconda" Plan, 11; genesis of, 250–52; premises, 249–50; defects, 252–53; abandoned, 254

Anderson, Maj. Robert, 236, 239–40

Anti-Masonry, 101

Anton Lizardo, 150

Arago (ship), 263–64

Archer, William S., 71

Arctic (ship), 92

Armstrong, John (secretary of war), 31, 33–34, 36, 38, 40–41, 181

Army Reduction Act of 1821, 61, 75, 118

Army Reduction Board, 59–60

Army, U.S.: bureaus, independence of, 119; defection of Southern officers during Civil War, 242; demobilization after War of 1812, 59–61; desertion, 38, 170, 182; expansion of during Civil War, 246–47; loyalty of enlisted men during Civil War, 242; managerial reforms, 62–63; mobilization during Civil War, 247–48; officers, low caliber of, 8, 12, 59–60, 134–35; organizational defects, 247; punishments, 38, 121–22; regulations, 223; size of, 6 (1807), 1 (1808), 17 (1812), 59 (1816), 102 (1838), 134 (1845), 216–17 (1855), 234 (1860), 1 (1861); social composition, 8, 38, 121, 170; uniforms, 6–7, 39, 43, 46–47, 114; tactical manuals, 40, 61–63; weaponry and tactics, 39–40, 218

Aroostook "war," 108–10

Atkinson, Gen. Henry, 85

Bad Axe, Battle of, 85

Baltimore riots: 1812, 16; 1861, 245–46

Barber, Capt. James, 18

Barbour, James (secretary of war), 78

Barcelona incident, 104

Bates, Edward, 309n15

Beauregard, Pierre G. T., 150, 156, 164, 178–79, 181, 187, 243, 254–56, 259–60

Belknap, William, 203

Bell, John, 116–17, 231

Benton, Thomas Hart, 87–88, 134, 143–44

Blackhawk War, 83–85

Black Rock, 15, 20

Blair, Francis P., 97–99

Blair, Montgomery, 239–40, 309n15

Bliss, Cap. William, 135

Boyd, Gen. John P., 31–32, 36

Brady, Gen. Hugh, 104

Breckenridge, John J., 231

Brevet rank, 77–78

Bribery scheme, 173–74

Brock, Sir Isaac, 18, 21, 23, 28